Fifth Edition

Questions & Answers to Help You Pass the Real Estate
APPRAISAL EXAMS

Jeffrey D. Fisher • Dennis S. Tosh

Dearborn
Real Estate Education

This publication is designed to provide accurate and authoritative information in regard to the subject matter covered. It is sold with the understanding that the publisher is not engaged in rendering legal, accounting, or other professional service. If legal advice or other expert assistance is required, the services of a competent professional should be sought.

President: Mehul Patel
Vice President of Product Development & Publishing: Evan M. Butterfield
Editorial Director: Kate DeVivo
Development Editor: Tom Selley
Director of Production: Daniel Frey
Production Editor: Caitlin Ostrow
Production Artist: Virginia Byrne
Creative Director: Lucy Jenkins
Assistant Product Manager: Erica Smith

Published by Dearborn™ Real Estate Education
30 South Wacker Drive
Chicago, Illinois 60606-7481
(312) 836-4400
www.dearbornRE.com

Printed in the United States of America

08   09   10   10 9 8 7 6 5 4 3 2 1

The Library of Congress has cataloged the fourth edition as follows:

Fisher, Jeffrey D.
    Questions & answers to help you pass the real estate appraisal exams / Jeffrey D. Fisher, Dennis S. Tosh.—4th ed.
        p. cm.
    ISBN 0-7931-9179-3
    1. Real property—Valuation—Examinations, questions, etc. I. Title: Questions and answers to help you pass the real estate appraisal exams. II. Title: Real estate appraisal exams. III. Tosh, Dennis S. IV. Title.
    HD1387.F54 2003
    333.33'2'076—dc22   2004001300

Fifth edition ISBN-13: 978-1-4277-6616-8
Fifth edition ISBN-10: 1-4277-6616-9

CONTENTS

ABOUT THE AUTHORS

Jeffrey D. Fisher, PhD, is Director of the Center for Real Estate Studies, and the Charles H. and Barbara F. Dunn Professor of Finance and Real Estate at the Kelley School of Business at Indiana University in Bloomington. He served as President and a member of the board of directors of the American Real Estate and Urban Economics Association (AREUEA) from 1984 to 1990.

Dr. Fisher has a doctorate in real estate from Ohio State University and is coauthor of *The Language of Real Estate Appraisal, Income Property Valuation,* and *Income Property Appraisal* in Dearborn's appraisal line.

Dr. Fisher has been actively involved in many real estate–related industry associations. He has developed and presented numerous seminars for both the American Society of Appraisers and The Appraisal Institute. He was a founding trustee of The Appraisal Foundation.

Dennis S. Tosh, PhD, recently retired as Professor and holder of the J. Ed Turner Chair of Real Estate at the University of Mississippi. He earned his doctorate in real estate and land economics from Georgia State University and is the author and coauthor of numerous textbooks and articles on real estate and real estate education, including *Uniform Standards of Professional Appraisal Practice: Applying the Standards,* 13th Edition.

Dr. Tosh has served as President of Rho Epsilon and was a member of the board of directors of the Real Estate Educators Association. Dr. Tosh has been on the teaching faculty for several appraisal and banking associations. He has helped develop tests and course materials for numerous state appraisal boards for appraiser licensing and certification. He was a founding trustee of The Appraisal Foundation.

PREFACE

During the past 20 years we have seen significant changes in the real estate appraisal profession. Every state has enacted regulations that require appraisers to become licensed and certified in conformance with the Financial Institutions Reform, Recovery, and Enforcement Act of 1989 (FIRREA). These regulations apply to all appraisers, regardless of prior education and experience.

Whether you are already a practicing appraiser or are entering the profession for the first time, this study guide can help you prepare for the licensing and certification exams. Appraisal examinations tend to focus on definitions, concepts, techniques, and application of typical appraisal assignments. Consequently, this guide includes areas of study that even experienced appraisers can benefit from reviewing. Regardless of what other courses you have taken or materials you have studied, practicing with sample test questions can be an important part of your preparation.

Based on our experience writing exam questions of the type used by professional testing companies on appraisal exams, we have prepared the fifth edition of *Questions and Answers to Help You Pass the Real Estate Appraisal Exams* in a manner we felt would best prepare readers for the licensing and certification exams. We also hope that readers, in addition to passing the exams, become better appraisers by studying this book.

A number of people have been very helpful in the preparation of this study guide. We would like to thank Cynthia Hull, Program Manager for Certification and Licensure, Hagerstown Community College, and John Henry Saunders, The Real Estate Academy, Inc. We would also like to thank Charles A. Hicks, Jr., RES, Central Piedmont Community College; Jeri Meteer, Hinds Community College; Margaret L. Sullivan, National Association of Independent Fee Appraisers; and Dwight E. Norris for their valuable assistance in the revision of this text. We would especially like to thank and acknowledge the assistance of Paige Mueller, who helped with the development and editing of the test questions and preparation of the glossary. We would also like to thank J. H. Hinton, Judith Meadows, and William Pastuszek, Jr., for their input to the second edition, as well as Barry Diskin, Kennard Howell, Beverly Pearson, George Potter, and Bill Rayburn, who provided us with valuable suggestions in the first edition.

Jeffrey D. Fisher, PhD
Dennis S. Tosh, PhD

The Appraisal Profession

INTRODUCTION: THE NEW ERA OF FEDERAL LEGISLATION

This book was written to prepare readers to take an examination to become state-licensed and state-certified appraisers[1] under the requirements of federal legislation. This legislation was part of the Financial Institutions Reform, Recovery and Enforcement Act (FIRREA) of 1989, often referred to as the S&L Bailout Bill. The regulations require the use of state-certified appraisers for certain real estate transactions that involve federal, financial, and public policy interests. The provisions for this requirement are included in Title XI of FIRREA, titled "Real Estate Appraisal Reform Amendments."

FEDERALLY COVERED TRANSACTIONS

As indicated above, certain transactions affecting the federal government currently require state-licensed and/or state-certified appraisers. These transactions are referred to as "federally related transactions." A large number of real estate transactions involve the federal government. First, federally related transactions involve any institution regulated or insured by one of the following five regulatory agencies: the Federal Reserve System (FRS), the Office of the Comptroller of the Currency (OCC), the Federal Deposit Insurance Corporation (FDIC), the Office of Thrift Supervision (OTS), and the National Credit Union Administration (NCUA). Second, federally related transactions include any transaction involving the following three agencies: the Federal National Mortgage Association (Fannie Mae), the Federal Home Loan Mortgage Corporation (Freddie Mac), and the Resolution Trust Corporation (RTC).

---

1 In this book, the term *state-certified appraiser* refers to an appraiser certified as either a residential or general appraiser by a state under the provisions of Title XI, Real Estate Appraisal Reform Amendments, of the Financial Institutions Reform, Recovery, and Enforcement Act of 1989.

Thus we see that many transactions have been affected by the legislation. For example, the financial institution making the loan is likely regulated by one of the named regulatory agencies; or the lender may want to sell the loan in the secondary market, which usually would involve either Fannie Mae or Freddie Mac.

STATE-CERTIFIED AND LICENSED APPRAISERS

Under the federal legislation, as of December 31, 1992, either state-certified or licensed appraisers must be used for federally related transactions. According to the legislation, state-certified appraisers *must* be used for transactions of $1,000,000 or more. Furthermore, transactions under $1,000,000 may require the use of a state-certified appraiser if so directed by the particular federal agency. For federally related transactions that do not require a state-certified appraiser, a licensed appraiser must be used. The differences between a licensed appraiser and a state-certified appraiser are explained below.

State-Certified Appraisers

Under the federal legislation, each state has enacted legislation that allows appraisers to become certified in that state. Appraisers can become either residential or general state certified by meeting specific experience and education requirements and by passing an examination offered by their state. According to the federal legislation, topics covered by the state examinations must be consistent with criteria determined by the Appraiser Qualifications Board (AQB) of The Appraisal Foundation. The Appraisal Foundation was established in December 1987 by the appraisal profession as a private nonprofit corporation to promulgate uniform standards of appraisal practice[2] and to establish qualification criteria for the certification of appraisers. Thus, we now have a system where the appraisal profession establishes criteria for appraiser licensing and certification, but with oversight from the federal government.

Contact information for The Appraisal Foundation is:

> The Appraisal Foundation
>
> Suite 1111
>
> 1155 15th Street, NW
>
> Washington, DC 20005-3517
>
> Phone: 202-347-7722
>
> Fax: 202-347-7727
>
> *www.appraisalfoundation.org*

---

2   The *Uniform Standards of Professional Appraisal Practice* (USPAP) were first developed by an ad hoc committee of nine appraisal organizations. The standards provide guidelines that appraisers should follow in developing and communicating their appraisal.

Residential and General Certification

There are two levels of state certification: certified residential and certified general. The appraiser certified for residential property is expected to understand appraisal principles and practices that bear on the appraisal of one-family to four-family residential properties such as single-family residences, duplexes, and the like. Although these properties may be held for investment purposes, the nature of the income is not as complex as for larger residential income properties or most nonresidential properties (office buildings, shopping centers). Thus only a minimum knowledge of concepts and techniques associated with the analysis of income is required for residential certification. The general level of certification *includes* that required for residential certification, *plus* an understanding of certain concepts and techniques that are important in the appraisal of income property. That is, the main difference between residential and general certification is the degree to which the appraiser needs to understand how to appraise income property, especially application of the income approach. This will be evident from the study outline in Chapter 3.

Educational Requirements for Certification

In addition to passing an exam, certain minimum educational requirements must be met prior to attaining certification. These requirements include both classroom hours and experience.

Cost of Certification

States charge a fee for giving the certification exams. This fee varies from state to state depending on how the exam is administered. There is also an annual or biannual registration fee, which is charged to the appraiser for maintaining the license and inclusion of his or her name in a national directory.

Licensed Appraisers

Federally related transactions that *do not* require either certified residential or certified general appraisers involve licensed appraisers. The AQB has established experience, education, and examination requirements for any person wishing to become a licensed appraiser. Thus licensing represents the minimum requirements for appraisal of properties involving federally related transactions. States also require appraisers to meet minimum criteria for all appraisals done within the state, whether they involve federally related transactions or not.

Trainee Appraisers

In recent years, states have established a trainee licensee category for people with no documented appraisal experience who want to enter the appraisal profession. Trainee appraisers may gain appraisal experience by affiliating themselves with a certified appraiser who serves as the trainee's supervising appraiser. The supervising appraiser is responsible for the actions of the trainee under his or her supervision. Many people work as an appraiser apprentice while completing the minimum experience requirement. Currently, there are no examination requirements for the appraiser trainee classification.

PROFESSIONAL DESIGNATION

Prior to the federal legislation, appraisers who wanted to demonstrate achievement of a certain level of professionalism could do so only by becoming designated by a national appraisal association. Such designation generally involves taking courses offered by that organization and passing exams covering the course material, as well as a comprehensive exam covering the material in all the courses. Furthermore, the appraiser's experience is usually evaluated by the organization and must meet certain criteria before a designation is awarded. Most designated appraisers must follow the *Uniform Standards of Professional Appraisal Practice* (USPAP) discussed earlier.

With the new government regulation, certification status shows that the appraiser has achieved a minimum level of experience and education. However, membership in one or more of the national appraisal organizations is still desirable for several reasons. First, most appraisal organizations have educational and experiential requirements for designation that exceed those required for state certification. Thus becoming designated allows the appraiser to improve professional skills beyond the minimum level.

Second, appraisal associations offer continuing education through a variety of seminars designed to keep members up-to-date. These seminars also allow appraisers to interact and share professional experiences. Most associations publish newsletters and hold periodic meetings designed to keep members informed.

Third, some lenders historically have required that appraisers be designated with a recognized appraisal organization. Because designation with many of the appraisal organizations demands more education and experience than does state certification, many lenders are still likely to require that appraisers be designated as well as certified.

Because a number of appraisal organizations award designations and their requirements vary considerably, we recommend that readers find out more about the organizations' requirements before joining. Talking with other local appraisers, especially those who work for lenders, is a good way to determine what organization to join.

THE APPRAISAL FOUNDATION

Purpose of The Appraisal Foundation

The Appraisal Foundation was formed in 1987 by eight of the national appraisal organizations to be a source of uniform standards for the appraisal profession. The same appraisal organizations that formed The Appraisal Foundation developed a set of *Uniform Standards of Professional Appraisal Practice* (USPAP) as part of an ad hoc committee prior to formation of the Foundation. The responsibility for modifying those standards was then turned over to the Foundation after it was formed. To carry out this responsibility, the Foundation has an Appraisal Standards Board (ASB).

Each appraisal organization that is a member of the Foundation has adopted the uniform standards as its own appraisal standards. The standards provide guidelines for developing an appraisal and communicating the appraisal report to the intended user.

The Foundation also has an Appraiser Qualifications Board (AQB) whose purpose is to develop qualifications for states to follow for licensing and certification of appraisers as discussed earlier. They include educational requirements for appraisers as well as an outline of the scope of appraisal concepts and techniques with which licensing and certification applicants should be familiar. The state-administered exams for licensing and certification cover the outline of material recommended by the Foundation. Chapter 3 includes a study outline based on information recommended by the AQB.

Membership of The Appraisal Foundation

The appraisal organizations that are members of The Appraisal Foundation are referred to as appraisal sponsors of the Foundation. In addition to these sponsors, affiliate sponsors of the Foundation, comprised of nonappraisal organizations, have an interest in the appraisal profession. Affiliate sponsors include education-oriented associations and associations representing various real estate professional groups. Each sponsor appoints one member of the Board of Trustees. The sponsors of the Foundation are listed on the top of page 7.

WHY ARE APPRAISALS NEEDED?

There are a number of reasons an appraiser is asked to prepare a report giving an opinion about a particular property. Following is a brief discussion of some situations where appraisals may be required.

Loans

When a mortgage loan is made, that loan is secured by the real estate. Lenders want to be reasonably sure that the amount of the loan does not exceed the value of the real estate. Typically, the loan will be some percentage of the value of the real estate (e.g., 80 percent). Thus, an appraiser may be asked to estimate the value of the property for the purpose of estimating market value. The appraiser might be a staff member of the institution making the loan (e.g., a bank) or a fee-based independent appraiser who works for an appraisal company engaged by the financial institution.

Property Tax Assessment

Property taxes are ad valorem, which means that the tax is based on the value of the property being taxed; that is, property taxes are based on the assessed value of the real estate. Depending on the laws of a particular tax jurisdiction, the assessed value may be based on the full market value of the property or some percentage of that market value. The taxing jurisdiction will use an appraisal to determine the assessed value of the property. Appraisers on the staff of the local government's assessment office will conduct the appraisals. If a property owner disagrees with the assessment, another appraiser might be hired to help contest the assessment.

Condemnation

Condemnation occurs when property is taken for public use through the power of eminent domain. Because the owner of eminent domain property must be justly compensated, an appraiser would be employed to recommend an appropriate price to be paid by the government. An owner who disagrees with the recommended price could employ another appraiser to estimate a value. The final price would then be decided through negotiation or court settlement.

Establishing an Asking Price

Sellers of real estate often use an appraisal to estimate the value of a property so they know what price to ask. Real estate is also frequently sold through auction, and an appraisal may be used to help determine a minimum bid price for the property.

Insurance Claims

An appraiser might be used to estimate the loss in value of real estate for insurance purposes. Depending on the nature of the policy, this value may be based on the replacement cost of the property.

Inheritance Tax

Depending on the size of the estate, an inheritance tax might be due on the value of the property. This value is often estimated by an appraiser.

Divorce Settlements

Often real estate is involved in a divorce settlement. If the parties cannot agree on division of the assets, an appraiser might be employed to establish a value of the real estate to help the judge estimate a fair settlement.

Auxiliary Services

In addition to the traditional ways in which appraisers are called upon to render value opinions, appraisers also perform a number of other real estate–related services. Examples of such services include market analysis, cost benefit analysis, feasibility studies, and investment analysis. These types of services are normally undertaken by individuals who have specialized in a certain property type such as industrial parks, shopping malls, or golf courses.

WHO EMPLOYS APPRAISERS?

It should be obvious, then, that many different situations arise where appraisals may be used to establish the value of real estate. A variety of organizations might employ an appraiser. Lending institutions such as commercial banks, savings banks, life insurance companies, and pension funds employ fee appraisers on an as-needed basis. Similarly, real estate developers often employ fee appraisers. Many utilities (electric, gas, water, and telephone) also have appraisers on staff.

SPONSORING ORGANIZATIONS OF THE APPRAISAL FOUNDATION

Appraisal Sponsors	Affiliate Sponsors
American Society of Appraisers	American Bankers Association
American Society of Farm Managers & Rural Appraisers	Farm Credit Council
Appraisal Institute	Mortgage Insurance Companies of America
Appraisers Association of America	National Association of REALTORS®
International Association of Assessing Officers	
International Right of Way Association	
Massachusetts Board of Real Estate Appraisers	
National Association of Independent Fee Appraisers	
National Association of Master Appraisers	

Large national companies, such as oil companies, food chains, department stores and other retailers, and hotel and motel chains may employ appraisers to help find new sites and to monitor their property taxes. Similarly, large nonprofit organizations may employ full-time staff appraisers.

A variety of federal, state, and local government agencies employ appraisers. Examples include the General Services Administration, FHA, VA, state departments of transportation, and assessors' offices.

In addition to private organizations and public agencies that employ appraisers, there are local firms that specialize in providing appraisal services. These range from large national appraisal firms to single-person offices that usually specialize in a particular geographic area. Many real estate brokerage firms and accounting firms also provide appraisal services.

FEES FOR APPRAISER SERVICES

As with any profession, fees vary greatly depending on the education, experience, ability of the appraiser, and the complexity of the appraisal assignment. Appraisals for smaller residential properties are frequently completed on forms, although they may be prepared in a narrative format for complex properties. Appraisals for larger multifamily residential properties and for nonresidential properties (e.g., commercial and industrial) are usually prepared as a narrative report.

As a rough guideline, the fee for a single-family residential property appraisal prepared on a form ranges from $250 to $600 for a property in an area with an active market and recent sales of highly comparable properties. However, the fee would increase as the complexity of the assignment increases—especially if a narrative report is prepared. Fees for the appraisal of nonresidential properties generally range from $2,000 to $25,000 depending on the complexity of the assignment.

It should be noted that one of the primary reasons for the implementation of appraiser licensing and certification is to elevate the level of the appraisal profession. All appraisers are expected to follow the *Uniform Standards of Professional Appraisal Practice* (USPAP) promulgated by The Appraisal Foundation. With these standards come higher expectations for the quality of the appraisal report.

The Appraisal Examinations

As discussed in Chapter 1, the appraisal profession has undergone significant changes in terms of state licensure and state certification of real estate appraisers. An integral part of the regulatory process is the testing of appraisers on those topics believed to be important in understanding real estate valuation and appraisal principles. Jurisdictions test that knowledge by giving appraisal examinations to those who specialize in the appraisal of residential real estate, as well as to those who have a broader and more general real estate appraisal practice.

As required by your state certification program, you will be taking one of three appraisal examinations: (1) licensing, (2) certified residential, or (3) certified general. Some jurisdictions have an appraisal trainee designation, which may or may not require a written examination. Prior to taking any of the examinations, familiarize yourself with the specific topics covered on the examination you will be taking.

SOURCES OF INFORMATION

The best and certainly the most reliable source of information is the administrative agency in your state charged with licensing and certifying appraisers. This agency may be known as the real estate appraisers examination board or a real estate appraisal committee; or it may be part of the real estate commission. Regardless of its name, information about specifics of the examination(s) and qualifications for sitting can be obtained by contacting the appropriate agency. (The name, address, and telephone number of each state real estate appraisal board is listed in Appendix A.) In addition to your state administrative agency, professional real estate appraisal organizations and societies are a good source of information. Many readers may already be active members of such organizations. Your local chapter, as well as your national office, may be able to answer general questions about examination dates, location, and other particulars.

Finally, fellow real estate appraisers in your area may have already taken the examination required in your jurisdiction. They may be able to assist you in terms of what needs to be done prior to your taking one of the examinations. You should, however, be wary of hearsay information from anyone not directly involved in the licensing or certification process. Oftentimes information is given and repeated to the extent that what is presented as fact may be more fiction than truth. If there is any question about licensing and certification requirements, the best and most reliable source of information is the administrative agency overseeing the appraisal certification program in your state.

THE EXAMINATIONS

Both the licensing and certification examinations are comprised of objective multiple-choice questions. In some jurisdictions, the questions are contained in a test booklet; a separate answer or scoring sheet is provided for recording answers to each question. In other jurisdictions the examinations are taken through an electronic computer-type machine. Because the total score on an examination is based on the percentage of questions answered correctly, it is better to guess at an answer rather than simply leave it blank.

To complete the examination successfully, you must know basic terminology of real estate valuation and appraisal. In addition, you will have to solve problems that illustrate numerous appraisal techniques, procedures, and analysis. You will be expected to know how to work with a calculator and, in some jurisdictions, how to use compound interest rate tables. Again, any questions as to the specific topics covered should be directed to the appropriate administrative agency.

The Licensing and Certified Residential Examinations

The licensing and residential examinations are intended to test your knowledge of real estate valuation and appraisal as it relates to the appraisal of one-family to four-family residential real estate and basic property such as residential rentals. As such, the examinations are comprised of questions that require knowledge of basic principles of real estate as related to valuation. Although the specific examination you will take may vary somewhat from the one given in other jurisdictions, the broad subcategories will include those discussed in the following sections.

Valuation Principles and Market Characteristics   You are expected to have a working knowledge of real estate valuation and appraisal terminology. Such terms as *market value, cost, assessed value,* and *value in use* are included on the licensing and certified residential examinations to see if you have a clear and correct understanding of their definitions. In addition, numerous appraisal principles and concepts such as the economic principles of highest and best use, substitution, conformity, and contribution are included. Questions dealing with the characteristics of real estate markets, as well as the different types of space, are also included. The role of money and capital markets and the basic terminology that relates to financing should be clearly understood by appraisers; as such, this area is also tested on the licensing and certified residential examinations. In short, you must know basic real estate terminology, principles of economics and value concepts, and the terminology that corresponds with these principles.

Legal Considerations   United States law defines legal rights and interests in real estate by indicating the extent of real property ownership. This ownership involves an aggregate of rights, privileges, and powers guaranteed and protected by the government. Ownership of land entails both ownership and duties. In addition, property ownership is subject to various restrictions by the public. Anyone attempting to estimate the value of real estate must fully understand the legal considerations that affect land use, ownership, and, therefore, value. An important component of both the licensing and certified residential examinations deals with legal considerations in appraisal. The distinction between real and personal property should be clear. The numerous limitations on real estate ownership, both private and public, are covered on the examinations, as are the various legal rights and interests in real estate. Traditional forms of property ownership, as well as special ownership forms (condominiums, cooperatives, and time-sharing), need to be understood. In addition, terminology and basic concepts of legal descriptions, which are part of every appraisal assignment, are tested.

Highest and Best Use Analysis and Property Description   An understanding of highest and best use, including the four tests for estimating highest and best use, is essential in the appraisal of real estate. Regardless of the final form an appraisal assignment takes, every appraisal should be based on a systematic, step-by-step approach. Such an approach is normally referred to as the valuation process, and a thorough understanding of each step in the process serves as a basis for examination questions. Property description (including land characteristics, architectural styles, and types of construction) is also covered on the exams.

Traditional Approaches to Value   Anyone desiring to be licensed or certified as a real estate appraiser is expected to know and be able to apply the three traditional approaches to value. Accordingly, the examinations include a thorough coverage of the cost approach, the sales comparison approach, and, for the licensing and certified residential examinations, the basics of the income approach. The relevance and limitations of these approaches should be known as well as the specific steps to be followed in applying a specific approach to an appraisal assignment. Certainly the terminology associated with these approaches needs to be understood, as does the basic mathematics involved with specific steps in the approaches.

Valuation of Partial Interests and Appraisal Math/Statistics   Real estate is not always held in fee simple by one person. Partial interests can be created in various ways, such as life estates, leases, or easements. Ownership forms such as time-shares, cooperatives, and condominiums also create partial interests. Thus the appraiser needs to know how to value these partial interests.

Appraisal is mathematical as well as statistical by nature. Even though this may apply more to income property, the licensed or certified residential appraiser must also be familiar with statistical concepts, such as mean, median, and mode, and be able to calculate percentages, rates, and areas.

Appraisal Standards and Ethics   As was noted in Chapter 1, a set of *Uniform Standards of Professional Appraisal Practice* (USPAP) has been developed by the Appraisal Standards Board of The Appraisal Foundation. Those standards, as well as additions that may have been made to the standards by a particular jurisdiction, are subjects covered on the examination. Those standards should be thoroughly reviewed and understood. A copy of the uniform standards can be obtained by contacting The Appraisal Foundation, Suite 1111, 1155 15th Street, NW, Washington, DC 20005; (202) 347-7722 *(www.appraisalfoundation.org)*.

State-Specific Topics   An important component of the examination consists of those topics that are part of understanding appraisals and specific appraisal assignments. The examinations include an area commonly referred to as state-specific or special topics; for instance, the requirements to be licensed, hearing procedures, and the appraisal rules and regulations of that jurisdiction. For those pursuing a licensure or certification in a state that has enacted specific statutes or rules and regulations unique to that particular jurisdiction, you will be expected to know those components of state law related to the appraisal of real estate and the appraisal process. This includes any terminology unique to that particular state. A copy of the appraisal regulations applicable in your jurisdiction can be acquired from the appraisal regulatory agency (see Appendix A, "State Real Estate Appraisal Boards").

The Certified General Examination

As you would expect, the certified general examination is directed toward those persons who have expanded their practice beyond the appraisal of one-family to four-family residential real estate. Thus the examination encompasses a much broader (as well as a much deeper) coverage of the basics of valuation and appraisal. All of the material expected to be understood by applicants for the licensing or certified residential examinations is certainly expected to be known by persons taking the certified general examination. In fact, the level of difficulty of the test questions will be greater on the certified general examination than on the residential examination. The certified general examination covers the income approach to value much more rigorously than do the other examinations. In addition to knowing the relevance and limitations of the income approach as well as how to reconstruct an operating statement, persons sitting for the certified general examination should also know operating statement ratios, be able to perform mortgage calculations, and know how to estimate cash flow. The numerous direct capitalization techniques, as well as discounted cash flow capitalization, need to be understood. In the case of discounted cash flow, compound interest concepts are included. Finally, the subject of leased fee and leasehold valuation comprises a much greater portion of the certified general examination than it does on the licensed or certified residential examinations. Besides being able to identify the interest created by a lease, a person taking the certified general examination should understand lease provisions and the valuation considerations associated with leased fee and leasehold interests. Many examination questions dealing with the income approach to value will be based on a block of information. You will have to solve problems and perform mathematical calculations. You may have to work with compound interest tables. An understanding of certain formulas and how they are used may also be required.

In addition to the higher level of difficulty of the questions appearing on the certified general examination, the type of questions in regard to professional standards of conduct and practice are also more detailed. Anyone desiring to be certified as a certified general appraiser must have a clear and complete understanding of the uniform standards and how they relate to the valuation and appraisal of all types of appraisal assignments. Again, any specific questions dealing with what should be studied prior to taking the general certified examination should be directed to the proper administrative agency. Do not rely on hearsay.

ORGANIZATION OF THIS STUDY GUIDE

The remaining chapters of this book are designed to help you prepare for any of the three examinations. Chapter 3 contains a study outline of the topics you can expect to be covered on the exams. The outline indicates which topics apply only to the licensing or certified residential exam versus those topics that apply to all three exams. Parts I through VIII of the study outline include material that all state exams are likely to include.

Chapters 4 through 11 contain diagnostic exams that cover the eight parts of the content outline relevant to all state exams. The diagnostic exams allow the reader to review the material likely to be covered on exams by studying questions that are similar to the type of question that will be on state exams. The answers to each question, along with a brief explanation, are included at the end of each chapter. We recommend that the reader first attempt to answer the question without looking at the answer. For many of the questions it is almost as important to know why the wrong answers are wrong! This is because multiple-choice questions often purposely include one or more answers that the test writer knows might be picked by a student who does not completely understand the concept or calculations. In general, each question in the diagnostic exam focuses on only one of the topics listed in the study outline. Only in a few cases will a particular question cover more than one topic at the same time.

Chapters 12 and 13 include two practice licensing and certified residential exams. Use them to check your mastery of the material likely to be included on both licensing and certified residential exams. Similarly, Chapters 14 and 15 include two practice certified general exams. Answers for all of these exams, along with a brief explanation, are also provided.

We have also included "Quick Review" questions, designated by a gray box design element, which are questions that convey the essential points of each chapter. These questions should be used as a review tool only after the entire exam has been completed. These quick review questions are not meant to replace the entire exam.

◎ For Chapters 9 and 10 only, gray-box quick review questions featuring a **bull's-eye** are for the **licensing** and **certified residential** exams. The gray-box questions *without the bull's-eye are for the certified general exam.*

Appendix A lists Real Estate Appraisal Boards by state. Appendix B contains compound interest tables with the six functions of a dollar. The tables can be used for solutions to those problems that require the use of compound interest calculations. Tables based on both annual and monthly compounding are provided. Of course, most readers will prefer to use a financial calculator since it is allowed while taking the exam. Check ahead of time to find out whether your state has any limitations on the type of financial calculators you can use during the examination.

A glossary contains key terms and concepts covered by the study outline and the diagnostic and practice exams. The glossary can be used to check definitions of unfamiliar terms used in the study outline and test questions. Reviewing all the terms in the glossary is also an excellent way to study material that is likely to be included on an exam.

TEST-TAKING STRATEGY

There is no sure-fire secret that can assure you of successfully completing the examination. What can be noted is that certain suggestions may offer you better insight into the examinations and how best to approach them. In addition, the following steps should be taken to improve the likelihood of your successful completion of the exam.

Before the Examination

If you have already reviewed the requirements necessary for licensure or certification, you will note that both the licensing and certification designations require a significant number of clock hours of course work directly related to appraisal principles and practices. Therefore, you should be familiar with that material and certainly should review the outlines, test questions, explanations, and examples covered during those courses. In addition, you should review an appraisal glossary such as the one included in this study guide to reacquaint yourself with the valuation terms that may not be part of your current vocabulary. As you would expect, an examination such as the one you are going to take relies a great deal on an understanding of the basic terminology associated with the subject, in this case, valuation and appraisal. You certainly are aware of the fact that real estate principles, and more specifically real estate valuation, encompass numerous terms and concepts.

In addition to reviewing the subject matter covered in your courses, familiarize yourself with the specifics of the examination you are going to take. As noted earlier, the administrative agency in your state can make this information available to you. In most jurisdictions, a booklet of information has been prepared that explains the specifics of the examination. You need to know the number of questions contained on the examination, the time allowed for the exam, when and where the examination will be given, and what identification you might need.

Once you know the examination specifications, begin to prepare for the exam. Practice answering appraisal questions such as the ones included in the diagnostic and sample examinations in this book. Remember that the actual examination you take is based on correct answers. There is no place for judgment or opinion. The examination assumes each question has only one correct answer. Be prepared, but do not be exhausted when it is time to take the examination. If you cram and study too much, you are apt to make careless errors. You want to be fresh and confident, not exhausted and nervous. Take a watch to the examination so you can monitor your time. Remember that the examination is graded on the number of questions answered correctly; thus you are at a distinct disadvantage if you do not answer all questions. Be sure your calculator is functioning properly and has fresh batteries (you certainly would not want a dead calculator just when you start working the math problems). Taking extra pencils is a good idea, although taking your own scratch paper is generally disallowed. Finally, make sure you are on time. Arriving a little early is not a bad idea, but showing up late may result in your not being allowed to take the examination as scheduled.

During the Examination

Read the Instructions Carefully   Quite often when filling out a form, the tendency is to jump right in and begin writing. The fear of not having enough time and forgetting everything causes test takers to rush, rush, rush. Even though you will have found out beforehand the exact format of the questions and how to complete the test, you should still read the introductory material included with the examination and listen carefully to any instructions given by the exam administrator.

Fill in All Preliminary Information   Include your name, address, and other personal information on the examination or test booklet. If you have an identification number or registration number, that too will need to be included; do not leave any of this portion of the examination blank. If information is requested that you do not know, check to see if the examination can still be taken without providing that information.

Read the Questions Carefully   By the time you actually begin reading the test questions, you will know the exact number of questions included as well as the total time allowed to complete the examination. Thus you will know on average how much time you can allocate to each question. There should be no reason to rush through the questions. You should have ample time to read and answer each one.

Do Not Jump to Quick Conclusions   Questions on the appraisal licensing and certification examinations require careful analysis. Even though a certain multiple-choice answer may look good, examine all choices before reaching a conclusion. Unfortunately you may find that with some questions, one or more of the incorrect choices also looks good. What you will discover—and this is certainly illustrated with the sample questions throughout this study guide—is that the incorrect choices are not always obviously wrong to someone who does not know the material. Questions involving mathematical and statistical calculations are deliberately written so that incorrect choices can appear to be the correct answer. For example, a question that requires you to know that there are 43,560 square feet in an acre as part of solving the problem may have an incorrect choice based on your using 45,360 square feet in an acre. In hurrying through the calculation, you could make such a mistake easily.

Be Careful of Certain Cue Words   Multiple-choice examinations often include the use of certain cue words such as *always, never, except, only,* and *without exception.* When you see such words in a question, a yellow light should come on and you should proceed with caution. This does not mean that the question is tricky or difficult; rather, it simply requires more thought and consideration before selecting an answer.

Be Careful of "Sounds-Like" Words   Real estate valuation and appraisal terminology are full of terms that are similar in sound and, in many instances, in meaning. Think about the following terms: lessor-lessee, condominium-cooperative, gross income-net income. In each of these examples, the terms are different in meaning yet related to a similar topic. A portion of a test question could read as follows: "The lessor agrees to . . . ." In this instance, you would have to know who the lessor is; if you are not sure about the difference between the lessor and the lessee, you could not answer this question correctly.

Work the Problems Carefully   Do not try to guess the answer before working the problem. Questions included on appraisal examinations are generally written so that once you read the stem (the question itself) you will, in most instances, know what the question is testing and you could probably write down the correct answer even before looking at the choices. Some applicants are in such a hurry to answer the questions that they find an answer they think matches the question before first reading the question and working the problem. They may come up with a great answer; unfortunately, it is incorrect.

Do Not Concern Yourself with Rounding Errors   More than likely you will use a calculator to assist with the questions and problems that require quantitative calculations. This is fine and calculators are strongly recommended. You may find, however, that the particular calculator you are using rounds or truncates the decimal place at 2 or 3 places, whereas someone else may have a financial calculator that carries the decimal up to 20 places. Do not let this bother you; quantitative questions are not concerned solely with where you round your answer. For example, the question may involve calculating the property tax due on a parcel of land. The answer depends on an assessed value and a tax (or mileage) rate. The correct answer could be $410.88. However, when you examine the choices for this problem, you may find the closest answer is $410 or $411. What you would *not* find in this problem would be both $410 and $411 offered as different choices. The incorrect choices will be incorrect for reasons other than rounding errors. For example, you calculate the property tax to be $410.88 while the only possible choice is $411, then choose the $411. The examination is not intended to test your ability in rounding numbers, nor is it intended to test your calculator's internal operating procedure.

Budget Your Time   Before taking the examination, you will know the number of questions included as well as the amount of time you have to complete the exam. If the examination in your jurisdiction consists of 150 questions and you have six hours to complete it, then that is 360 minutes, or more than two minutes per question. While that may not seem like a great deal of time—and in fact it may not be for certain questions or problems—the majority of questions will not take the time allotted on a per question basis. Realistically, the first time through the examination should not take the full time allotted. If you have six hours, then three hours into the examination you should probably have answered significantly more than half the questions. If you find this is not the case, then you should consider increasing the speed of reading and working the questions so you will be certain at least to attempt to answer all of the questions. Otherwise, not only will you not finish the examination, you will not have time to go back and check for errors or complete questions omitted the first time through the examination.

Guess Intelligently   There is no better advice for taking a multiple-choice examination than to guess intelligently. The fact is, you will see questions on the examination for which you do not know the correct answer. You may not have ever heard of the subject matter, or you may know a little bit about the terminology but not enough to answer the question correctly. What do you do? One approach taken by some examinees is: "Well, I chose A last time, so I will pick B this time." This is not a sound approach, and the result of such action will mean your chance of correctly guessing the answer is exactly one in four, which are not very good odds. The end result of such an approach is that if there are 20 questions that you cannot answer and you simply pick one of the four choices at random, you will probably answer correctly 5 of them and will therefore miss 15 questions. However, think what will happen to your success rate, and thus your chances of passing the examination, if you can simply eliminate one of the four choices. Your chances are now one in three, and thus you could answer 7 of the 20 questions correctly instead of only 5. The difference between 5 correct and 7 correct out of 20 may not seem significant, but it could mean the difference between passing and failing the examination. What if you can eliminate two of the four choices? Under the same circumstances, you should be able to answer 10 of the 20 questions, which is five more than if you simply pick a letter at random. Most people who fail a multiple-choice examination come reasonably close to making the minimum passing score. Therefore, had students who missed a passing score by only one or two points simply been able to answer one or two additional questions correctly, they would have passed the examination.

Do Not Leave Blank Answers   Make sure you put something down for each question. The score on the examination is based on the number of questions correctly answered. Those left blank are counted wrong and their value is exactly the same as those incorrectly answered. For the appraisal examination, a question is either right or wrong, and blanks are counted as wrong answers.

Keep Working   The appraisal examination is certainly an important one for you; otherwise, you would not have spent the time and effort to prepare yourself properly. There is no need to finish early. No extra points are given to persons who turn their examinations in first. If you finish before time, go back over the exam. Use all of the time given and use it wisely.

Do Not Change Answers for the Sake of Changing   More than likely you will have time to review your examination. If an error is obvious, then certainly you want to make the correction. However, do not change answers just for the sake of changing. Quite often your first instinct is the best one, and what you put down the first time through the exam may be the best choice.

When You Are Finished, Stop and Relax   Hopefully, you will complete the examination successfully as well as meet the other requirements for licensing or certification. However, if you do not pass the examination the first time, it is not the end of the world. If you must retake the exam, you will be in a much better position the second time around in terms of knowing the types of questions and how they are worded. Plan on retaking the examination as soon as possible; during the interim, do what's necessary to ensure successful completion of the examination. Good luck!

Study Outline*

PART I: VALUATION PRINCIPLES AND REAL ESTATE MARKETS

I. Influences on Real Estate Value (% of Tests: Licensed Residential = 5%; Certified Residential = 5%; Certified General = 5%)
   A. Physical and environmental
   B. Economic
   C. Governmental
   D. Social

II. Types of Value (% of Tests: Licensed Residential = 5%; Certified Residential = 5%; Certified General = 6%)
   A. Market value or value in exchange
   B. Price
   C. Cost
   D. Investment value
   E. Value in use
   F. Assessed value
   G. Insurable value
   H. Going-concern value

III. Economic Principles (% of Tests: Licensed Residential = 5%; Certified Residential = 5%; Certified General = 6%)
   A. Anticipation
   B. Balance
   C. Change
   D. Competition
   E. Conformity
   F. Contribution

---

*   The residential licensing and certified residential exams are likely to cover the topics in Parts I through V and the topics noted by an asterisk under Parts VI through IX. The certified general exam is likely to cover all the topics in this outline.

      G. Increasing and decreasing returns
      H. Substitution
      I. Supply and demand
      J. Surplus productivity

IV. Real Estate Markets and Analysis (% of Tests: Licensed Residential = 4%; Certified Residential = 4%; Certified General = 5%)
      A. Characteristics of real estate markets
          1. Availability of information
          2. Changes in supply vs. demand
          3. Immobility of real estate
          4. Segmented markets
          5. Regulations
      B. Absorption analysis
          1. Demographic data
          2. Competition
          3. Absorption
          4. Forecasts
          5. Existing space inventory
          6. Current and projected space surplus
          7. New space
      C. Role of money and capital markets
          1. Competing investments
          2. Sources of capital
      D. Real estate financing
          1. Mortgage terms and concepts
          2. Mortgage payment plans
          3. Types of mortgages

PART II: LEGAL CONSIDERATIONS

V. Legal Considerations in Appraisal (% of Tests: Licensed Residential = 5%; Certified Residential = 5%; Certified General = 4%)
      A. Real estate vs. real property
      B. Real property vs. personal property
          1. Fixtures
          2. Trade fixtures
          3. Machinery and equipment
      C. Limitations on real estate ownership
          1. Private
              a) Deed restrictions
              b) Leases
              c) Mortgages
              d) Easements
              e) Liens
              f) Encroachments

2. Public
   a) Police power
      (1) Zoning
      (2) Building and fire codes
      (3) Environmental regulations
   b) Taxation
      (1) Property tax
      (2) Special assessments
   c) Eminent domain
   d) Escheat
D. Legal rights and interests
   1. Fee simple estate
   2. Life estate
   3. Leasehold interest
   4. Leased fee interest
   5. Other legal interests
      a) Easement
      b) Encroachment
E. Forms of property ownership
   1. Individual
   2. Tenancies and undivided interests
   3. Special ownership forms
      a) Condominium
      b) Cooperative
      c) Time-sharing
F. Legal descriptions
   1. Metes and bounds
   2. Government survey
   3. Lot and block
G. Transfer of title
   1. Basic types of deeds
   2. Recordation

PART III: HIGHEST AND BEST USE ANALYSIS, PROPERTY DESCRIPTION, AND THE VALUATION PROCESS

VI. **Highest and Best Use Analysis (% of Tests: Licensed Residential = 9%; Certified Residential = 9%; Certified General = 9%)**
   A. Four tests
      1. Physically possible
      2. Legally permitted
      3. Economically feasible
      4. Maximally productive
   B. Vacant site or as if vacant
   C. As improved
   D. Interim use
   E. Application of highest and best use

VII. **Property Description and the Valuation Process (% of Tests: Licensed Residential = 11%; Certified Residential = 11%; Certified General = 10%)**
   A. Definition of the problem
      1. Purpose and use of appraisal
      2. Interests to be appraised
      3. Type of value to be estimated
      4. Date of the value estimate
      5. Limiting conditions
   B. Collection and analysis of data
      1. National and regional trends
      2. Economic base
      3. Local area and neighborhood
         a) Employment
         b) Income
         c) Trends
         d) Access
         e) Locational convenience
      4. Site and improvements
         a) Market analysis
         b) Geographic characteristics of the land/site
         c) Improvements—architectural styles/types of construction
   C. Analysis of highest and best use
   D. Application and limitations of each approach to value
      1. Sales comparison
      2. Cost
      3. Income capitalization
   E. Reconciliation and final value estimate
   F. The appraisal report

PART IV: SALES COMPARISON APPROACH

VIII. **Sales Comparison Approach (% of Tests: Licensed Residential = 15%; Certified Residential = 15%; Certified General = 10%)**
   A. Research and selection of comparables
      1. Data sources
      2. Verification
      3. Units of comparison
         a) Income
            (1) Potential gross income multiplier
            (2) Effective gross income multiplier
            (3) Overall rate
         b) Size
            (1) Square foot
            (2) Acres
            (3) Other
         c) Utility (examples only)
            (1) Rooms
            (2) Beds
            (3) Other

    B. Elements of comparison
        1. Property rights conveyed
           a) Easements
           b) Leased fee/leasehold
           c) Mineral rights
           d) Others
        2. Financing terms and cash equivalency
           a) Loan payment
           b) Loan balance
        3. Conditions of sale
           a) Arm's-length sale
           b) Personalty
        4. Market conditions at time of contract and closing
        5. Location
        6. Physical characteristics
    C. Adjustment process
        1. Sequence of adjustments
        2. Dollar adjustments
        3. Percentage adjustments
        4. Paired sales analysis
    D. Reconciliation
    E. Application of sales comparison approach

PART V: VALUATION METHODS AND THE COST APPROACH

    IX. Site Value (% of Tests: Licensed Residential = 5%; Certified Residential = 5%; Certified General = 4%)
    A. Sales comparison
    B. Land residual
    C. Allocation
    D. Extraction
    E. Ground rent capitalization*
    F. Subdivision analysis*
        1. Development cost: direct and indirect
        2. Contractor's overhead and profit
        3. Forecast absorption and gross sales
        4. Entrepreneurial profit
        5. Discounted value conclusion
    G. Plottage and assemblage

    X. Cost Approach (% of Tests: Licensed Residential = 9%; Certified Residential = 9%; Certified General = 6%)
    A. Concepts and definitions
    B. Steps in cost approach

---

* Only these topics from this part of the outline are likely to be on the licensed residential and certified residential exams.

1. Reproduction vs. replacement cost
    a) Comparative unit method
    b) Unit-in-place method
    c) Quantity survey method
    d) Cost service index
2. Accrued depreciation
    a) Types of depreciation
        (1) Physical deterioration
            (a) Curable and incurable
            (b) Short-lived and long-lived
        (2) Functional obsolescence
            (a) Curable and incurable
            (b) Superadequacy
            (c) Defects and deficiency
        (3) External obsolescence
            (a) Locational
            (b) Economic
    b) Methods of estimating depreciation
        (1) Age-life method
        (2) Break-down method and sequence of deductions
        (3) Market extraction of depreciation
C. Application of the cost approach

PART VI: INCOME APPROACH

XI. **Income Approach (% of Tests: Licensed Residential = 7%; Certified Residential = 7%; Certified General = 15%)**
    A. Estimation of income and expenses*
        1. Gross market income*
        2. Effective gross income*
            a) Vacancy*
            b) Collection loss*
        3. Operating expenses*
            a) Fixed expenses*
            b) Variable expenses*
            c) Reserve for replacements*
        4. Net operating income*
    B. Operating statement ratios
        1. Operating expense ratio*
        2. Net income ratio
        3. Break-even ratio
    C. Direct capitalization
        1. Relevance and limitations*
        2. Overall capitalization rate*
        3. Gross income (rent) multiplier and net income ratio*
        4. Band of investment (mortgage equity) techniques*

---

* Only these topics from this part of the outline are likely to be on the licensed residential and certified residential exams.

    5. Residual techniques

        a) Land (building value given)

        b) Building (land value given)

        c) Equity (mortgage value given)

D. Cash flow estimates (before tax only)

    1. Operating years

        a) Estimating NOI with a change in NOI

        b) Estimating NOI using lease information

        c) Cash flow (NOI less mortgage payment)

    2. Reversion

        a) Estimating resale with a change in value

        b) Estimating resale with a terminal capitalization rate

        c) Cash flow (sale price less mortgage balance)

        d) Deduction for costs of sale and legal fees to calculate net reversion

E. Measures of cash flow

    1. Equity dividend rate (cash on cash rate)

    2. Debt coverage ratio

F. Discounted cash flow capitalization (DCF)

    1. Relevance and limitations

    2. Potential gross income and expense estimates

        a) Market vs. contract

        b) Vacancy and lease commissions

        c) Tenant improvements and concessions

    3. Discount rates and yield rates (definition and concept but no calculations of yield rate)

    4. Discounting cash flows (from operations and reversion where all cash flows are projected in dollar amounts and tables or calculators can be used)

PART VII: VALUATION OF PARTIAL INTERESTS AND APPRAISAL MATH/ STATISTICS

XII. Valuation of Partial Interests (% of Tests: Licensed Residential = 1%; Certified Residential = 1%; Certified General = 1%)

A. Interests created by a lease

    1. Leased fee*

    2. Leasehold*

    3. Subleasehold

    4. Renewal options

    5. Tenant improvements

    6. Concessions

B. Lease provisions

    1. Overage rent

    2. Expense stops

    3. Net leases

    4. Minimum rent

    5. Percentage rent

---

*   Only these topics from this part of the outline are likely to be on the licensed residential and certified residential exams.

6. CPI adjustments
7. Excess rent
C. Other partial interests*
   1. Life estates*
   2. Undivided interest in commonly held property*
   3. Easements*
   4. Time-shares*
   5. Cooperatives*
   6. Leased fee estate*
   7. Leasehold estate*

XIII. **Appraisal Math and Statistics (% of Tests: Licensed Residential = 3%; Certified Residential = 3%; Certified General = 4%)**
A. Compound interest concepts
   1. Future value of $1
   2. Present value of $1
   3. Future value of an annuity of $1 per period
   4. Present value of an annuity of $1 per period
   5. Sinking fund factor
   6. Installment to amortize $1 per period (loan constant)
B. Statistical concepts used in appraisal
   1. Mean*
   2. Median*
   3. Mode*
   4. Range*
   5. Standard deviation*

PART VIII: APPRAISAL AND ETHICS*

XIV. **Uniform Standards of Professional Appraisal Practice (USPAP) (%of Tests: Licensed Residential = 16%; Certified Residential = 16%; Certified General = 15%)**
A. Preamble
B. Ethics Rule
C. Competency Rule
D. Scope of Work
E. Jurisdictional Exception Rule
F. Definitions
G. Standard 1—Real Property Appraisal, Development
H. Standard 2—Real Property Appraisal, Reporting
I. Standard 3—Appraisal Review, Development and Reporting
J. Standards 4–10**

---

*   Only these topics from this part of the outline are likely to be on the licensed residential and certified residential exam. (Note: In some jurisdictions, compound interest concepts are covered on all examinations.)

** Standards 4–10 of the USPAP are not covered on the majority of state exams.

PART IX: STATE-SPECIFIC TOPICS *

    A. Definitions
    B. Exemptions
    C. Qualifications for licensing
    D. Creation of regulatory agency
    E. Maintaining license
    F. Denial, suspension, revocation of license
    G. Hearing procedures
    H. Renewal requirements
    I.   Uniform standards
    J.   Rules and regulations

---

*   State-specific topics are not covered in this book. Contact the appropriate regulatory agency in your state for information on state-specific topics. Each jurisdiction can provide you with a copy of applicable appraisal regulation in that jurisdiction. See Appendix A for the contact information of state real estate appraisal boards.

Valuation Principles and Real Estate Markets and Analysis

KEY TERMS

absorption rates	deed of trust	mortgagor
amortized mortgage	economic forces	market value (value in exchange)
anticipation	feasibility study	
assessed value	going-concern value	opportunity cost
balance	governmental forces	physical/environmental forces
blanket mortgage	increasing and decreasing returns	
buydown		price versus cost
change	insurable value	social forces
competition	investment value	substitution
conformity	liquidation value	supply and demand
consistent use theory	market analysis	surplus productivity
contribution	mortgagee	value in use

DIAGNOSTIC EXAM I*

1. An estimate of the rate at which a particular type of space will be sold each year is referred to as
   A. absorption.
   B. rentup.
   C. presales.
   D. occupancy.

2. What term is used for a transaction in which all parties to the transaction are dealing from equal bargaining positions?
   A. Anticipation
   B. Open market
   C. Arm's-length
   D. Secondary market

3. Which appraisal concept (principle) implies that land should *NOT* be valued on the basis of one use while improvements are valued on the basis of a different use?
   A. Balance
   B. Anticipation
   C. Consistent use
   D. Substitution

4. Which statement is *TRUE* regarding the relationship between the market value of a property and its sales price at the time the property sold?
   A. They are the same at that point in time.
   B. The sales price will always exceed market value.
   C. The market value will always exceed the sales price.
   D. The sales price could be more or less than the market value, depending on the motivations of the buyer and seller and details of the transaction.

5. An appraisal of the price that a property would sell for based in a quick sale would normally be estimating what type of value?
   A. Market value
   B. Use value
   C. Going-concern value
   D. Liquidation value

6. A neighborhood's life cycle consists of which four stages?
   A. Growth, stability, decline, and disintegration
   B. Growth, stability, decline, and revitalization
   C. Growth, stability, displacement, and gentrification
   D. Stability, decline, gentrification, and revitalization

7. Which factor is *NOT* normally considered to have an effect on the demand for real estate?
   A. Demographic data
   B. Number of vacancies
   C. Fire and police protection
   D. Transportation facilities

8. Primary data refers to
   A. the main data used by the appraiser.
   B. data collected by the appraiser.
   C. data that have a direct impact on value.
   D. data published by a reliable source.

9. Social characteristics that affect real estate values include which classification of people?
   A. Race
   B. Religion
   C. National origin
   D. None of the above

---

* We have included "quick review" questions, designated by a gray-box design element, that convey the essential points of each chapter. These questions should be used as a review tool only after the entire exam has been completed. These quick review questions are not meant to replace the entire exam.

10. Which feature represents physical data that must be considered by the appraiser?
    A. Easements
    B. Plottage
    C. Public restrictions
    D. Utility connections

11. If a real estate development happens to go bankrupt, who would get money back first from liquidation?
    A. Debt financiers
    B. Equity financiers
    C. Consultants to the project
    D. Developers

12. What term *BEST* identifies the most probable price as of a given date for which specified property rights should sell to a knowledge-able buyer in a competitive market?
    A. Market value
    B. Value in use
    C. Market price
    D. Investment value

13. What is meant by the term *surplus productivity*?
    A. The excess in revenues received above the market rate
    B. The income attributable to land rent that remains after labor, capital, and manage-ment have been compensated
    C. The income received after operating expenses, taxes, and debt service have been paid
    D. The income received after the marginal level of productivity is reached

14. Which condition is *NOT* an economic force that affects real estate?
    A. Building codes
    B. Desire
    C. Effective purchasing power
    D. Supply and demand

15. All of these classes of persons are protected under the Federal Fair Housing Act *EXCEPT*
    A. race.
    B. national origin.
    C. sex.
    D. age.

16. The term *investment value* is *BEST* described as value to whom?
    A. A typical investor
    B. A particular investor
    C. A user
    D. A lender

17. A set of percentages indicating the proportion of site value attributable to each additional amount of depth in the lot is referred to as
    A. depth tables.
    B. metes and bounds.
    C. standard parallel tables.
    D. quadrangle percentages.

18. The interest or value that the owner has in real estate after the liens against it is referred to as
    A. capital.
    B. debt.
    C. principal.
    D. equity.

19. The legally and physically possible use that, at the time of appraisal, is *MOST* likely to produce the greatest land value is known as
    A. highest and best use.
    B. investment value.
    C. going-concern use.
    D. fee simple use.

20. Which land use is generally *NOT* considered income property?
    A. Hotels
    B. Undeveloped land
    C. Office buildings
    D. Apartment buildings

21. What term is used for the act or process of developing an opinion of value?
    A. Appraisal
    B. Market analysis
    C. Investment analysis
    D. Feasibility analysis

22. A study of the supply and demand conditions in a specific area for a specific type of property is referred to as
   A. assemblage.
   B. projection analysis.
   C. economic base.
   D. market analysis.

23. According to common income taxation terminology, which land use is residential property?
   A. Hotel
   B. Office building
   C. Apartments
   D. Apartments and hotels

24. Risk resulting from uncertainty in rents, vacancies or operating expenses is referred to as
   A. business risk.
   B. operating risk.
   C. economic risk.
   D. interest risk.

25. Risk due to uncertainty in future interest rates is referred to as
   A. mortgage risk.
   B. financial risk.
   C. underwriting risk.
   D. interest risk.

26. Risk due to the use of debt financing is referred to as
   A. interest risk.
   B. financial risk.
   C. leverage risk.
   D. equity risk.

27. A collection of retail stores with a common parking area and generally one or more large department, discount, or food stores, and sometimes including an enclosed mall or walkway, is commonly referred to as a
   A. mall.
   B. retail complex.
   C. mixed-use development.
   D. shopping center.

28. A large national tenant that occupies space in a shopping center is often referred to as a(n)
   A. discount tenant.
   B. anchor tenant.
   C. department store.
   D. mall tenant.

29. What term applies to a designation of the U.S. Census Bureau for metropolitan areas with a central city having a specified minimum population and including all counties that are economically linked to the central city?
   A. Central business district
   B. Neighborhood
   C. Township
   D. Metropolitan statistical area (MSA)

30. Which value BEST reflects investment value?
   A. Value to a typical buyer or seller
   B. Value to a specific buyer or seller
   C. Value for insurance purposes
   D. Value for property tax purposes

31. Federal fair housing laws are administered by which government agency?
   A. Attorney General
   B. Department of Housing and Urban Development
   C. Federal Reserve System
   D. Department of Human Resources

32. One important characteristic of land that adds to the land's value is its
   A. mobility.
   B. divisibility.
   C. stability of value.
   D. reversionary use.

33. The term market value is MOST closely associated with which term?
   A. Value in use
   B. Assessed value
   C. Intrinsic value
   D. Value in exchange

34. What is the distinction between the terms *market price* and *market value*?
    A. Market price is synonymous with replacement cost, while market value is the same as assessed value.
    B. Market price is what the seller asks for, while market value is what the buyer actually pays.
    C. Market price is what the property sells for, while market value is what the sales price should be to a typical buyer.
    D. Market price is what is currently owed on the property, while market value is what is actually paid for the property.

35. Which condition is *NOT* a basic assumption in the definition of market value?
    A. The seller receives cash or its equivalent.
    B. Both the buyer and the seller are knowledgeable about current market conditions.
    C. The value will be as of a specific date.
    D. The property will sell promptly.

36. Under which condition would an appraiser appraise the value of the property as of a future date?
    A. If the current use is the highest and best use
    B. If the appraiser uses all three approaches to value
    C. If the market is stable and there is no inflation
    D. If the value is appropriately defined for a future date of the value

37. The term *market value* is sometimes explained as a theoretical economic concept. Part of the definition of *market value* addresses how payment is made. In the common definition of *market value,* the method of payment is assumed to be in what form?
    A. Cash to the seller
    B. Cash to the buyer
    C. Purchase-money mortgage by the seller
    D. No financing by the buyer

38. Which condition is assumed in the normal definition of *market value*?
    A. The stated value is as of a future date.
    B. The property will sell promptly.
    C. Payment will be made in cash or its equivalent.
    D. Only the buyer is knowledgeable as to the potential uses of the property.

39. In valuation theory, the economic concept that considers the usefulness of property is known as
    A. situs.
    B. linkage.
    C. plottage value.
    D. functional utility.

40. Which principle best describes the effect of an international airport on the value of a nearby residential subdivision?
    A. Substitution
    B. Highest and best use
    C. Externalities
    D. Conformity

41. The fundamental economic (valuation) principle underlying the sales comparison (market) approach to value is known as
    A. anticipation.
    B. conformity.
    C. highest and best use.
    D. substitution.

42. What type of analysis identifies land uses that are legally permissible, physically possible, and financially feasible?
    A. Sensitivity
    B. Highest and best use
    C. Feasibility
    D. Supply and demand

43. The highest and best use of a parcel of land will result in which action?
    A. Highest floor area ratio
    B. Greatest building value
    C. Largest building size
    D. Greatest present value of the land

44. In considering the highest and best use of a parcel of land to be improved with an office building, the appraiser determines the optimal land to building ratio for the parcel. Which economic principle does this illustrate?
    A. Anticipation
    B. Balance
    C. Contribution
    D. Substitution

45. The income approach to value is based primarily on which economic principle?
    A. Anticipation
    B. Conformity
    C. Highest and best use
    D. Substitution

46. What economic principle would explain that when several houses with essentially the same utility are available, the one with the lowest price will attract the greatest demand?
    A. Anticipation
    B. Highest and best use
    C. Substitution
    D. Surplus productivity

47. An appraiser estimates the income for several possible uses of a vacant site for the purpose of estimating how that income contributes to the value of the land. This is an example of
    A. reconciliation.
    B. highest and best use analysis.
    C. market analysis.
    D. regression analysis.

48. Included in the definition of highest and best use are certain tests or criteria that must be met. Which condition is *NOT* a criterion in determining the highest and best use of land?
    A. Physically possible
    B. Legally permissible
    C. Financially feasible
    D. Socially acceptable

49. An existing site has an improvement on it such as a building. Which statement *BEST* describes the highest and best use of that site?
    A. It cannot be determined.
    B. It is automatically the current use because the site is improved.
    C. It may be different from the current use.
    D. If the improvement is a residence, then the land does not have a highest and best use.

50. An estimate of the accrued depreciation is an important part of the cost approach to value. Which economic principle is the foundation on which estimating accrued depreciation is based?
    A. Anticipation
    B. Balance
    C. Contribution
    D. Substitution

51. The sales comparison approach involves a step undertaken by the appraiser to adjust for such items as square footage, age, quality of construction, etc. What economic principle is the foundation on which this adjustment process is undertaken?
    A. Anticipation
    B. Contribution
    C. Substitution
    D. Surplus productivity

52. Which commonly accepted economic principle is used to explain that when several parcels of property with substantially the same utility are available on the market, the one with the lowest asking price will attract the greatest demand?
    A. Anticipation
    B. Balance
    C. Contribution
    D. Substitution

53. The use of a parcel of real estate that generates the largest residual land value is known as that parcel's
    A. efficient use.
    B. highest and best use.
    C. intrinsic use.
    D. income use.

54. The term used to explain the difference between the value of a parcel of land and the outstanding balance on an existing mortgage is known as
    A. sales price.
    B. equity.
    C. fee simple.
    D. escheat.

55. The financial device used to maximize cash flow using other people's money is commonly referred to as
    A. liquidity.
    B. equity.
    C. leverage.
    D. tax shelter.

56. Which statement is correct in regard to an increase in the loan-to-value ratio for a loan to finance the purchase of a parcel of land?
    A. The selling price of the land must be higher.
    B. The selling price of the land must be lower.
    C. The equity required of the borrower must be lower.
    D. The equity required of the borrower must be higher.

57. To achieve positive leverage, mortgage money would have to be obtained at an interest rate that is
    A. equal to the prime rate.
    B. equal to the property yield.
    C. more than the property yield.
    D. less than the property yield.

58. Liquidity is normally defined as the
    A. difference between income and expenses.
    B. purchasing power of an asset.
    C. ease of converting an asset into cash.
    D. difference between value and outstanding debt.

Questions 59 and 60 are based on the following information:

Certain properties have a very limited number of uses, perhaps only one use. In the case of a heavy manufacturing plant, the highest and best use probably is to continue the present use.

59. This is an example of which type of property?
    A. Nonconforming use property
    B. Special purpose property
    C. Variance property
    D. Interim use property

60. Which of the traditional approaches to value is normally considered the most applicable for this type of property?
    A. Cost approach
    B. Comparable sales approach
    C. Income capitalization approach
    D. Gross income multiplier approach

APPLICATION-STYLE QUESTIONS

Questions 61 through 65 are based on the following information:

Your appraisal assignment, a residential property, requires you to collect a great deal of information due to the uniqueness of the property; thus, you have to spend a significant amount of time collecting cost and sales data. In addition to having good road access, the subject property is also conveniently located near a shopping center and two schools.

61. The cost and sales data you collect as part of this appraisal assignment is an example of what type of data?
    A. Primary
    B. Secondary
    C. Intrinsic
    D. Supplementary

62. The fact that the subject property has good access to schools, shopping, and roads favorably impacts the time-distance necessary to travel. This economic concept is commonly explained as
    A. obsolescence.
    B. linkage.
    C. appreciation.
    D. regression.

63. One of the sales properties you look at as a possible comp is located on a busy street. Its value, therefore, is negatively impacted by the high traffic flow. This negative impact on value is commonly explained as the principle of
    A. anticipation.
    B. substitution.
    C. externalities.
    D. highest and best use.

64. If in your analysis you conclude that similar properties are selling for around $300,000, what economic principle explains that the market will probably pay no more than $300,000 for the subject property?
    A. Substitution
    B. Anticipation
    C. Externalities
    D. Linkage

65. The subject property, as well as the three properties surrounding it, are prime candidates for a developer to purchase, have them all rezoned commercial, and establish a different use that would result in income for the new owner. In this scenario, the developer would be basing his decision on what economic principle?
    A. Externalities
    B. Depreciation
    C. Amortization
    D. Anticipation

ANSWERS TO DIAGNOSTIC EXAM I

1. **A.** *Absorption* is a general term for either sale or leasing of new space that comes on the market. The term *rentup* would apply only to space that is leased.

2. **C.** An arm's-length transaction is one where both buyer and seller are acting in their own best interests and are not under duress to act. It can be a private transaction, i.e., not on the open market and still be considered an arm's-length transaction.

3. **C.** Based on the highest and best use theory, improvements must contribute to land value to have value themselves. Therefore, land and improvements are valued separately on the same use.

4. **D.** The market value represents the price a typical buyer should pay for the property, whereas the sales price represents the actual price a specific buyer paid for the property. They may not be the same.

5. **D.** This is a liquidation value. Market value does not assume that a quick sale occurs; it assumes a reasonable time on the open market.

6. **B.** Growth is a period during which a neighborhood gains public favor and acceptance. Stability, the following stage, describes a period with no large increases or decreases in demand. Decline describes a stage of diminishing demand, and revitalization occurs when the neighborhood is renewed with increasing demand. Gentrification describes a process in which neighborhood properties are purchased and renovated; this is not included in the normal life cycle of a neighborhood.

7. **B.** The number of vacancies affects the supply of real estate. For example, developers are less likely to create more space if vacancy levels are already high.

8. **B.** Primary data refers to any data collected by the appraiser, including information that does not have a direct impact on the value of the property. Secondary data is that collected and published by another party (e.g., census data or multiple listing services).

9. **D.** Race, religion, and national origin of owners/tenants have not been shown to have a direct impact on value and should never be included in an appraisal assignment.

10. **D.** Easements, plottage, and public restrictions are actions or agreements. Utility connections are physically present on a property.

11. **A.** Debt financiers receive priority over equity holders because of the legal position held by the lender(s).

12. **A.** Market value is the value to a typical buyer, whereas investment value is the value to a specific buyer.

13. **B.** Surplus productivity is the concept on which residual valuation techniques are based. Land receives any surplus income after providing a return on the building.

14. **A.** Forces that affect real estate include social, economic, government, and environmental factors. Economic forces affect real estate values through changes in supply and demand, population wants and needs, purchasing power, employment and wage levels, new development, and existing stock and prices. Building codes are considered a governmental force.

15. **D.** Age is not a protected class under the Federal Fair Housing Act. Age is protected under the Equal Credit Opportunity Act.

16. **B.** Investment value is for a particular investor who may or may not be typical. Value to a typical investor is a description of market value.

17. **A.** Depth tables are sometimes used as a means of indicating the proportion of site value to each additional amount of depth. The reader should be aware of the inherent weakness in reaching valuation conclusions from depth tables.

18. **D.** Equity is an owner's interest in property. Equity equals the difference between the property value and the debt value.

19. **A.** The highest and best use is measured as the use that produces the greatest residual income to the land.

20. **B.** Undeveloped land is not considered income property. Hotels, office buildings, and apartment buildings all have the ability to produce income.

21. **A.** According to the definitions in the Uniform Standards of Professional Appraisal Practice, an appraisal is the act or process of developing an opinion of value. The other types of analyses do not necessarily estimate value.

22. **D.** Market analysis is important in appraisal assignments since it identifies the market supply and demand for a particular type of real estate.

23. **C.** In income taxation terminology, rental units used for dwelling purposes not of a transient nature (hotel, motel) are considered residential property. Other types of real estate income property are nonresidential property. Note: To qualify as residential property, at least 80 percent of a building's income should be derived from dwelling units.

24. **A.** Risk due to uncertainty in the operations of a property or business is known as business risk. A fluctuation in cash flows due to changes in the operations of a property will affect the return to the investor.

25. **D.** Interest risk is caused by fluctuations in interest rates, which may cause changes in debt payments or property value.

26. **B.** Financial risk arises from the method of financing chosen. If an investor uses all equity to purchase a property, financial risk does not exist.

27. **D.** The term *shopping center* refers to the small stores and anchors present in the center. The term *mall* refers to the small stores and common areas. A mixed-use development refers to a complex that contains different types of real estate such as retail, office, and hotel.

28. **B.** Anchor tenants are usually department stores in larger shopping centers. However, smaller centers often have grocery or discount stores as an anchor.

29. **D.** A metropolitan statistical area (MSA) is an area with a central city having a specified minimum population. A neighborhood is a group of complementary land uses. A district is a type of neighborhood that has homogeneous land use, and a central business district is the core of the city where the major businesses are concentrated. A township is a measurement of land containing 36 square miles of land.

30. **B.** Investment value is for a specific buyer or investor. Market value is value to a typical buyer. Value to a lender would tend to be based more on minimizing the likelihood of becoming an owner through default. Value to a user could reflect noninvestment criteria.

31. **B.** Federal fair housing laws are administered by the Department of Housing and Urban Development (HUD).

32. **B.** Real estate involves legal rights and interests that may be divided and sold separately. The economic impact is that different users, such as tenants, may have legal interests in real estate without ownership. Therefore, different legal interests may result in different values being placed on the property.

33. **D.** Market value is a type of value in exchange in that it reflects the value that a willing buyer and a willing seller in a free market should agree on.

34. **C.** Market price and market value do not refer to the same thing. Market price is what the property sells for, while market value is what the sales price should be to the typical buyer.

35. **D.** The concept of the term *market value* does not assume that the property in question will necessarily sell promptly. Current market conditions may in fact mean that the property will remain on the market for an extended period of time. The other three choices are all included in the underlying assumptions of market value.

36. **D.** Proposed projects often require an estimate of value upon completion of the project. In these situations the value should be clearly defined as an estimate of future (prospective) value. Note: Although this is an estimate of future market value, it is usually not defined as *market value*.

37. **A.** Assumed in the definition of *market value* is the fact that the price is stated in terms of cash or its equivalent to the seller. If the seller agrees to take back financing via a purchase-money mortgage, at less than current market rates, then this is not cash or its equivalent.

38. **C.** Market value is defined as the price in terms of cash or its equivalent upon which a willing buyer and a willing seller will agree, where neither is under undue pressure to act and both are knowledgeable as to market conditions and are acting in their own best interest. A prompt sale of the property is not assumed in the definition of *market value*.

39. **D.** Functional utility attempts to consider and measure the usefulness of property.

40. **C.** Influences outside a property's boundaries that may have an effect on its value are called externalities.

41. **D.** The principle of substitution states that the maximum value of an item (for example, a house) is set by the cost of acquiring an equally desirable substitute.

42. **B.** *Highest and best use* analysis identifies uses that are legally permissible, physically possible, and financially feasible.

43. **D.** Highest and best use is explained as that specific use of land that will generate the highest present value of the land.

44. **B.** The principle of balance states that there is an ideal equilibrium in assembling and using the factors of production. In this example, the appraiser has determined the balance between the land and the building.

45. **A.** The principle of anticipation is the basis on which the income approach is derived. The principle states that value changes in expectation of some future benefit or detriment affecting the property.

46. **C.** The principle of substitution would explain why the maximum value of a parcel of real estate is set by the cost of acquiring an equally desirable substitute. Thus the lowest priced house among equals in terms of utility will attract the greatest demand.

47. **B.** Highest and best use analysis involves analyzing income for alternative uses of a site to determine which use maximizes land value.

48. **D.** Included in the criteria for highest and best use is a use that is (1) physically possible, (2) legally permissible, (3) financially feasible, and (4) maximally productive. Whether a specific use is socially acceptable is not part of the criteria for estimating highest and best use.

49. **C.** The highest and best use of land may be different from the existing use. In theory, every parcel of land has a highest and best use, and the fact that the current use is residential would not mean that a highest and best use does not exist.

50. **C.** The principle of contribution states that the value of a component part of a piece of property is equal to what that component adds to the total value, less any costs incurred. This principle is the basis on which accrued depreciation is subtracted from replacement or reproduction cost when using the cost approach to value.

51. **B.** The principle of contribution is an economic principle that states that the value of a component part of a piece of property is equal to what the component part adds to the total value. For example, square footage is a normal adjustment since the value of property is directly related to size. Likewise, age and quality of construction also influence value.

52. **D.** The principle of substitution states that the maximum value of a parcel of real estate is set by the cost of acquiring an equally desirable substitute. For example, a house would not sell for $125,000 if equally desirable substitutes were available for $100,000.

53. **B.** Highest and best use is that use that will result in the greatest residual land value. Every parcel of real estate has a highest and best use, which may (and often does) change over time.

54. **B.** Equity is defined as the difference between value and current debt. Equity may be greater or less than the original purchase price.

55. **C.** Leverage is the use of borrowed money to finance all or part of the purchase price of an item such as real estate.

56. **C.** Equity is the difference between the value of property and the amount borrowed; thus, an increase in the loan-to-value ratio would mean less equity on the part of the borrower.

57. **D.** Leverage can be either positive or negative. For positive leverage to be achieved, the cost of the borrowed capital (mortgage money) would have to be less than the property yield. If the cost of the borrowed capital is greater, then negative leverage exists.

58. **C.** Liquidity is the ease with which an asset may be converted into cash. Quite often real estate is thought of as being nonliquid; however, under certain conditions, real estate investments may be quite liquid.

59. **B.** Properties that have a very limited number of uses, perhaps as few as one, are referred to as special purpose properties.

60. **A.** The cost approach has historically been appropriate in estimating the value of special purpose properties.

61. **A.** Primary data is information collected by the appraiser that is not available in a published source.

62. **B.** Linkage is the time-distance relationship between a property or neighborhood and other destinations, such as schools, work, or shopping.

63. **C.** The concept of externality is an economic principle that states that forces outside a property's boundaries may have a positive or negative effect on its value.

64. **A.** The principle of substitution states that a buyer will pay no more for a property than the cost of obtaining an equally desirable substitute.

65. **D.** The economic principle of anticipation states that value is created by the expectation of benefits to be received in the future.

5

Legal Considerations

KEY TERMS

adverse possession

air rights

bundle of rights

condemnation

condominium

cooperative

deed restriction

easement

eminent domain

encroachment

escheat

fee simple estate

fixture

general warranty deed

government (rectangular)
  survey system

joint tenancy

lease

leased-fee estate

leasehold estate

lien

life estate

lot-and-block system

metes-and-bounds
  system

millage rate

monument system

nonconforming use

personal property

police power

quitclaim deed

real estate

real property

special warranty deed

taxation

tenancy

tenancy by the entirety

tenancy in common

time-share

trade fixtures

variance

zoning

DIAGNOSTIC EXAM II*

1. The following partial legal description is given: "Beginning at the intersection of Highway 6 and going in a northerly direction for approximately 500 feet to a gravel road, then along the gravel road for approximately 1,000 feet to the property line of . . ." This description is an example of which legal method of land description?
   A. Monuments
   B. Lot-and-block
   C. Government survey
   D. Subdivision plat

2. Which statement is *FALSE* in regard to the mathematics of legal descriptions?
   A. A section of land contains 640 acres.
   B. There are 36 sections in a township.
   C. An acre contains 46,360 square feet.
   D. A square mile contains 640 acres.

3. The S 1/2 of the NW 1/4 of the SE 1/4 of a section of land contains how many acres?
   A. 20
   B. 40
   C. 160
   D. 640

4. In the government survey method of land description, an area six miles by six miles is referred to as a
   A. section.
   B. township.
   C. quadrant.
   D. plat.

5. The legal right to remove items such as topsoil or coal from land belonging to another is known as a(n)
   A. easement.
   B. profit.
   C. escheat.
   D. emblement.

6. When a deed of trust is used in the financing of real estate, the person making a pledge of the property being financed as security for the debt is known as the
   A. mortgagee.
   B. trustor.
   C. trustee.
   D. beneficiary.

7. When two or more individual parcels are legally encumbered by one mortgage and one of the parcels is to be freed from the encumbrance, the instrument used is a(n)
   A. partial release of mortgage.
   B. satisfaction agreement.
   C. subassignment of mortgage.
   D. estoppel certificate.

8. A tax assessment is intended to accomplish which result?
   A. Set the maximum price paid at a foreclosure sale
   B. Establish the asking price of property when listed for sale by owner
   C. Aid in the determination of how much property tax is due
   D. Determine market value

9. Which statement is *NOT* necessarily correct about a local zoning ordinance?
   A. Zoning can establish height restrictions on buildings.
   B. Zoning prevents decline in property values within a certain zoning district.
   C. Zoning is often used to separate incompatible land uses.
   D. Zoning establishes setback requirements for improvements on land.

---

* We have included "quick review" questions, designated by a gray-box design element, that convey the essential points of each chapter. These questions should be used as a review tool only after the entire exam has been completed. These quick review questions are not meant to replace the entire exam.

10. The three parties involved in a deed of trust are
    A. trustee, trustor, beneficiary.
    B. trustee, beneficiary, principal.
    C. beneficiary, principal, agent.
    D. trustee, trustor, benefactor.

11. Legally speaking, a condominium can be which type of property?
    A. Residential
    B. Commercial
    C. Industrial
    D. All of the above

12. A planned unit development (PUD) could *BEST* be explained by which statement?
    A. A means by which a developer can develop a large tract of land in various stages
    B. A type of special land use that allows a mixture of different land uses or densities
    C. A type of land use financed with government-backed securities
    D. Any land use in which land is dedicated to a homeowners association

13. Which component would *NOT* be found in a metes-and-bounds legal description method?
    A. Point of beginning
    B. Degrees, minutes, and seconds
    C. Range lines
    D. Benchmark

14. An easement in which no dominant estate exists, but rather only a servient estate exists, is known as a(n)
    A. easement by necessity.
    B. easement appurtenant.
    C. public easement.
    D. easement in gross.

15. The process of changing the use of a building from an apartment complex to a condominium form of ownership is normally referred to as a(n)
    A. conversion.
    B. proration.
    C. interim use.
    D. variance.

16. An easement in gross is defined as the right to use the land of another. What is the only requirement of an easement in gross?
    A. Recording of the easement in the public land records
    B. An annual payment for use of the easement
    C. No dominant estate
    D. At least two parcels of land, the dominant and servient estates

17. A mortgage secured by a legal claim against two or more separate properties is referred to as a
    A. wraparound mortgage.
    B. participation mortgage.
    C. blanket mortgage.
    D. ground lease mortgage.

18. In regard to zoning, which statement is correct?
    A. Zoning ordinances are always more restrictive than deed restrictions.
    B. A nonconforming use and a variance refer to the same thing.
    C. Zoning normally establishes land-use districts and provides for different restrictions within each district.
    D. Exclusionary zoning and spot zoning refer to the same thing.

19. The property tax due on real estate is calculated by what method?
    A. Dividing the tax rate by the assessed value
    B. Multiplying the tax rate by the assessed value
    C. Dividing the tax rate by the most probable sales price
    D. Multiplying the tax rate by the most probable sales price

20. Determining whether a specific article is
    a fixture would include all of these tests
    EXCEPT
    A. how the article is attached.
    B. the intention of the person who attached
       it.
    C. the cost of the article.
    D. the method of attachment.

21. If an area in a city were changed to residen-
    tial zoning, a commercial property already in
    use in the zone would normally be permitted
    as a(n)
    A. spot zone variance.
    B. exception.
    C. nonconforming use.
    D. variance.

22. In the rectangular survey method of land
    description, an area one mile by one mile is
    referred to as a
    A. plat.
    B. monument.
    C. section.
    D. township.

23. The E 1/2 of the NE 1/4 of the NW 1/4 of a
    section of land contains how many acres?
    A. 10
    B. 20
    C. 40
    D. 640

24. Which item would normally *NOT* be consid-
    ered a fixture?
    A. Wall-to-wall carpeting
    B. Area rug
    C. Storm door
    D. Built-in dishwasher

25. The extension of some improvement or
    object, such as a building or driveway, across
    the legal boundary of an adjoining tract of
    land is referred to as a(n)
    A. easement.
    B. emblement.
    C. encroachment.
    D. profit.

26. The portion of a condominium that is owned
    in severalty is referred to as a
    A. common element.
    B. limited common element.
    C. unit.
    D. cooperative.

27. Which statement is correct in regard to a
    condominium form of ownership?
    A. A condominium is a legal form of prop-
       erty ownership.
    B. A condominium provides each unit
       owner with a proprietary lease.
    C. A condominium provides the same legal
       interest as a cooperative.
    D. A condominium may not be owned by
       tenants in common.

28. In an agricultural lease in which there is
    unexpected termination of the lease, normally
    the lessee retains the legal right to
    A. receive a ground rent.
    B. recover any emblements.
    C. recover the encumbrances at harvest time.
    D. seek a reversion agreement.

29. The legal right of the state to acquire prop-
    erty of a decedent who died without a will
    and without heirs is referred to as
    A. eminent domain.
    B. escheat.
    C. dedication.
    D. devise.

30. If a building site has a floor-area-ratio (FAR) of 5:1, what is the maximum height for a building that covers one-fourth of the total lot?
    A. 1 story
    B. 4 stories
    C. 5 stories
    D. 20 stories

31. A geographic area used to physically separate two incompatible uses, such as a residential subdivision and an industrial park, is commonly referred to as a
    A. nonconforming use.
    B. variance.
    C. planned unit development.
    D. buffer zone.

32. Which technique gives a developer the legal right and flexibility to mix land uses and land-use intensities in the development of a tract of land?
    A. PUD
    B. VRM
    C. FRS
    D. PLAM

33. For property tax purposes, a church or hospital would normally be considered an
    A. easement.
    B. emblement.
    C. equalization factor.
    D. exemption.

34. A local tax levied against a property owner for the paving of a road running directly in front of the property is referred to as a
    A. road tax.
    B. special assessment tax.
    C. prescriptive easement tax.
    D. homeowners tax.

35. If the owner of the adjoining residential property paves a driveway that extends onto the subject property, legally the driveway is referred to as a(n)
    A. easement.
    B. emblement.
    C. encroachment.
    D. leasehold.

36. If property taxes are $320.25 and the assessed value is $8,725, what is the tax rate?
    A. $0.0367/$100
    B. $3.67/$100
    C. $36.70/$100
    D. $367/$100

37. Which statement *BEST* describes a lien?
    A. A personal privilege to pass over or cross the property of another
    B. A slanting structure placed against the primary building on a lot
    C. A legal claim upon the property of another as security for some debt or charge
    D. The difference between value and debt on a property

38. An indirect form of property ownership in which individuals own shares of a legal entity such as a corporation, which in turn owns the real estate, is known as a
    A. time-sharing agreement.
    B. condominium.
    C. cooperative.
    D. community property entity.

39. A tenant's right or legal interest in a cooperative form of ownership is considered
    A. real property.
    B. personal property.
    C. realty.
    D. fixtures.

40. Which statement *BEST* describes the typical ownership rights of the purchaser of a condominium?
    A. Owns shares of a corporation that owns the property
    B. Owns a tenancy in common in the unit occupied as well as common areas
    C. Has fee simple ownership in the unit occupied plus a joint tenancy in shared areas
    D. Has fee simple ownership in the unit occupied plus a tenancy in common in the shared areas

41. Which definition is appropriate for the term *real estate*?
    A. Land and anything permanently attached to the land
    B. Property that is not encumbered by leases
    C. Buildings and other improvements
    D. Buildings and fixtures

42. Which term applies to an item that originally was personal property but has become real property as a result of being attached to a building?
    A. Real property
    B. Fixture
    C. Appendix
    D. Chattel

43. Which term refers to the rights of a person who owns a property but has leased it to someone else?
    A. Leased fee estate
    B. Leasehold estate
    C. Fee simple estate
    D. Lessee's estate

44. Which definition is *MOST* appropriate for the term *easement*?
    A. A legal document used to secure the performance of an obligation
    B. An agreement that grants the right to exclusive possession and use of real estate of an owner's property
    C. An instrument that transfers ownership interest in real property to another party
    D. A nonownership real property interest that grants a second party the right to use an owner's land

45. In a lease, the term *landlord* refers to the
    A. lessee.
    B. lessor.
    C. limited partner.
    D. mortgagee.

46. The lender who makes a mortgage loan is referred to as the
    A. grantor.
    B. mortgagor.
    C. mortgagee.
    D. grantee.

47. The term *mortgagor* refers to which person?
    A. Grantor
    B. Trustee
    C. Lender
    D. Borrower

48. The term *real property* refers to
    A. the physical land and structures (appurtenances) affixed to it.
    B. the physical land and structures affixed to it, not including fixtures.
    C. land and buildings, including fixtures.
    D. all rights, interests, and benefits inherent in the ownership of physical land and the structures affixed to it.

49. If the density of land development permitted by deed restrictions is more restrictive (less density) than that allowed by zoning, then the land can
    A. be developed only to the density allowed in the deed.
    B. be developed only to the density allowed in the zoning.
    C. not be developed.
    D. be developed to the density allowed in the zoning after a deed certificate is filed.

50. Eminent domain gives the government the right to
    A. acquire interests in private property without the consent of the owner.
    B. regulate property to protect public safety and health.
    C. acquire interests in private property when an owner dies without a will or known heirs.
    D. create zoning ordinances.

51. If a parcel of land is described as "Lot 42 of Southridge Subdivision," it is being described by which legal description?
    A. Geodetic survey system
    B. Lot-and-block system
    C. Metes-and-bounds system
    D. Government survey system

52. The term *metes-and-bounds* refers to
    A. a method for describing property.
    B. an appraisal of a property.
    C. the transportation to a site.
    D. the linkages to a property.

53. Which limitation is *NOT* a power of the government?
    A. Deed restrictions
    B. Taxation
    C. Police power
    D. Escheat

54. Which statement differentiates personal property from real property?
    A. Real property is the physical structure affixed to the land; personal property includes property affixed to the structure.
    B. Real property includes all interests, benefits, and rights from the ownership of real estate; personal property includes only physical items.
    C. Real property includes all interests, benefits, and rights from the ownership of a physical structure affixed to the land; personal property includes movable items.
    D. Real property is the physical structure affixed to the land; personal property includes movable items.

55. The process of physically taking private property for public use or purpose is referred to as
    A. eminent domain.
    B. police power.
    C. condemnation.
    D. escheat.

56. Which method of legal description does *NOT* typically define real property?
    A. Metes-and-bounds system
    B. Rectangular survey system
    C. Quantity survey system
    D. Lot-and-block system

57. The term *leasehold estate* refers to which rights or responsibility?
    A. The rights of the owner of a property that has been leased
    B. The rights of the tenant who has leased property
    C. The rights of the owner of a property that is not currently leased
    D. The responsibility of a trustee who holds the lease

58. The term *leased-fee estate* refers to which rights or responsibility?
    A. The rights of the owner of a property that has been leased
    B. The rights of the tenant who has leased property
    C. The rights of the owner of a property that is not currently leased
    D. The responsibility of a trustee who holds the lease

59. A clause in a deed that limits the use of real estate is referred to as a
    A. carryover clause.
    B. subordination clause.
    C. veto clause.
    D. deed restriction.

60. A provision in a deed stipulating that alcoholic beverages not be sold on the land for 20 years is an example of a
    A. deed of confirmation.
    B. deed restriction.
    C. deed in trust.
    D. cession deed.

61. The highest form of an estate under which the owner can use the property at will and dispose of it without restriction is commonly referred to as
    A. leased fee.
    B. highest and best use.
    C. life estate.
    D. fee simple.

62. Improvements, or personal property so attached to the land as to become part of the real estate, are referred to as
    A. fixtures.
    B. chattels.
    C. real property.
    D. real estate.

63. Determining whether an item is a fixture includes all of these tests *EXCEPT*
    A. intent of the parties.
    B. method of annexation.
    C. relation of the item in respect to the real estate.
    D. amount paid for the property.

64. Which survey method refers to the rectangular system of land surveying in which land is divided into 36-square-mile townships?
    A. Rectangular breakdown survey method
    B. Government survey method
    C. Metes-and-bounds survey method
    D. Quadrangular line survey method

65. Which term is *NOT* synonymous with the other three?
    A. Fee
    B. Fee simple
    C. Fee simple absolute
    D. Fee simple determinable

66. The walls between two condominium units are normally considered to be
    A. individual unit elements.
    B. common elements.
    C. limited common elements.
    D. proprietary lease elements.

67. One who rents property to another under a lease agreement is referred to as the
    A. lessee.
    B. lessor.
    C. tenant.
    D. mortgagee.

68. Legally speaking, the term *real estate* refers to
    A. buildings only.
    B. ownership rights in land or buildings.
    C. land and everything attached to it.
    D. land only.

69. The right of a lessor to possess leased property upon the termination of a lease is known as the right of
    A. termination.
    B. covenant.
    C. remainder.
    D. reversion.

70. The legal mechanism by which local governments regulate the use of privately owned real property to prevent conflicting land uses and promote orderly development is known as
    A. escheat.
    B. zoning.
    C. deed restrictions.
    D. eminent domain.

APPLICATION-STYLE QUESTIONS

Questions 71 through 75 are based on the following information:

During the inspection of the subject property, an appraiser observes a number of things that could impact the market value of the property. The neighborhood comprises one-half section of land. In interviewing the property owner, the appraiser finds out that the next-door neighbor has the legal right to park his travel van on the back of the subject property. The subject property also has an underground swimming pool as well as a portable hot tub. Deed restrictions require a setback of 50 feet from the road, but in checking the zoning requirements, the appraiser confirms that city zoning only requires a 20-foot setback.

71. Due to the easement that the adjoining property has, the subject property would be referred to as what kind of estate?
    A. Dominant
    B. Servient
    C. Dominating
    D. Leasehold

72. If there are 320 lots in the neighborhood, all of equal size, how many acres is the subject property?
    A. 1/4
    B. 1/2
    C. 1
    D. 10

73. What kind of property is the underground swimming pool legally considered to be?
    A. Real
    B. Personal
    C. Leasehold
    D. Leased fee

74. What kind of property is the portable hot tub legally considered to be?
    A. Real
    B. Personal
    C. Leasehold
    D. Leased fee

75. Given the setback requirements of the deed restrictions and the zoning ordinance, what is the minimum setback requirement that the property must meet?
    A. 20 feet
    B. 50 feet
    C. 70 feet
    D. Since there is a conflict, the property owner may choose which setback to follow.

ANSWERS TO DIAGNOSTIC EXAM II

1. **A.** The monuments method of legally describing land relies on the use of both artificial as well as natural monuments. In some jurisdictions this method is considered less exact than a description by the other normally accepted methods of describing land.

2. **C.** An acre of land contains 43,560 square feet. A section of land, which is a square mile, contains 640 acres; there are 36 sections in a township.

3. **A.** 640 × 1/2 × 1/4 × 1/4 = 20 acres.

4. **B.** A township is six miles by six miles, or 36 square miles. There are 36 sections in a township, and a quadrant is one-fourth of a section.

5. **B.** A profit, the right to remove something from the land of another, is considered a real property right.

6. **B.** The trustor is the borrower under a deed of trust. The lender (mortgagee) is the beneficiary and the person representing the lender is the trustee.

7. **A.** A partial release clause, often included in a mortgage covering more than one parcel of real estate, allows the borrower (such as a developer) to have certain parcels released from the mortgage upon repayment of a specified dollar amount.

8. **C.** The assessment of property is one of the steps necessary in determining how much property tax will be due from a specific property. Assessment value has no direct bearing on either listing price, market value, or what property will sell for at foreclosure.

9. **B.** Nothing in regard to the establishment of a zoning ordinance guarantees that property values may not decline. The other three choices are all normally included in a zoning ordinance.

10. **A.** The three parties in a deed of trust are the trustee (attorney, lender representative), the trustor (borrower), and the beneficiary (lender).

11. **D.** A condominium is a legal form of property ownership and does not refer to a specific style such as residential. Any style or type of real estate use could be under a condominium form of ownership.

12. **B.** A planned unit development allows a developer flexibility of design and land use by allowing a mixture of different land uses or densities. Many modern zoning ordinances allow for planned unit developments.

13. **C.** Range lines are part of the government survey method of legally describing land. The other three choices are all part of the metes-and-bounds method.

14. **D.** An easement in gross is the personal right to use the land of another. Such an easement involves only one parcel of land, referred to as the servient estate.

15. **A.** A conversion occurs when a building currently under one form of ownership is changed or converted into a different form of ownership. Many buildings in the United States have been converted into a condominium form of ownership.

16. **C.** Because an easement in gross is the right to use the land of another, no dominant estate is required, just a servient estate. While it should be recorded in the public land records, it may not be. An annual payment for use of the easement is not a requirement.

17. **C.** A loan covering the financing of two or more properties is the basic definition of a blanket mortgage. Such financing is often used by a developer to cover more than one parcel of land under the same mortgage.

18. **C.** Normally, zoning establishes land-use districts and provides for different restrictions and standards within each district. Use districts are divided into such categories as (1) residential, (2) commercial, (3) industrial, and (4) agricultural. A zoning ordinance is not necessarily less or more restrictive than a deed restriction. The four terms—*nonconforming use, variance, exclusionary zoning,* and *spot zoning*—all have entirely different meanings.

19. **B.** Property tax is calculated by multiplying the tax rate or millage rate by the assessed value of the property.

20. **C.** To determine whether a specific item is a fixture, certain historical tests have been applied. Those tests include the intent of the party attaching the object, the adaptation of the object, the method of attachment, and the relationship of the parties. The cost of the article is not a determining factor.

21. **C.** A nonconforming use is a preexisting use of land that does not conform to the present zoning ordinance. Ordinarily, a nonconforming use is permitted to remain.

22. **C.** A township is a physical division of land into a six-by-six-mile area containing 36 sections, each section equal to one square mile.

23. **B.** A section of land contains 640 acres. Thus 640 × 1/2 × 1/4 × 1/4 = 20 acres.

24. **B.** One of the tests used in determining whether an item is a fixture concerns the manner of attachment. Wall-to-wall carpeting, storm doors, and built-in dishwashers are all attached in such a manner as to attach them to the real property; thus they are fixtures. An area rug is not a fixture and is thus considered to be personal property.

25. **C.** An encroachment is the extension of some improvement or object such as a building or driveway across the legal boundary of an adjoining tract of land.

26. **C.** A unit is that portion of a condominium intended for the exclusive use and possession of the individual unit owner. Neither common elements nor limited common elements are owned in severalty. In a cooperative, the individual unit is not owned by the individual.

27. **A.** A condominium is a legal form of property ownership that may be owned by tenants in common. A cooperative is different from a condominium in that in a cooperative, tenants enter into a proprietary lease and do not legally own the individual units.

28. **B.** Emblements are crops that require annual planting and are considered a form of personal property. In an indefinite lease, if notice is given to terminate the lease, the tenant is entitled to harvest the crops even after the end of the lease term.

29. **B.** One of the public limitations on real estate is the legal right or claim of government to ownership of property left by a deceased property owner who leaves no will and no descendants or heirs.

30. **D.** A FAR of 5:1 means that five square feet of floor space may be constructed on one square foot of land. Thus a building that covers one-fourth of the total lot could have a maximum height of four times five, or 20 stories.

31. **D.** The purpose of a buffer zone is to provide for the "blending" of the two uses. The buffer can be created by distance and by barriers, such as fences or the planting of trees and bushes.

32. **A.** A PUD (planned unit development) is a type of exception or special land use permitted under many modern zoning ordinances. Such flexibility allows the developer to use different land uses or

densities and thus make more efficient use of open spaces and the physical aspects of the land.

33. **D.** Normally such land uses as churches, schools, and hospitals are exempt from the payment of property taxes.

34. **B.** A special assessment is levied against property by a local jurisdiction when the property receives a special benefit, such as the paving of a road or the addition of sidewalks, which differs significantly from the benefit that the public at large receives.

35. **C.** An encroachment is defined as a part of real estate that physically intrudes on, overlaps, or tresspasses on the property of another.

36. **B.** $320.25 ÷ $8,725 = 0.036705 or $3.67 per $100.

37. **C.** A lien is a legally recognized right to enforce a claim, such as unpaid property taxes or an outstanding mortgage debt, on property. Liens can be specific (such as mortgages) or general (such as state and federal income taxes).

38. **C.** A cooperative is an indirect form of property ownership in which individuals own shares of a corporation that in turn holds the legal title to the real estate. A cooperative is different from a condominium, where individual owners actually hold title to the real estate.

39. **B.** In a cooperative form of ownership, the tenant's legal rights or interests are considered to be personal, not real property.

40. **D.** Normally the condominium owner has fee simple title to the unit and tenancy in common in shared areas. Corporate ownership is used by a cooperative, not a condominium. Joint tenancy (which has right of survivorship) would not be practical for the shared areas in a condominium.

41. **A.** Real estate includes land and things that are permanently attached to the land, such as buildings and other improvements to the land. Real property includes all interests, benefits, and rights associated with the ownership of real estate and is often distinguished from "personal property"; that is, property not permanently attached to land, such as furniture and personal belongings.

42. **B.** The manner of attachment is one test used to determine whether an item is a fixture or is personal property. Examples of fixtures include built-in appliances and wall-to-wall carpet.

43. **A.** The leased fee estate refers to the rights of the lessor or landlord in real estate that the landlord has leased.

44. **D.** An easement simply gives one party the right to use another party's land. It does not transfer ownership. Easements are often created to give an owner access to the land by way of a different owner's land.

45. **B.** The landlord is referred to as the lessor. The tenant is referred to as the lessee.

46. **C.** The lender is referred to as the mortgagee. The person or company taking out the loan is the mortgagor.

47. **D.** The person or company taking out the loan is the mortgagor. The lender is referred to as the mortgagee.

48. **D.** Real estate is the physical land and appurtenances, including structures, affixed thereto. Real property includes the rights, interests, and benefits included in the ownership of real estate.

49. **A.** If both zoning ordinances and deed restrictions exist, the most restrictive takes precedence.

50. **A.** Eminent domain gives the government the right to acquire private property for public use upon just compensation.

Condemnation is the act of enforcing the right of eminent domain.

51. **B.** The lot-and-block system is used typically in subdivisions where lots are drawn by surveyors and identified and numbered.

52. **A.** Metes-and-bounds is a method of legally describing a property. This is the oldest known method of surveying and involves describing the property's boundaries in terms of reference points. The survey starts with one point and moves through a series of other points before finally returning to the point of beginning. *Bounds* refer to the points and *metes* refer to the direction one moves between the points.

53. **A.** Deed restrictions are private limitations placed on land. Taxation, police power, and escheat are all public limitations (powers) of government.

54. **C.** Real estate is the physical structure. Real property includes all interests, benefits, and rights from the ownership of real estate. Personal property is not permanently affixed to the real estate.

55. **C.** Condemnation is the process of taking private property for public use or purpose; the power to do so is eminent domain.

56. **C.** The quantity survey system is a system of estimating building costs by duplicating the contractor's method of developing a bid.

57. **B.** The term *leasehold* is the legal term for the rights of a tenant who has leased the property from the owner who has a leased-fee estate.

58. **A.** The term *leased-fee estate* is the legal term for the estate held by the owner of the property, who has leased it to someone else.

59. **D.** Deed restrictions are placed in deeds to limit the use that can be made of real estate.

60. **B.** Deed restrictions are placed in deeds to limit the use that can be made of real estate. Prohibiting the sale of alcoholic beverages could be included as a deed restriction.

61. **D.** Fee simple is the highest ownership recognized by law. Highest and best use is not a type of estate.

62. **A.** Fixtures are personal property that has been permanently attached to the real estate so as to become real property.

63. **D.** The cost of an item is not a determining factor in deciding whether it is a fixture. The remaining choices are all tests in determining if an item is a fixture.

64. **B.** Also known as the rectangular survey system, this method measures land by east-west lines called base lines and north-south lines called principal meridians. Standard parallels and guide meridians are drawn every 24 miles to adjust for the curvature of the earth.

65. **D.** The greatest ownership recognized by law is referred to as fee, fee simple, or fee simple absolute. Fee simple determinable is a legal interest created to exist only until the occurrence or nonoccurrence of a particular event.

66. **C.** Limited common elements are those portions of a condominium that are jointly owned by all unit owners but under the exclusive control or possession of only some of the unit owners. Examples would include walls between two units or enclosed courtyards.

67. **B.** The lessor (landlord) rents or leases the property to the lessee (tenant).

68. **C.** Real estate is the physical land. Real property is the ownership rights in the land.

69. **D.** A reversion is the legal right of an owner to the property rights upon termination of the lease. A remainder refers to a situation in which the property reverts to someone else. In the case of leased property, the legal interest reverts to the lessor upon termination of the lease.

70. **B.** Zoning is a mechanism of police power. Deed restrictions are private, not public.

71. **B.** Since the easement is on subject property, it burdens the property and the subject property is the servient estate.

72. **C.** A section of land contains 640 acres. The neighborhood is one-half of one section and since each lot is of equal size, the subject property is one acre in size.

73. **A.** The underground swimming pool is considered to be part of the real estate and is thus real property.

74. **B.** The portable hot tub is not considered to be part of the real estate and is thus personal property.

75. **B.** When there are both deed restrictions and zoning ordinances, the most restrictive must be followed; therefore the minimum setback requirement is 50 feet.

CHAPTER 6

Highest and Best Use Analysis and Property Description

KEY TERMS

economic base analysis
excess land
financially feasible
general data
highest and best use
interim use
legally permissible

limiting conditions
maximally productive
most profitable
neighborhood life cycle
  (stages)
physically possible
plottage

primary data
reconciliation
secondary data
specific data
surplus land
surplus productivity

DIAGNOSTIC EXAM III*

1. The allocation of value between land and building is referred to as
   A. absorption.
   B. abstraction.
   C. extrapolation.
   D. interpolation.

2. The act or process of developing an opinion of value is referred to as a(n)
   A. market analysis.
   B. investment analysis.
   C. appraisal.
   D. extraction.

3. Which condition is NOT correct in regard to a building that is the highest and best use of a vacant site?
   A. It will not have any locational obsolescence.
   B. It is the use that maximizes the value of the land.
   C. It has to conform to current building codes.
   D. All of the above are correct.

4. An appraiser who resolves a dispute in regard to a specific opinion of value is commonly referred to as
   A. a review appraiser.
   B. an arbitrator.
   C. a condemnator.
   D. none of the above, because it is unethical for an appraiser to get involved in disputes regarding value.

5. Highest and best use analysis is used to determine which action?
   A. The type of property to put on a site
   B. The amount of capital to invest in a site for improvements
   C. Whether any existing building on a site should be demolished
   D. All of the above

6. Which condition should have no influence on an appraiser's compensation?
   A. The complexity of the assignment
   B. The value estimated in the appraisal
   C. The expenses required to complete the appraisal
   D. The time required to complete the appraisal

7. The term topography refers to the
   A. process of mapping an area by metes and bounds.
   B. process of developing a legal description for a site.
   C. configuration of the surface of the land.
   D. soil condition of a site.

8. What is meant by the concept of consistent use?
   A. Land cannot be valued on a basis other than the highest and best use.
   B. Land must be used in a fashion consistent with use of similar land.
   C. Improvements cannot be valued based on a use that is different from the land.
   D. Improvements must be built in a manner consistent with current building codes.

9. The term economic base analysis can be described as a(n)
   A. analysis of the economic activity of a community that allows it to attract income from outside its boundaries.
   B. analysis of population trends in a community.
   C. compilation of demographic data for comparable areas.
   D. analysis of how interest rates will affect the base rent on a property.

---

*   We have included "quick review" questions, designated by a gray-box design element, that convey the essential points of each chapter. These questions should be used as a review tool only after the entire exam has been completed. These quick review questions are not meant to replace the entire exam.

10. Which statement is *FALSE* in the definition of *interim use*?
    A. An interim use is not the current highest and best use.
    B. The highest and best use of an interim use property is expected to change in the future.
    C. The immediate development of an interim use property to its future highest and best use is probably not financially feasible.
    D. An interim use may contribute to property value depending on factors such as income produced and expected demolition costs, if any.

11. Special purpose properties can be valued on the basis of either of two highest and best uses. These two highest and best uses are
    A. value in use and value in exchange.
    B. value in use and speculative use.
    C. value in exchange and interim use.
    D. interim use and legally nonconforming use.

12. Which appraisal approach(es) can be used for considering the value of excess land?
    A. Cost approach only
    B. Sales comparison and income approaches
    C. Cost approach and income approach
    D. Income approach only

13. When reconciling an appraisal, the appraiser should review the objective of the appraisal and the legal interests being appraised because
    A. if all three approaches do not give the same value, there was an error in the report.
    B. the market value will vary depending on the investor.
    C. the value may vary greatly depending on the interest being appraised or the definition of use.
    D. the value should equal the value needed to receive financing.

14. Which statement is *TRUE* in regard to reconciling the appraisal?
    A. The value should reflect market data only if the market value is being defined.
    B. Market data should be used only in the sales comparison approach.
    C. The appraiser should never use subjective judgments.
    D. The relationship of the final value estimate to market perceptions should be considered.

15. Which term *BEST* describes what a real estate appraiser does in rendering an opinion on the value of a tract of land?
    A. Determines value
    B. Calculates value
    C. Estimates value
    D. Predicts value

16. The primary reason an appraiser analyzes a neighborhood is to
    A. identify the area on a zoning map.
    B. identify and evaluate factors that may influence property values.
    C. satisfy requirements of FHA/VA.
    D. determine assessed value for tax purposes.

17. Which physical unit *MOST* clearly defines the term *neighborhood* as used by an appraiser?
    A. A section of land
    B. The area defined by a zoning district
    C. The area served by a single public school district
    D. A grouping of similar land uses within accepted geographic boundaries

18. Which action *BEST* describes what is required of the appraiser in the reconciliation step of the appraisal process?
    A. Averaging the indicated values of the three approaches to derive a final value estimate
    B. Choosing the highest value indication of the three approaches to derive a final value estimate
    C. Placing the most emphasis on the value estimate of the approach(es) considered most reliable by the appraiser
    D. Choosing the value closest to what the appraiser assumed the value would be prior to undertaking the assignment

19. In regard to an appraisal assignment, which factor primarily determines which approach(es) should be given the most weight in the reconciliation step of the appraisal process?
    A. The time allowed to finish the assignment
    B. The compensation received by the appraiser
    C. The nature of the assignment and the quality of available data
    D. The amount of outstanding debt against the property

20. What step in the appraisal process must be performed before the highest and best use analysis is done?
    A. Collection of data
    B. Application of approaches to value
    C. Reconciliation
    D. Report preparation

21. The process by which the appraiser resolves the indicators of value into a final estimate of the defined value is known as
    A. averaging.
    B. reconciliation.
    C. capitalization.
    D. recapitulation.

22. In regard to real estate market analysis, a feasibility study relates *MOST* closely to
    A. accrued depreciation.
    B. economic success.
    C. income tax shelter.
    D. likelihood of a change in zoning.

23. One of the necessary steps in the appraisal process is the application of the various approaches to value. Which statement is correct?
    A. After determining which of the approaches to value is the most suitable, the appraiser should never use any of the other approaches.
    B. Approaches to value should be used only if their use results in the same value derived when the first approach chosen was used.
    C. All of the traditional approaches to value must be used with every appraisal assignment.
    D. The various approaches to value may indeed result in different estimates of value.

24. In which approach to value is information that is obtained in the marketplace used as part of the approach?
    A. Sales comparison approach
    B. Cost approach
    C. Income approach
    D. All of the above approaches

25. The very nature on which area and neighborhood analysis is done as part of the appraisal assignment means that the person doing the analysis must be
    A. objective.
    B. subjective.
    C. a resident of the area being analyzed.
    D. a nonresident of the area so as not to be biased by previous information and knowledge.

26. A neighborhood can be defined or explained in many different ways. Which condition is *NOT* an acceptable means by which an appraiser can define a neighborhood?
    A. Income levels
    B. Natural boundaries
    C. Race
    D. Political boundaries or districts

27. One of the necessary steps in the appraisal process is referred to as reconciliation. Which statement *BEST* describes the objective of this step?
    A. It establishes the time frame within which market data will be collected and analyzed.
    B. It sets both the upper limit and the lower limit within which the value estimate will be made.
    C. It provides for a single and final estimate of value to be made.
    D. It outlines the correct appraisal process that will be followed for a specific appraisal assignment.

28. Reconciliation is a necessary step in the appraisal process. Which reason is *NOT* a justification for including reconciliation as part of the appraisal process?
    A. Real estate markets are not perfect and are purely competitive.
    B. The appraisal process requires six steps, no more and no less.
    C. The exact data necessary for each approach to value may not be available.
    D. Application of different approaches to value may result in different estimates of value.

29. The final value estimate as reported by an appraiser is *BEST* described by which statement?
    A. It is an average of the three approaches to value.
    B. It is always the value set by the sales comparison approach since this is the best approach to use.
    C. It is part of the definition step in the appraisal process.
    D. It is an opinion of the appraiser supported by documentation and analysis.

30. Assume you are appraising a property. After applying the various approaches to value, you derive significant differences in the indications of value. Which action would *NOT* be appropriate?
    A. Correct mathematical mistakes
    B. Review collection of data and how it was analyzed
    C. Revise the data to come up with one value for all approaches
    D. Check application of the approach(es) used

31. Which step would be the final one taken in the appraisal process?
    A. Definition of the problem
    B. Collection and analysis of the data
    C. Application of the approaches to value
    D. Reconciliation

32. There are various types of appraisal reports. Which type might *NOT* be considered an appraisal report?
    A. Narrative report
    B. FNMA/FHLMC form report
    C. Personal letter of opinion
    D. Form report

33. The appraisal process involves a number of steps that should be followed by an appraiser. The first step in the appraisal process is
    A. collection and analysis of data.
    B. definition of the problem.
    C. application of the approaches to value.
    D. reconciliation and final value estimate.

34. Private limitations, such as deed restrictions, and public limitations, such as zoning ordinances, are important influences on real estate. A discussion of such limitations would more than likely appear in what part of an appraisal report?
    A. Definition of the problem
    B. Definition of market value
    C. Analysis of highest and best use
    D. Reconciliation and final value estimate

35. Which item would be included in the minimum requirements of an appraisal report?
    A. Photographs of the property
    B. Table of contents
    C. A detailed letter of transmittal
    D. Signed certification statement

36. Which statement *BEST* describes an appraisal?
    A. The sales price agreed on between buyer and seller
    B. The amount of the loan
    C. An unbiased opinion of value
    D. An exact prediction of value

37. In an analysis of highest and best use, the appraiser must consider which criterion?
    A. The physically possible
    B. The legally permissible
    C. The financially feasible
    D. All the above criteria

38. If applicable, the technique of capitalizing income is performed in which step of the appraisal process?
    A. Definition of problem
    B. Highest and best use analysis
    C. Application of approaches to value
    D. Reconciliation

39. Comparing the physical components of comparable properties to those of the subject property is part of which of the steps in the appraisal process?
    A. Defining the problem
    B. Collecting data
    C. Analyzing data
    D. Reconciling of valuation approaches

40. Which statement is the *MOST* accurate concerning what an appraiser does in regard to value?
    A. The appraiser creates value.
    B. The appraiser knows the true value.
    C. The appraiser guarantees value.
    D. The appraiser estimates value.

APPLICATION-STYLE QUESTIONS

Questions 41 through 45 are based on the following information:

You have been asked by a financial institution to appraise a ten-acre tract of land that has one house located on the property. Recently the land was rezoned highway commercial but it is currently being used as a residence. The property has excellent frontage access to a busy highway.

41. Given the uniqueness of this property, in terms of the appraisal process, what should the appraiser do first?
    A. Define the problem
    B. Collect the necessary data
    C. Reconcile the data
    D. Conduct site analysis

42. If the property had remained zoned as single family, which highest and best use "test" would *NOT* permit the property to be used for a commercial use?
    A. Physically possible
    B. Legally permissible
    C. Economically feasible
    D. Most profitable

43. As commercial property, the site is worth $500,000, while as residential property, the lot is only worth $50,000 and the house is worth $100,000. What HABU concept prohibits the appraiser from valuing the property at $500,000 (commercial value of lot) plus $100,000 (value of the house) for a total property value of $600,000?
    A. Nonconforming use
    B. Variance use
    C. Economic use
    D. Consistent use

44. If your appraisal assignment is to estimate the market value of the subject property, implicit in the definition of *market value* is that the land will be used as
    A. highway commercial.
    B. residential.
    C. either commercial or residential.
    D. Market value assumes nothing regarding highest and best use.

45. More than likely, in the appraisal report the appraiser would explain the current use of the property as residential as a(n)
    A. nontimely use.
    B. nonconforming use.
    C. interim use.
    D. persistent use.

ANSWERS TO DIAGNOSTIC EXAM III

1. **B.** This is an appraisal method whereby the appraiser estimates the land value of any improved property by deducting, or abstracting, the value of any site improvements from the overall sales price of the property. The amount remaining is the estimated sales price, or indicated value, of the land. This is also called the allocation or extraction method.

2. **C.** Appraisal is the act or process of developing an opinion of value. A market analysis examines real estate market conditions. An investment analysis is usually considered to be the study of a particular acquisition price.

3. **D.** Criteria for determining the highest and best use are (1) physically possible, (2) legally permissible, (3) financially feasible, and (4) maximally productive.

4. **B.** An arbitrator resolves disputes. A review appraiser analyzes the reports of other appraisers to determine if the conclusions drawn are consistent and defensible, but does not resolve disputes.

5. **D.** Highest and best use analysis can be used to determine several factors. The analysis is usually based on land as though vacant or on property as improved. Purposes of completing a highest and best use analysis include identifying comparable sales of land or property; estimating a separate land value; and identifying the use of the property that can be expected to produce the highest overall return for each dollar of capital invested. Therefore, all of the answers given are correct.

6. **B.** It is unethical for an appraiser to base compensation on the value to be estimated.

7. **C.** Topography refers to the land's contour, soil condition, drainage, and general usefulness. The nature of the topography may affect the value of the site.

8. **C.** In highest and best use analysis, improvements must contribute to the land value to have a value themselves. Improvements that do not contribute to land value may have an interim use or a negative value. The concept of consistent use is especially important in valuing properties with temporary or interim uses.

9. **A.** Economic base analysis measures the economic activity of a community that allows it to attract income from outside its boundaries. The analysis includes, but is not limited to, population, demographic, and interest rate data.

10. **A.** An interim use is the *current* highest and best use of the property as improved, although the highest and best use is expected to change in the future. For instance, a cornfield on the edge of an area being developed into residential subdivisions may be at its highest and best use now as a cornfield. However, after infrastructure (zoning, for example) is in place, the highest and best use may be as residential homes. If the field produced more income than other similar vacant lots, the interim use of farming contributes value to the property.

11. **A.** Because special use properties have a limited number of uses or only one use, they may have to be valued on the basis of an alternative use in periods of low demand. Value in use refers to the value based on the current use of the property, which is the usual method of valuing special purpose properties. Value in exchange refers to the value of the property based on an alternative use.

12. **B.** Both the sales comparison approach and the income approach can be used for considering the value of excess land. The cost approach cannot be used to obtain a value for land.

13. **C.** The value will probably vary slightly depending on which approach was used due to the natural variations in data. However, in reconciling the values, this variance should be minor and be explainable. The value may vary greatly depending on the interest being appraised. The appraiser will also double-check the interest being appraised in the reconciliation process. Market value does not vary by investor or qualifications for financing.

14. **D.** The appraiser should always consider market data and perceptions. Some subjective judgments will have to be used in reconciling the alternate conclusions, because some differences in value will occur between the approaches.

15. **C.** An appraisal is merely an opinion as to the worth of the property and is thus an estimate on the part of the appraiser.

16. **B.** Neighborhood analysis is an integral part of the appraisal process. The purpose of neighborhood analysis is to identify and evaluate any factor(s) that may influence neighborhood property values.

17. **D.** A neighborhood is a grouping of similar land uses within accepted geographic boundaries. Although possibly important, neither a zoning district nor a public school district defines a neighborhood.

18. **C.** One of the necessary steps an appraiser must undergo during the appraisal process is reconciliation of the valuation approaches. The purpose is to assist the appraiser to reach a rational conclusion regarding the value of the property being appraised.

19. **C.** Both the nature of an appraisal assignment and the quality of available data are important factors in determining which of the approaches to value will be given the most weight in the reconciliation step of the appraisal process.

20. **A.** Data must be collected before the highest and best use analysis is undertaken.

21. **B.** The process of resolving the indicators of value into a final value estimate is referred to as reconciliation. Reconciliation is not the same as averaging, and the two terms should not be confused.

22. **B.** A feasibility study is a detailed analysis of a real estate project to determine the most profitable use of the property and the likelihood of that particular use being an economic success.

23. **D.** Because traditional approaches to value are based on entirely different assumptions and techniques, the application of those approaches may—and in fact generally does— result in different estimates of value. Such results do not imply that a specific approach should not be used just because different estimates of value are generated.

24. **D.** All three traditional approaches to value rely on information obtained in the marketplace. The type of information obtained may be different and may have different applications for each of the approaches.

25. **A.** Any analysis done by an appraiser should be objective. Whether the appraiser is a resident of the area is not the determining factor in who should undertake the analysis.

26. **C.** An appraiser should never consider the racial composition of an area in either defining a specific neighborhood or in rendering an opinion as to the estimate of value.

27. **C.** Reconciliation allows for a single and final estimate of value. This step is an important one in the appraisal process and should not be taken until the necessary preceding steps have been completed.

28. **B.** There is no exact number of steps to be included in the appraisal process. However, any appraisal process followed should contain reconciliation, which allows for a single and final estimate of

value to be made. If real estate markets were perfect, all necessary data available, and different approaches resulted in the same exact estimate of value, reconciliation would not play the same role in the appraisal process that it plays today.

29. **D.** The final value estimate is an opinion of the appraiser. It should be supported with the correct documentation and analysis as necessary. It does not involve a simple averaging of the three approaches nor does it involve a certain approach because that is always the best approach. The final value estimate is not part of the definition of the problem.

30. **C.** An appraiser should never revise or rework the data so it results in a value estimate that "fits" what is being done. The fact that different approaches may and often do result in different value estimates does not mean that the approaches are incorrect.

31. **D.** Reconciliation, which is the second from last step in the appraisal process, cannot and should not be done until the other steps have been completed.

32. **C.** A personal letter of "opinion" is generally not considered to be an appraisal report. The uniform standards do allow oral and letter "reports" if specific guidelines are followed.

33. **B.** The first step in the appraisal process is for the appraiser to define the problem. The other choices in this question are all steps in the appraisal process.

34. **C.** Included in the definition of highest and best use is that legal use and as such both the private and public limitations, such as deed restrictions and zoning ordinances, should be included in the analysis of highest and best use.

35. **D.** A minimum requirement of all appraisals is a signed certification statement. Photographs, a table of contents, and a letter of transmittal often are included in various appraisal reports.

36. **C.** An appraisal is an opinion of value substantiated with knowledge and market analysis. Further, an appraisal should be unbiased.

37. **D.** Certain criteria must be met in determining the highest and best use of a parcel. Those criteria include what is physically possible, legally permissible, and financially feasible. The fourth criteria is what is maximally productive.

38. **C.** Capitalizing income is part of the income approach to value and is thus performed as part of the approaches to value.

39. **C.** A necessary step in the appraisal process is the analysis of data. During this step would be the correct and proper time to compare the physical components of comparables to those of the subject property.

40. **D.** An appraisal is an opinion of value; therefore, an appraiser estimates value. The appraiser does not create, guarantee, or suggest that he or she knows the *true* value!

41. **A.** The first step in the appraisal process, regardless of the appraisal assignment, is to define the problem.

42. **B.** Highest and best use assumes that the use of the land is legally possible; thus, in this example, the land would have to be used as residential.

43. **D.** Consistent use is an appraisal concept that states that land and improvements to the land must be valued on the same basis. Improvements to the land (such as the house) must contribute to land value (under its highest and best use) in order to have any value themselves.

44. **A.** Implicit in the definition of *market value* is the assumption that the land will be used under its highest and best use.

45. **C.** Interim use is a use in which the highest and best use is expected to change in the future although the future use is not currently legally, financially, or physically possible.

Sales Comparison Approach

KEY TERMS

adjusted sales price	dollar adjustment	property rights conveyed
arm's-length transaction	elements of comparison	subject property
cash equivalency	market conditions	time adjustment
comparable	paired sales analysis	units of comparison
conditions of sale	percentage adjustment	

DIAGNOSTIC EXAM IV *

1. The sales comparison approach involves various elements of comparison. Which element is *NOT* one employed in this approach?
   A. Cost
   B. Property rights being conveyed
   C. Conditions of sale
   D. Date of sale

2. The increase or decrease in the sales price of a comparable property to arrive at an indicated value for the property being appraised is referred to as
   A. fudging.
   B. adjustments.
   C. reconciliation.
   D. capitalization.

3. What rental unit of comparison is of primary importance in appraising office buildings with multiple tenants?
   A. Rent per room per year
   B. Rent per floor per year
   C. Rent per square foot of net rentable area per year
   D. Rent per cubic foot of gross leasable area per year

4. Paired data sets analysis could *BEST* be used to estimate which factor?
   A. Value of location
   B. Regression analysis
   C. Age of the property
   D. Reproduction cost new

5. A good unit of comparison for an apartment building would be rent per
   A. room.
   B. floor.
   C. cubic foot of storage area.
   D. lineal foot of road frontage.

6. A regression gives the following information to estimate monthly rent for apartments in a college town.

   > Rent = 25 + (75 × Rooms) + (50 × Students) – (25 × Distance)

   Where:
   Rooms is the number of rooms in the apartment.
   Students is the percent of students in the apartment building (0 = 0 percent, 1.00 = 100 percent).
   Distance is the distance from the periphery of campus.

   The rent for an apartment with three rooms, 100 percent students, and one mile from campus would be
   A. $250.
   B. $275.
   C. $300.
   D. $350.

7. Tools for applying the sales comparison approach to value include which technique?
   A. Paired sales analysis
   B. Multiple regression
   C. Graphic analysis
   D. All of the above techniques

---

*   We have included "quick review" questions, designated by a gray-box design element, that convey the essential points of each chapter. These questions should be used as a review tool only after the entire exam has been completed. These quick review questions are not meant to replace the entire exam.

8. The following information is given:

   Transaction price of a comparable property is $100,000.

   As a percent of the above comparable price it is determined that

   ■ financing of subject is 5 percent less desirable because the comparable had a below-market loan;
   ■ conditions of sale are 15 percent better for the subject;
   ■ market conditions are now 15 percent worse than when the comparable sold;
   ■ the location of the subject is 10 percent better; and
   ■ the physical characteristics of the subject are 5 percent worse.

   The indicated value of the subject is
   A. $97,041.
   B. $97,506.
   C. $99,275.
   D. $101,703.

9. Linear regression typically would *NOT* be used for which purpose?
   A. To determine an adjustment in the sales comparison approach for comparable sales
   B. To complete a mass appraisal of a residential area for tax assessment
   C. To test for the effect of a flood on home values
   D. To perform sensitivity analysis on changes in income in the income approach to value

10. Simple regression analysis is used to show the relationship between two variables on a straight-line basis. However, most appraisal data have a curvilinear relationship; i.e., if the value of one property characteristic is plotted against another, the result is a curved line instead of a straight line necessary for regression. What should an appraiser do if a curvilinear relationship is found?
    A. Do not use a regression analysis
    B. Fit the curve to a straight line drawn through or closest to the greatest number of points
    C. Use a spreadsheet instead
    D. Use only data that fit on a straight line

11. In the sales comparison approach, how is the appropriate unit of comparison chosen?
    A. Price per square foot is always used.
    B. Price per square foot is used except for hotels, for which the price per room is used.
    C. It depends on the appraisal problem. The appraiser should apply all appropriate units of comparison, explain differences in wide variation in the results, and choose the most reliable unit.
    D. It depends on the extent to which each comparable property differs from the subject property.

12. Which element includes typical adjustments made in the sales comparison approach?
    A. Property rights, financing, conditions of sale, location
    B. Property rights, financing, capitalization rate, location
    C. Financing, physical characteristics, date of sale, income
    D. Physical characteristics, capitalization rate, date of sale, location

13. Normally, the proper sequence of adjustments in the sales comparison approach is
    A. property rights, conditions of sale, market conditions, financing, location, and physical characteristics.
    B. financing, conditions of sale, market conditions, property rights, location, and physical characteristics.
    C. property rights, financing terms, conditions of sale, market conditions, location, and physical characteristics.
    D. physical characteristics, location, property rights, financing, conditions of sale, and market conditions.

14. Which statement is correct in regard to the paired sales technique?
    A. Adjustments should be made by dollar amounts and not by percentages.
    B. Adjustments should be made by dollar amounts or percentages, depending on how the adjustment is derived from the market.
    C. The paired sales technique should not be used unless a large quantity of data can be utilized.
    D. To measure the effect of a single characteristic, only one adjustment should be made.

15. The dollar value or percentage amounts that, when added to or subtracted from the sales price of a comparable to provide an indication of the value of a subject property, are referred to as
    A. comparables.
    B. adjustments.
    C. multipliers.
    D. sales.

16. An appraisal is to be made of a three-bedroom house. One comparable with two bedrooms sold for $150,000. The appraiser makes an adjustment of $20,000 to the comparable to account for the difference in the number of bedrooms. The adjusted sales price of the comparable is
    A. $130,000.
    B. $150,000.
    C. $170,000.
    D. $190,000.

17. When value is estimated by analyzing sales prices of similar properties (comparables) recently sold, this is referred to as which approach to value?
    A. Income approach
    B. Sales comparison approach
    C. Cost approach
    D. Sales value approach

18. The subject property is a three-bedroom, two-bath house. Two recently sold comparables are found. The appraiser, using the sales comparison approach, sets up the following table:

Subject	Comparable 1	Comparable 2
Sales Price	$169,500	$169,000
Date of Sale	½ month ago	3 months ago (+2,000)
3 Bedrooms	3 Bedrooms	3 Bedrooms
2 Baths	2 Baths	2 Baths

What is the best estimate of the appraised value of the subject property?
    A. $160,000
    B. $165,000
    C. $170,000
    D. $175,000

19. The sales comparison or market approach is very popular in the appraisal of residential property. Which statement is *TRUE* in regard to this approach as it applies to residential property?
    A. When selecting comparables, it is not necessary to consider the quality of construction.
    B. When using the sales comparison approach, the appraiser compares the comparable properties to the subject property.
    C. Comparable sales data that are more than six months old should never be used by an appraiser.
    D. The sales prices of comparables are always conclusive evidence of market value in the area.

20. A sale of residential property from one member of a family to a close relative normally would be described as which type of sale?
    A. Normal market sale
    B. Distorted sale
    C. Arm's-length sale
    D. Illegal sale

21. Each acceptable approach to value has certain limitations. Which condition is a limitation when using the sales comparison approach?
    A. The approach is based on historical data.
    B. There may be too many comparables.
    C. An active market may exist.
    D. Both buyers and sellers may be knowledgeable.

22. The sales comparison approach is based on a very sound economic assumption that an informed buyer would pay _____ for the property being purchased than what that buyer would pay to acquire an existing property with the same benefits and utility.
    A. less
    B. no more
    C. more
    D. considerably less

23. For an appraiser using the sales comparison approach to value, which type of market would *BEST* provide confidence and reliability in using such an approach?
    A. Seller's market
    B. Buyer's market
    C. Active market
    D. Inactive market

24. Regression analysis is a statistical technique sometimes employed by tax assessors to study the relationship between sales prices and property characteristics, that is, number of square feet of living area, age of the property, date of sale, etc. To which traditional approach to value is this most similar?
    A. Sales comparison approach
    B. Cost approach
    C. Income approach
    D. Gross rent multiplier

25. Which statement is *FALSE* in regard to a comparable being used as part of the sales comparison approach to value?
    A. It should approximate the subject property in terms of size, age, and quality of construction.
    B. It should have sold as recently as possible to the date of the appraisal.
    C. It must be in the same neighborhood as the subject property to be considered a comparable.
    D. It must be adjusted to the subject property for differences that can be identified by the appraiser.

26. Which statement is correct in regard to the sales comparison approach?
    A. The comparables are adjusted to the subject property.
    B. The subject property is adjusted to the comparables.
    C. The sales comparison approach is never used for income-producing property.
    D. The sales comparison approach will always result in an estimate of value less than the estimate derived by the cost approach.

27. When using the sales comparison approach to value, an appraiser may identify differences between the subject property and the comparables. If so, the dollar value of a positive feature present in the subject property but not present in the comparables is _____ while the dollar value of a feature in the comparables but not in the subject property is _____.
    A. subtracted, added
    B. added, subtracted
    C. subtracted, subtracted
    D. added, added

28. With the sales comparison approach, the estimated sales price of a comparable property after additions and/or subtractions have been made to the actual sales price for improvements and deficiencies, when compared to the subject property, is referred to as the
    A. market value.
    B. actual sales price.
    C. adjusted sales price.
    D. economic price.

29. The appropriate time adjustment to make for a comparable property that sold three years ago for $80,000 and has increased in value at a 4 percent annual compound rate is what amount?
    A. Less than $9,600
    B. $9,600
    C. Less than $9,989
    D. $9,989

30. A comparable property is identical to the subject property being appraised. The comparable sold six months ago for $100,000. As the appraiser, you must make an adjustment for the time difference between the subject property and the comparable. You have found a paired sale of two houses, one of which sold one year ago for $80,000 and the other sold yesterday for $88,000. What is the proper estimated adjusted sales price for your comparable?
    A. $88,000
    B. $100,000
    C. $105,000
    D. $110,000

31. The appraisal assignment involves a residence with 6 bedrooms, 3 bathrooms, 2 fireplaces, and a tennis court. Recently the following houses in the neighborhood have sold:

    Comparable 1: sales price $143,000; 5 bedrooms; 3 bathrooms; 2 fireplaces; tennis court
    Comparable 2: sales price $163,000; 7 bedrooms; 4 bathrooms; 4 fireplaces; tennis court
    Comparable 3: sales price $124,000; 4 bedrooms; 2 bathrooms; 2 fireplaces; no tennis court
    Current market information places the following values on certain features:

    Bedroom: $7,000
    Bathroom: $4,000
    Fireplace: $1,000
    Tennis court: $8,000

    What is the indicated value of the subject property?
    A. $100,000
    B. $143,000
    C. $143,333
    D. $150,000

32. A comparable property being used in an appraisal assignment sold one year ago for $125,000. Its overall quality makes it 10 percent more valuable today than the subject property. Property values have increased 5 percent annually in the marketplace. Given the above information, what is the indicated value of the subject property?
    A. $119,318
    B. $125,000
    C. $131,250
    D. $144,375

33. The geographic limitation for selecting and using comparable sales depends on the
    A. time given to complete the appraisal assignment.
    B. size of the subject property.
    C. nature and type of property being appraised.
    D. fee being paid for the appraisal.

34. In using the sales comparison approach, what consideration should an appraiser give to "sales contracts pending closing" on other properties?
    A. They should never be used.
    B. They are used to render a final opinion of value.
    C. They should be used when they are considered to be competitive with the subject property.
    D. They should be used only if they were part of a multiple listing service.

35. When using the sales comparison approach, which property should be adjusted by the appraiser?
    A. The subject property to the comparables
    B. The comparables to the subject property
    C. The cost approach to the market approach
    D. The comparables to the assessed value of the subject property

36. The general principles and procedures underlying the sales comparison approach are applicable to which type of property?
    A. Single-family residential only
    B. Single-family and multifamily residential only
    C. Land sales only
    D. Any type property except special purpose property

37. In using the sales comparison approach, which condition often cannot be adapted to the adjustment process?
    A. Terms of financing
    B. Location
    C. Time of sale
    D. Non-arm's-length transaction

38. Normally, what is the foremost consideration in the initial attempt to eliminate sales that do not meet the minimum criteria for being a legitimate comparable in the sales comparison approach?
    A. Location
    B. Time of sale
    C. Age of property
    D. Considerations of sale

39. A comparable sale sold for $100 per square foot. Market investigation indicates that the following adjustments to the price of the comparable are appropriate:

    Time adjustment +8 percent
    Physical adjustment –5 percent
    Age adjustment –6 percent

    What is the indicated value from the comparable sale?
    A. $96.12
    B. $97.30
    C. $108.00
    D. $119.00

40. Using paired sales is a technique an appraiser sometimes employs in the sales comparison approach. Which procedure is inappropriate when using the paired sales technique?
    A. Pairing very similar properties in very dissimilar locations
    B. Pairing very similar properties with very dissimilar times of sale
    C. Pairing very similar properties with very dissimilar physical features
    D. Pairing very dissimilar properties with very similar locations

41. What is the primary difference between the sales comparison approach and the market data approach?
    A. None, they refer to the same approach.
    B. The sales comparison approach is a direct approach, and the market data approach is an indirect approach.
    C. Adjustments must be made when using the sales comparison approach but not when using the market data approach.
    D. The sales comparison approach is used for residential property, and the market data approach is used for income-producing property.

APPLICATION-STYLE QUESTIONS

Use the following sales adjustment grid to answer questions 42 through 45.

COMPARABLES

Characteristic	Subject	1	2	3	4
Sales Price		$168,000	$180,000	$186,000	$189,000
Financing	Conv	Conv	Conv	Conv	Conv
Sale Date	1/2008	1/2008	1/2008	1/2008	1/2008
Square Feet	1,700	1,600	1,800	1,800	1,800
Exterior	Alum	Brick	Alum	Alum	Brick
Fireplace	1	1	1	1	1
Basement	Full	Full	Full	Full	Full
Age	16	20	20	18	20
Lot Size	18,700	18,700	18,700	18,700	18,700
Garage	2	2	2	2	2

42. The adjustment for size should be $ _____ per square foot.
   A. $60
   B. $90
   C. $105
   D. $125

43. The adjustment for a brick exterior should be $ _____.
   A. $3,000
   B. $9,000
   C. $10,000
   D. $12,000

44. The adjustment for age should be $ _____ per year.
   A. $3,000
   B. $4,000
   C. $5,000
   D. $6,000

45. The best estimate of sales price for the subject property would be $ _____.
   A. $168,000
   B. $181,500
   C. $189,000
   D. $199,500

ANSWERS TO DIAGNOSTIC EXAM IV

1. **A.** Cost is not an element of comparison used in the sales comparison approach to value.

2. **B.** When using comparable properties, the appraiser may have to make certain adjustments to arrive at an indicated value. Obviously the appraiser should not "fudge" to get the answer sought. Reconciliation refers to arriving at a final estimate of value after considering the results from all three approaches—not "adjustments" made to specific properties. Capitalization refers to conversion of income into value.

3. **C.** Rent per square foot of net rentable area per year is a typical comparison unit for office buildings. Rent per room is used for hotels.

4. **A.** Paired data sets are sets of comparables that are similar except for one factor. The difference in the sales price among the similar properties can be attributed to the differing factor. However, the appraiser should use caution when using this technique; usually several characteristics will vary between comparable properties, and a series of sales price adjustments have to be made to isolate the effect of one characteristic.

5. **A.** Rent per room, rent per apartment, or rent per square foot of gross or leasable area can be used as comparison units for apartments.

6. **B.** Rent = 25 + (75 × 3) + (50 × 1.00) − (25 × 1) = $275.

7. **D.** Paired sales analysis, multiple regression, and graphic analysis can all be used in the sales comparison approach to estimate value.

8. **A.** Comparables are always adjusted to the subject property; the subject property is never adjusted to the comparables.

$100,000
− 5 percent

$95,000
+ 15 percent

$ 109,250
− 15 percent

$92,862
+ 10 percent

$102,148
− 5 percent

= $97,041

Note: Some appraisers may have been taught to net the physical and locational adjustments, i.e., 10 percent minus 5 percent. That is NOT the same as adjusting up by 10 percent to get $102,148 (1.1 × 92,862), then adjusting down by 5 percent to get $97,041 (102,148 × 0.95).

9. **D.** Regression analysis provides an understanding of the relationship among different market variables. Sensitivity analysis is used to determine the sensitivity of a model to change in the variables.

10. **B.** Data can be manipulated to fit a straight line to provide a better understanding of the data in regression analysis.

11. **C.** Different comparison units are used for different types of properties. For example, price per room is used for hotels. Price per square foot of leasable space is most often used for office space. Apartments are usually based on price per room, price per apartment, or, sometimes, price per square foot of leasable or gross space.

Warehouses can be based on price per square foot or price per cubic foot of space.

12. **A.** The elements of comparison in the sales comparison approach are real property rights conveyed, financing terms, conditions of sale, date of sale (market conditions), and location and physical characteristics. Adjustments should be made in this order.

13. **C.** The proper sequence of adjustments in the sales comparison approach is property rights, financing terms, conditions of sale, market conditions, location, and physical characteristics. Note that the adjustments for location and physical characteristics are made simultaneously.

14. **B.** The type of adjustment used in the paired sales analysis depends on how the information is derived from the market. Usually several adjustments will have to be made to isolate the effect of one variable. The analysis is more reliable if a large amount of data is available. However, if only a limited amount of data exists, other methods should be relied on to determine the effectiveness of this approach.

15. **B.** Adjustments are additions or subtractions made in the sales comparison approach to account for differences between the comparables and the subject property.

16. **C.** Add $20,000 to the price of the comparable because the subject property contains one extra bedroom: $150,000 + $20,000 = $170,000.

17. **B.** Analyzing sales prices of similar properties is part of the market approach, also referred to as the market comparison or sales comparison approach.

18. **C.** Using either comparable results in an adjusted price of $170,000.

19. **B.** Comparable properties are always compared to the subject property. The subject property is never adjusted to the comparables. Quality of construction is important, and there is no absolute time lapse that results in comparable sales not being appropriate for analysis. Sales price and market value do not necessarily refer to the same thing.

20. **B.** Generally a sales transaction between relatives is not considered a market sale or an arm's-length sale. Rather, such a sale is considered a distorted sale; if such a transaction is used as a comparable sale in the sales comparison approach to value, then the specifics of the sale would need to be investigated before such a transaction could be used as a comparable. A sale between relatives is not an illegal sale.

21. **A.** The sales comparison approach is based on taking the sales prices of comparable properties as the starting point of adjusting those sales. These prices are historical data and as such may have to be adjusted to reflect current market value. The other choices are not weaknesses; in fact, they are all strengths or advantages that, if they exist, add to the reliability of the sales comparison approach.

22. **B.** The sales comparison approach assumes that a person would pay no more for property than the price at which he or she could acquire an existing property that would generate the same satisfaction or utility.

23. **C.** The sales comparison approach has the most reliability placed on it when the market is active, that is, when it has a lot of buyers and a lot of sellers. Generally the more active the market, the more reliability can be placed on the sales comparison approach.

24. **A.** The sales comparison approach is also based on information from sales of other properties. Adjustments to the comparables are based on differences in size, age, time of sale, etc.

25. **C.** Location is an important criterion in using comparables, but a comparable does not have to be in the same neighborhood to be used. The other choices are all correct in terms of what makes an acceptable comparable.

26. **A.** In the sales comparison approach, the comparables are always adjusted to the subject property; the subject property is never adjusted to the comparables. The sales comparison approach is used with property that is generating income; never can an assumption be made that one approach will always result in a higher estimate of value than another approach.

27. **B.** In using the sales comparison approach, adjustments are made to the comparables for features either present or not present in the subject property. If the subject property has a feature that is not present in the comparable, the dollar value is added, while the dollar value of a feature present in the comparable but not present in the subject property is subtracted.

28. **C.** In theory, the adjusted sales price is what a comparable property would sell for if it were exactly equal to the subject property in terms of all of its features, location, age, etc. What the comparable(s) actually sold for is the actual sales price, which may or may not be market value.

29. **D.** $80,000 × (1.04)^3 = $89,989. During the three years the property has increased in value by $9,989.

30. **C.** $88,000 ÷ $80,000 = 1.10, a 10 percent increase in one year or 5 percent in six months; $100,000 × 1.05 = $105,000.

31. **D.** Adjusted sales prices of the three comparables would be

    Comparable 1 ($143,000 + $7,000 = $150,000)
    Comparable 2 ($163,000 − $7,000 − 4,000 − $2,000 = $150,000)

    Comparable 3 ($124,000 + $14,000 + $4,000 + $8,000 = $150,000)

    The indicated value would be $150,000.

32. **A.** $125,000 × 1.05 = $131,250; $131,250 ÷ 1.10 = $119,318.

    Note: Because the comparable was expressed as 10 percent better than the subject (i.e., the comparable is worth 110 percent of subject), we must divide the price that the comparable would have sold for today by 1.10 to estimate the subject's value. This is NOT the same as multiplying by 1 − 0.10, or 0.90.

33. **C.** The type and location of comparables used in the sales comparison approach are dependent on the nature and type of property being appraised.

34. **C.** The sales comparison approach is based on choosing comparables. Comparables, by definition, should be competitive with the subject property.

35. **B.** When using the sales comparison approach, the appraiser should always adjust the comparables to the subject property.

36. **D.** The sales comparison approach is applicable so long as there are comparable properties, regardless of the specific type property. There are typically no comparable sales for special-purpose properties.

37. **D.** Adjustments that are often part of the sales comparison approach include such items as terms of financing, location, and time of sale. Non-arm's-length transactions are difficult to adapt to the adjustment process and should not be used.

38. **D.** The sales comparison approach is based on using comparable properties as a basis for rendering an opinion as to the value of the subject property. The foremost consideration in choosing comparables is the

circumstances of the sale of the comparable. For example, was it an arm's-length transaction?

39. **A.** $100 \times 1.08 = \$108.00$; $\$108 \times 0.89 = \$96.12$.

Note: In this case we should NOT divide $108 by 1.11 to get $97.30.

40. **D.** When using the paired sales technique as part of the sales comparison approach, an appraiser must use similar properties. Pairing very dissimilar properties, even though they have very similar locations, is inappropriate.

41. **A.** The terms *sales comparison approach* and *market data approach* refer to the same technique for estimating value.

42. **C.** Compare #1 and #4.

43. **B.** Compare #2 and #4.

44. **A.** Compare #2 and #3.

45. **B.** Start with any comparable and adjust to find the estimated value of the subject property. Starting with comparable number 1, the estimate of value for the subject property is:

Square foot adjustment: 100 square feet $\times$ \$105/square foot = \$10,500

Brick adjustment: –\$9,000

Age adjustment: 4 years $\times$ \$3,000 per year = \$12,000

$$\begin{array}{r} \$168,000 \text{ (Sales price of comparable 1)} \\ + \$10,500 \text{ (Square foot difference)} \\ - \$9,000 \text{ (No brick)} \\ + \underline{\$12,000} \text{ (Age adjustment)} \\ \$181,500 \end{array}$$

Site Valuation Methods and the Cost Approach

KEY TERMS

access

accrued depreciation

actual age

age-life method

allocation versus
  extraction technique

break-down method

comparative unit method

curable versus incurable

defects versus
  deficiencies

direct cost versus
  indirect cost

economic life

economic obsolescence

effective age

external obsolescence

floodplain

frontage

functional obsolescence

ground rent
  capitalization

land residual technique

physical deterioration

physical life

plottage

quantity survey method

remaining economic life

replacement versus
  reproduction cost

site improvements

subdivision development
  technique

superadequacy

tract

topography

unit-in-place method

DIAGNOSTIC EXAM V *

1. What type of depreciation is generally *NOT* curable?
   A. Physical
   B. Functional
   C. External
   D. Internal

2. What term is used to denote the cost of an exact duplication of the property?
   A. Replacement cost
   B. Reproduction cost
   C. Original cost
   D. Construction cost

3. Land that is *NOT* necessary for the primary improvements is referred to as
   A. plottage land.
   B. offsite land.
   C. excess land.
   D. residual land.

4. Which statement applies to corner influence?
   A. Corner sites have a higher value per square foot than other sites.
   B. Corner sites are preferable to interior properties.
   C. Corner sites have greater utility than other sites.
   D. Corner influence tables can sometimes be used to determine how a corner site affects the property's value.

5. The term *plottage value* can be defined as the
   A. incremental value created by combining two or more sites to produce greater utility.
   B. value associated with the plot of land on which the improvement is built.
   C. value of a plot of land according to tax rolls.
   D. total value of a parcel of land that has been subdivided.

6. If a building layout or style fails to meet market tastes or standards due to changes in design and technological advances, the building suffers from
   A. external obsolescence.
   B. incurable depreciation.
   C. functional obsolescence.
   D. curable physical deterioration.

7. The remaining economic life of a building is equal to the
   A. total period of time in which real estate improvements contribute to property value.
   B. estimated period of time over which improvements will continue to contribute to property value.
   C. number of years since construction was completed.
   D. estimated period of time remaining until repairs will have to be made.

8. Which method is *NOT* an acceptable means of estimating building costs?
   A. Unit-in-place method
   B. Quantity survey method
   C. Break-down method
   D. Comparative unit method

* We have included "quick review" questions, designated by a gray-box design element, that convey the essential points of each chapter. These questions should be used as a review tool only after the entire exam has been completed. These quick review questions are not meant to replace the entire exam.

9. The building cost estimate method that finds a cost per unit of area or volume based on known costs of similar structures that are adjusted for time and physical differences is known as the
   A. unit-in-place method.
   B. quantity survey method.
   C. break-down method.
   D. comparative unit method.

10. Methods of estimating accrued depreciation include
    A. economic age-life, modified economic age-life, sales comparison, break-down method.
    B. economic age-life, comparative unit, sales comparison, break-down method.
    C. economic age-life, modified economic age-life, quantity survey, break-down method.
    D. economic age-life, modified economic age-life, sales comparison, comparative unit method.

11. The method of measuring accrued depreciation by analyzing each cause of depreciation separately and then adding the separate estimates to arrive at the total is known as the
    A. break-down method.
    B. economic age-life method.
    C. modified economic age-life method.
    D. comparative unit method.

12. Which condition is an example of external obsolescence?
    A. Location in a neighborhood that is in the decline phase of its life cycle
    B. A roof that leaks
    C. A ceiling that is too high based on current standards
    D. Light fixtures that do not meet current building codes

13. Economic obsolescence can be measured by
    A. capitalizing the income or rent loss attributable to the negative influence.
    B. calculating the actual age of the improvments.
    C. applying the ratio of effective age to estimated total physical life to the reproduction or replacement cost of each component.
    D. subtracting functional obsolescence from total replacement cost.

14. What is meant by *accumulated depreciation*?
    A. The amount of capital recapture written off on the accounting statements
    B. The sum of the annual accumulated depreciation since the building was purchased
    C. The accumulated depreciation on the land since the building was constructed
    D. The difference between a structure's reproduction or replacement cost and its market value as of the date of the appraisal

15. A building was purchased for $100,000. The annual straight-line depreciation expense is $2,500. The accumulated depreciation in three years is
    A. $2,500.
    B. $5,000.
    C. $7,500.
    D. $92,500.

16. A charge against the reproduction cost (new) of an asset for the estimated wear and obsolescence is referred to as
    A. physical obsolescence.
    B. functional obsolescence.
    C. economic obsolescence.
    D. depreciation.

17. The estimated reproduction cost (new) of a theater being appraised is $1,200,000. Wear and tear sustained during its life is estimated at $100,000. Functional obsolescence caused by lack of air-conditioning and high ceilings causes an estimated loss of $100,000. It is in a decaying area of the city, and economic obsolescence is estimated at $100,000. Total depreciation is
    A. $100,000.
    B. $200,000.
    C. $300,000.
    D. $400,000.

18. What term refers to the loss of value from all causes outside the property itself?
    A. Economic depreciation
    B. Functional obsolescence
    C. Physical obsolescence
    D. Superadequacy

19. A private home may drop in value when an industrial plant is built nearby. This is an example of what form of depreciation?
    A. Functional obsolescence
    B. Economic obsolescence
    C. Physical depreciation
    D. Incurable functional obsolescence

20. The total period of time for which real estate improvements are expected to generate more income than operating expenses cost is referred to as the
    A. depreciable life.
    B. effective age.
    C. remaining operating life.
    D. economic life.

21. The term *economic obsolescence* denotes the same thing as
    A. economic base.
    B. superadequacy.
    C. economic function.
    D. external depreciation.

22. The age of a property based on the amount of wear and tear it has sustained is referred to as
    A. effective age.
    B. actual age.
    C. physical age.
    D. depreciable age.

23. What term is used for a standard measurement of land, applied at the frontage of its street line, and for lots of generally uniform depth in downtown areas?
    A. Acre
    B. Front foot
    C. Quadrangle
    D. Depth-frontage ratio

24. Loss of value from all causes within the property, except those due to physical deterioration, is referred to as
    A. depreciation.
    B. internal obeselescence.
    C. functional obsolescence.
    D. obsolescence.

25. A poor floor plan or outdated plumbing fixtures are types of
    A. curable physical depreciation.
    B. functional obsolescence.
    C. economic obsolescence.
    D. incurable physical depreciation.

26. A plot of land already prepared for or underlying a structure or development is generally referred to as a
    A. site.
    B. lot.
    C. plat.
    D. subdivision.

27. A tract of land divided into lots suitable for home-building purposes is referred to as a
    A. subdivision.
    B. section.
    C. township.
    D. quadrangle.

28. The term *wear and tear* refers to
    A. external obsolescence inherent in the aging of a building.
    B. physical deterioration of property as the result of use, weathering, and age.
    C. all obsolescence incurred by a building as it ages.
    D. functional obsolescence.

29. The subject property being appraised cannot provide the same utility as that provided by a new structure designed for similar use. Such obsolescence is referred to as
    A. locational obsolescence.
    B. functional obsolescence.
    C. economic obsolescence.
    D. environmental obsolescence.

30. The difference between a building's economic life and its remaining economic life is the
    A. effective age.
    B. actual age.
    C. economic age.
    D. chronological life.

31. Physical deterioration results from
    A. deferred maintenance.
    B. federal income tax depreciation.
    C. functional utility.
    D. economic obsolescence.

32. In the cost approach to value, which step would an appraiser take in estimating value?
    A. Estimate the net operating income of the property
    B. Determine the value of the land using the assessed value and tax rate
    C. Estimate the accrued depreciation
    D. Calculate the acquisition price of the construction material used when the structure was built

33. What is the total area of a parcel of land that measures 80 feet by 62.5 feet?
    A. 5,000 ft.
    B. 5,000 sq. ft.
    C. 5,000 cubic ft.
    D. 5,000 sq. miles

34. Under which circumstances would the lack of central air-conditioning most likely be considered a functional deficiency in a dwelling?
    A. The cost of replacement is high.
    B. The dwelling has never been occupied.
    C. Comparable properties have central air-conditioning.
    D. The dwelling is less than ten years old.

35. Under which condition might the cost approach to value be a poor indicator of value?
    A. There is functional obsolescence.
    B. The unit-in-place method is used.
    C. Accrued depreciation is substantial.
    D. Any market data are available.

36. The cost approach to value is more reliable when the improvement is
    A. highest and best use.
    B. new and highest and best use.
    C. highest and best use and suffers no functional obsolescence.
    D. new, has no accrued depreciation, and is the highest and best use.

37. Under which condition is the cost approach to value a poor or inappropriate indication of value?
    A. When there are numerous land sales
    B. When there is substantial accrued depreciation
    C. When there is any functional obsolescence
    D. When the property generates income

38. Which action *BEST* explains the cost approach to value?
    A. Subtracting total depreciation from the purchase price
    B. Adding land value to depreciated improvement value
    C. Multiplying historic cost by an inflation factor
    D. Capitalizing income attributable to the accrued depreciation

39. How is land (site) value treated under the cost approach to value?
    A. At present use if currently improved
    B. At its highest and best use as if vacant
    C. At highest and best use if the cost of demolition is less than 50 percent of the land cost
    D. At present use so long as it is not economical to demolish the building

40. Accrued depreciation is calculated as the difference between what it would cost to replace the building new and the
    A. current assessed value.
    B. current market value.
    C. current insured value.
    D. accumulated depreciation allowed for tax purposes.

41. Accrued depreciation is defined as the difference between the reproduction or replacement cost of an improvement, such as a building, and its value as of the
    A. date of original construction.
    B. time of the most recent sale.
    C. present.
    D. time any financing is approved.

42. The actual number of elapsed years since a structure was originally built is referred to as that building's
    A. economic life.
    B. chronological age.
    C. remaining economic life.
    D. effective age.

43. When using the cost approach to value, an appraiser generally treats the contractor's overhead and profit as
    A. direct costs.
    B. indirect costs.
    C. opportunity costs.
    D. inapplicable, because contractor's overhead and profit are not considered when the cost approach to value is being used.

44. An active railroad line running behind the property lines of lots in a residential subdivision would *BEST* be described as what type of obsolescence?
    A. Functional curable
    B. Functional incurable
    C. Economic curable
    D. Economic incurable

45. The poor layout of offices in a commercial building would be an example of curable or incurable
    A. physical obsolescence.
    B. functional obsolescence.
    C. economic obsolescence.
    D. locational obsolescence.

46. With the cost approach to value, the site is valued as if
    A. vacant and available to be used under its highest and best use.
    B. its current use is its only use.
    C. vacant and available for any use that will generate income.
    D. occupied and being used under its existing use.

47. Which statement *BEST* describes the use of depth tables by appraisers?
    A. Depth tables are a sophisticated mathematical model employed by appraisers when using the income approach to value.
    B. Depth tables generally can be used to reflect market activity in metropolitan areas.
    C. An appraiser should place little reliance on the use of depth tables without first testing market behavior.
    D. The use of depth tables is superior to any other mathematical technique, such as simple or multiple regression, because depth tables are precise and easily obtained.

48. There are numerous techniques available to estimate reproduction or replacement cost of a building. The most detailed and precise technique is the
    A. comparative unit method.
    B. builder's (trade break-down) method.
    C. unit-in-place method.
    D. quantity survey method.

49. Numerous items must be considered and incorporated into the cost approach to value. Which item would *NOT* be considered under the cost approach?
    A. Replacement cost
    B. Functional obsolescence
    C. Vacancy allowance
    D. Physical wear and tear

50. A building feature *NOT* fully valued by the marketplace, such as 24-karat gold faucets in the bathroom, is normally referred to as a(n)
    A. physical deterioration.
    B. underimprovement.
    C. superadequacy.
    D. nonconforming use.

51. While appraising a single-family residence you observe the following: run-down and vacant buildings around the subject property, a roof that needs replacing, and undersized bedrooms with no windows. You have observed (respectively)
    A. economic obsolescence, physical deterioration, and functional obsolescence.
    B. functional obsolescence, physical deterioration, and economic obsolescence.
    C. economic obsolescence, physical deterioration, and locational obsolescence.
    D. economic obsolescence, physical deterioration, and economic obsolescence.

52. The age of a building as indicated by its physical condition and utility compared to the building's useful life is referred to as
    A. actual age.
    B. chronological age.
    C. effective age.
    D. economic age.

53. The age-life method is a method of estimating accrued depreciation by applying to a property's reproduction cost new the ratio of the property's effective age to its
    A. economic age.
    B. actual age.
    C. chronological age.
    D. economic useful life.

54. Physical deterioration of a building would be the direct result of
    A. functional utility.
    B. deferred maintenance.
    C. tax depreciation.
    D. locational obsolescence.

55. With the cost approach to value, a decrease in value as a result of deferred maintenance is referred to as
    A. accelerated depreciation.
    B. functional obsolescence.
    C. physical deterioration.
    D. economic obsolescence.

56. Economic obsolescence of residential property could be the result of
    A. an increase in FHA or VA interest rates.
    B. construction of a warehouse on the adjoining lot.
    C. passage of a more restrictive zoning ordinance barring property in the area from commercial use.
    D. increases in the cost of construction.

57. Under which condition is an item of accrued depreciation considered to be curable?
    A. The cost to cure is less than the replacement cost new.
    B. The cost to cure is less than the reproduction cost new.
    C. The cost to cure is less than the expected increase in value.
    D. The item can be physically replaced or repaired.

58. Which method of estimating the cost of reproducing a building new is the most detailed and time consuming?
    A. Cost break-down method
    B. Comparative unit method
    C. Quantity survey method
    D. Unit-in-place method

59. You are estimating the total cost of constructing a sidewalk around the exterior of a building. The building covers an area 30 feet by 45.5 feet. The sidewalk will be 3.5 feet wide and 3 inches deep. Concrete costs $45 per cubic yard, and labor costs are $2 per square foot. What is the total cost of the sidewalk?
    A. $1,155.00
    B. $1,395.75
    C. $1,444.50
    D. $2,112.40

60. In estimating the value of a single-family residence, the appraiser concludes that 24 percent of the total estimated value of the property is attributable to the land. If the value of the property is estimated to be $150,000, what is the estimated value of the land?
    A. $0
    B. $36,000
    C. $114,000
    D. $150,000

61. What is the percentage of accrued depreciation for a 12-year-old building that has a total economic life of 50 years and a remaining economic life of 40 years?
    A. 12 percent
    B. 20 percent
    C. 24 percent
    D. 50 percent

62. The difference between the reproduction cost new of the improvements and their present value is known as
    A. accelerated depreciation.
    B. accrued depreciation.
    C. physical deterioration.
    D. cost of improvements.

63. When a property's value is decreased because of a structural feature that is considered undesirable by today's standards, the property is said to be suffering from
    A. functional obsolescence.
    B. functional obsolescence, curable.
    C. functional obsolescence, incurable.
    D. locational obsolescence.

64. If an industrial building needs improved modern lighting, which costs $30,000, and if the improvement would result in an increase in value to the building of $30,000, the depreciation is referred to as
    A. functional obsolescence, curable.
    B. functional obsolescence, incurable.
    C. locational obsolescence, curable.
    D. a superadequacy, incurable.

65. Which cost is the measure of physical curable deterioration?
    A. The cost of restoring the item to new or reasonably new condition
    B. The cost of the item as if new less functional obsolescence
    C. The cost of the item as if new plus functional obsolescence
    D. The cost of the item as if new less the cost of any superadequacy

66. What valuation principle is the foundation on which the cost approach to value is based?
    A. Anticipation
    B. Balance
    C. Highest and best use
    D. Substitution

67. When an appraiser uses the straight-line method for estimating physical deterioration in the cost approach, what assumption has been made?
    A. The physical deterioration and functional obsolescence of the improvements are the same.
    B. The effective age of the improvements and the remaining economic life are the same.
    C. Deterioration occurs at a constant average annual rate.
    D. Deterioration occurs at a compounded annual rate.

68. An appraiser estimates the amount of accrued depreciation by calculating the difference between the estimate of reproduction cost new and the indicated value derived by the sales comparison or income approach. This appraiser has used the
    A. direct method for estimating accrued depreciation.
    B. indirect method for estimating accrued depreciation.
    C. break-down method for estimating accrued depreciation.
    D. summation method for estimating accrued depreciation.

69. The age of a building, as indicated by its physical condition and utility compared to its useful life contrasted to its chronological age, is referred to as
    A. actual age.
    B. effective age.
    C. economic age.
    D. given age.

70. A *superadequacy* is defined as
    A. land being used more efficiently than its highest and best use.
    B. a feature of a building that is not fully valued by the marketplace.
    C. a building whose effective life is less than its actual age.
    D. real estate generating an abnormal rate of return.

71. A means by which an appraiser estimates the reproduction or replacement cost of a building by grouping the cost by stages of construction is known as which cost-estimating method?
    A. Comparative unit method
    B. Builder's method
    C. Unit-in-place method
    D. Quantity survey method

APPLICATION-STYLE QUESTIONS

Questions 72 and 73 are based on the following information:

A newly completed state highway has directed traffic from a road on which the subject property is located. As a result of the new road, the subject property is renting for $.50 per square foot less than it was prior to the opening of the new highway. The typical gross income multiplier for property in this area is 9. The building on the subject property contains 25,000 square feet.

72. What is the amount of accrued depreciation attributable to the new highway?
    A. $12,500
    B. $25,000
    C. $112,500
    D. $225,000

73. In the cost approach to value, this type of depreciation would be classified as
    A. physical deterioration.
    B. functional obsolescence.
    C. interior deterioration.
    D. economic obsolescence.

Questions 74 and 75 are based on the following information:

Central air-conditioning is lacking in a house located in an area where most houses contain central air-conditioning. If central air-conditioning were included in estimating reproduction cost new, it would add $4,000 in costs. However, to add a central air-conditioning system to the subject property will cost $5,000, but doing so will add more than $5,000 to the value of the house.

74. How is this depreciation properly classified?
    A. Physical deterioration
    B. Functional obsolescence, curable
    C. Functional obsolescence, incurable
    D. Economic obsolescence

75. What is the estimate of depreciation attributable to this feature?
    A. $1,000
    B. $1,000 less depreciation already taken
    C. $4,000 less depreciation already taken
    D. $5,000

Questions 76 through 80 are based on the following information:

An appraiser has been asked to estimate the value of a newly constructed 3,000-square-foot home located in a neighborhood where the surrounding houses are between three and five years of age. The appraiser estimates that reproduction cost is $150 per square foot and that the site is worth $67,500. The only loss in value that the appraiser believes exists is that rather than a two-car garage, the subject property has a one-car garage. The appraiser believes this loss is $15,000.

76. What is the reproduction cost of the house?
    A. $300,000
    B. $450,000
    C. $500,000
    D. $517,500

77. What is the site/building ratio?
    A. 10%
    B. 15%
    C. 20%
    D. 85%

78. The one-car garage deficiency is an example of which type of depreciation?
    A. Physical
    B. Functional
    C. Economic
    D. External

79. The effective age of the house is
    A. zero.
    B. one year.
    C. three to five years.
    D. greater than five years.

80. Based on the cost approach, what is the appraised value of the property?
    A. $450,000
    B. $502,500
    C. $517,500
    D. $600,000

ANSWERS TO DIAGNOSTIC EXAM V

1. **C.** External or locational depreciation is generally not curable.

2. **B.** Reproduction cost is the current cost of constructing an exact duplicate. Although sometimes reproduction cost is referred to as if it is synonymous with replacement cost, the two are different. Replacement cost refers to a building that has the same functional ability but possibly is of different size, materials, or design.

3. **C.** When a site is larger than that needed to support its improvements, the extra land is referred to as excess land. Vacant sites may also have excess land if the area of the land is larger than that needed for the highest and best use.

4. **D.** Corner sites may have a higher or lower value than other properties, depending on the use and utility associated with the corner influence. In mass appraisals, corner influence tables can be developed mathematically to measure the amount of value associated with a corner location.

5. **A.** The combination of two or more sites does not necessarily produce incremental value. An incremental value, or plottage, results only if the combination of the sites also creates greater utility. Plottage is important in appraising farmland where smaller lots may not be able to support newer and larger farm equipment.

6. **C.** Functional obsolescence results from a deficiency in design and technological advances.

7. **B.** The remaining economic life refers to the estimated number of years of usefulness of a structure.

8. **C.** The break-down method is a means of measuring accrued depreciation.

9. **D.** In the comparative unit method, the appraiser finds comparable properties that were recently constructed. The value of the site is subtracted from each comparable to find the value of the improvements. Adjustments are made for time and physical differences. Then the value is divided by the area or volume to find a dollar-per-unit measure. In addition, a unit-cost figure can be developed from a recognized cost service.

10. **A.** Accrued depreciation is estimated by various methods. Common methods are economic age-life, modified economic age-life, sales comparison, and break-down.

11. **A.** The break-down method separately measures five types of depreciation: curable physical deterioration, incurable physical deterioration, curable functional obsolescence, incurable functional obsolescence, and external obsolescence.

12. **A.** Economic obsolescence results from negative influences outside the site, such as location in a neighborhood that is in the decline phase of its life cycle.

13. **A.** External obsolescence is any loss in value due to adverse factors outside the subject property. Such obsolescence can be measured by capitalizing the income or rental loss attributable to the negative influence.

14. **D.** Accumulated (accrued) depreciation refers to the difference between a structure's reproduction or replacement cost and its market value as of the date of the appraisal.

15. **C.** 3 years × $2,500 per year = $7,500.

16. **D.** Depreciation is defined as a loss in utility, and thus value, from any cause. Depreciation may be physical, functional, or economic.

17. **C.** Physical deterioration: $100,000
    Functional obsolescence: $100,000
    External obsolescence: + $100,000
    Total $300,000

18. **A.** Economic or external depreciation refers to the loss of value from all causes outside the property itself.

19. **B.** Economic obsolescence occurs when factors outside the property cause negative influences on the value of the property.

20. **D.** The economic life of an improvement refers to the time period over which the improvement generates more income than the cost incurred in generating the income. Economic life is sometimes referred to as useful life.

21. **D.** Economic obsolescence and external depreciation refer to the same thing.

22. **A.** Effective age refers to the age of an item as indicated by its physical condition and utility compared to its useful life. The effective age will probably be less than the actual age if the item is rehabilitated or it has above-average maintenance, and vice versa.

23. **B.** A front foot is a measurement of property frontage where each foot extends the depth of the property.

24. **D.** Obsolescence can be either functional or external. Depreciation refers to the loss of value from all causes within the property, including physical deterioration.

25. **B.** Functional obsolescence or depreciation results from outdated or defective design.

26. **A.** A site is land that has been improved for a specific purpose.

27. **A.** A subdivision is a tract of land divided into lots suitable for home building. Section, township, and quadrangle refer to legal descriptions of land prepared under the rectangular survey system.

28. **B.** Wear and tear refers to physical deterioration.

29. **B.** Functional obsolescence is defined as a loss in value within a structure due to changes in design, market standards, or technological advances.

30. **A.** The difference between the economic life of a building and that building's remaining economic life is the effective age.

31. **A.** Failure to properly maintain a property may result in physical deterioration of that property. Physical deterioration has nothing to do with functional or economic obsolescence, nor is it related to federal income tax depreciation.

32. **C.** One of the necessary steps in the cost approach to value requires an estimate of accrued depreciation. The other three choices are not part of the cost approach to value.

33. **B.** 80 feet × 62.5 feet = 5,000 square feet.

34. **C.** Functional deficiency (obsolescence) is defined as a loss in value within a structure due to changes in tastes, preferences, technical innovations, or market standards. If the comparable properties have central air-conditioning, then the subject property is functionally deficient if it does not have central air-conditioning.

35. **C.** The greater the amount of accrued depreciation, the more subjective the cost approach to value becomes. The fact that there may be functional obsolescence would not preclude its use.

36. **D.** The greatest reliability can be placed on the cost approach to value when the improvements are new, there is no accrued depreciation, and the land is being used under its highest and best use.

37. **B.** The cost approach to value is weakened as the amount of accrued depreciation increases, regardless of whether the depreciation is physical, functional,

or economic. A substantial amount of accrued depreciation significantly weakens the cost approach to value.

38. **B.** The cost approach to value requires the appraiser to add the estimated value of the land to the depreciated value of the improvements.

39. **B.** When using the cost approach to value, the appraiser values the land (site) at its highest and best use as if vacant. If the current use is not the highest and best use, the building suffers a loss in value.

40. **B.** Accrued depreciation is defined as any diminishment or loss of value from the original time of construction to the present and is calculated as the difference between what it would cost to replace the building new and the current market.

41. **C.** Accrued depreciation is the difference between reproduction or replacement cost and the value as of the present.

42. **B.** The actual age and the chronological age of a building refer to the same thing as measured by a standard calendar.

43. **A.** The contractor's overhead and profit are usually included as direct costs because typically they are included in the construction contract. However, the developer or entrepreneurial profit is not considered a direct cost and is added to the direct and indirect costs to find a total value.

44. **D.** A railroad line, which is beyond the boundary of the subject property, is considered economic obsolescence and thus by definition is incurable.

45. **B.** Poor layout is an example of functional obsolescence. It may be curable or incurable, depending on the cost of correcting the defect and what the correction would add to value.

46. **A.** With the cost approach to value, one of the necessary steps is to estimate the value of the site as if vacant and available

for use under the land's highest and best use. Such a use may or may not be the land's current use.

47. **C.** Depth tables are sometimes used by appraisers or tax assessors to estimate the value of a particular parcel of land. However, the use of such tables should be undertaken only after careful analysis of market behavior; otherwise, little reliance can be placed on such techniques.

48. **D.** The quantity survey method, which is the most detailed and precise technique for estimating replacement or reproduction cost, requires calculating the quantity and the cost of each material item plus the total cost of installation. The remaining choices are all less detailed techniques for estimating replacement or reproduction cost.

49. **C.** The vacancy allowance, and its impact on income, is part of the income approach to value; it is not considered when using the cost approach to value. All three of the remaining choices are items incorporated into the cost approach.

50. **C.** Both residential and income-producing property may contain items or features that are not fully valued by the marketplace. These features are referred to as superadequacies and are considered as functional obsolescence when estimating value by the cost approach.

51. **A.** Vacant buildings around the subject property are an example of economic obsolescence. A roof that needs replacing is physical deterioration, and small bedrooms with no windows are examples of functional obsolescence.

52. **C.** The effective age of a building may be quite different from that building's actual age. For example, a 10-year-old building could have an effective age of 30 years because of poor or deferred maintenance. Likewise, the same building with proper maintenance and upkeep could have an effective age of only 6 years.

53. **D.** The age-life method is one of the means by which accrued depreciation can be estimated as part of the cost approach to value. The ratio is the property's effective age to its economic useful life.

54. **B.** Physical deterioration is a result of wear and tear, deferred maintenance, or both.

55. **C.** Physical deterioration is defined as any loss in value due to the impairment of physical conditions. Deferred maintenance is an example of physical deterioration.

56. **B.** Economic obsolescence is defined as a loss in value due to factors or conditions outside the subject property. The construction of a warehouse on an adjoining lot could be an example of economic obsolescence.

57. **C.** An item of accrued depreciation is considered curable when the cost to correct the defect is either equal to or less than the expected increase in value. The item is considered incurable if the cost of correction is greater than the expected increase in value.

58. **C.** The quantity survey method is one of the ways in which the replacement or reproduction cost of a building can be estimated. This approach involves totaling the cost of each individual part to be used in the construction and is the most detailed method of cost estimating.

59. **B.** Sidewalk dimensions are 577.5 square feet, 144.38 cubic feet, or 5.35 cubic yards. Therefore: $5.35 \times \$45 = \$240.75$ concrete cost; $577.5 \times \$2 = \$1,155$ labor cost; $\$1,155 + \$240.75 = \$1,395.75$ total cost.

60. **B.** The total value of property is equal to the value of the land plus the value of the improvements: $\$150,000 \times 0.24 = \$36,000$ land value.

61. **B.** If property has a remaining economic life of 40 years and a total economic life of 50 years, the percentage of accrued depreciation is $10 \div 50$, or 20 percent.

62. **B.** Accrued depreciation is the difference between the reproduction cost new of the improvements and the present value of the improvements.

63. **A.** Functional obsolescence in defined as a loss in value within a structure due to changes in such things as technical innovations or market standards.

64. **A.** Functional obsolescence is considered curable if the cost of correcting the defect is either equal to or less than the increase in value resulting from correcting the defect. Thus, a defect that costs $30,000 to correct and adds $30,000 to value is considered curable.

65. **A.** Physical curable deterioration is measured by the cost of restoring the item in question to new or reasonably new condition.

66. **D.** The principle of substitution, which is the foundation of the cost approach to value, states that the value of a parcel of real estate is set by the cost of acquiring an equally desirable substitute.

67. **C.** One of the means of estimating physical deterioration is a straight-line method. An assumption when using such a method is that deterioration or wear and tear occurs at a constant average annual rate.

68. **B.** Estimating accrued depreciation by the indirect method involves calculating the difference between the estimate of reproduction cost new and the estimate of value derived by one of the other approaches to value.

69. **B.** The effective age of an item is indicated by the item's physical condition and utility compared to its useful life. Effective age should not be confused with actual age or chronological age.

70. **B.** A superadequacy is defined as a feature of a building that is not fully valued by the marketplace. A custom-built home in a neighborhood of speculative-built houses might suffer from superadequacies.

71. **C.** Numerous techniques are used to estimate replacement or reproduction cost. The unit-in-place method estimates value by grouping the cost by stages of construction.

72. **C.** 25,000 × $.50 = $12,500; $12,500 × 9 = $112,500.

73. **D.** Economic obsolescence is defined as any loss in value due to factors outside the subject property, such as a change in the road network, which causes rent per square foot to decrease.

74. **B.** If a property suffers from lack of central air-conditioning, which would cost $5,000 to correct but would add more than $5,000 to the value of the property, the depreciation is classified as curable functional obsolescence.

75. **A.** An item of accrued depreciation that would cost $5,000 to correct now, but only $4,000 if included in the reproduction cost new of the improvements, suffers from $1,000 ($5,000 − $4,000) of depreciation.

76. **B.** 3,000 × $150 = 450,000.

77. **B.** $67,500/$300,000 = 0.15.

78. **B.** The one-car garage deficiency is an example of functional obsolescence.

79. **A.** Since the house is new, it has an effective age of zero.

80. **B.** $450,000 + $67,500 − $15,000 = $502,500.

CHAPTER 9

Income Approach

KEY TERMS

band of investment technique

break even ratio

capitalization rate

cash flow

direct capitalization

discount rate

discounted cash flow

effective gross income (EGI)

equity dividend rate

fixed expenses

gross income multiplier (GIM)

gross rent multiplier (GRM)

gross (potential) income

net operating income (NOI)

operating expense ratio (OER)

operating expenses

overall rate of capitalization

potential gross income

rate of return

reserves for replacement

return "on" versus return "of" investment

reversion

vacancy and bad debt allowance

variable expenses

yield capitalization

DIAGNOSTIC EXAM VI*

1. Which statement *BEST* describes the amount of adjustment an appraiser should make for vacancy allowance in a property?
   A. 5 percent of gross income
   B. 1 percent for each year the property has been rented
   C. Somewhere between 5 percent and 10 percent
   D. The amount will vary with each property

2. ◎ When a property's vacancy and credit loss is subtracted from the property's gross (potential) income, which type of income is derived?
   A. Effective gross income
   B. Net operating income
   C. Taxable income
   D. Cash flow income

3. Which return would be included in the capitalization rate established by the appraiser for a property with a declining building value and a constant land value?
   A. Return on the land and building
   B. Return on the land and building and recapture of the building
   C. Return on the land and building and recapture of the land and building
   D. Return on the land and building and recapture of the land

4. ◎ A building with an annual net operating income of $8,000 is valued at $80,000. What is the estimated value of the building if the capitalization rate is increased by one percentage point?
   A. $53,300
   B. $72,700
   C. $80,000
   D. $80,900

5. An annual net income of $20,000 capitalized at a rate of 18 percent indicates a value _____ the value indicated by capitalizing a net income of $10,000 at a rate of 9 percent.
   A. less than
   B. equal to
   C. greater than
   D. indeterminable to

6. ◎ Which expense (cost) is *NOT* considered by an appraiser in estimating the net operating income of a particular property?
   A. Property insurance
   B. Mortgage payments
   C. Property management fees
   D. Upkeep and maintenance

7. ◎ Assume the property being appraised has an unusually high degree of risk and uncertainty associated with its ability to generate income. In applying the income approach to value, the capitalization rate used will more than likely be
   A. lower, thus resulting in a lower value.
   B. lower, thus resulting in a higher value.
   C. higher, thus resulting in a lower value.
   D. higher, thus resulting in a higher value.

8. A previously appraised building with an annual net operating income of $8,000 was valued at $80,000. What is the current estimate of value if the capitalization rate has been increased by 200 basis points?
   A. $66,700
   B. $78,500
   C. $80,000
   D. $100,000

---

*   We have included "quick review" questions, designated by a gray-box design element, that convey the essential points of each chapter. These questions should be used as a review tool only after the entire exam has been completed. These quick review questions are not meant to replace the entire exam. For Chapters 9 and 10 only, gray-box quick review questions featuring a **bull's-eye** are for the **licensed** and **certified residential** exams. The gray-box questions *without the bull's-eye are for the certified general exam.*

9. ◎ In addition to the income generated by rents, what else does the income approach always require the appraiser to analyze?
   A. Total debt service
   B. Pretax cash flow
   C. Operating expenses
   D. After-tax cash flow

10. When appraising income-producing property, the appraiser often needs to estimate the replacement allowance. When doing so, the appraiser should avoid duplication with certain items that may already have been included in which expense category?
    A. Fixed expenses
    B. Repair and maintenance
    C. Property management fees
    D. Insurance and taxation escrow accounts

11. An office building contains 100,000 square feet of net leasable space. The appraiser has information on operating expenses and an appropriate capitalization rate. Which calculation is required to complete the income approach to value?
    A. Land value
    B. Replacement cost
    C. Effective gross income
    D. Accrued depreciation

12. A ten-unit apartment complex has been purchased for $500,000. A 75 percent loan has been obtained. Vacancy allowance, operating expenses, reserve accounts, and debt service equal $47,500 annually. How much must each unit rent for monthly to generate a 10 percent dividend rate?
    A. $475
    B. $480
    C. $500
    D. $600

13. ◎ The basic equation used in the income approach to value is
    A. rate divided by income equals value.
    B. income divided by rate equals value.
    C. rate times income equals value.
    D. rate plus income equals value.

14. ◎ The operating expense ratio for income-producing property can be calculated by dividing stabilized expenses by
    A. gross income.
    B. net income.
    C. debt service.
    D. cash flow.

15. The mathematical process of converting investment inflows or an income stream into a present value is commonly referred to as
    A. compounding.
    B. discounting.
    C. amortization.
    D. equity reduction.

16. A debt coverage ratio shows the relationship between the debt service of the mortgage loan on a property and the
    A. gross income of the property.
    B. effective gross income of the property.
    C. net operating income of the property.
    D. cash flow of the property.

17. One of the standard techniques used by appraisers when analyzing the income of property is to divide the income being generated between the land and the improvements and then to capitalize the residual income to the improvements into a value estimate. Such a technique is referred to as the
    A. land residual technique.
    B. building residual technique.
    C. property residual technique.
    D. plottage residual technique.

18. ◎ In analyzing the market by using a gross rent multiplier (GRM) technique, value is estimated by
    A. dividing market rent by gross rent multiplier.
    B. dividing market rent by net income.
    C. multiplying operating expenses by gross rent multiplier.
    D. multiplying market rent by gross rent multiplier.

19. In reconstructing an income statement for an apartment complex, you estimate that potential gross income is $500,000 and vacancy and bad debt allowance equal 6 percent. If operating expenses are $205,000, what is the operating expense ratio based on effective gross income (rounded)?
    A. 41 percent
    B. 44 percent
    C. 45 percent
    D. Operating expense ratio cannot be determined without knowing the amount of the mortgage payment.

20. The income approach to value
    A. is based on the principle of anticipation.
    B. translates the ability of property to generate income into an indication of value.
    C. requires an estimate of net operating income of property.
    D. All of the above are correct.

21. ◎ An industrial warehouse that generates monthly gross income of $8,000 is being appraised. If prior market analysis has determined that an annual gross income multiplier for this type of property is 9.5, what is the subject property's estimated value?
    A. $76,000
    B. $760,000
    C. $800,000
    D. $912,000

22. A property with a net operating income of $30,500 was appraised at $350,000. At what rate was the income capitalized (rounded)?
    A. 0.08
    B. 0.008
    C. 0.09
    D. 0.009

23. Normally, the financial compensation of a property manager to cover property management fees is based on a percentage of
    A. effective gross income.
    B. net income.
    C. pretax cash flow.
    D. after-tax cash flow.

24. An office building with a net income of $10,000 was valued at $100,000. Given the same net income, what will the estimate of value be if the capitalization rate increases by one full percentage point?
    A. $90,909
    B. $99,010
    C. $100,000
    D. $111,111

25. Which statement is *MOST* descriptive of what occurs with a capitalization rate used in the income approach to value?
    A. The capitalization rate increases when the risk increases.
    B. The capitalization rate decreases when the risk increases.
    C. The capitalization rate increases when the risk decreases.
    D. The capitalization rate remains the same as long as there is positive net income.

26. The three basic components of the capitalization formula used in the income approach to value are
    A. sales comparison, cost, income.
    B. physical, functional, economic.
    C. gross income, effective gross income, net operating income.
    D. value, net income, rate.

27. When a property's vacancy loss and bad debt allowance are subtracted from potential income, which cash flow is derived?
    A. Effective gross income
    B. Net operating income
    C. Pretax income
    D. Taxable income

28. A small apartment complex valued at $300,000 earns a monthly net income of $3,000. What is the overall capitalization rate?
    A. 1 percent
    B. 6 percent
    C. 12 percent
    D. 20 percent

29. Net operating income minus debt service equals
    A. potential gross income.
    B. effective gross income.
    C. pretax cash flow.
    D. after-tax cash flow.

30. ◎ An office building is valued at $1,000,000 when net income is capitalized at a rate of 12 percent. If total operating expenses are 40 percent of effective gross income, what is effective gross income?
    A. $133,333
    B. $200,000
    C. $300,000
    D. $1,000,000

31. The term *amortization* refers to
    A. periodic repayment of debt.
    B. debt service constant.
    C. difference between value and debt.
    D. decrease in value of real estate.

32. In the income approach, value can be estimated by applying an overall capitalization rate to
    A. gross sales price.
    B. net operating income.
    C. effective gross income.
    D. before-tax cash flow.

33. A property has NOI (net operating income) of $15,000, debt service of $10,000, and sold for $100,000. What is the overall capitalization rate?
    A. 10 percent
    B. 15 percent
    C. 5 percent
    D. 25 percent

34. Which rate is most analogous to the concept of return on capital?
    A. Amortization rate
    B. Interest rate
    C. Capitalization rate
    D. Reversion rate

35. ◎ Which cash flow is *NOT* an operating expense?
    A. Mortgage interest
    B. Property tax
    C. Property management fees
    D. Maintenance

36. What economic condition would tend to result in overall capitalization rates that decrease from one year to the next?
    A. An increase in the level of interest rates
    B. A decrease in the level of interest rates
    C. A change in market conditions toward higher rent levels
    D. A change in tax laws that are unfavorable for real estate

37. What reaction would generally be *TRUE* for overall capitalization rates for properties that are purchased with favorable financing?
    A. Unaffected
    B. Lower
    C. Higher
    D. Cannot be determined

38. If a property has an overall rate of 8 percent, what is the net income multiplier?
    A. 8 percent
    B. 8
    C. 12.5
    D. 12.5 percent

39. The annual expenses for the first year of ownership of a property are expected to be $35,000. Expenses are projected to increase 6 percent per year. What will the expenses be during the fifth year of ownership?
    A. $44,187
    B. $45,550
    C. $46,838
    D. $49,648

40. A loan has a current balance of $200,000. The interest rate on the loan is 12 percent, and monthly payments are $2,082.90. How many years will it take to fully amortize the loan?
    A. 8 years
    B. 23 years
    C. 27 years
    D. 96 years

41. Funds deposited in a sinking fund are expected to earn interest at a nominal rate of 12 percent per year, but with interest compounded monthly. What is the effective annual rate?
    A. 1 percent
    B. 12 percent
    C. 12.7 percent
    D. 13 percent

42. What is the present value of a 40-year net income of $10,000 per year if payments are in advance and the income is discounted at a rate of 12 percent?
    A. $82,330
    B. $82,438
    C. $92,210
    D. $92,330

43. A building is expected to have a remaining economic life of 25 years. The appraiser believes that a typical investor would require a 10 percent rate of return to invest in the building. What is the appropriate building capitalization rate using the straight-line method?
    A. 10 percent
    B. 10.4 percent
    C. 12.5 percent
    D. 14 percent

44. A property is expected to have net operating income during the first year of $50,000, which is projected to increase at a rate of 4 percent per year over a five-year holding period. The property value is also projected to increase at a rate of 4 percent per year. The appraiser believes that a 14 percent discount rate is appropriate. What is the estimated value of the property?
    A. $184,054
    B. $292,150
    C. $357,143
    D. $500,000

45. A property is purchased for $100,000. Net operating income is currently $10,000 per year and is expected to remain level for the next five years. What yield will an investor earn if the property is sold for $110,000 after five years?
    A. 10.00 percent
    B. 10.52 percent
    C. 11.26 percent
    D. 11.59 percent

46. A property was recently purchased for $100,000. Net operating income is currently $10,000 per year and is expected to remain level for the next five years. What can be said about the investor's yield if the property is sold for less than $100,000 after five years?
    A. It will be more than 10 percent.
    B. It will be less than 10 percent.
    C. It will equal 10 percent.
    D. It could be more or less than 10 percent.

47. The seller of a property provides a purchase-money mortgage for $50,000 at an 8 percent interest rate with monthly payments over a 15-year term. Immediately after the loan is made, the loan is sold to an investor at a price of $40,000. What yield will be earned by the purchaser of the loan, assuming that it runs for the full term?
    A. 8.00 percent
    B. 10.00 percent
    C. 10.91 percent
    D. 11.91 percent

48. A sinking fund is to be established to replace a roof estimated to cost $20,000 in 15 years. How much must be set aside each year if the account earns 8 percent per year?
    A. $737
    B. $1,235
    C. $1,333
    D. $2,337

49. A property purchased today for $120,000 is projected to increase in value by 5 percent per year. How much is it projected to sell for after ten years?
    A. $174,000
    B. $180,000
    C. $186,159
    D. $195,467

50. ◎ A reconstructed statement of net operating income should include which item?
    A. Tax depreciation
    B. Management charges
    C. Additions to capital
    D. Mortgage interest payments

51. Capitalization is the process used to
    A. establish reproduction cost.
    B. establish mortgage payments.
    C. establish a depreciation schedule.
    D. convert income into an estimate of value.

52. To obtain an estimate of value, the overall capitalization rate is divided into
    A. effective gross income.
    B. net operating income.
    C. before-tax cash flow.
    D. after-tax cash flow.

53. Dividing the before-tax cash flow for a property by the equity dividend rate results in which value?
    A. Value of the property
    B. Value of the equity position
    C. Reversion value
    D. Loan value

54. A property has operating expenses that are 32 percent of gross income, which is $125,000. Using a 14 percent capitalization rate, what is the value of the property?
    A. $607,143
    B. $892,857
    C. $1,178,571
    D. $1,313,025

55. When calculating net operating income, which expense is *NOT* a proper deduction from gross income?
    A. Maintenance expense
    B. Income tax expense
    C. Insurance expense
    D. Management expense

56. The conversion of estimated future income into a present value estimate is referred to as
    A. reversion.
    B. direct capitalization.
    C. discounting.
    D. guessing.

57. The mortgage loan constant is the ratio of the loan payment to
    A. loan amount.
    B. loan term.
    C. interest rate.
    D. net operating income.

58. Why do lenders examine the debt coverage ratio?
    A. It is required by government regulation.
    B. It indicates the safety of the loan.
    C. It indicates the value of the property.
    D. It indicates how fast the loan will be repaid.

59. When comparable land sales are *NOT* available to the appraiser, what technique might be used to estimate land value?
    A. Highest and best use
    B. Land residual
    C. Property residual
    D. Building residual

60. ◎ In the context of real estate operating expenses, what is meant by the term *fixed expenses*?
    A. Expenses that never change
    B. Expenses that are fixed for the holding period
    C. Expenses that do not vary with the level of occupancy
    D. Expenses that are guaranteed by the seller

61. Which event is likely to cause an appraiser to use a lower overall capitalization rate to estimate the value for a property?
    A. Higher than normal risk
    B. Lower than normal operating expenses
    C. Higher than average net operating income
    D. Higher than normal expectations for future increases in property value

62. How would the income from renting garage space in an apartment building be handled by an appraiser?
    A. It would be included as "other income" in calculating potential gross income.
    B. It would be ignored because the income from a garage is derived from personal property.
    C. It would be deducted from net operating income.
    D. It would be used to reduce the operating expenses.

63. ◎ Which item is *NOT* one of the categories of operating expenses that might be included in a reconstructed operating statement?
    A. Fixed expenses
    B. Variable expenses
    C. Replacement allowance
    D. Mortgage debt service

64. An allowance for vacancy and collection loss is usually estimated as a percentage of
    A. potential gross income.
    B. effective gross income.
    C. net operating income.
    D. operating expenses.

65. The lump sum that an investor receives at the termination of an investment is referred to as the
    A. remainder.
    B. reversion.
    C. lump sum.
    D. gain.

66. Which term would refer to a financing technique where the developer, builder, or seller makes a payment to the lender to reduce the loan payments for the purchaser?
    A. Subsidy
    B. Buydown
    C. Discount
    D. Lowdown

67. What is the meaning of a *participation mortgage*?
    A. The lender participates in the income from the mortgaged property beyond a fixed return.
    B. The lender participates in the equity ownership of the property.
    C. The lender participates in the income from the property tenants.
    D. The lender participates in the operating costs of the property.

68. The term *cash-on-cash return* is synonymous with
    A. yield rate.
    B. internal rate of return.
    C. discount rate.
    D. equity dividend rate.

69. Which term indicates the amount by which the net proceeds from the resale of an asset exceed the adjusted cost, or book value, of the item?
    A. Adjusted basis
    B. Reversion
    C. Capital gain
    D. Before-tax cash flow from sale

70. Which term refers to a rate of return on capital used to convert future payments or receipts into present value?
    A. Capitalization rate
    B. Equity dividend rate
    C. Mortgage constant
    D. Discount rate

71. What term describes the use of debt capital to acquire an income-producing asset?
    A. Liquidation
    B. Leverage
    C. Joint venture
    D. Syndication

72. Which expense is *NOT* included in the calculation of net operating income?
    A. Property taxes
    B. Utilities
    C. Interest expense
    D. Repairs

73. Which expense is *NOT* included in the calculation of net operating income?
    A. Maintenance
    B. Property taxes
    C. Property insurance
    D. Federal income taxes

74. ◎ The term *effective gross income* can be defined as
    A. income after the effect of financing.
    B. gross potential income less an allowance for vacancy and collection.
    C. income actually collected after all operating expenses.
    D. potential gross income from space that can actually be rented.

75. The term *before-tax cash flow* can best be defined as
    A. net operating income less interest expenses.
    B. net operating income less mortgage payments (principal and interest).
    C. actual cash flow available to the investor after all cash expenses except federal income taxes.
    D. gross income less mortgage payments.

76. Which calculation is the best definition of *debt coverage ratio*?
    A. Net operating income divided by the interest expenses
    B. Net operating income divided by the mortgage payment
    C. Property value divided by the loan balance
    D. Mortgage payment divided by the before-tax cash flow

77. The band of investment technique is used to calculate
    A. internal rate of return.
    B. overall capitalization rate.
    C. yield rate.
    D. mortgage rate.

78. For a fully amortized loan, what is the relationship between the annual loan constant and the annual interest rate on the loan?
    A. The loan constant will be lower than the interest rate.
    B. The loan constant will be equal to the interest rate.
    C. The loan constant will be higher than the interest rate.
    D. There is no relationship between the loan constant and the interest rate.

79. A property is projected to have net operating income of $10,000 per year for the next five years. At the end of the fifth year, the property is expected to be sold for $100,000. Using a 12 percent discount rate, what is the present value of the projected income and resale proceeds?
    A. $86,711
    B. $87,116
    C. $92,790
    D. $103,925

80. Given the following information:

    Loan-to-value ratio: 0.75
    Mortgage constant: 0.11
    Net operating income: $60,000
    Annual debt service: $49,000

    What is the overall rate?
    A. 6.7 percent
    B. 8.2 percent
    C. 10.1 percent
    D. 13.5 percent

81. The use of overall capitalization rates derived from analysis of comparable sales is referred to as what type of capitalization?
    A. Direct capitalization
    B. Yield capitalization
    C. Overall capitalization
    D. Rate capitalization

82. Given the following information:

    Sales price: $500,000
    Loan-to-value ratio: 0.80
    Interest rate: 11 percent
    Mortgage term: 25 years

    What is the monthly mortgage payment?
    A. $3,920
    B. $4,901
    C. $47,496
    D. $59,370

83. Which operating expense is *NOT* normally considered as a fixed expense?
    A. Real estate taxes
    B. Fire insurance
    C. Property management
    D. Reserve for replacements

84. The term *fixed expenses* refers to expenses that
    A. are expected to be constant for the term of ownership.
    B. are fixed by terms of a lease.
    C. do not vary with the level of occupancy of the property.
    D. do not vary from typical market rates.

85. ◎ Value is created by the anticipation of
    A. market rent.
    B. gross income.
    C. current benefits.
    D. future benefits.

86. Which rate is *NOT* a yield rate?
    A. Internal rate of return
    B. Interest rate
    C. Discount rate
    D. Equity dividend rate

87. What is the definition of *annual mortgage constant*?
    A. Annual debt service divided by the net operating income
    B. Annual debt service divided by the loan principal
    C. Internal rate of return of the mortgage
    D. Mortgage principal divided by the value of the property

88. Capitalization is the process of
    A. forecasting future yields of a property.
    B. calculating value from price.
    C. deducting expenses to find net assets.
    D. converting income into a value indication.

89. Which item is normally a legitimate operating expense for an income property?
    A. Rubbish removal
    B. Owner's entrepreneurial profit
    C. Tax depreciation
    D. Debt service

90. The annual pretax cash flow (net operating income less debt service) received by a property owner is known as
    A. equity dividend.
    B. gross income.
    C. taxable income.
    D. equity yield.

110. In regard to capitalizing the rent on a property that has leases with overages, which statement is *MOST* correct?
     A. The base rent and overage should be capitalized with the same capitalization rate.
     B. The base rent and overage should be capitalized with different capitalization rates.
     C. The overages should not be capitalized.
     D. A higher capitalization rate should be used for the base rent than for the overage.

111. When is an overall rate equal to the equity dividend rate?
     A. There is either no loan on the property or the overall rate is equal to the mortgage constant.
     B. The overall rate cannot be equal to the equity dividend rate unless there is no loan.
     C. The property value is not changing over time.
     D. The property is highly leveraged.

112. A property produces an annual income of $50,000 when fully leased. Vacancies are currently running at 15 percent. The sales price is $240,000. What is the potential gross income multiplier?
     A. 0.18
     B. 0.21
     C. 4.80
     D. 5.65

113. A small office building valued at $300,000 earned a net operating income of $52,000 annually. What is the direct capitalization rate?
     A. 3 percent
     B. 5.2 percent
     C. 17.3 percent
     D. 20 percent

114. Which term refers to a mortgage that allows the lender to receive compensation based on the performance of the property?
     A. Joint venture mortgage
     B. Participation mortgage
     C. Partnership mortgage
     D. Option mortgage

115. Which explanation *BEST* describes the meaning of the term *overall capitalization rate?*
     A. The ratio of the property's net operating income to the value of the property
     B. The rate of return earned by an investor over a holding period
     C. The rate used to determine the capital gains tax for a property
     D. The ratio of the property's mortgage payment to the loan amount

116. Which term refers to the ratio of a property's first-year cash flow to the amount of equity invested?
     A. Equity investment rate
     B. Reversion rate
     C. Equity dividend rate
     D. Overall capitalization rate

117. An apartment building is estimated to have a market value of $5,000,000. Potential gross income is $1,000,000, vacancy loss is $50,000, and operating expenses are $350,000. What is the effective gross income multiplier?
     A. 0.19
     B. 0.20
     C. 5.26
     D. 8.33

118. A loan is made for $100,000. The loan has monthly payments of $908.70. The first month's interest is $833.33, and the principal (amortization) is $75.37. What is the annual mortgage constant?
     A. 0.01
     B. 0.09
     C. 0.10
     D. 0.11

119. An appraiser collects the following information:

    Net operating income: 70,000
    Land capitalization rate: 0.09
    Building capitalization rate: 0.12
    Land-to-value ratio: 0.35

    What is the *BEST* estimate of the value of the property?
    A. $293,747
    B. $639,269
    C. $666,667
    D. $696,517

120. An appraiser collects the following information:

    Net operating income: $38,000
    Loan amount: $273,000
    Annual mortgage payment: $28,700
    Equity dividend rate: 0.08

    What is the *BEST* estimate of the value of the property based on the financing specified above?
    A. $116,250
    B. $358,750
    C. $389,250
    D. $475,000

121. A property has net operating income of $10,000. The total annual payment on the mortgage is $9,000, which consists of $8,000 in interest and $1,000 in principal. What is the debt coverage ratio?
    A. 0.80
    B. 0.90
    C. 1.11
    D. 1.25

122. A loan has an initial balance of $50,000. The nominal annual interest rate is 10 percent. Payments are $500 per month. What is the balance of the loan after three months?
    A. $49,662
    B. $49,748
    C. $49,833
    D. $49,917

123. Two properties have the same net operating income and are considered to be very similar in all respects, except property *B* is more risky than property *A*. What should be true for the relationship between the overall capitalization rates for the two properties?
    A. The capitalization rate for property *B* will be higher than for property *A*.
    B. The capitalization rate for property *B* will be lower than for property *A*.
    C. The capitalization rate would not be affected by differences in risk.
    D. The capitalization rate could be higher or lower, depending on the type of risk.

124. A property has a net income ratio of 0.7 and a gross income multiplier of 9. Using this information, what is the overall capitalization rate?
    A. 6.3 percent
    B. 7.8 percent
    C. 12.9 percent
    D. 14.0 percent

125. A property has an equity dividend rate of 6 percent, a mortgage constant of 10 percent, and a loan-to-value ratio of 70 percent. Using this information, what is the overall capitalization rate?
    A. 6.4 percent
    B. 7.2 percent
    C. 8.8 percent
    D. 12.4 percent

126. A property is purchased that has a 10 percent overall capitalization rate and a mortgage constant of 11 percent. What can be concluded about the equity dividend rate?
    A. The equity dividend rate will be less than 10 percent.
    B. The equity dividend rate will be between 10 percent and 11 percent.
    C. The equity dividend rate will be higher than 11 percent.
    D. Nothing can be concluded about the equity dividend rate.

127. ◎ What *BEST* describes a fixed expense?
    A. Expenses that do not vary with the level of occupancy
    B. Expenses that are a fixed percent of occupancy
    C. Expenses that do not change over time
    D. Expenses that are fixed by the landlord

128. Which term describes the result of subtracting vacancy and collection loss from potential gross income?
    A. Net potential income
    B. Net operating income
    C. Effective cash flow
    D. Effective gross income

129. ◎ In direct capitalization, what is the relationship between value and the cap rate?
    A. Higher cap rate, higher value
    B. Higher cap rate, lower value
    C. Higher cap rate, no value impact
    D. Lower cap rate, lower value

130. A series of equal periodic payments or receipts is referred to as a(n)
    A. mortgage payment.
    B. annuity.
    C. principal.
    D. cash flow.

131. An annuity that is received at the beginning of each period is referred to as a(n)
    A. annuity in arrears.
    B. annuity in advance.
    C. acceleration annuity.
    D. prepayment annuity.

132. An income property appraisal technique where the overall interest rate is derived from weighting mortgage and equity rates is referred to as
    A. discounting.
    B. band of investment.
    C. yield capitalization.
    D. discounted cash flow analysis.

Questions 133 and 134 are based on the following information:

Smith purchases land for $10,000 and erects a store for $80,000. Her tax basis is $90,000.

133. If Smith then sells the property for $95,000, what is the gain?
    A. $2,500
    B. $5,000
    C. $15,000
    D. $85,000

134. If Smith instead depreciates the property, what amount is depreciable?
    A. $80,000
    B. $90,000
    C. $95,000
    D. $100,000

135. ABC Corporation purchases a building for $100,000, then depreciates it by $10,000 on corporate financial statements. What is the book value?
    A. $80,000
    B. $90,000
    C. $100,000
    D. $110,000

136. What is meant by *capital gain*?
    A. The sales price less accumulated depreciation
    B. The book value less accumulated depreciation
    C. The gain on the sale of a capital asset
    D. The gain on the sale of property after the mortgage balance, taxes, and sales costs are subtracted

137. Jones purchases investment land for $10,000. Thirteen months later, she sells it for $14,000. What is the capital gain?
    A. $307
    B. $2,400
    C. $4,000
    D. $10,000

138. Able purchases investment land for $10,000 and sells it two years later for $8,000. The $2,000 difference is treated as
   A. capital gain.
   B. capital loss.
   C. adjusted basis.
   D. accumulated depreciation.

139. The debt coverage ratio is most often used as a(n)
   A. underwriting criterion.
   B. appraisal criterion.
   C. investment criterion.
   D. sales criterion.

140. Annual debt service for a mortgage loan on a certain office building is $10,000. The property generates $25,000 in annual gross rent and requires $7,000 for expenses of operation, leaving $18,000 net operating income. The debt coverage ratio is
   A. 0.70.
   B. 1.42.
   C. 1.80.
   D. 2.50.

141. A loan that requires both interest and principal with each payment, such that the level payment will be adequate for full amortization over the loan's term, is referred to as a(n)
   A. constant amortization mortgage.
   B. junior mortgage.
   C. annuity mortgage.
   D. direct reduction mortgage.

142. Collins borrows $50,000 at 10 percent interest over a 30-year term, using a direct reduction mortgage. The monthly principal and interest payment is
   A. $435.16.
   B. $438.79.
   C. $4,821.78.
   D. $5,303.96.

143. The difference between the face amount of an obligation and the amount advanced or received is referred to as the
   A. discount.
   B. interest.
   C. capital gain.
   D. book value.

144. Smith sells land for $100,000 and receives a $60,000 mortgage at 7 percent interest as part of the payment. Smith then sells the mortgage (the right to collect payments on the mortgage) at a $15,000 discount. What does Smith receive from the sale of the mortgage?
   A. $40,000
   B. $45,000
   C. $55,000
   D. $85,000

145. Amounts paid to the lender at the time of origination of a loan, to account for the difference between the market interest rate and the lower face rate of the note, are referred to as
   A. management fees.
   B. discount points.
   C. discount rate.
   D. amortization points.

146. Loan applications for conventional mortgages are being made at 9 percent. The current rate on an FHA loan is 8.5 percent with four discount points added to compensate for the lower face rate of interest. If the loan is for $50,000, how much of an additional down payment will be required at closing to cover the points?
   A. $200
   B. $500
   C. $2,000
   D. $6,840

147. Jones borrows $10,000 on a one-year bank loan. He pays two discount points and a 10 percent face interest rate. He repays the loan at the end of the year, with interest. What can be said about Jones's effective rate?
   A. It will be less than 10 percent.
   B. It will be greater than 10 percent.
   C. It would have been greater if he had no discount points.
   D. It equals the loan constant.

148. The use of borrowed money to complete an investment purchase is referred to as
    A. underwriting.
    B. mortgage leverage.
    C. debt servicing.
    D. financial leverage.

149. A mortgage that has priority as a lien over all other mortgages is referred to as a(n)
    A. junior mortgage.
    B. first mortgage.
    C. initial mortgage.
    D. primary mortgage.

150. A property costing $100,000 is financed with a first mortgage of $75,000, a second mortgage of $15,000, and $10,000 in cash. If the borrower defaults and the property is sold upon foreclosure for $80,000, the holder of the first mortgage will receive
    A. $0.
    B. $65,000.
    C. $75,000 plus legal expenses.
    D. $80,000.

151. A loan secured by real property featuring an interest rate that is constant for the term of the loan is referred to as a(n)
    A. adjustable-rate mortgage.
    B. fixed-rate mortgage.
    C. constant amortization mortgage.
    D. nonadjustable-rate mortgage.

152. ◎ Total income from property before any expenses are deducted is referred to as
    A. operating income.
    B. gross income.
    C. before-tax cash flow.
    D. equity income.

153. ◎ The difference between potential gross income and effective gross income is
    A. vacancy.
    B. collection loss.
    C. operating expenses.
    D. vacancy and collection loss.

154. Which item is *NOT* included in effective gross income?
    A. Other income (e.g., vending machines)
    B. Vacancy
    C. Operating expenses
    D. Collection loss

155. A building with 10,000 net rentable square feet of floor space rents for an average of $10 per square foot. Concession outlets in the lobby produce an additional $20,000 in annual income. An average 5 percent vacancy rate is maintained. What is the effective gross income?
    A. $95,000
    B. $114,000
    C. $115,000
    D. $119,000

156. What ratio results when the sales price is divided by the contract rental rate?
    A. Gross rent multiplier (GRM)
    B. Net operating income (NOI)
    C. Actual rent multiplier (ARM)
    D. Operating sales ratio (OSR)

157. ◎ The sales price of a property is $40,000, and the gross monthly contract rent is $400. What is the GRM (gross rent multiplier) based on monthly rent?
    A. 0.01
    B. 0.12
    C. 8.33
    D. 100

158. The method of appraising real estate based on the property's anticipated future income is referred to as a(n)
    A. capitalization approach.
    B. income approach.
    C. anticipation approach.
    D. overall rate approach.

159. A property is expected to produce a net operating income of $100,000 yearly. Recent sales data indicate that the capitalization rate for comparable properties is 10 percent. By application of the income approach, the property has a market value of
    A. $194,872.
    B. $614,457.
    C. $851,356.
    D. $1,000,000.

160. A loan that does *NOT* require amortization is referred to as a(n)
    A. fixed-interest loan.
    B. flat-payment loan.
    C. negative amortization loan.
    D. interest-only loan.

161. Land was bought with a five-year interest-only loan of $100,000 at 12 percent. The interest of $12,000 was paid annually for four years. What is the balance of the loan at the end of the fifth year?
    A. $40,000
    B. $52,000
    C. $100,000
    D. $112,000

162. A $50,000 mortgage loan is made at a 12 percent contract interest rate and four discount points with monthly payments over 30 years. What is the effective interest rate?
    A. 11.00 percent
    B. 11.48 percent
    C. 12.55 percent
    D. 13.15 percent

163. The term *interest rate* would *NOT* normally refer to which concept?
    A. The cost of money
    B. A capitalization rate
    C. The rate of return on an investment
    D. A yield rate

164. The annual rate of earnings on an investment that equates the value of cash returns with cash invested and considers the application of compound interest factors is known as the
    A. external rate of return (ERR).
    B. internal rate of return (IRR).
    C. financial management rate of return (FMRR).
    D. compound annual rate (CAR).

165. Smith received $3,000 per year for five years on a $10,000 loan investment. What is the IRR (internal rate of return) in the nearest percent?
    A. 3 percent
    B. 15 percent
    C. 20 percent
    D. 30 percent

166. An investment is expected to provide income of $1,000 per year for ten years. At the end of ten years the investment has no value. At an interest rate of 10 percent, the present value of the investment is
    A. $5,759.
    B. $6,145.
    C. $9,557.
    D. $75,671.

167. The use of borrowed funds to increase purchasing power and, ideally, to increase the profitability of an investment is referred to as
    A. leverage.
    B. banker's acceptance.
    C. reserve banking.
    D. commercial paper.

168. A written instrument that creates a lien on real estate as security for the payment of a specific debt is referred to as a
    A. lease.
    B. mortgage.
    C. mortgagee.
    D. contract.

169. The percentage ratio between the annual debt service and the loan principal is referred to as a(n)
    A. debt coverage ratio.
    B. equity dividend rate.
    C. interest ratio.
    D. mortgage constant.

170. A loan of $10,000 at 12 percent interest for five years requires annual payments of $2,774. The mortgage constant is
    A. 11.00 percent.
    B. 12.00 percent.
    C. 26.57 percent.
    D. 27.74 percent.

171. Which term explains an increase in the outstanding balance of a loan resulting from the failure of periodic debt service payments to cover required interest charged on the loan?
    A. Bankruptcy
    B. Negative amortization
    C. Negative leverage
    D. Leverage

172. A loan is originated at 15 percent interest with a maturity of 30 years. The interest rate may be adjusted each six months, but monthly payments remain constant at $632. After six months, the interest rate is raised to 16.5 percent, which would require a monthly payment of $692 to fully amortize the loan. What is *TRUE* of the amortization at the new interest rate?
    A. The amortization is positive.
    B. The amortization is negative.
    C. Because of the negative amortization, the loan will never be paid off with the higher interest rate.
    D. Because of the positive amortization, the loan will be paid off faster.

173. A situation in which a property owner must make an outlay of funds to operate a property is referred to as negative
    A. cash flow.
    B. amortization.
    C. leverage.
    D. debt service.

174. Income from property or business after operating expenses have been deducted, but before deducting income taxes and financing expenses (interest and principal payments), is referred to as
    A. equity dividend.
    B. before-tax cash flow.
    C. effective gross income.
    D. net operating income.

175. An investment measure that subtracts the present value of cash outflows from the present value of cash inflows using a specified discount rate is referred to as
    A. profitability index.
    B. net present value.
    C. present value.
    D. internal rate of return.

176. An investment measure that divides the present value of cash inflows by the present value of cash outflows using a specified discount rate is referred to as
    A. net present value.
    B. profitability index.
    C. present value.
    D. investment index.

177. A written instrument that acknowledges a debt and promises to repay the obligation is referred to as a
    A. deed.
    B. note.
    C. mortgage.
    D. trust.

178. A mortgage that covers two or more pieces of property pledged as security is known as a
    A. participation mortgage.
    B. convertible mortgage.
    C. blanket mortgage.
    D. shared appreciation mortgage.

179. A loan is given on an office building. In addition to a fixed payment of principal and interest, the lender is entitled to 2 percent of gross rental income. This is an example of what kind of mortgage?
    A. Gross loan
    B. Participation loan
    C. Percentage loan
    D. Shared appreciation mortgage

180. What is the term used to explain the amount of time required for cumulative estimated future income from an investment to equal the amount initially invested?
    A. Return on investment
    B. Return of investment
    C. Payback period
    D. Holding period

181. The purchase of an apartment building requires an equity investment of $20,000. Annual cash flow is expected to be $2,000. What is the payback period for the investment?
    A. Cannot be determined without knowing the interest rate
    B. 10 years
    C. Depends on the economic base in future years
    D. 20 years

182. The use of borrowed funds that increases the return on an investment is referred to as
    A. positive leverage.
    B. negative leverage.
    C. cash equivalency.
    D. positive amortization.

183. ◎ The amount of income that could be produced by real estate, assuming no vacancies or collection losses, is referred to as
    A. cash flow.
    B. net operating income.
    C. potential gross income.
    D. effective gross income.

184. What is the present value of an annuity of $1 per year after ten years, discounted at 12 percent?
    A. $0.29
    B. $0.32
    C. $5.65
    D. $5.94

185. Financial statements showing what is expected to occur are referred to as
    A. pro forma statements.
    B. income statements.
    C. balance sheets.
    D. accounting statements.

186. What term is sometimes used in appraisal for a method of estimating the value of property based on estimated future income and the reversionary value of the building and land?
    A. Compounded cash flow
    B. Property residual technique
    C. Land residual technique
    D. Reversionary residual technique

187. In general, the percentage relationship between the earnings and the price paid for an investment is referred to as the
    A. capitalization rate.
    B. rate of return.
    C. financial management rate of return.
    D. investment rate.

188. The term *reversionary factor* is sometimes used to express the mathematical factor that indicates the
    A. value of the reversion in relation to the initial cost.
    B. value of the reversion in relation to the adjusted basis.
    C. present worth of a stream of equal cash flows.
    D. present worth of one dollar to be received in the future.

189. A loan is made in which an existing loan is retained and an additional loan, larger than the existing loan, is made. The new lender accepts the obligation to make payments on the old loan. This is an example of what kind of mortgage?
   A. Senior mortgage
   B. Wraparound mortgage
   C. Equity mortgage
   D. Negative amortization mortgage

190. The term *yield to maturity* is similar to which term?
   A. Capitalization rate
   B. Adjusted internal rate of return
   C. Internal rate of return
   D. Equity dividend rate

191. ◎ To estimate effective gross income, which items are required?
   A. Potential gross income and operating expenses
   B. Potential gross income and vacancy and collection loss
   C. Gross income, operating expenses, and debt service
   D. Gross income and operating expenses

192. ◎ In real estate appraising, what is meant by the term *capitalization*?
   A. The initial funds invested in a project
   B. Conversion of income into an estimate of value
   C. Value resulting from any one of the three approaches
   D. Determination of the amount of capital available for investment

193. When calculating an equity dividend rate based on the first year of ownership, which type of information is required?
   A. Purchase price
   B. Purchase price, loan amount, and before-tax cash flow
   C. Purchase price and net operating income
   D. Equity invested and net operating income

194. An income property sells for $175,000 and has a gross income of $20,000. What is the gross income multiplier?
   A. 0.09
   B. 0.11
   C. 8.75
   D. 11.42

195. ◎ Which item is an example of an out-lay that might be included in a reserve for replacements?
   A. Building replacement at the end of its economic life
   B. Roof replacement when it is worn out
   C. Allowance for painting
   D. Refinancing fees

APPLICATION-STYLE QUESTIONS

Questions 196 through 199 are based on the following information:

An office building recently sold for $2,000,000. Given the following information:

Gross (potential) income: $400,000
Vacancy factor: 8 percent
Expenses: 45 percent of effective gross income
Annual mortgage payment: $165,000
Equity: $500,000

196. What is the indicated gross income multiplier?
    A. 4
    B. 5
    C. 7.5
    D. 10.12

197. What is the overall rate of return for the property?
    A. 8.3 percent
    B. 9 percent
    C. 10 percent
    D. 10.12 percent

198. What is the equity dividend rate or cash-on-cash rate of return?
    A. 5 percent
    B. 7.48 percent
    C. 9 percent
    D. 10.12 percent

199. What is the indicated loan-to-value ratio?
    A. 25 percent
    B. 75 percent
    C. 90 percent
    D. 100 percent

Questions 200 and 201 are based on the following information:

You are appraising a property in an area where mortgages are available on similar properties for 75 percent of the sales price with mortgage constants of 10 percent. Research reveals that investors who are willing to invest the remaining 25 percent of the sales price require a 15 percent equity dividend rate.

200. Using the band of investment method, calculate the proper capitalization rate to be used for the subject property.
    A. 0.1000
    B. 0.1125
    C. 0.1375
    D. 0.1500

201. If the subject property in the previous question has a net operating income of $55,000, what is its indicated value using the capitalization rate from the band of investment analysis?
    A. $367,000
    B. $400,000
    C. $489,000
    D. $550,000

Questions 202 through 204 are based on the following information:

Building value:	$1,000,000
Net operating income:	$167,000
Building capitalization rate:	14 percent
Land capitalization rate:	9 percent

202. What is the residual income to the land?
    A. $27,000
    B. $77,000
    C. $90,000
    D. $140,000

203. What is the value of the land?
  A. $90,000
  B. $192,857
  C. $300,000
  D. $855,555

204. What is the total value of the property?
  A. $1,090,000
  B. $1,192,857
  C. $1,300,000
  D. $1,855,555

Questions 205 through 208 are based on the following information collected by an appraiser:

Potential gross income: $100,000
Vacancy and collection loss: 15 percent
Operating expenses: $30,000
Mortgage payment: $37,000
Property value: $500,000
Loan-to-value ratio: 0.70

205. What is the net operating income?
  A. $45,000
  B. $55,000
  C. $70,000
  D. $85,000

206. What is the overall capitalization rate?
  A. 0.07
  B. 0.11
  C. 0.12
  D. 0.17

207. What is the before-tax cash flow (equity dividend)?
  A. $18,000
  B. $33,000
  C. $55,000
  D. $59,500

208. What is the equity dividend rate?
  A. 0.10
  B. 0.11
  C. 0.12
  D. 0.13

Questions 209 and 210 are based on the following information:

A proposed land investment requires $10,000 cash now and is expected to be resold for $25,000 in four years. For the risks involved, the investor seeks a 20 percent discount rate.

209. What is the net present value?
  A. $0
  B. $46
  C. $2,056
  D. $12,056

210. What is the profitability index?
  A. 0.21
  B. 0.40
  C. 1.21
  D. 2.50

ANSWERS TO DIAGNOSTIC EXAM VI

(Many of the answers contain references to the tables in Appendix B. The symbols used to refer to the tables are included in the Glossary.)

1. **D.** There is no absolute number or adjustment that can be used for vacancy allowance. One of the responsibilities of the appraiser in analyzing the market is to estimate what the specific number should be for the subject property.

2. **A.** Gross (potential) income minus vacancy and credit allowance equals effective gross income.

3. **B.** The capitalization rate would explicitly include a return on both the land and the building as well as a recapture of the building.

4. **B.** $8,000 net operating income and $80,000 value means the capitalization rate used was 10 percent. If the capitalization rate is increased by one percentage point, the new value would be $8,000 ÷ 0.11, or $72,700 (rounded).

5. **B.** $20,000 ÷ 0.18 = $111,111. $10,000 ÷ 0.09 = $111,111. Because both the net income and the rate of capitalization for the second property were exactly one-half those for the first property, the value would remain constant.

6. **B.** Mortgage (debt) payments are not part of the calculation to estimate net operating income. The remaining three choices are all subtracted from effective gross income to estimate net operating income.

7. **C.** As risk and uncertainty increase, the capitalization rate is normally increased. Because there is an inverse relationship between the capitalization rate chosen and the value estimate, an increase in the capitalization rate will result in a lower value.

8. **A.** $8,000 ÷ $80,000 = 10 percent capitalization rate; 0.10 + 0.02 = 0.12 (new capitalization rate); $8,000 ÷ 0.12 = $66,700 (rounded). Note: 200 basis points is two percentage points.

9. **C.** The income approach to value includes an analysis of income and operating expenses. Debt service, pretax cash flow, and after-tax cash flow are not necessary for the income approach to value.

10. **B.** The appraiser needs to analyze all expenses carefully when using the income approach to value. One reason is to make sure that certain items are not being either counted twice or eliminated completely. One area where careful attention should be given concerns replacement allowances, which could have mistakenly been placed in a repair and maintenance category.

11. **C.** A necessary part of the income approach to value includes the calculation of the effective gross income. Accrued depreciation, replacement cost, and land value are all part of the cost approach to value.

12. **C.** $500,000 × 0.75 = $375,000 loan; thus the equity is $125,000. A 10 percent return on equity would be $12,500 per year. $12,500 + $47,500 = $60,000 gross income. $60,000 ÷ 12 = $5,000 per month 10 = $500 per unit per month.

13. **B.** The basic equation used in the income approach to value is V = I ÷ R, or value equals net income divided by the rate of capitalization.

14. **A.** The operating expense ratio shows the relationship between operating expenses and gross income. In some examples, an appraiser will see that effective gross income has been used rather than gross income.

15. **B.** Discounting involves the process of converting future dollars or income into a present value or worth. Compounding is just the opposite, namely, converting present income or dollars into a future worth or value. Amortization is the repayment of debt over time in a series of periodic payments.

16. **C.** The debt coverage ratio shows the relationship between debt service and net operating income.

17. **B.** The building residual technique is a method used in appraising income-producing property to estimate the total value of the property when the value of the land is known. The income not attributable to the land is assumed to be attributable to the building.

18. **D.** A gross rent multiplier is a technique used to estimate market value by multiplying the market rent by the gross rent multiplier. The resulting number is an estimate of what the value would be, based on the gross rents and sales prices of other properties.

19. **B.** $500,000 × 0.06 = $30,000 vacancy allowance. $500,000 − $30,000 = $470,000 effective gross income. $205,000 ÷ $470,000 = 0.436 (rounded to 44 percent).

20. **D.** The income approach to value is based on the principle of anticipation, which states that value changes in expectation of some future benefit or detriment affecting the property. The translation of the ability of property to generate income into an indication of value as well as an estimate of net operating income are both part of the income approach to value.

21. **D.** $8,000 × 12 = $96,000 annual gross income. $96,000 × 9.5 = $912,000.

22. **C.** Capitalization rate = income ÷ value; $30,500 ÷ $350,000 = 0.087 (rounded to 0.09 or 9 percent).

23. **A.** Normally with income-producing property, the owner will employ someone to manage the property. Compensation for such a person is usually a percentage of effective gross income, which serves as an incentive to the property manager to keep the space fully occupied and collect all rents.

24. **A.** Rate of capitalization equals net income divided by value: $10,000 ÷ $100,000 = 0.10, or 10 percent. By increasing the capitalization rate by one full percentage point, $10,000 ÷ 0.11 = $90,909.

25. **A.** The capitalization rate is directly related to the amount of risk associated with the investment. Normally as the risk perception increases, the capitalization rate is increased to reflect that uncertainty.

26. **D.** The basic formula used in the income approach to value is V (value) = I (net income) ÷ R (rate).

27. **A.** Potential (gross) income minus vacancy and land debt allowance equals effective gross income. This is one of the necessary calculations in reconstructing an operating statement for income-producing property.

28. **C.** $3,000 × 12 = $36,000 per year. $36,000 ÷ $300,000 = 0.12 or 12 percent.

29. **C.** Net operating income minus debt service (mortgage payments) equals pretax or before-tax cash flow.

30. **B.** $1,000,000 × 0.12 = $120,000 net operating income. $120,000 ÷ 0.6 = effective gross income of $200,000.

31. **A.** Amortization refers to the repayment of a financial obligation, such as a mortgage, over a period of time in a series of periodic installments.

32. **B.** The overall capitalization rate can only be applied to NOI. The basic formula is V = I ÷ R. In this formula, *I* denotes net

operating income and R is the overall capitalization rate.

33. **B.** $15,000 ÷ $100,000 = 15 percent. The debt service does not enter into the calculation of an overall capitalization rate.

34. **B.** Return on capital is like an interest rate; it is a rate of return on the amount of capital invested in the project.

35. **A.** Mortgage interest is not an operating expense, although it is a cash flow. Mortgage interest is paid off after NOI is calculated.

36. **B.** A capitalization rate implicitly includes a return on capital for investors. Lower interest rates would result in investors requiring a lower return and thus a lower capitalization rate.

37. **B.** All else being equal, one would expect overall rates to be lower for properties purchased with favorable financing because a higher price would be paid for a property with the same NOI.

38. **C.** The net income multiplier is the reciprocal of the overall rate. Thus $1 ÷ 0.08 = 12.5$.

39. **A.** Note that expenses increase for four years (year 1 to year 5). Thus what needs to be calculated is the future value of $35,000 after compounding at 6 percent per year for four years. $35,000 \times (1.06)^4 = $44,187.

40. **C.** $200,000 = $2,082.90 × (MPVIFA, 12 percent, years). $200,000 ÷ $2,082.90 = 96.02. 96.02 on 12 percent monthly table = 27 years.

    Calculator Solution:
    PV = – 200,000
    i = 12% ÷ 12 = 1%
    PMT = 2,082.90
    FV = 0

    Solve for n = 324 months or 324 ÷ 12 = 27 years

41. **C.** Twelve percent compounded monthly is equivalent to 1 percent per month. After 12 months, a deposit of $1 would increase to $1.126825 (see column 1 of the monthly compound interest tables for 12 percent). Thus the effective annual rate is 12.6825 percent.

    Calculator Solution:
    PV = 1
    n = 12
    i = 12% ÷ 12 = 1%

    Solve for FV = 1.126825

    Effective annual rate is 1.126825 – 1 = 0.126825 or 12.7%

42. **D.** $10,000 + $10,000 × (PVIFA, 12 percent, 39 years) = Present Value. $10,000 + $10,000 × 8.233030 (from table column 5) = $92,330.

43. **D.** The straight-line method develops a capitalization rate by adding an allowance for return of capital to the discount rate (return on capital). In this case, the return of capital would be 1/25 or 4 percent. Thus the capitalization rate would be 10 percent plus 4 percent = 14 percent. This method of capitalization is not in common use today.

44. **D.** The important thing to recognize is that because NOI and property value are increasing at the same compound rate (in this case 4 percent per year), a shortcut method can be used to estimate the value. The capitalization rate is equal to the discount rate minus the rate of increase in income and property value. Thus the capitalization rate is 14 percent – 4 percent = 10 percent. Therefore, the property value is $50,000 ÷ 0.10 = $500,000.

45. **D.** $100,000 = $10,000 × (PVIFA, ? percent, 4 years) + $120,000 × (PVIF, ? percent, 5 years) ? percent = between 11 percent and 12 percent from tables

    Calculator Solution:
    PV = – 100,000
    PMT = 10,000

n = 5
FV = 110,000

Solve for i = 11.59%

46. **B.** The yield must be less than 10 percent because the yield would be exactly 10 percent if the property sold for $100,000. That is, if the property value does not change over time (neither increase nor decrease), and the NOI is level, the yield rate will be equal to the NOI divided by the purchase price.

47. **D.** $50,000 = PMT × (MPVIFA, 8 percent, 15 years)

$50,000 = PMT × 104.640592
$50,000 ÷ 104.640592 = $477.83 = PMT
$40,000 = $477.83 × (MPVIFA, ? percent, 15 years)
$40,000 ÷ $477.83 = 83.7125 = MPVIFA, ? percent, 15 years
MPVIFA, ? percent 15 years = approximately 12 percent from tables

Calculator Solution:
PV = – 50,000
n = 15 × 12 = 180
i = 8% ÷ 12 = 0.66667%

Solve for PMT = 477.83

Do not clear calculator

PV = 40,000

Solve for i = 0.99274%

Multiply i by 12 for annual rate

0.99274% × 12 = 11.91%

48. **A.** $20,000 = PMT × (FVIFA, 8 percent, 15 years)

$20,000 = PMT × 27.152114

$20,000 ÷ 27.152114 = $736.59 = PMT

Calculator Solution:
FV = 20,000
n = 15
i = 8%

Solve for PMT = $736.59 or $737

49. **D.** $120,000 × (1.05)^{10} = $195,467

50. **B.** Management expenses should be included as an operating expense even for properties managed by the owner. The other expenses listed are not operating expenses.

51. **D.** Income can be capitalized to a value estimate by either direct capitalization techniques or yield capitalization. Direct capitalization uses a single year's income or an average of several years' income and finds a property value by dividing the income estimate by an income rate or by multiplying the income by an income multiplier. Use of the overall rate to find property value is an example of direct capitalization. Yield capitalization converts future cash flows into a present value by discounting the cash flows at a rate that reflects the investment's income pattern, value change, and yield rate. Discounted cash flow is an example of yield capitalization.

52. **B.** An overall rate is always applied to net operating income (NOI).

53. **B.** The value of the equity position is calculated by dividing the before-tax cash flow by the equity dividend rate. The value of the equity position would have to be added to the amount of the loan (value of the mortgage position) to arrive at a total value of the property.

54. **A.** NOI ÷ R_o = V

$125,000 × 0.32 = $40,000

$125,000 – $40,000 = $85,000

$85,000 ÷ 0.14 = $607,143

55. **B.** Federal income taxes are not a deduction for net operating income. They are used only to calculate after-tax cash flow.

56. **C.** Discounting or discounted cash flow analysis is the process of finding the present value of future cash flows. It should be based on *reasonable estimates* of the future income, not on guessing. While this is capitalization, it is not *direct*

capitalization. Direct capitalization (e.g., use of overall capitalization rates derived from the market) does not involve discounting estimated future income; direct capitalization uses current income.

57. **A.** By definition, the mortgage loan contract is the ratio of the loan payment to the loan amount.

58. **B.** The debt coverage ratio (DCR) is an indication of the safety or "riskiness" of the loan. Lenders want to be reasonably sure that the NOI is sufficient to cover the debt service so that the owner's capital will not have to be used to repay the loan.

59. **B.** The land residual technique can be used. Land value is estimated by assuming it is used under its highest and best use. However, this is not a technique for estimating land value per se.

60. **C.** The distinction between fixed and variable expenses is based on whether the expense varies with the level of occupancy. For example, property taxes are considered a fixed operating expense because they will not change if occupancy (vacancy) changes. However, they are not necessarily constant over a holding period and certainly not forever.

61. **D.** Higher than normal expectations for future increases in property value make the property more valuable today relative to the current net operating income. Thus, all else being equal, a lower capitalization rate would be justified. (Lower capitalization rates result in higher property values.) Higher than normal risk would require a higher rate of return and thus a lower property value, which requires a higher overall capitalization rate. Lower than normal operating expenses would not affect the choice of a capitalization rate because the capitalization rate is applied to income that is the net of operating expenses.

62. **A.** Income from renting a garage space is an example of "other income" that would normally be included in the calculation of potential gross income because the garage is in the apartment building. If the garage is not part of the building (i.e., it was a separate structure), then the appraiser would have to specify whether the garage was included with the property being appraised.

63. **D.** Mortgage debt service is not a deduction in the calculation of NOI. Although not all appraisers include a replacement allowance, it is an appropriate expense in calculation of NOI. Some appraisers do not include a replacement allowance because they handle the need for replacements in a different manner. For example, with a discounted cash flow analysis, the cost of the replacement would be part of the cash flow in the year it was expected to occur.

64. **A.** Vacancy and collection loss is typically based on potential gross income. Deducting vacancy and collection loss from potential gross income results in effective gross income. Thus it would not make sense to estimate it as a percent of effective gross income, and certainly not net operating income or operating expenses.

65. **B.** *Reversion* is the term used to denote the lump sum an investor receives at the termination of an investment. It is probably historically based on the legal concept of reversion, which refers to the rights of the lessor to the property at the end of a lease. That is, the lessor receives income from the lease until the lease expires and the reversion rights at the end of the lease. However, this is an oversimplification because properties may be sold before the lease expires, and the proceeds are still referred to as the reversion.

66. **B.** The term *buydown* denotes payment by the seller or the purchaser to the lender in order to reduce the loan payments (interest rate) for the purchaser. Appraisers must be aware of properties that sell with loans with subsidized financing like buydowns because the property is likely

to have sold at a higher price than the market value of the real estate.

67. **A.** A participation mortgage means that the lender participates in income from the property (e.g., a percentage of the net operating income). It is not an ownership position per se. Sometimes the term *equity kicker* is used for participation, but this is a misnomer.

68. **D.** The terms *cash-on-cash return, equity dividend rate, equity capitalization rate,* and *cash flow rate* are synonymous.

69. **C.** The term *capital gain* is used primarily in income tax computations to indicate the amount by which the net proceeds from the resale of an asset exceed the book value of the item.

70. **D.** A discount rate is a return on capital.

71. **B.** Debt capital is usually used in expectation of a higher rate of return on the equity investment. When the investor's equity yield rate increases with the use of debt capital, the leverage is said to be favorable or positive. Conversely, if the investor's equity yield rate decreases with borrowed funds, the leverage is said to be unfavorable or negative.

72. **C.** Interest expense is a financing cost and is not deducted when calculating net operating income. NOI is before any costs associated with the financing of the property.

73. **D.** Federal income taxes are not deducted to calculate net operating income. NOI is a before-tax measure of income.

74. **B.** Effective gross income includes an allowance for vacancy and collection but does not deduct any operating expenses or financing costs.

75. **C.** The term *before-tax cash flow* is usually meant to consider all cash inflows and outflows that affect the owner except federal income taxes. Answer B would be

correct *if* there were no other cash inflows or outflows, e.g., tenant improvement expenses.

76. **B.** The debt coverage ratio (DCR) is a measure of the extent to which NOI exceeds the mortgage payment. Lenders typically require the DCR to be greater than some minimum ratio (e.g., 1.1 or 1.2).

77. **B.** The band of investment technique is used to calculate the overall capitalization rate. It is typically measured by the weighted average of the mortgage constant and the equity capitalization rate or by the weighted average of the land capitalization rate and the building capitalization rate. The average is weighted by the loan-to-value ratio or land value to total property value ratio, respectively.

78. **C.** The loan constant must be higher than the interest rate to allow for amortization of the loan. An interest-only loan would have a constant equal to the interest rate. If the constant were less than the interest rate, it would be a negative amortization loan.

79. **C.** V = \$10,000 × (PVIFA, 12 percent, 4 years) + \$110,000 × (PVF, 12 percent, 5 years) V = (\$10,000 × 3.037349) + (\$110,000 × 0.567427) = \$92,790.

    Calculator Solution:
    PMT = 10,000
    FV = 10,000
    n = 5
    i = 12%

    Solve for PV = 92,790

80. **C.** $R_O = R_M \times M \times DCR$

    DCR = \$60,000 ÷ \$49,000 = 1.2245

    $R_O = 0.11 \times 0.75 \times 1.2245 = 0.101$

81. **A.** When overall capitalization rates are calculated by using information obtained directly from comparable sales, the technique is referred to as direct capitalization.

82. **A.** $\$500,000 \times 0.80 = \$400,000 =$ value of loan

    $\$400,000 = PMT \times$ (MPVIFA, 11 percent, 25 years)

    $\$400,000 = PMT \times 102.029044$ (from table column 5)

    $\$400,000 \div 102.029044 = PMT = \$3,920$

83. **C.** Property managers are typically paid a percentage of the actual income collected and thus property management expenses are considered variable expenses.

84. **C.** Fixed expenses include items such as insurance, taxes, and advertising, which do not vary with the level of occupancy. Variable expenses change with the level of occupancy and include expenses such as utilities and maintenance.

85. **D.** The notion that value is created by the anticipation of future benefits is the premise of discounted cash flow analysis.

86. **D.** The equity dividend rate equals the before-tax cash flow to the investor divided by the equity. Because this is the ratio of one year's income to value, the equity dividend rate is a direct capitalization ratio and not a yield rate.

87. **B.** The mortgage constant equals the loan payment (debt service) divided by the initial loan principal.

88. **D.** Income can be converted to a value estimate by direct capitalization, which considers only the first year's income or an average of incomes, or by yield capitalization, which discounts the future benefits of the property to find a present value estimate.

89. **A.** The removal of rubbish is a legitimate operating expense. Debt service, owner's entrepreneurial profit, and tax depreciation are not operating expenses.

90. **A.** The equity dividend equals the cash flow available to the equity investor. This term is synonymous with the terms *pre-tax cash flow* or *before-tax cash flow*.

91. **B.** $\$70,000 \times 0.10 = \$7,000 =$ income to the land

    $\$30,000 - \$7,000 = \$23,000 =$ residual income to the building

    $\$23,000 \div 0.09 = \$255,556$

92. **C.** DCR = annual NOI ÷ annual mortgage payment

    $DCR = \$120,000 \div (\$9,000 \times 12) = 1.11$

93. **C.** The income approach, especially yield capitalization, is based on the present value of future cash flows. Therefore a reasonable estimate of actual cash flows is necessary to compute a value. Future cash flows may vary from those shown on previous accounting statements.

94. **C.** $GIM = \$210,000 \div \$24,000 = 8.75$

95. **C.** $R_O = \$18,000 \div \$140,000 = 0.129$

96. **D.** Corporate taxes are never considered as operating expenses. A reserve for replacements might be considered.

97. **A.** $\$500,000 \times 0.12 = \$60,000$

98. **B.** $\$26,000 \div 0.10 = \$260,000 =$ total property value

    $\$260,000 - \$175,000 = \$85,000 =$ land value

    $R_O = L \times R_L + (1 - L) \times R_B$

    $L = \$85,000 \div \$260,000 = 0.327$

    $0.10 = 0.327 \times R_L + 0.673 \times 0.11$

    $0.026 = 0.327 \times R_L$

    $0.079 = R_L$

99. **D.** $\$30,000 \div \$64,000 = 0.47$

100. **B.** The gross income multiplier (GIM) equals the value of the property divided by the gross income. It can be used to calculate the overall rate by the following

formula: $R_O = (1 - OER) \div EGIM$; where OER (operating expense ratio) equals the operating expenses divided by the effective gross income multiplier (EGIM).

101. **B.** Management fees are usually computed as a percent of effective gross income. Effective gross income includes vacancy, which is related to the ability of the management to find new tenants.

102. **A.** $R_O = M \times R_M + (1 - M) \times R_E$

$R_O = 0.75 \times 0.1275 + 0.25 \times 0.09$
$= 0.1181$

$V = NOI \div R_O = \$10,000 \div 0.1181$
$= \$84,656$

103. **C.** $\$50,000 \times 0.1275 = \$6,375 =$ income to mortgage

$\$10,000 - \$6,375 = \$3,625 =$ income to equity

$\$3,625 \div 0.09 = \$40,278 =$ equity value

$\$40,278 + \$50,000 = \$90,278$

104. **B.** $EGIM = Value \div EGI$

$5.5 = Value \div \$185,000$

$5.5 \times \$185,000 = \$1,017,500$

105. **C.** $NIR = NOI \div EGI$

$GIM = V \div EGI$

$V = GIM \times 1 \div NIR \times NOI$

$V = 7.5 \times 1/0.6 \times \$240,000 = \$3,000,000$

106. **A.** $EGIM = V \div EGI = 6$ from question; therefore, $EGI \div V = 1 \div 6$

$NOI = 0.63 \times EGI$ from question
$(1 - 0.37 = 0.63)$

$R_O = NOI \div V$

therefore, $R_O = 0.63 \div 6 = 0.105$

107. **C.** $R_O = L \times R_L + (1 - L) \times R_B$

$R_O = 0.25 \times 0.08 + 0.75 \times 0.12$

$R_O = 0.110$

108. **C.** Wraparound mortgages have been used to obtain additional financing without taking out a new second mortgage and without disturbing the existing mortgage. Interest rates on the wraparound mortgage tend to be higher than interest rates on the existing mortgage.

109. **C.** $\$500,000 \times (1 - 0.7) = \$150,000 =$ equity
$\$12,000 \div \$150,000 = 0.08$

110. **B.** Because different risks are associated with each type of rent, different capitalization rates should be used to reflect the difference in risk.

111. **A.** $R_O = M \times R_M + (1 - M) \times R_E$

Therefore, if $M = 0$, R_E must equal R_O.

Also, if $R_O = R_M$ then $R_O = R_E$, which means the leverage is zero (neither positive nor negative).

112. **C.** $PGIM = V \div PGI$

$PGIM = \$240,000 \div \$50,000$

$PGIM = 4.80$

113. **C.** $\$52,000 \div \$300,000 = 0.173.$

114. **B.** A participation mortgage allows the lender to participate in income from the property during the operating years and/or gain from the sale of the property.

115. **A.** The overall capitalization rate is a ratio of NOI to price or value. It is based on a single year's NOI, usually the first year of ownership. The overall capitalization rate is not a rate of return over a holding period because it does not consider changes in NOI and value over time. The ratio of the mortgage payment to the loan amount is sometimes referred to as a mortgage capitalization rate but not an overall capitalization rate.

116. **C.** Equity dividend rate refers to the ratio of a property's first-year cash flow to the amount of equity invested. It may also be referred to as the equity capitalization rate.

117. **C.** Effective gross income (EGI)
= $1,000,000 - $50,000 = $950,000

EGIM = V ÷ EGI = $5,000,000
÷ $950,000 = 5.26

118. **D.** A mortgage constant is the ratio of the total payment (principal and interest) to the amount of the loan. Constants are normally stated on an annual basis even if the payments are actually made monthly.

$908.70 × 12 = $10,904 total annual payment

$10,904 ÷ $100,000 = 0.109

119. **B.** $R_O = L \times R_L + (1 - L) \times R_B$

$R_O = 0.35 \times 0.09 + 0.65 \times 0.12 = 0.1095$

$V = NOI \div R_O = \$70,000 \div 0.1095$
$= \$639,269$

120. **C.** $38,000 - $28,700 = $9,300 = residual income to the equity

$9,300 ÷ 0.08 = $116,250 = value of the equity

$116,250 + $273,000 = $389,250

121. **C.** DCR = NOI ÷ debt service; debt service includes principal and interest

DCR = $10,000 ÷ $9,000 = 1.11

122. **B.**

Month	Beg. Balance	Payment	Interest	Prin. Paid	End. Balance
0					50,000.00
1	50,000.00	500	416.67	83.33	49,916.67
2	49,916.67	500	415.97	84.03	49,832.64
3	49,832.64	500	415.27	84.73	49,747.91

Beginning balance equals the ending balance of the previous pay period.

Payment equals $500 as given.

Interest equals the monthly rate of 10 percent ÷ 12 times the beginning balance.

Principal paid equals the payment minus the interest.

Ending balance equals the beginning balance minus the principal paid.

Calculator Solution:
PMT = 500
PV = - 50,000
i = 10 ÷ 12 = 0.833333%
n = 3

Solve for FV = 49,747.91

123. **A.** All else being equal, investors will require a higher rate of return for properties with higher risk. To earn a higher rate of return for property B, the investor would have to pay a lower price, resulting in a higher overall capitalization rate.

124. **B.** The overall rate equals the net income ratio divided by the gross income multiplier.

0.7 ÷ 9 = 0.0778

125. **C.** $R_O = M \times R_M + (1 - M) \times R_E$

$R_O = 0.7 \times 0.1 + 0.3 \times 0.06 = 0.088$

126. **A.** The equity dividend rate will be less than 10 percent because there is unfavorable leverage on an income basis. When the overall rate is less than the mortgage constant, the equity dividend rate will be less than the overall rate.

127. **A.** Fixed expenses do not vary with the level of occupancy.

128. **D.** Potential gross income – vacancy and collection loss = effective gross income. Effective gross income – operating expenses = net operating income.

129. **B.** There is an inverse relationship between a cap rate and value; thus, the higher the cap rate, the lower the value.

130. **B.** An annuity is a series of equal payments or receipts. Annuity tables are available for calculating present and future values of annuities (*see* Appendix B).

Note: Sometimes a series of payments or receipts that change according to a predictable pattern is also referred to as an annuity.

131. **B.** Annuity received at the beginning of each year is known as an annuity in advance. Annuity in arrears is an annuity that is received at the end of each period.

132. **B.** The band of investment technique involves an overall interest rate derived from both mortgage and equity rates. The formula is: $R_O = M \times R_M + (1 - M) \times R_E$; where M = loan value ÷ property value, R_M = mortgage constant and R_E = equity dividend rate.

133. **B.** The capital gain equals the sale price minus the adjusted basis. The adjusted basis equals the original cost minus accumulated depreciation. Therefore, the gain is $95,000 – $90,000. This example assumes no depreciation.

134. **A.** The cost basis of improvements is depreciable; the $10,000 basis of the land remains because land is not depreciable.

135. **B.** The initial book value was $100,000 and is now $90,000.

$100,000 – $10,000 = $90,000

136. **C.** Capital gain is the gain on the sale of a capital asset.

137. **C.** She reports the $4,000 profit as a long-term capital gain on her income tax return.

$14,000 – $10,000 = $4,000

138. **B.** If land is sold for less than the purchase price, the difference is known as a capital loss. (Note: There are limitations on the amount of loss that can be used to offset ordinary income.)

139. **A.** The debt coverage ratio is the ratio between the net operating income and the debt service. It gives an indication of how well the cash flows from the property can cover the debt payments and is used as an underwriting criterion.

140. **C.** 1.80, calculated by the following formula:

NOI ÷ Debt service = DCR

$18,000 ÷ $10,000 = 1.8

141. **D.** In a direct reduction mortgage, a portion of the principal and interest is paid off in systematic installments. The payments are usually of equal amounts.

142. **B.** A payment of $438.79 will fully amortize (pay off) $50,000 over 30 years at an interest rate of 10 percent.

Calculator Solution:
PV = – 50,000
i = 10 ÷ 12 = 0.833333%
n = 30 × 12 = 360

Solve for PMT = 438.79

143. **A.** The difference between the face amount of an obligation and the amount received is a discount. Discounts of this type can be seen in mortgage markets where an investor will purchase a secondary mortgage at a discount. In this case, the original lender will want to sell the loan and will thus sell the loan at the current published mortgage discount rate. The discount should increase the effective yield to the buyer.

144. **B.** $60,000 – $15,000 = $45,000.

145. **B.** Discount points (or points) are fees paid to a lender to account for the difference between the market interest rate and the contract or face rate.

146. **C.** The 4 points equal 4 percent of $50,000, which is $2,000.

147. **B.** When discount points are charged, then the effective rate is greater than the face rate. If the borrower received only $9,800 at the start of the loan and repaid $10,000 through the loan payments, the effective rate was greater than 10 percent; it was approximately 12.25 percent.

148. **D.** The use of borrowed money to complete a purchase is known as leverage. Financial leverage can be favorable or unfavorable to the borrower; that is, it could increase or decrease the investor's rate of return.

149. **B.** A first mortgage has priority, as a lien over all other mortgages. In cases of foreclosure, the first mortgage will be satisfied before other mortgages.

150. **C.** The holder of the first mortgage receives the full amount of the unpaid principal plus legal expenses. The second mortgage holder will receive any excess after the first mortgage has been fully satisfied.

151. **B.** A fixed-rate mortgage is one in which the interest rate is the same throughout the term of the loan. The amount of amortization can, and usually does, change with each payment.

152. **B.** Gross income is the total income before any expenses are deducted. Gross income can be either potential (before vacancy) or effective (after allowance for vacancy and collection loss).

153. **D.** Potential gross income minus vacancy and collection loss equals effective gross income.

154. **C.** Effective gross income is before deduction for operating expenses. Deducting operating expenses results in net operating income (NOI). Other income is included in effective gross income.

155. **C.**

Total rent income	$100,000	(10,000 × 10)
Concession income	20,000	
Potential gross income	$120,000	
Vacancy loss	− 5,000	(0.05 × $100,000)
Effective gross income	$115,000	

156. **A.** The gross rent multiplier (GRM) is derived by dividing the sales price by the contract rental rate.

157. **D.** The GRM = $40,000 ÷ $400 = 100. Note: The GRM may also be expressed on an annual basis; e.g., $40,000 ÷ $4,800 annual rent results in a GRM of 8.333.

158. **B.** The term *capitalization* refers to converting income into value when using the income approach. Use of an overall rate is only one way of applying the income approach. Income can also be discounted using a discount rate.

159. **D.** $NOI ÷ R_O = V$

$$\$100,000 ÷ 0.10 = \$1,000,000$$

160. **D.** If no amortization occurs, the principal of the loan is not paid off. Therefore, only interest is paid. This does not mean that the principal is never paid. Some sort of balloon payment at the end of the loan period will require payment of the principal.

161. **C.** The balance is $100,000, assuming the interest of $12,000 has already been paid.

162. **C.** $50,000 = PMT × (MPVIFA, 12 percent, 30 years)

$50,000 = PMT × 97.218331

$514.31 = PMT

$50,000 × 0.04 = $2,000

$50,000 − $2,000 = $48,000

$48,000 = $514.31 × (MPVIFA, ? percent, 30 years)

$48,000 ÷ $514.31 = 93.3289 = (MPVIFA, ? percent, 30 years)

(MPVIFA, ? percent, 30 years) = between 12 and 13 percent (from table)

Calculator Solution:
PV = − 50,000
i = 12% ÷ 12 = 1%
n = 30 × 12 = 360
Solve for PMT = 514.31

Do not clear calculator

PV = – 48,000 (amount loaned after 4 points)

Solve for i = 1.04619

Multiply by 12 for annual rate

1.04619 × 12 = 12.55%

163. **B.** An interest rate refers to the cost of borrowing money. It is also a yield rate and is the return on an investment. However, it is conceptually quite different from a capitalization rate.

164. **B.** The internal rate of return equates the value of cash returns with cash outlays.

165. **B.** $10,000 = $3,000 × (PVIFA, ? percent, 5 years)

$10,000 ÷ $3,000 = 3.33 = (PVIFA, ? percent, 5 years)

(PVIFA, ? percent, 5 years) = between 15 and 16 percent from table (column 5)

166. **B.** From the Annual Compound Interest Tables for 10% Annual Interest Rate, page 227, column 5, $1,000 × 6.1446 = $6,145. Note: the factor 6.1446 from tables is sometimes referred to as the Inwood annuity factor.

Calculator Solution:
PMT = 1,000
n = 10

Solve for PMT = 438.79
i = 10%
PV = 6,145

167. **A.** Positive leverage refers to a situation in which borrowed funds increase the profitability of the project. However, borrowing may also cause the profitability of the project to decrease. This situation is referred to as negative leverage.

168. **B.** A mortgage is the written security for payment of a debt.

169. **D.** The formula is: Annual debt service ÷ loan principal = mortgage constant.

170. **D.** 2,774 ÷ 10,000 = 0.2774 or 27.74 percent

171. **B.** When the loan payment is less than the interest incurred for the period, the result is negative amortization. Thus the interest not paid by the payment is added to the principal of the loan, and the loan principal increases. Payments are usually increased in a later period to pay off the principal.

172. **B.** As a result of the higher interest rate, $687 is required to pay interest. The $55 difference between the $632 payment and the interest due is added to the principal in month 7 as negative amortization.

173. **A.** When a property owner must make an outlay of funds to operate a property, the property is said to be generating negative cash flow. An inflow of funds (payments received) is referred to as positive cash flow.

174. **D.** Gross income – operating expenses = net operating income (NOI).

175. **B.** Net present value is derived by subtracting the present value of cash outflows from the present value of cash inflows using a specified discount rate. The term *present value* refers only to the present value of cash inflows.

176. **B.** A profitability index is derived by dividing the present value of cash inflows by the present value of cash outflows using a specified discount rate. The profitability index can be used in a similar fashion as the net present value since they are based on the same information. The net present value subtracts the present value of cash outflows from the present value of cash inflows.

177. **B.** A note represents the promise to repay debt. A mortgage makes the property collateral for a note. However, a note can exist without a mortgage, in which case the note would be unsecured.

178. **C.** A blanket mortgage is one in which the lender receives two or more pieces of property as security for the debt.

179. **B.** A participation loan is one in which the lender is entitled to a portion of the property's income or part of the proceeds from sale. Because the lender participates in the income stream provided by the property, the loan is not a shared appreciation loan.

180. **C.** The payback period is the time required for cumulative income to equal the initial investment. In computing the payback period, simply add the cash flows from each year until the sum of the cash flows equals the initial investment. The period of time it takes to reach this point is called the payback period.

181. **B.** By receiving $2,000 per year, it will take 10 years to gain back the initial $20,000 investment. Mathematically, $20,000 ÷ $2,000 = 10.

182. **A.** Positive leverage occurs when the use of borrowed funds (other people's money) increases the return on an investment. Negative leverage arises where the use of borrowed funds decreases the return on an investment.

183. **C.** Potential gross income is the amount of gross receipts if all available income is collected.

    Potential gross income – vacancy = effective gross income.

    Effective gross income – operating expenses = net operating income.

184. **C.** From the Annual Compound Interest Tables for 12 percent Annual Interest Rate, page 229, column 5, $1 × 5.650223 = $5.65

    Calculator Solution:
    PMT = 1
    i = 12%
    n = 10

    Solve for PV = 5.65

185. **A.** Pro forma statements show expected *future* cash flows, which can then be used in the income approach to estimate property value. Income and balance sheets are accounting statements that show prior cash flows.

186. **B.** The property residual technique, used in the valuing of income-producing property, is based on estimated future income and the reversionary value of both the building and the land. This is a misnomer because nothing is actually a "residual" as in the case of a land or building residual technique.

187. **A.** A capitalization rate shows the percentage relationship between the earnings and the price of an investment. The capitalization rate equals the net operating income divided by the property price.

188. **D.** The reversionary factor is the same as the factor for the *present value of one*. The formula is: Reversionary factor = $1 \div (1 + i)^n$ where i = interest rate and n = number of years (or periods).

189. **B.** A wraparound mortgage is one in which additional financing is acquired by placing the additional funds in a secondary position to the existing debt and thus the new mortgage "wraps around" the existing mortgage. The existing loan generally carries an interest rate below the rate available on new loans. Consequently, the yield to the wraparound lender is higher than the rate charged on the new loan.

190. **C.** *Yield to maturity* refers to the internal rate of return on an investment.

191. **B.** By definition, effective gross income is equal to potential gross income less vacancy and collection loss.

192. **B.** Capitalization applies to the use of the income approach to convert income into an estimate of value. It could involve using capitalization rates, such as an overall rate or discount rates.

193. **B.** Purchase price minus loan amount equals equity invested. The equity dividend rate is found by dividing the before-tax cash flow (NOI less debt service) by the equity invested.

194. **C.** $175,000 ÷ $20,000 = 8.75.

195. **B.** Reserves are intended for long-lived items that must be replaced before the end of the economic life of the property. An example would be replacement of a worn-out roof.

196. **B.** The gross income multiplier is calculated by dividing the gross (potential) income by the sales price. In this example, the GIM would be $2,000,000 ÷ $400,000 = 5.

197. **D.** The overall rate of return cannot be calculated without estimating net operating income (NOI). In this problem the NOI is $202,400. This is calculated by subtracting the vacancy allowance as well as the expenses from the gross income. Net operating income divided by sales price equals the overall rate of return for the property: $202,400 ÷ $2,000,000 = 10.12.

198. **B.** The equity dividend rate is calculated by dividing the cash flow (net operating income minus debt service) by equity. In this problem the cash flow is $37,400 and the equity is $500,000. The equity dividend rate is 7.48 percent.

199. **B.** The loan-to-value ratio is the relationship between the amount of money borrowed and the value of the property. In this problem the amount borrowed ($1,500,000) and the sales price ($2,000,000) indicate a loan-to-value ratio of 75 percent.

200. **B.** $(0.75 \times 0.1) + (0.25 \times 0.15) = 0.075 + 0.0375 = 0.1125$.

201. **C.** Value = Income ÷ Capitalization Rate; V = $55,000 ÷ 0.1125 or $489,000 (rounded).

202. **A.** $1,000,000 × 0.14 = $140,000

$167,000 − $140,000 = $27,000

203. **C.** $27,000 ÷ 0.09 = $300,000.

204. **C.** $1,000,000 + $300,000 = $1,300,000.

205. **B.** $100,000 − $15,000 ($100,000 × 0.15) − $30,000 = $55,000.

206. **B.** R_o = $55,000 ÷ $500,000 = 0.11.

207. **A.** $55,000 − $37,000 = $18,000.

208. **C.** Equity = $500,000 × (1 − 0.7) = $150,000 $18,000 ÷ $150,000 = 0.12.

209. **C.** The $25,000 amount to be received in four years, when discounted by 20 percent annually, is worth $12,056 now. The investment costs $10,000, so the net present value is $2,056.

210. **C.** $12,056 ÷ $10,000 = 1.21.

CHAPTER 10

Valuation of Partial Interests and Appraisal Math/Statistics

KEY TERMS

annual debt service
compounding versus
   discounting
concessions
excess rent
expense stops
leased fee
leasehold
life estate
future value of $1

future value of an
   annuity of $1 per
   period
gross lease
installment to amortize
   $1 per period
mean
median
mode
mortgage constant
net lease

overage rent
percentage rent
present value of $1
present value of an
   annuity of $1 per
   period
range
sinking fund factor
standard deviation
sublease
time-share

DIAGNOSTIC EXAM VII *

1. ◎ Which term is *NOT* a type of average or measure of cental tendency?
   A. Mean
   B. Median
   C. Mode
   D. Standard deviation

2. ◎ In statistical analysis, the median is a useful appraisal tool because it defines the
   A. range of the data.
   B. average.
   C. midpoint.
   D. most frequently occurring statistic.

3. The Smith family lives in their own house. The property tax rate is 32 mills and the tax rate is baed on 40 percent of the appraised value. There is also a $5,000 homestead (homeowner's) exemption. What is their tax bill if the Smith house is appraised for $100,000?
   A. $660
   B. $1,120
   C. $1,280
   D. $3,040

4. A vacant lot is subject to a property tax of $2.10/$100 of assessed value. What would the tax rate be if it were expressed in mills?
   A. 0.21 mills
   B. 2.1 mills
   C. 21 mills
   D. 210 mills

5. The JET Development Company purchased the S ½ of the S ½ of the NE ¼ of Section 22. If the company paid $480,000 for the land, what was the cost per acre?
   A. $4,000
   B. $6,400
   C. $12,000
   D. $24,000

6. If the price of land is $20,000 per acre, what is the price of the S ½ of the NE ¼ of the NE ¼ of a section?
   A. $200,000
   B. $400,000
   C. $800,000
   D. $1,280,000

7. If the market value of land is $5,000 per acre, what is the value of the S ½ of the NW ¼ of a section?
   A. $400,000
   B. $640,000
   C. $800,000
   D. $3,200,000

8. A multilevel apartment complex you are appraising contains a total of 700 rental units comprised of 140 efficiency units; the remainder is comprised of one-, two-, and three-bedroom units. The percentage of the units that are *NOT* efficiency units is
   A. 20 percent.
   B. 40 percent.
   C. 75 percent.
   D. 80 percent.

9. ◎ A vacant lot measuring 100 feet by 160 feet is what percentage of an acre?
   A. 16 percent
   B. 37 percent
   C. 43 percent
   D. 63 percent

10. ◎ Two vacant lots have the same width. Lot *A* is 500 feet deep and lot *B* is 1,250 feet deep. If lot *A* is 10 acres, what is the size of lot *B?*
    A. 4 acres
    B. 10 acres
    C. 20 acres
    D. 25 acres

*   We have included "quick review" questions, designated by a gray-box design element, that convey the essential points of each chapter. These questions should be used as a review tool only after the entire exam has been completed. These quick review questions are not meant to replace the entire exam. For Chapters 9 and 10 only, gray-box quick review questions featuring a **bull's-eye** are for the **licensed** and **certified residential** exams. The gray-box questions *without the bull's-eye are for the certified general exam.*

11. ◎ While property is being leased, the leased fee interest is held by whom?
    A. Lessor
    B. Lessee
    C. Grantor
    D. Grantee

12. In which lease arrangement does the lessee agree to pay rent and assume the financial responsibility of certain costs of operation so as to provide the lessor with a guaranteed annuity?
    A. Gross lease
    B. Percentage lease
    C. Net lease
    D. Reappraisal lease

13. There are numerous types of net leases. Ordinarily, a net lease would *NOT* require the lessee to be responsible for which expense?
    A. Property tax
    B. Insurance premium on the contents
    C. Day-to-day maintenance expenses
    D. Mortgage debt service

14. A commercial building leases for $4,000 per month. If the dimensions of the space being leased are 45 feet by 60 feet, what is the annual rate of rent per square foot?
    A. $2.25
    B. $4.00
    C. $16.67
    D. $17.78

15. Which type of lease agreement allows the lessee the opportunity to know exactly how much rent will be due and payable each period during the term of the lease?
    A. Gross
    B. Net
    C. Percentage
    D. Reappraisal

16. If wall-to-wall carpeting is installed in an individual unit by a tenant without permission of the landlord, upon termination of the lease the landlord acquires ownership of the carpet by what legal right?
    A. Accessibility
    B. Accession
    C. Accretion
    D. Escheat

17. Under a lease agreement, the lessor often includes what type of clause in a long-term lease so as to be compensated for inflation?
    A. Acceleration
    B. Escalation
    C. Exculpatory
    D. Subordination

18. A tenant in a warehouse pays an annual rent of $2.75 per square foot. If the tenant pays a monthly rent of $4,354, how large is the warehouse in square feet?
    A. 1,900 square feet
    B. 4,354 square feet
    C. 19,000 square feet
    D. 27,500 square feet

19. ◎ A lease creates two legal interests, the
    A. leased fee estate and the fee simple estate.
    B. leased fee estate and the leasehold estate.
    C. leasehold estate and the fee simple estate.
    D. leasehold estate and the ground rent.

20. What legal interest in real estate is valued by adding the present worth of the contract rent and the present worth of the reversion at the end of the lease?
    A. The fee simple estate
    B. The leasehold estate
    C. The leased fee estate
    D. The reversionary estate

21. What party to a lease owns the legal interest known as the leasehold estate?
    A. Lessor
    B. Lessee
    C. Mortgagee
    D. Fiduciary

22. What party to a lease owns the legal interest known as the leased fee estate?
    A. Lessor
    B. Lessee
    C. Mortgagee
    D. Fiduciary

23. How does the value of a parcel of real estate owned in fee simple and unencumbered compare to the value of the same parcel subject to a long-term lease?
    A. Must be exactly equal to the sum of the leasehold and leased fee values
    B. Is always less than the sum of the leasehold and leased fee values
    C. Is always greater than the sum of the leasehold and leased fee values
    D. May be less than or greater than the sum of the leasehold and leased fee values

24. The rent received by the lessor over and above the minimum rent stated in a percentage lease is referred to as
    A. excessive rent.
    B. overage income.
    C. equity rent.
    D. sweetener.

25. For income-producing property, the ratio of leasable space to total space is referred to as the
    A. efficiency ratio.
    B. proficiency ratio.
    C. equity ratio.
    D. land-to-building ratio.

26. A percentage lease is one in which a portion or all of the rent is based on a certain percentage of
    A. market value.
    B. sales price.
    C. sales.
    D. assessed value.

27. A rental agreement in which the lessor pays the property taxes, property insurance, and maintenance expenses is commonly referred to as a(n)
    A. gross lease.
    B. net lease.
    C. net net lease.
    D. all-encompassing lease.

28. An existing tenant in an office building has four years remaining on a lease. The tenant assigns the right to possess the premises to a third party for three years. This action is legally known as a(n)
    A. assignment.
    B. sublease.
    C. escheat.
    D. adverse possession.

29. A tenant is the owner of which legal interest?
    A. Leasehold
    B. Leased fee
    C. Remainder
    D. Reversion

30. In a sublease agreement, the sublessee owes rent to whom?
    A. Lessor
    B. Lessee
    C. Landlord
    D. Freehold holder

31. In which type of lease does the lessee agree to pay rent and bear certain costs of operation to provide the lessor a guaranteed annuity?
    A. Flat lease
    B. Net lease
    C. Percentage lease
    D. Sandwich lease

32. An 80-foot by 90-foot space in an office building rents for $12 per square foot. If the tenant signs a three-year lease, no rent is due for the first three months. Under these conditions, what is the average rent paid by the tenant per month over the full term of the lease?
    A. $6,600
    B. $7,200
    C. $79,200
    D. $86,400

33. In a sublease, the sublessor holds what type of lease?
    A. Security lease
    B. Subordinated lease
    C. Sandwich lease
    D. Leased fee lease

34. A two-story office building leases for $16 per square foot. The first floor is 80 feet by 100 feet, and the second floor is 80 feet by 80 feet. What is the annual rent for the building?
    A. $19,200
    B. $128,000
    C. $230,400
    D. $256,000

35. A small retail clothing store in a neighborhood shopping center is leased for $500 per month plus 2 percent of gross sales over $50,000. If total rent paid for the year is $8,000, what are total gross sales for the year?
    A. $50,000
    B. $150,000
    C. $100,000
    D. $200,000

36. In collecting and analyzing market data, an appraiser discovers that the market rent exceeds the contract rent for the subject property. Who benefits directly from this difference?
    A. Landlord
    B. Leasehold
    C. Leased fee
    D. Mortgagee

37. When market rent exceeds contract rent, which legal interest or person benefits most directly?
    A. Leased fee estate
    B. Landlord
    C. Tenant
    D. Lessor

38. What is meant by the term *overage rent?*
    A. Rent that is over the market rent
    B. Percentage rent above a guaranteed minimum rent
    C. Rent used to calculate an overall rate
    D. Rent that is above average

39. What is meant by the term *expense stop?*
    A. A limit on operating expenses that will be paid by the owner
    B. A limit on operating expenses that will be paid by the tenant
    C. A method that protects the lessee from increases in operating expenses
    D. An expense ceiling over which the lessor will pay operating expenses

40. What is meant by the term *escalation clause?*
    A. A clause in a mortgage specifying how payments increase over time
    B. A clause in a mortgage relieving the borrower of personal liability
    C. A clause in the lease requiring the tenant to pay costs of maintaining the escalator
    D. A clause in a lease that specifies how the rent will automatically increase over time

41. An assessment ratio is the ratio of the assessed value of a property to what other measure of value?
    A. Loan
    B. Investment
    C. Market
    D. Cost

42. In which lease are all expenses paid by the tenant?
    A. Gross lease
    B. Rental lease
    C. Flat lease
    D. Net lease

43. Which term applies to the excess of contract rent over market rent?
    A. Excess rent
    B. Percentage rent
    C. Overage rent
    D. Surplus rent

44. What is meant by the term *percentage rent?*
    A. Rent received based on a percent of the contract rent
    B. Rent received based on a percent of the base rent
    C. Rent received based on a percent of sales
    D. Rent received based on a percent of net operating income

45. Which statement is *TRUE* in regard to a percentage lease?
    A. It is usually used in industrial properties.
    B. It specifies the amount of contract rent to be received above market rent.
    C. It is calculated by multiplying a percentage specified in the lease by the sales generated from the property.
    D. It is calculated by multiplying a percentage specified in the lease by the base rent.

46. What term is used to identify the rent that probably would be obtained for a specific property in the current rental market?
    A. Market rent
    B. Minimum rent
    C. Contract rent
    D. Long-term rent

47. What term is used to identify rent paid over the guaranteed minimum rent?
    A. Market rent
    B. Excess rent
    C. Overage rent
    D. Percentage rent

48. Which statement is *TRUE* in regard to rent?
    A. Contract rent is typically used to find the fee simple value of a property.
    B. Contract rent is higher than economic rent.
    C. Economic rent is typically used to find the fee simple value of a property.
    D. Economic rent is equal to contract rent minus market rent.

49. *Percentage rent* is defined as the
    A. amount of contract rent above market rent.
    B. amount of rent paid above the minimum rent.
    C. rent received based on a portion of sales.
    D. rent received based on an inflation index.

50. *Excess rent* is defined as the
    A. amount of contract rent above market rent.
    B. amount of rent paid above the minimum rent.
    C. rent received based on a portion of sales.
    D. rent received based on an inflation index.

51. ◎ The value of a property estimated for property tax purposes is referred to as
    A. market value.
    B. tax value.
    C. going-concern value.
    D. assessed value.

52. Space in an office building rents for $1,200 per month. If the dimensions of the space are 45 feet by 20 feet, what is the annual rent per square foot?
    A. $1.33
    B. $12.00
    C. $16.00
    D. $20.00

53. Which term refers to a tax based on the value of the item being taxed?
    A. Market value tax
    B. Ad valorem tax
    C. Assessed tax
    D. Value tax

54. The minimum rent due under a lease that has a percentage or participation requirement is referred to as the
    A. base rent.
    B. percentage rent.
    C. flat rent.
    D. gross rent.

55. Yummy Yogurt leases space in Southwood Mall. Under the lease, Yummy Yogurt must pay a base rent of $2,000 per month plus 5 percent of all sales revenue over $50,000 per month. What is the total rent for the month if Yummy Yogurt has sales of $60,000 this month?
    A. $2,500
    B. $3,000
    C. $4,500
    D. $5,000

56. In economics, the cost commanded by a factor of production that is unique or inelastic in supply is referred to as
    A. economic rent.
    B. market rent.
    C. fixed cost.
    D. supply cost.

57. A contract in which, for a payment called rent, a person who is entitled to the possession of real property transfers those rights to another for a specific period of time is referred to as a
    A. lease.
    B. deed.
    C. mortgage.
    D. trust.

58. Jones leases property to Smith under a long-term lease. The contract rent required by the lease is lower than market (economic) rents. The difference in rents will probably add value to
    A. Smith's leasehold.
    B. Jones's leasehold.
    C. Jones's leased fee estate.
    D. Smith's leased fee estate.

59. The rent a comparable unit would command if offered in a competitive market is referred to as
    A. comparable rent.
    B. base rent.
    C. contract rent.
    D. market rent.

60. ◎ Long rents an apartment to Towns for $400 per month. Similar units are renting for $450 per month. The apartment's market rent is
    A. $50 per month.
    B. $400 per month.
    C. $450 per month.
    D. $506 per month.

61. In a building or project, what term applies to the floor space that may be rented to tenants; i.e., the area upon which rental payments are based?
    A. Gross leasable area
    B. Gross rentable area
    C. Net leasable area
    D. Common area

62. A lease whereby, in addition to the rent stipulated, the lessee (tenant) pays such expenses as taxes, insurance, and maintenance is referred to as a
    A. gross lease.
    B. base lease.
    C. flat lease.
    D. net lease.

63. ◎ A town assesses a property tax at the rate of $0.50 per $100 of market value. How much tax is paid on property valued at $100,000?
    A. $50
    B. $500
    C. $5,000
    D. $50,000

64. A lease held by a lessee who becomes a lessor by subletting is referred to as a
    A. sublease.
    B. double lease.
    C. sandwich lease.
    D. middle lease.

65. What is meant by the term *tax shelter?*
    A. An investment that produces passive income
    B. An investment that produces tax advantages for the investor through deductions for cost recovery, taxes, and interest
    C. An investment that produces after-tax income that is greater than before-tax income
    D. An investment that continually produces cash losses

APPLICATION-STYLE QUESTIONS

Questions 66 through 70 are based on the following information:

An apartment complex is the subject of an appraisal assignment. The appraiser has found the following information in regard to four recent sales of similar apartments:

Sale #1—20 units; gross annual income of $72,000; gross building area of 19,000 sq. ft.; sales price of $352,800

Sale #2—38 units; gross economic income of $125,400; gross building area of 38,000 sq. ft.; sales price of $627,000

Sale #3—45 units; gross annual income of $170,000; gross building area of 46,125 sq. ft.; sales price of $884,520

Sale #4—28 units; gross annual income of $97,440; gross building area of 25,200 sq. ft.; sales price of $516,432

66. What is the range of the gross income multipliers?
    A. 0.2
    B. 0.4
    C. 5.0
    D. 5.3

67. What is the range of the indicated sales price per square foot?
    A. $3.99
    B. $5.00
    C. $20.00
    D. $20.49

68. What is the mean sales price per unit?
    A. $15,000
    B. $16,667
    C. $18,060
    D. $21,043

69. What is the mean gross income multiplier?
    A. 4.9
    B. 5.0
    C. 5.1
    D. 5.3

70. If the property being appraised is most comparable to sale #4, what is the indicated value by the GIM of the subject property with a gross income of $85,000 per year?
    A. $416,500
    B. $425,000
    C. $442,000
    D. $450,500

ANSWERS TO DIAGNOSTIC EXAM VII

1. **D.** The mean, median, and mode are all types of averages or measures of central tendency. The standard deviation is a measure of the variability of the data around the mean.

2. **C.** Median is the middle or midpoint of the observations. Appraisers use various statistical techniques in their analyses, and by finding the median, appraisers have identified the point at which one-half of the observations are greater and one-half of the observations are less.

3. **B** $100,000 × 0.40 = $40,000; $40,000 − $5,000 = $35,000; $35,000 × 0.032 = $1,120.

4. **C.** $2.10/$100 = 0.021; 0.021 = 21 mills.

5. **C.** 640 × ½ × ¼ = 40 acres; $480,000/40 = $12,000.

6. **B.** A section of land contains 640 acres. Thus, 640 × ½ × ¼ × ¼ = 20 acres.

7. **A.** 640 × ½ × ¼ × $5,000 = $400,000. There are 640 acres in a section of land, so the value of this particular parcel would be based on one-half of one-fourth of 640 times the value per acre.

8. **D.** 140 ÷ 700 = 20 percent efficiency units. The remaining units would comprise 80 percent of the total.

9. **B.** 100 × 160 = 16,000 ÷ 43,560 = 0.3673 or 37 percent.

10. **D.** Because both lots have the same width, the ratio between lot *A* and lot *B* is that lot *B* is two and one-half times the size of lot *A*. Therefore, since lot *A* contains 10 acres, lot *B* contains two and one-half times that, or 25 acres.

11. **A.** The landlord's (lessor's) interest is referred to as a leased fee interest, while the legal interest of the tenant (lessee) is referred to as a leasehold interest.

12. **C.** There are various types of net leases; the primary purpose of a net lease is to provide the landlord (lessor) with a specified payment during the term of the lease. Gross, percentage, or reappraisal leases could not provide that certainty.

13. **D.** A net lease would normally not require the tenant (lessee) to be responsible for mortgage debt service. Such an expense would be the responsibility of the lessor (landlord).

14. **D.** 45 × 60 = 2,700 square feet of leasable space. $4,000 × 12 = $48,000 per year in rent. $48,000 ÷ 2,700 = $17.78 annual rent per square foot.

15. **A.** Under a gross lease, the amount of the payment is certain and thus the tenant (lessee) knows the amount that will be due and payable.

16. **B.** Accession is the legal right that entitles the owner of the land to all that is added either intentionally or by mistake. In this instance, the carpeting belongs to the landlord upon the termination of the lease.

17. **B.** An escalation clause allows the landlord to increase the amount of rent due. This should not be confused with an acceleration clause, which is normally included in a mortgage by the lender for the purpose of demanding all future principal repayments due if and when the borrower is in default on the mortgage.

18. **C.** $4,354 × 12 = $52,248; $52,248 ÷ $2.75 = 19,000 square feet (rounded).

19. **B.** The two legal interests created by a lease are the leased fee estate and the leasehold estate.

20. **C.** The leased fee estate is the landlord's (lessor's) interest in leased property. That legal interest is equal to the present value

of the contract rent plus the present worth of the reversion at the end of the lease.

21. **B.** The leasehold estate is the legal interest of the tenant (lessee). The legal interest of the landlord (lessor) is referred to as the leased fee estate.

22. **A.** The leased fee estate is the legal interest of the landlord (lessor). The legal interest of the tenant (lessee) is referred to as the leasehold estate.

23. **D.** The value of the leasehold estate plus the value of the leased fee estate may be less than, equal to, or greater than the value of the same property when unencumbered by a lease.

24. **B.** The amount paid over and above the minimum rent in a percentage lease is referred to as overage income.

25. **A.** The efficiency ratio of a building shows the relationship between leasable space and total space. For example, an office building with 50,000 square feet may be only 70 percent efficient, since 15,000 square feet of the building are used for entrances, hallways, or elevators.

26. **C.** A percentage lease is one in which the lessor receives a percentage of sales as part or all of the rental payment for the lease of the property. In some instances, percentage leases may be based on profit, but they are never based on market value, sales price, or assessed value.

27. **A.** A lease in which the landlord (lessor) pays such expenses as property taxes, property insurance, and maintenance expenses is referred to as a gross lease. A net lease or a net net lease is one in which the tenant (lessee) pays a portion or all of these expenses.

28. **B.** A sublease is a lease agreement in which the lessee (tenant) transfers some of the legal interest in the leased property to a

third party (sublessee) but retains some reversionary interest. An assignment occurs when one party transfers all legal interest to another party.

29. **A.** A leasehold is the legal interest that a lessee (tenant) has in property by virtue of a lease. A leased fee is the legal interest of the lessor (landlord).

30. **B.** A sublease is a lease agreement in which the lessee (tenant) transfers some of the interest in the leased property to a third party (sublessee) but retains some reversionary interest. In a sublease agreement, the sublessee owes rent to the lessee (sublessor).

31. **B.** A net lease imposes an obligation on the lessee (tenant) to pay such costs as real estate taxes, insurance, and maintenance as agreed to between the lessor and the lessee. Thus the lessor receives a fixed amount, which may be treated as an annuity.

32. **A.** $80 \times 90 = 7,200$ square feet. $7,200 \times \$12 = \$86,400$ per year. $\$86,400 \times 2.75 = \$237,600$ total rent due for 3 years but only collected for 2 years and 9 months. (No rent is due the first 3 months.) $\$237,600 \div 36 = \$6,600$ average rent due per month over 3 years.

33. **C.** In a sublease the sublessor (original tenant) has a sandwich lease, and no direct legal relationship is created between the lessor and the sublessee. A sublease is really an estate within an estate.

34. **C.** $(80 \times 100) + (80 \times 80) = 14,400$ square feet. $14,400 \times \$16 = \$230,400$ annual rent.

35. **B.** $\$500 \times 12 = \$6,000$ minimum rent due. $\$8,000 - \$6,000 = \$2,000$ rent attributable to gross sales. $\$2,000 \div 0.02 = \$100,000$ gross sales over $\$50,000$. $\$100,000 + \$50,000 = \$150,000$ total gross sales.

36. **B.** If the market rent is greater than the contract rent, the tenant benefits. The legal interest that a tenant has in property is referred to as a leasehold.

37. **C.** The tenant (leaseholder) benefits directly when market rent exceeds contract rent. The owner (lessor) who has the leased fee estate incurs the opportunity cost associated with the lower contract rent.

38. **B.** Overage rent refers to rent that is above a guaranteed minimum rent, which results from percentage leases where the lessor receives additional rent based on a percentage of the tenant's sales. The percentage is normally based on sales usually above a specified amount. The total rent, including the overage rent, may be above or below the market rate for that space.

39. **A.** Expense stops are used in leases to place an upper limit on expenses that will be paid by the owner. Any expenses incurred above the expense stop must be paid by the tenant or lessee. This protects the owner from increases in expenses in times of unexpected inflation and helps keep the NOI from decreasing over time due to increasing expenses.

40. **D.** The term *escalation clause* is used in leases and specifies how the lease payments increase (escalate) over time. An exculpatory clause in a mortgage relieves the borrower of personal liability. A graduated payment mortgage has payments that increase over time, although there are other mortgage types that can have increasing payments.

41. **C.** The assessment ratio is the ratio of assessed value to the market value of the property. The market value may or may not be equal to the cost.

42. **D.** The term *net lease* is often used when all operating expenses are passed through to the tenant (lessee). Sometimes the term *net net net lease* or *triple-net lease* is used to indicate that property taxes, insurance, and maintenance expenses are passed through to the tenant.

43. **A.** Excess rent occurs in situations favorable to the lessor, such as a strong rental market, an advantageous location, or exceptional management. Excess rent is often capitalized at a higher rate in the income capitalization method of appraisal to reflect the higher risk associated with the excess payments.

44. **C.** Percentage rent is typically used in retail leases and is normally based on a percent of sales.

45. **C.** A percentage rent is usually used in retail leases in which the tenant pays a base rent plus a percentage of sales over a specified level and is normally calculated by multiplying a percentage specified in the lease by the sales generated from the property.

46. **A.** Market rent, also referred to as economic rent, is the rent most likely obtained for a specific property in the current rental market. The market rent can be derived from comparable properties at the same date as the appraisal.

47. **C.** The rent paid over the guaranteed minimum rent is referred to as overage rent. Overage rent is a contract rent, whereas excess rent is not. Overage may be part of market rent, excess rent, or both.

48. **C.** A fee simple interest assumes no leases. Therefore contract rent, the rent specified in a lease, cannot be used to value a fee simple interest. Economic (market) rent is the appropriate cash flow to find the fee simple value.

49. **C.** Percentage rent is typically used in retail leases and is the rent received based on a portion of sales.

50. **A.** Excess rent should not be confused with overage rent. Excess rent is the difference between contract and market rent. Overage

rent is the difference between total rent and base rent specified in a contract.

51. **D.** Assessed value refers to the value of a property according to tax rolls. It is usually calculated in some relation to market value but will not necessarily equal market value.

52. **C.** $45 \times 20 = 900$ square feet. $\$1,200 \times 12 = \$14,400$ annual rent. $\$14,400 \div 900 = \$16$ per square foot.

53. **B.** Property taxes are ad valorem taxes; the term *ad valorem* means according to value.

54. **A.** Base rent is the guaranteed price property would sell for based on rent called for in a lease that has a percentage or participation requirement.

55. **A.** $\$60,000 - \$50,000 = \$10,000 =$ sales on which rent will be based. $\$10,000 \times 0.05 = \$500 =$ percentage or overage rent. $\$2,000 + \$500 = \$2,500$ total rent.

56. **A.** The portion of rental income attributable to the land is often considered economic rent, since the land will exist no matter what the rental rate.

57. **A.** A lease is an agreement by which one party entitles another party to possession of a property for a period of time and with the payment of rent. The one transferring the rights is known as a lessor or, more commonly, the landlord. The one to whom the rights are transferred is the lessee or, more commonly, the tenant.

58. **A.** Smith, the tenant, has a leasehold; Jones, the landlord, has a leased fee estate. The favorable terms of the lease will normally add value to the leasehold and reduce the value to the leased fee.

59. **D.** Market rent is the rent a comparable unit would command if offered in a competitive market. Market rent can be derived from comparable properties at the time of the appraisal.

60. **C.** The market rent is the rent that a property would most probably command in the open market. In this case, that would be $450. The contract rent is $400.

61. **C.** Net leasable area refers to the floor space rented to tenants. Generally net leasable area excludes common areas and space devoted to the heating, cooling, and other equipment of a building.

62. **D.** A net lease is one in which the lessee (tenant) pays certain expenses associated with the property. The landlord's rent receipt is thereby net of those expenses. Sometimes the term *net net net lease* is used to indicate that taxes, insurance, and maintenance are all net. In practice, various levels of net leases are often used to designate arrangements where the tenant pays only some types of expenses and the landlord pays other types. In such cases, the actual category that is net must be specified.

63. **B.** $\$0.50 \div \$100 = \$0.005$ per dollar; $\$0.005$ per dollar $\times \$100,000 = \$500$.

64. **C.** A tenant (lessee) who becomes a lessor is known as a sandwich leaseholder. Typically the sandwich leaseholder is neither the owner nor the user of the property.

65. **B.** A tax shelter is thought of as an investment that produces tax advantages for the investor through deductions for cost recovery, taxes, and interest. The tax reform of 1986 reduced many of the tax shelters through real estate. However, a property does not necessarily have to produce negative cash flows to provide tax reductions.

66. **B.** The gross income multipliers for each sale are calculated by dividing the sales price by the gross annual income. In this example, the GIMs are as follows: 4.90, 5.00, 5.20, and 5.30. Thus, the range is $5.30 - 4.90 = 0.40$.

67. **A.** Sales price per square foot for each sale is calculated by dividing the sales price by the number of square feet. In this example, the sales prices per square foot for the four sales are as follows: $18.57, $16.50, $19.18, and $20.49, with a range of $3.99 ($20.49 – $16.50).

68. **C.** The mean sales price per unit is calculated by dividing the sales price by the number of units. In this example, the four sales prices per unit are as follows: $17,640, $16,500, $19,656, and $18,440. The mean (average) is $18,060.

69. **C.** The gross income multiplier is calculated by dividing the sales price by the annual gross income. In this example, the four GIMs are as follows: 4.90, 5.00, 5.20, and 5.30. The average is 5.10.

70. **D.** Using sale #4, the GIM would be $516,432 ÷ $97,440 = 5.30; 5.30 × $85,000 = $450,500.

Appraisal Standards and Ethics

KEY TERMS

advisory opinions
appraisal
appraisal practice
appraisal review
appraiser
assignment results
assumption
certification statement
competency rule
confidential information
confidentiality

contingency fee
definitions
ethics rule
extraordinary assumption
hypothetical condition
intended use
intended user
jurisdictional exception rule
limiting condition
market value

preamble
record-keeping provision
report
scope of work rule
self-contained versus summary versus restricted use
signature
statements on standards
workfile

DIAGNOSTIC EXAM VIII*

1. The Scope of Work Rule states that the appraiser
   A. may not perform anything less than a self-contained appraisal report.
   B. advise the client that the assignment calls for something less than the work required by the requirements of the borrower.
   C. advise the client as to which approach to value is least important in the appraisal.
   D. must disclose the scope of work in the report.

2. When the value opinion to be developed is market value, an appraiser must analyze all sales of the property being appraised that occurred within what minimum time period?
   A. One year
   B. Three years
   C. Five years
   D. No specific time period is mentioned.

3. All of these conditions are appraisal requirements required by Standard 1 *EXCEPT*
   A. identify the client but not other intended users.
   B. identify the type and definition of value.
   C. base projections of future rent and expenses on public record data.
   D. explain and support the exclusion of any of the usual valuation approaches.

4. Which term is used to describe "the act or process of developing an analysis, recommendation, or opinion to solve a problem, where an opinion of value is a component of the analysis leading to the assignment results"?
   A. Cash flow analysis
   B. Appraisal consulting
   C. Economic base analysis
   D. Appraisal

5. Which term is used to describe "a study of the cost-benefit relationship of an economic endeavor"?
   A. Cash flow analysis
   B. Appraisal consulting
   C. Feasibility analysis
   D. Market analysis

6. Any appraiser who signs a certification on an appraisal report prepared by another
   A. is not responsible for the contents of the report.
   B. must have contributed at least 50 percent to the report.
   C. must have physically inspected the property.
   D. accepts full responsibility for all elements of the certification.

7. What rule or standard requires that the appraiser, in reviewing an appraisal and reporting the results of that review, must develop and report a credible opinion as to the quality of another appraiser's work and must clearly disclose the scope of the work performed in the assignment?
   A. Standard 1
   B. Standard 2
   C. Standard 3
   D. Competency Rule

8. According to USPAP, when the purpose of an assignment is to develop an opinion of market value, the appraiser must also develop an opinion of
   A. minimum exposure time.
   B. maximum exposure time.
   C. reasonable exposure time.
   D. no exposure time.

---

*   We have included "quick review" questions, designated by a gray-box design element, that convey the essential points of each chapter. These questions should be used as a review tool only after the entire exam has been completed. These quick review questions are not meant to replace the entire exam.

9. An appraiser is employed by the owner of an industrial park to estimate market value for the purpose of a property tax appeal. The appraisal report is completed on April 15, 2006. On June 2, 2007, the appraiser testifies in court on behalf of the property owner. The state supreme court rules in favor of the owner with final disposition on November 11, 2007. At a minimum, the appraiser must keep her records until
   A. June 2, 2009.
   B. November 11, 2009.
   C. April 15, 2011.
   D. November 11, 2012.

10. The requirement that the appraiser must have the knowledge and experience to complete the appraisal assignment is part of which USPAP rule?
    A. Preamble
    B. Ethics
    C. Conduct
    D. Competency

11. What term is used to describe "that which is contrary to what exists but is supposed for the purpose of analysis"?
    A. Hypothetical condition
    B. Appraisal consulting
    C. Economic base analysis
    D. Appraisal

12. The following statement would appear in which section of an analysis: "My compensation is not contingent upon the reporting of a predetermined value"?
    A. Contingent and limiting conditions
    B. Letter of transmittal
    C. Certification statement
    D. Assumptions and limiting conditions

13. Each written or oral appraisal report must include all of these items *EXCEPT*
    A. state the qualifications of the appraiser.
    B. clearly and accurately set forth the appraisal in a manner that will not be misleading.
    C. contain sufficient information to enable the intended users of the appraisal to understand it properly.
    D. define the value to be estimated.

14. The purpose of the *Uniform Standards of Professional Appraisal Practice* is to
    A. guarantee professionalism in appraisers and analysts.
    B. hold off government regulation.
    C. establish requirements for professional appraisal practice.
    D. present information that will be useful to appraisers.

15. What term defines "the act or process of developing and communicating an opinion about the quality of another appraiser's work"?
    A. Analysis
    B. Feasibility study
    C. Appraisal review
    D. Examination of content

16. According to the definitions included in the USPAP, "the party or parties who engage an appraiser in a specific assignment" are referred to as the
    A. employer.
    B. client.
    C. customer.
    D. intended user.

17. The term *market value* is defined as the _____ price a property should bring in an open and competitive market.
    A. most probable
    B. most accurate
    C. average
    D. highest

18. According to the Ethics Rule, confidential factual data obtained from the client may be disclosed to certain individuals. An example of these individuals mentioned in the USPAP would include
    A. persons authorized by the owner of the property being appraised.
    B. any certified appraiser.
    C. a prior owner of the property being appraised.
    D. third parties as may be authorized by due process of law.

19. The Ethics Rule is divided into four sections. Which activity is *NOT* one of the four sections?
    A. Confidentiality
    B. Record keeping
    C. Competence
    D. Management

20. Which one of these requirements is *NOT* part of Standard 1?
    A. If single-family residential property is being appraised, then the sales comparison approach must be used and fully explained.
    B. The type of value being estimated must be defined.
    C. Identify any extraordinary assumptions necessary in the assignment.
    D. The appraiser must not commit a substantial error of omission or commission that significantly affects an appraisal.

21. In developing a real property appraisal, Standard 1 requires an appraiser must analyze certain instruments related to the property being appraised current as of the effective date of the appraisal. Which instrument is *NOT* specifically mentioned as one to be examined?
    A. Agreements of sale
    B. Mortgages
    C. Options
    D. Listings

22. In the certification statement, as required by Standard 2, the appraiser should include all of these statements *EXCEPT*
    A. "My actual compensation for this assignment is $ _____."
    B. "My compensation is not contingent upon the reporting of a predetermined value . . ."
    C. "I have no (or the specified) present or prospective interest in the property . . ."
    D. "I have (or have not) made a personal inspection of the property . . ."

23. In regard to Standard 2, which statement is *FALSE?*
    A. Both level of information and content are addressed in Standard 2.
    B. Any communication must be in a manner that is not misleading.
    C. Recognized techniques must be used in the development of the appraisal.
    D. Each written real property appraisal report must contain a certification.

24. Standard 2 requires the appraiser to include certain minimum requirements in the appraisal report. Which item is *NOT* required to be included in the report?
    A. The date of the appraisal report
    B. The definition of market value
    C. The intended use of the appraisal
    D. The effective date of the appraisal

25. According to Standard 2 all written appraisal reports must include the effective date of the appraisal. Which statement is correct in regard to the effective date?
    A. The effective date establishes the context of the value estimate.
    B. The effective date and the date of the appraisal report will always be the same date.
    C. The effective date cannot be a date later than the date of the appraisal report.
    D. The effective date cannot be a date prior to the date of the appraisal report.

26. According to the definitions included in the USPAP, a "report" includes which means of communication?
    A. Oral communication only
    B. Written communication only
    C. Oral or written communication
    D. Means of communication not defined in the USPAP

27. Scope of work includes, but is not limited to,
    A. the extent to which the property is identified.
    B. the extent to which tangible property is inspected.
    C. the type and extent of data researched.
    D. All of the above actions are part of the Scope of Work Rule.

28. All of these actions are requirements of Standard 1 *EXCEPT*
    A. define the value being considered.
    B. adequately identify the real estate.
    C. identify the effective date of the appraisal.
    D. use all three recognized approaches to value regardless of the assignment.

29. An appraisal performed for the purpose of confirming whether the completed improvements and/or market conditions are consistent with the assumptions and statements made in an earlier prospective appraisal is commonly referred to as a(n)
    A. recertification of value.
    B. update of an appraisal.
    C. evaluation.
    D. restricted appraisal.

30. Which action on the part of the appraiser is *NOT* a requirement of Standard 1?
    A. Define the value being estimated
    B. Always value the property under its highest and best use
    C. Identify and consider the effect on value of any personal property included in the appraisal
    D. Identify the real property interest to be valued

31. USPAP recognizes various types of appraisal reports. Which type is *NOT* recognized?
    A. Self-contained
    B. Summary
    C. Limited
    D. Restricted use

32. An assumption directly related to a specific assignment, which, if found to be false, could alter the appraiser's opinions or conclusions, is referred to under the USPAP as a(n)
    A. extraordinary assumption.
    B. hypothetical assumption.
    C. appraisal assumption.
    D. jurisdictional exception.

33. The operative words in Standard 2 that result in the actions of the appraiser being referred to as an appraisal are
    A. confirmation and reporting of data.
    B. analyses, opinions, and conclusions.
    C. certification statement.
    D. application of the approaches to value.

34. In regard to Standard 2, which statement is correct?
    A. Standard 2 requires a certification statement.
    B. Standard 2 addresses oral as well as written appraisal reports.
    C. The content and level of information required in the appraisal report are the subject of Standard 2.
    D. All of the above statements are correct.

35. Which product of the Appraisal Standards Board (ASB) has the least direct impact on a licensed or certified appraiser?
    A. Standards
    B. Standards rules
    C. Statements on standards
    D. Advisory opinions

36. The Scope of Work Rule addresses the importance of the appraiser recognizing and communicating assignment conditions. Which item can affect the scope of work in an assignment?
    A. Extraordinary assumptions
    B. Hypothetical conditions
    C. Jurisdictional exceptions
    D. All of the above items are mentioned in the Scope of Work Rule.

37. According to the Ethics Rule, which statement is correct?
    A. Whenever an appraiser develops an opinion of value, acceptance of compensation contingent on the reporting of a predetermined value is ethical.
    B. When an opinion of value is necessary as part of a consulting assignment, contingent compensation is always ethical.
    C. To promote and preserve the public trust inherent in professional appraisal practice, an appraiser must observe the highest standards of professional ethics.
    D. An appraiser can, without violation of the USPAP, communicate assignment results in a misleading or fraudulent manner.

38. In regard to the Competency Rule, which statement is correct?
    A. This rule does not permit the appraiser taking the necessary steps to complete the assignment competently.
    B. The burden of proof is on the owner of the property to decide if the appraiser is competent.
    C. The Competency Rule only extends to residential property.
    D. The burden of disclosure is on the appraiser to report the lack of knowledge and/or experience to the client before accepting the assignment.

39. The "interests, benefits, and rights inherent in the ownership of real estate" is the normal definition for which term?
    A. Real estate
    B. Real property
    C. Personal property
    D. Fixtures

40. Which person or entity is specifically mentioned as someone to whom an appraiser may disclose confidential factual data obtained from a client?
    A. Any reader of the appraisal report
    B. State enforcement agencies and such third parties as may be authorized by due process of law
    C. Appraisers who have previously rendered an opinion of value on the subject property
    D. Prior owners of the appraised property

41. According to the USPAP, which requirement is part of Standard 1?
    A. The appraiser must not render services in a careless or negligent manner.
    B. Prior to accepting an appraisal assignment, the appraiser must possess the knowledge and experience necessary to complete the assignment or take specific alternatives.
    C. The appraiser must protect the confidential nature of the appraiser-client relationship.
    D. The appraisal report must contain sufficient information to enable the person(s) who receive or rely on the report to understand it properly.

42. Which statement is correct in regard to Standard 1 as it relates to the production of a credible appraisal?
    A. Changes in the construction/development field have little impact on the appraisal profession.
    B. Social changes have no effect on appraisal theory and practice.
    C. Each appraiser must continuously improve his or her skills.
    D. In order to show proficiency, each appraiser must have, as a minimum, ten hours of continuing education each year.

43. Standard 1 requires the appraiser to
    A. include a certification statement.
    B. define market value.
    C. use the sales comparison approach if the subject property is single-family residential.
    D. None of the above requirements are part of Standard 1.

44. Which statement is correct in regard to Standard 2 as it relates to self-contained appraisal reports?
    A. Communication must be in a manner that is not misleading.
    B. Recognized techniques must be used in the development of the appraisal.
    C. Proper communication extends to all readers of the report.
    D. Form but not content is addressed in this standard.

45. Standards Rule 2-3 addresses the certification statement in an appraisal report. Which statement is correct in regard to Standards Rule 2-3?
    A. Not including a certification statement in the report is always permitted.
    B. The certification statement must be in a clearly marked separate section of the report.
    C. Each written appraisal report must contain a certification statement.
    D. The certification statement should identify whether the sketches in the appraisal report are drawn to scale.

46. In regard to the provisions and requirements of Standard 2, which statement is correct?
    A. All of the standards rules of Standard 2 cover the appraisal.
    B. Standard 2 only addresses written appraisal reports.
    C. The content and level of information required in a report are the subject of Standard 2.
    D. Standard 2 makes a certification statement optional by the appraiser.

47. Standards Rule 2-2(a) requires that each self-contained real property appraisal report contain certain minimum requirements. Which item is required to be included in the report?
    A. The names of all possible readers of the report
    B. The definition of market value as per the USPAP Glossary
    C. The real property interest appraised
    D. The date of the last sale of the property

48. The certification statement required as per Standard 2 includes mention of persons involved in the appraisal assignment other than the person signing the report. In regard to those persons, which statement is correct?
    A. There should be a statement as to how much anyone providing significant professional assistance was compensated.
    B. The amount of time spent by each person providing significant professional assistance must be stated.
    C. The name of each person providing significant professional assistance must be stated.
    D. The names of persons providing clerical assistance must be included.

49. Standards Rule 2-3 addresses the appraiser who signs a certification as part of the appraisal report. In terms of this standards rule, which statement is correct?
    A. Standards Rule 2-3 is directed toward the state regulatory agency that reviews experience requirements for appraisers.
    B. Standards Rule 2-3 addresses the responsibilities of an appraiser who signs any part of the appraisal report.
    C. Using a conditional label next to the signature of the employer or supervisor automatically exempts that individual from adherence to these standards.
    D. The employer signing the report is as responsible as the individual preparing the appraisal for the content and conclusions of the appraisal and the report.

50. Which statement is correct in regard to the standards rules?
   A. Standards rules are much shorter than the standards.
   B. Standards rules are more specific in direction than the standards.
   C. None of the standards rules are followed by explanatory comments.
   D. Adherence to the standards rules is not required.

APPLICATION-STYLE QUESTIONS

Questions 51 through 55 are based on the following information:

Susan, a certified appraiser, has been asked by a financial institution to appraise a vacant lot in a subdivision for the purpose of estimating market value for a customer who wants to borrow money in order to purchase the lot. In inspecting the property, Susan assumed that the lot was zoned single-family residential since most of the surrounding properties contained houses; thus, she concluded that it was not necessary to disclose this assumption to the lender and did not include it in her appraisal report. In addition, she did not disclose to the lender that she actually owned the lot before selling it to the current owner.

51. Who is the appraiser's client in this transaction?
   A. The financial institution
   B. The potential borrower
   C. Both are clients.
   D. Neither are clients.

52. Once Susan completes the appraisal report, according to the USPAP, how many years must she keep her workfile on this assignment?
   A. One
   B. Three
   C. Five
   D. Per the USPAP, there is no minimum time period for record retention.

53. According to the USPAP, in assuming that the lot being appraised was zoned single-family residential, Susan was making what kind of assumption?
   A. Hypothetical
   B. Extraordinary
   C. Extravagant
   D. Normal

54. Since Susan saw no need to disclose her assumption regarding the zoning to the lender, what part of the USPAP has she violated?
   A. Ethics Rule
   B. Jurisdictional Exception Rule
   C. Standard 1
   D. Standard 2

55. The fact that Susan had previously owned the lot she is appraising should be disclosed in what part of her appraisal report?
   A. Certification statement
   B. Preamble
   C. Scope of work section
   D. Since she no longer owns the lot, she does not need to disclose anything to her client.

ANSWERS TO DIAGNOSTIC EXAM VIII

1. **D.** The Scope of Work Rule states that the appraiser must disclose the scope of work in the report.

2. **B.** S.R. 1-5(b) addresses the time period for analyzing all sales of the property being appraised, which as a minimum is three years.

3. **B.** S.R. 1-2(c) requires the appraiser to identify the type and definition of value.

4. **B.** Appraisal consulting involves developing an analysis where an opinion of value is a component.

5. **C.** Feasibility analysis describes a study of the cost-benefit relationship of an economic endeavor.

6. **D.** S.R. 2-3 states that an appraiser who signs a certification accepts full responsibility for the assignment results and the contents of the appraisal report.

7. **C.** Standard 3 addresses the disclosure of the nature of the review process undertaken.

8. **C.** S.R. 1-2(c) requires the appraiser, when estimating market value, to develop an opinion of reasonable exposure time.

9. **C.** The minimum period for retention of records is five years following preparation or two years after final disposition, whichever period expires last.

10. **D.** The Competency Rule requires the appraiser to have the knowledge and experience necessary to complete the appraisal assignment.

11. **A.** *Hypothetical condition* is the term used to describe that which is contrary to what exists but is supposed for the purpose of analysis.

12. **C.** S.R. 2-3 includes provisions for certification, which would include a compensation certification.

13. **A.** The qualifications of the appraiser are not required to be included in each written or oral analysis report. B and C are from S.R. 1-1, and D is from S.R. 2-2.

14. **C.** The purpose of the USPAP is to establish requirements for professional appraisal practice.

15. **C.** *Appraisal review* is defined as an act or process of developing and communicating an opinion about the quality of another appraiser's work that was performed as part of an appraisal, appraisal review, or appraisal consulting assignment.

16. **B.** The client is defined as the party or parties who engage an appraiser (by employment or contract) in a specific assignment.

17. **A.** Market value is defined as the most probable price a property should bring in an open and competitive market.

18. **D.** One of the three recognized persons to whom confidential factual data obtained from a client may be disclosed are third parties as may be authorized by due process of law. The owner of the property may not be the client.

19. **C.** The four sections of the Ethics Rule are conduct, management, confidentiality, and record keeping. Competency is a separate rule of the USPAP.

20. **A.** If applicable, the sales comparison should be used in appraising all types of property; however, nothing in the standards requires that any one of the approaches to value must be used in a particular appraisal assignment.

21. **B.** S.R. 1-5 requires the appraiser to analyze any current agreements of sale,
options, or listings of the subject property
current as of the effective date of the
appraisal, if such information is available
to the appraiser in the normal course of
business.

22. **A.** Nothing in the uniform standards requires
the appraiser to disclose the amount of
actual compensation being received. The
only mention of compensation concerns
the certification statement that the compensation is not contingent.

23. **C.** Using recognized techniques in the development of an appraisal is addressed in
Standard 1.

24. **B.** Standard 2 requires the appraiser to define
the value to be estimated. While market
value may be the value being estimated,
other types of value, such as investment
value, may be estimated.

25. **A.** The effective date establishes the context
of the value opinion and could be a date
prior to, equal to, or after the date of the
appraisal report.

26. **C.** The USPAP defines a report as "any communication, written or oral . . ."

27. **D.** The Scope of Work Rule includes a number of actions on the part of the appraiser.

28. **D.** Nothing in the USPAP requires the
appraiser to use all three approaches to
value.

29. **A.** A recertification of value confirms
whether completed improvements/market
conditions are consistent with earlier
prospective appraisal.

30. **B.** Standard 1 requires the appraiser when
necessary to develop an opinion on the
highest and best use of the real estate.

31. **C.** The three types of appraisal reports
are "self-contained," "summary," and
"restricted use."

32. **A.** An extraordinary assumption is an
assumption which, if found to be false,
could alter the appraiser's opinions or
conclusions.

33. **B.** The efforts of the appraiser that result in
his or her actions being referred to as an
appraisal are the analyses, opinions, and
conclusions.

34. **D.** Standard 2 addresses appraisal reports,
form and content, and certification.

35. **D.** Advisory opinions are informal responses
to requests the ASB receives for information. An advisory opinion does not
establish a new standard and is not
enforceable.

36. **D.** The Scope of Work Rule covers various
types of assignment conditions that affect
the scope of work.

37. **C.** As per the Ethics Rule, an appraiser has
the obligation to promote and preserve
public trust.

38. **D.** The Competency Rule requires the
appraiser to report the lack of knowledge
and/or experience to the client before
accepting the assignment.

39. **B.** The USPAP defines real property as the
interests, benefits, and rights inherent in
the ownership of real estate.

40. **B.** The Confidentiality section of the Ethics
Rule clearly identifies three persons (enti-
ties) to whom confidential factual data
obtained from a client can be disclosed.
Previous appraisers and/or owners of the
subject property are not listed, nor is any
reader of the appraisal report.

41. **A.** According to Standards Rule 1-1(c),
an appraiser must not render appraisal
services in a careless or negligent manner. Necessary knowledge and experience
is covered under the Competency Rule,
confidentiality is addressed in the Ethics Rule, and the appraisal report is the
subject of Standard 2.

42. **C.** The continuing education hours are part of the licensing/certification program of each jurisdiction, not the USPAP. Social changes and changes in the construction/development field both impact appraisal theory and practice.

43. **D.** Standard 1 covers the appraisal and not the appraisal report.

44. **A.** Using recognized techniques in the development of an appraisal is addressed in Standard 1. Proper communication extends to intended users, not all readers. Form is not addressed in the USPAP.

45. **C.** Standards Rule 2-3 does not require the certification statement to be in a separate section of the appraisal report. However, a good practice would be to have the statement identified in a way that makes it clear to the client and the intended users of the report exactly what is being certified by the appraiser. The accuracy of sketches is addressed as an assumption and limiting condition.

46. **C.** The content and level of information required in a report are the subject of Standard 2.

47. **C.** Standards Rule 2-2(a) requires the appraiser to define the value to be estimated. While market value may be the value being estimated, this is not always the case. Names of readers are not required, nor is the date of the last sale of the property.

48. **C.** While the names of persons providing professional assistance to the person signing the report must be stated, the amount of time spent by those persons does not have to be included in the certification. Names of persons providing clerical assistance do not have to be stated.

49. **D.** Standards Rule 2-3 does not address the responsibilities of a review appraiser as defined in the USPAP. A conditional label does not exempt the review appraiser from adherence to the standards. S.R. 2-3 concerns recertification.

50. **B.** The standards rules are lengthier than the standards, and many of them are followed by explanatory comments. Adherence is required.

51. **A.** Susan's client is the financial institution. A client is defined as the party or parties who engage an appraiser in a specified assignment.

52. **C.** According to the record-keeping section of the Ethics Rule, workfiles must be kept for a minimum of five years after preparation or at least two years after final disposition of any judicial proceeding, whichever period expires last.

53. **B.** An extraordinary assumption is defined as an assumption, directly related to a specific assignment, that if found to be false, could alter the appraiser's opinions and conclusions.

54. **D.** S.R. 2-2(a)(b)(c)(x) requires the appraiser to clearly and conspicuously state all extraordinary assumptions and hypothetical conditions.

55. **A.** Since Susan had previous legal interest in the property, she should disclose this fact to her client. In this case, the appropriate place to disclose this fact would be in the certification statement.

Licensed/Certified Residential Exam A

1. Which principle of value suggests that the maximum value of a property generally cannot exceed the cost of its replacement?
   A. Balance
   B. Substitution
   C. Anticipation
   D. Opportunity cost

2. Cost and market value are *MOST* likely to be similar under which condition?
   A. The property is new.
   B. The property is small.
   C. The property is special purpose.
   D. The property has no deferred maintenance.

3. What term is used to denote the time-distance relationships between a property or neighborhood and all other possible origins and destinations?
   A. Linkages
   B. Routes
   C. Access
   D. Trips

4. Which statement is *NOT* true in regard to real estate markets?
   A. Price is seldom equal to value.
   B. Supply and demand are seldom in balance.
   C. Supply adjusts more quickly than demand.
   D. There are many government regulations.

5. Highest and best use analysis is used to determine which factor?
   A. The type of property to put on a site
   B. The amount of capital to invest in a site for improvements
   C. Whether any existing building on a site should be demolished
   D. All of the above

6. The term *absorption rate* refers to
   A. an estimate of the expected annual sales or new occupancy of a particular type of land use.
   B. an estimate of the rate at which a type of real estate space will be sold or occupied.
   C. the rate at which the cash flows from a property will cover the initial investment in the property.
   D. the rate of return used to convert future payments into present cash values.

7. A property has a market value of $100,000. The owner currently owes $60,000 in mortgage loans against the property. The owner's equity is
   A. $40,000.
   B. $60,000.
   C. $140,000.
   D. $160,000.

8. Which explanation would be the *BEST* definition of market value?
   A. Value to a typical investor
   B. Value to any investor who is willing to purchase the property in the open market
   C. Value to the typical seller
   D. Value to the user who pays market rent

9. Which valuation concept is indicative of special-purpose properties, such as churches or schools, when the continuation of the special use is assumed?
   A. Value in exchange
   B. Value in use
   C. Value in perpetuity
   D. Book value

10. The term *market value* is *MOST* closely associated with which value concept?
    A. Highest sales price
    B. Value in exchange
    C. Value in use
    D. Assessed value

11. Which explanation *BEST* describes the term *market price?*
    A. The amount of money actually paid in a transaction
    B. The amount of the loan
    C. The amount of money necessary to replace the property
    D. Same as *market value*

12. Which economic principle best explains the occurrence of locational obsolescence resulting from a change in surrounding land use?
    A. Anticipation
    B. Conformity
    C. Contribution
    D. Substitution

13. What economic principle is best illustrated when an appraiser concludes that modernization of the plumbing system in the subject property will increase the value of the property by more than the cost of the modernization?
    A. Anticipation
    B. Balance
    C. Contribution
    D. Substitution

14. What economic principle suggests that the value of property is created and maintained when there is equilibrium in the supply, demand, and location of real estate?
    A. Balance
    B. Equilibrium
    C. Substitution
    D. Surplus productivity

15. Which statement is correct in regard to the highest and best use of a parcel of land?
    A. Unimproved land does not have a highest and best use.
    B. If the improvement to the land is a house, then the highest and best use is always residential.
    C. The highest and best use can change over time.
    D. Highest and best use is strictly an economic concept and is not influenced by physical or legal considerations.

16. Which land use would *NOT* be considered a single-purpose property?
    A. Nuclear power plant
    B. Grain elevator
    C. Golf course
    D. Cemetery

17. The total loan payment made on a parcel of real estate during any one year is generally referred to as
    A. debt service.
    B. equity.
    C. mortgage constant.
    D. cash flow.

18. Normally, the amount of money a lender will agree to lend against a specific parcel of real estate is based on which price or value?
    A. Contract price
    B. Appraised value
    C. Contract price or appraised value, whichever is less
    D. Assessed value

19. The test used to determine whether an article is a fixture depends on all of these conditions *EXCEPT*
    A. reasonable intent of the party attaching the object.
    B. adaptation of the object.
    C. cost of the item being attached.
    D. method of attachment.

20. The legal ownership rights in real estate are limited by all of these conditions *EXCEPT*
    A. private voluntary restrictions such as deed restrictions.
    B. the law of nuisance.
    C. supply of real estate in the marketplace.
    D. public limitations such as eminent domain.

21. Per the USPAP, that which is contrary to what exists but is supposed for the purpose of analysis is known as a(n)
    A. extraordinary assumption.
    B. extraordinary condition.
    C. hypothetical condition.
    D. hypothetical assumption.

22. The real property in a condominium form of ownership in severalty is referred to as a
    A. unit.
    B. common area.
    C. limited common area.
    D. cooperative.

23. Which action is an example of the legal right of government based on police power?
    A. Taxation
    B. Escheat
    C. Eminent domain
    D. Zoning

24. Property taxes levied by local governments are normally referred to as ad valorem taxes. The term *ad valorem* means
    A. ability to pay.
    B. according to value.
    C. according to most likely sales price.
    D. ability to collect the tax.

25. In a voluntary conveyance of real estate, the _____ conveys title to the property and the _____ receives the title.
    A. grantor, grantee
    B. grantee, grantor
    C. owner, seller
    D. grantee, granter

26. In which type of residential real estate uses could individual units *NOT* be mortgaged by the individual owner?
    A. Condominium
    B. Planned unit development
    C. Cooperative
    D. Duplex

27. If a commercial use such as a retail store is permitted to remain in business following a zoning change to residential use, the owner is said to have received a
    A. variance.
    B. nonconforming use.
    C. local exception.
    D. buffer zone use.

28. All legal rights, such as riparian rights or easements, that "go with the land" when title to the land is transferred are known as
    A. encroachments.
    B. seizings.
    C. appurtenances.
    D. easements.

29. An acre of land contains _____ square feet.
    A. 43,560
    B. 45,360
    C. 45,660
    D. 53,560

30. The voluntary conveyance of title to land from an individual private owner to a public agency such as the city or county is known as
    A. accretion.
    B. escheat.
    C. patent.
    D. dedication.

31. Numerous public and private limitations are placed on real property. Some are voluntary and others are involuntary. Which limitation is *NOT* an example of a private involuntary limitation?
    A. Encroachment
    B. Adverse possession
    C. Mechanic's or materialman's lien
    D. Deed restriction

32. According to the USPAP, at a minimum, how many years must an appraiser retain his or her workfile after preparation of the appraisal report?
    A. No minimum time is set.
    B. One
    C. Two
    D. Five

33. Reference to a plat map would be made in which legal description method?
    A. Lot and block
    B. Rectangular survey
    C. Street address
    D. Monuments

34. In regard to an easement, if there are two tracts of land, the one benefiting from the creation of the easement is known as the
    A. estate in net.
    B. appurtenant estate.
    C. servient estate.
    D. dominant estate.

35. The USPAP definition of *report* includes which means of communication?
    A. Oral communication only
    B. Written communication only
    C. Any communication, written or oral
    D. The USPAP does not define *report*.

36. Which term refers to the rights of a person who owns a property free and clear of any leases?
    A. Leased fee estate
    B. Leasehold estate
    C. Fee simple estate
    D. Lessee's estate

37. The Ethics Rule is divided into four sections. Which activity is one of those four sections?
    A. Scope of work
    B. Jurisdictional exception
    C. Record keeping
    D. Competency

38. When a building, a part of a building, or an obstruction physically intrudes, overlaps, or trespasses the property of another, this is referred to as an
    A. escheat.
    B. easement.
    C. encroachment.
    D. assemblage.

39. What term is used to identify recently sold or leased properties that are similar to a particular property being evaluated and used to indicate the value for the property being appraised?
    A. Subjects
    B. Comparables
    C. Relatives
    D. Outliers

40. An appraisal is best defined as
    A. an unbiased opinion of the most likely price for which a parcel of real estate would sell at a given date.
    B. an unbiased opinion of the nature, quality, value, or utility of an interest in real estate and related personalty.
    C. the process of developing an opinion as to the market value or other defined value of a specified interest in a specified point in time.
    D. the process of studying the nature, quality, or utility of an interest in real estate in which a value estimate is not necessarily required.

41. When identifying a neighborhood's boundaries, an appraiser should
    A. inspect the area's physical characteristics.
    B. draw preliminary boundaries on a map.
    C. test preliminary boundaries against socio-economic characteristics of the area's population.
    D. do all of the above.

42. Standard 1 of the USPAP requires an appraiser to analyze certain legal instruments dealing with the subject property if such information is available to the appraiser in the normal course of business. Which document is specifically mentioned as one to be analyzed?
    A. Agreement of sale
    B. Promissory note
    C. Deed of trust
    D. Installment sales contract

43. In the appraisal process, the property being appraised is referred to as the
    A. comparable property.
    B. assessed property.
    C. subject property.
    D. appraised property.

44. In the valuation process, which step identifies the items that contribute to a concise appraisal completed in a thorough and efficient manner?
    A. Definition of the problem
    B. Data collection and analysis
    C. Highest and best use analysis
    D. Reconciliation

45. The appraisal process undertaken by an appraiser consists of many steps. What is the correct first step in the appraisal process?
    A. Definition of the problem
    B. Collection and analysis of data
    C. Analysis of highest and best use
    D. Initial estimate of value

46. A common phrase included in all residential real estate appraisal forms includes the use of the "as of" date. Normally the "as of" date in an appraisal report refers to the date
    A. the appraisal assignment was accepted.
    B. the appraisal assignment is to be delivered.
    C. of the last inspection.
    D. the loan is to close.

47. The objective of undertaking an appraisal of real estate is to
    A. determine asking price.
    B. estimate value.
    C. establish loan value.
    D. identify legal rights and interests that may exist.

48. A technique used by market analysts and appraisers that attempts to measure the current economic activity and expected future economic growth in a specific geographic area is commonly referred to as
    A. basic industry analysis.
    B. nonbasic industry analysis.
    C. economic base analysis.
    D. site analysis.

49. In using the sales comparison approach, the appraiser finds that one of the comparables is superior to the subject property in terms of location. In this event, what adjustment will be made?
    A. The comparable will be adjusted upward.
    B. The comparable will be adjusted downward.
    C. The subject property will be adjusted upward.
    D. The subject property will be adjusted downward.

50. If comparable sale #1 sold for $200,000 and has a two-car garage, adding $10,000 to the value, and the subject property does not have a garage, the indicated value of the subject property would be found by
    A. adding $10,000 to the comparable sale.
    B. subtracting $10,000 from the comparable sale.
    C. adding $10,000 to the subject property.
    D. subtracting $10,000 from the subject property.

51. Normally, the sales comparison approach would be considered the most reliable when which condition exists?
    A. The property is new and unoccupied
    B. A high rate of inflation exists
    C. Obsolescence must be measured
    D. Access to reliable market data exists

52. When an appraiser is using the sales comparison approach, one of the elements of comparison that may have to be adjusted is often referred to as a time adjustment. What does the time adjustment provide?
    A. An adjustment for the period of time between when a listing is taken on property and when the property actually sells
    B. An adjustment between the date of sale of a comparable and the date of the appraisal to allow for any market changes over time
    C. An adjustment between the listing date of a comparable sale and the date the subject property is actually appraised
    D. An adjustment for the period of time between the actual sale of a comparable and the date the appraiser receives compensation for the appraisal assignment

53. Your appraisal assignment involves the estimation of value for a 100-foot by 180-foot parcel of land. You have identified and examined ten comparables that are similar to the subject property except for size differentials. You have developed a simple linear regression equation in which sales price (expressed in thousands of dollars) is the dependent variable and size (expressed in square feet) is the independent variable. The equation you have developed is: $Y_c = 10,000 + 1 (x)$. Using this equation and the information given, what is the indicated sales price for the subject property?
    A. $10,000
    B. $18,000
    C. $28,000
    D. $43,560

54. An appraiser has been asked to estimate the value of a lot. In the same neighborhood, the appraiser collects the following sales data:

Lot Sale	Sales Price	Time of Sale
1	$14,425	4 months ago
2	$14,705	2 months ago
3	$14,560	3 months ago

The price appreciation for lots is estimated to be at the rate of 1 percent per month (simple, not compounded). Given the above information, what is the estimated value of the subject property?
    A. $5,000
    B. $10,000
    C. $14,000
    D. $15,000

55. In appraising a property, the appraiser identifies a similar property that appears to be a very good comparable. The appraiser finds that when the comparable sold, very favorable financing was part of the sale. In regard to the comparable, what is the appropriate action?
    A. Don't use the sale under any condition
    B. Give the sale less weight than any of the other comparables
    C. Adjust the sales price for cash equivalency and explain
    D. Do nothing because the comparable sold and thus represents normal market activity

56. Deferred maintenance usually results in which loss in value?
    A. Incurable physical depreciation
    B. Curable physical depreciation
    C. Curable functional obsolescence
    D. Curable external obsolescence

57. The portion of land that is *NOT* necessary for the existing improvements is referred to as
    A. overimproved land.
    B. excess land.
    C. useless land.
    D. underimproved land.

58. What term applies to the effect on value of location or proximity to the intersection of two streets?
    A. Corner influence
    B. Amenity
    C. Externality
    D. Plottage

59. The term *site* refers to
    A. land that has been improved.
    B. land within a certain set of boundaries.
    C. a legal description of a plot of land.
    D. raw land with no improvements.

60. Functional obsolescence could be caused by
    A. a ceiling that is too high.
    B. deferred maintenance.
    C. a poor location.
    D. a worn-out roof.

61. _____ is the estimated cost at current prices to construct an exact replica of the building using the same standards, materials, design, and layout and including any deficiencies, superadequacies, and obsolescence as the subject building.
    A. Replacement cost
    B. Unit-in-place cost
    C. Reproduction cost
    D. Market cost

62. The building cost estimate method that replicates the contractor's development of a bid, and is the most comprehensive way to estimate building costs, is known as the
    A. unit-in-place method.
    B. quantity survey method.
    C. break-down method.
    D. comparative unit method.

63. The cost approach to value is generally most accurate when which situation exists?
    A. The building is old and suffers from a great deal of depreciation.
    B. The building is new and is being used under its highest and best use.
    C. The building is old and reproduction or replacement cost is not known.
    D. A vacant tract of land is being appraised.

64. Included in the cost approach to value is all of these components *EXCEPT*
    A. replacement cost.
    B. highest and best use of the land.
    C. acquisition cost.
    D. accrued depreciation.

65. A large tract of land measuring 2,200 feet by 800 feet sells for $32,000 per acre. What was the total selling price?
    A. $1,053,500
    B. $1,293,000
    C. $1,760,000
    D. $7,040,000

66. In the appraisal of real estate, the necessary step taken by the appraiser of valuing the land as if vacant is part of which approach to value?
    A. Cost
    B. Sales comparison
    C. Income capitalization
    D. Gross rent multiplier

67. In regard to accrued depreciation, which terms do *NOT* belong together?
    A. Physical deterioration—curable
    B. Functional obsolescence—incurable
    C. Economic obsolescence—curable
    D. Functional obsolescence—curable

68. Which statement is correct in regard to estimating the value of residential real estate?
    A. The highest and best use of a site with a newly constructed house properly located on the site is always its present use.
    B. The square footage of a single-family residence for purposes of using the cost approach to value is calculated by summing the interior heated and cooled areas of the structure.
    C. A newly constructed house cannot suffer from any type of depreciation.
    D. Total accrued depreciation is a loss in value from all causes.

69. The combining of two or more lots into a single ownership with the value of the assembled lots being more than the sum of the values of the individual lots is referred to as
    A. highest and best use.
    B. economic rent.
    C. escheat.
    D. plottage.

70. Superadequacies that might exist in a structure would be recognized and included in which type of depreciation?
    A. Physical deterioration
    B. Functional obsolescence
    C. Economic obsolescence
    D. Locational obsolescence

71. Another term used to denote the actual age of a building is
   A. chronological age.
   B. effective age.
   C. economic age.
   D. depreciated age.

72. A house being appraised has a total living area of 2,200 square feet. For a house of similar construction quality, a national cost service indicates a cost of $125 per square foot. The location multiplier is 0.94. The cost figures are five months old and the appraiser estimates that construction costs have increased 5 percent during this time period. What is the current estimated replacement cost of this house?
   A. $258,500
   B. $271,425
   C. $275,000
   D. $307,181

73. A building has a roof that originally had an expected life of 25 years. The roof's effective age is 15 years. A new roof will cost $10,000 to install. Using a straight-line method, what amount of depreciation would be charged for the roof?
   A. $4,000
   B. $6,000
   C. $8,000
   D. $10,000

74. The method of estimating total replacement cost of a building that measures the total square footage or cubic footage and multiplies this total by the current cost per square or cubic foot is referred to as which method?
   A. Comparative unit method
   B. Builder's method
   C. Unit-in-place method
   D. Quantity survey method

75. The basic capitalization formula used in the income approach to value contains three components. Those three components are
   A. market, cost, income.
   B. value, rate, income.
   C. physical, functional, economic.
   D. potential, gross, net income.

76. The term *amortization* refers to
   A. an increase in value of the property.
   B. a decrease in value of the property.
   C. periodic repayment of debt.
   D. assessment of property for tax purposes.

77. What is the gross income multiplier for a property with a current market value of $57,000 that rents for $500 per month?
   A. 9
   B. 9.5
   C. 10
   D. 10.5

78. The amount of debt payment due on a loan is a function of the amount borrowed, the interest charged, and the term of the loan. In regard to the term, which statement is *TRUE?*
   A. The longer the term, the greater the periodic payment.
   B. The longer the term, the less the periodic payment.
   C. The longer the term, the higher the interest rate charged and thus the higher the payment.
   D. The longer the term, the lower the interest rate charged and thus the higher the payment.

79. An appraiser must analyze all agreements of sale of the subject property if such information is available to the appraiser in the normal course of business going back how many years?
   A. One
   B. Three
   C. Five
   D. There is no minimum time period.

80. You have collected the following data on a comparable property, which you plan to use in estimating the gross rent multiplier for rental properties in a neighborhood: sales price $100,000, annual rent $6,000, annual property taxes $900, monthly mortgage payment $715.What is the monthly gross rent multiplier indicated by this property?
   A. 100
   B. 125
   C. 150
   D. 200

81. A mortgage loan for $30,000 at 9 percent for 30 years has been made. What is the amount of interest for the first month?
    A. $16.39
    B. $90.00
    C. $225.00
    D. $241.39

82. When payments on a loan are not sufficient to cover the interest on a loan, which of the following results is applicable?
    A. The loan has negative amortization.
    B. The loan will never get repaid.
    C. The loan has a debt coverage ratio less than one.
    D. The loan is a reverse annuity mortgage.

83. In regard to Standard 1 of the USPAP, which statement is *TRUE?*
    A. Standard 1 is directed toward the substantive aspects of reporting a competent appraisal.
    B. Standard 1 mirrors the appraisal report in the order of topics addressed.
    C. Standard 1 may be used by appraisers and clients as a convenient checklist.
    D. Standard 1 requires appraisal reports to be in writing.

84. What does the range of a group of variables indicate to the appraiser?
    A. The value of the highest sample
    B. The difference between the lowest and the highest values
    C. The average for the group
    D. The percentage variation from the mean

85. A reversion can follow which type of legal estates?
    A. Leasehold
    B. Fee simple
    C. Tenancy in common
    D. Fee simple absolute

86. Standard 1 of the USPAP requires the appraiser to
    A. include a certification statement.
    B. define *market value.*
    C. always use the sales comparison approach.
    D. do none of the above.

87. Which statement would be correct if contract rent is likely to exceed market rent for the term of the lease?
    A. The leasehold estate is not likely to have any value.
    B. The leased fee estate is probably less valuable than a fee simple estate in the property.
    C. The leasehold interest will be greater than the fee simple value.
    D. The leasehold value is not affected by the contract rent.

88. Which statement is correct in regard to assessed value?
    A. The assessed value must equal the market value.
    B. The assessed value is used primarily to calculate property taxes.
    C. The assessed value is used primarily to calculate property insurance.
    D. The assessed value will never exceed cost.

89. Which term refers to a lease used to sublease a property?
    A. Blanket lease
    B. Subordinated lease
    C. Sandwich lease
    D. Double lease

90. A father sells his home to his daughter and her husband. Such a sale would normally be described as which type of sale?
    A. Arm's-length sale
    B. Illegal sale
    C. Distorted sale
    D. Forced sale

91. Which reason is often given as a weakness or disadvantage of using the sales comparison approach?
    A. The market may be too active.
    B. There may be so many sales that the appraiser cannot find comparables.
    C. The sales comparison approach is based on historical information.
    D. A competitive and knowledgeable market may exist.

92. In collecting data, an appraiser concludes that comparable properties have increased in value at a 6 percent annual compound rate during the previous two years. The proper time adjustment to make for a comparable that sold two years ago for $100,000 is
    A. $6,000.
    B. $12,000.
    C. $12,360.
    D. $112,360.

93. Per the USPAP, disclosing any lack of knowledge or experience to the client is part of
    A. the Scope of Work Rule.
    B. Standard 4.
    C. Standard 1.
    D. the Competency Rule.

94. Which statement is *NOT* correct in regard to the Scope of Work Rule in the USPAP?
    A. The Scope of Work Rule only covers oral appraisal reports.
    B. The scope of work must include the research and analyses that are necessary to develop credible assignment results.
    C. The report must contain sufficient information to allow intended users to understand the scope of work performed.
    D. For each appraisal, the appraiser must identify the problem to be solved.

95. In the USPAP, all of these requirements are part of a self-contained appraisal report *EXCEPT*
    A. state the intended use of the appraisal.
    B. state the identity of the client and any intended users by name or type.
    C. state the type and definition of value.
    D. state all prior sales of the subject property.

96. Which rule or standard states that in reporting the results of a real estate appraisal, an appraiser must communicate each analysis, opinion, and conclusion in a manner that is not misleading?
    A. The Scope of Work Rule
    B. The Competency Rule
    C. Standard 2
    D. Standard 1

APPLICATION-STYLE QUESTIONS

Questions 97 through 100 are based on the following data:

Sale	Sales Price	Size (Sq. Ft.)
1	$150,000	2,000
2	$145,000	1,800
3	$150,000	2,000
4	$155,000	2,200
5	$152,500	2,100

97. What is the mean selling price?
    A. $149,500
    B. $150,000
    C. $150,500
    D. $152,500

98. What is the median selling price?
    A. $145,500
    B. $150,000
    C. $150,500
    D. $155,000

99. What is the mean price per square foot?
    A. $72.62
    B. $74.73
    C. $75.00
    D. $80.56

100. What is the mode selling price?
    A. $145,000
    B. $150,000
    C. $150,500
    D. $155,000

Questions 101 through 105 are based on the following information:

Your appraisal assignment involves a 2,500-square-foot house with a total economic life of 50 years and a remaining economic life of 35 years. Replacement cost is $190 per square foot. You estimate it would cost $10,000 for central air-conditioning since the house currently does not have it. The site and site improvements are worth $60,000.

101. Physical deterioration is estimated to be
  A. $47,500.
  B. $142,500.
  C. $147,500.
  D. $152,500.

102. What is the estimated depreciated cost of the improvements?
  A. $142,500
  B. $322,500
  C. $332,500
  D. $475,000

103. What is the estimated total value of the property?
  A. $142,500
  B. $322,500
  C. $382,500
  D. $475,000

104. If the property had central air-conditioning, the value would increase by $15,000 more than it is presently worth. How is this loss in value properly classified?
  A. Physical deterioration, curable
  B. Physical deterioration, incurable
  C. Functional obsolescence, incurable
  D. Functional obsolescence, curable

105. Suppose the sales comparison approach indicates that the market value of the improvements is $300,000. What would the difference between this and the replacement cost of the improvements indicate?
  A. Accelerated depreciation
  B. Accrued depreciation
  C. Physical deterioration
  D. Cost of improvements

ANSWERS TO RESIDENTIAL EXAM A

1. **B.** A replacement would be a substitute for the existing property.

2. **A.** Cost and market value are most likely to be similar when the property is new. However, for this to be true the property should be the highest and best use of the site. The cost approach must often be used for special-purpose properties due to lack of comparable sales for the sales comparison approach and lack of income to capitalize with the income approach. However, this does not mean that cost and market value are more similar with special-purpose properties than for new properties.

3. **A.** Linkage denotes the time-distance relationship between properties.

4. **C.** Because the amount of real estate available can change only as quickly as it can be built or renovated, supply changes more slowly than demand. Although the efficiency of the real estate market can be debated, it is usually considered true that price is seldom equal to value, and supply and demand are seldom in balance. It is also true that there are many government regulations.

5. **D.** Highest and best use analysis can be used to determine several factors. For vacant land it is used to determine the optimal use and amount of capital to invest in. It is also used to determine whether an existing improvement should be demolished. Therefore all of the answers are correct.

6. **B.** An absorption rate is the measure of the rate at which a type of real estate space will be sold or occupied.

7. **A.** $100,000 – $60,000 = $40,000.

8. **A.** Market value can be considered the value to a typical investor. A typical investor is not the same as any investor who is willing to purchase the property in the market. It must be the most likely or typical investor for the property being appraised.

9. **B.** Value in use is derived from a specific use of real estate and is not necessarily equal to the value estimate if the property were being used under its highest and best use. Value in exchange denotes how one item exchanges in the marketplace for other items.

10. **B.** Market value is defined as the price in terms of cash or its equivalent upon which a willing buyer and a willing seller will agree where neither is under any pressure, both are knowledgeable, and both are acting in their own best interest. Of the four choices given, market value is most closely associated with value in exchange.

11. **A.** Market price is the amount actually paid in a transaction. It is not the same as market value and may or may not be the same as the amount of the loan. Replacement cost and market price are two entirely different concepts.

12. **B.** If a property suffers from locational obsolescence, then the maximum value is not being achieved. The principle of conformity states that a parcel of land must be used in such a way as to conform to surrounding land use if maximum value is to be achieved.

13. **C.** The principle of contribution states that the value of a component part of a parcel of property, such as its plumbing system, is equal to what that component part adds to the total value, less any costs incurred.

14. **A.** The concept of equilibrium in the marketplace is explained by the principle of balance. The remaining three choices are all economic principles that influence land and how it is used.

15. **C.** The highest and best use of a parcel of land can change over time. The fact that the current use is residential does not imply that such use is indeed the highest and best use of the land. Both physical and legal concepts as well as economic concepts influence highest and best use.

16. **C.** A single-purpose property is defined as one in which the existing use is the only reasonable use that can be made of the site. A golf course, for example, normally involves a great deal of acreage that could, within reason, support any number of different land uses.

17. **A.** Debt service is defined as the periodic (monthly, quarterly, annually) payment necessary to pay the principal and interest on an amortized loan. This payment often is referred to as debt service on an operating statement.

18. **C.** Lenders normally make a loan decision based on the lower of the contract price or appraised value. Assessed value is not a primary factor in determining the amount of a loan.

19. **C.** Cost is not a criterion used in determining whether an item is a fixture or whether it is merely personal property.

20. **C.** Supply of real estate is an economic factor and not a legal consideration. The legal rights held in real estate are affected by all of the remaining three choices.

21. **C.** A *hypothetical condition* is defined as "that which is contrary to what exists, but is supposed for the purpose of analysis."

22. **A.** Individual ownership in a condominium is referred to as a unit. Common areas as well as limited common areas are held as tenants in common with others. A cooperative is a different type of ownership.

23. **D.** Zoning is a police power device used by government to divide a jurisdiction into districts and establish how land may be used within those districts.

24. **B.** The term *ad valorem* is a Latin phrase meaning "according to value." Local and state governments levy property taxes on real estate based on the assessed value of the property.

25. **A.** The person conveying title is known as the grantor; the person receiving the title is known as the grantee.

26. **C.** A cooperative is an indirect form of real estate ownership in which individuals own shares of a corporation, which in turn owns the real estate. Thus the individual owners cannot mortgage their units. The tenant's rights or interest in the cooperative is considered personal property.

27. **B.** A nonconforming use is a pre-existing use of land that does not conform to the present zoning ordinance.

28. **C.** An appurtenance is that which belongs to something and thus "passes" with the property. Riparian rights and easements pass with the land.

29. **A.** An acre of land contains 43,560 square feet.

30. **D.** Dedication is the donation of property by an owner to a public authority. Examples would include roads in a subdivision or land to be used as open space in a subdivision.

31. **D.** A deed restriction is a voluntary private limitation on real property. Encroachments, adverse possession, and mechanic's and materialman's liens are all examples of involuntary limitations.

32. **D.** Workfiles must, at a minimum, be retained for five years after preparation.

33. **A.** A plat map shows the specific location and boundaries of land that has been subdivided into individual lots. Each lot is assigned a lot-and-block number so that the lot can be easily identified when it is sold.

34. **D.** The dominant estate is the tract of land that benefits as a result of an easement on a servient estate, which is the estate burdened by the easement.

35. **C.** The USPAP defines a report as "any communication, written or oral, transmitted to the client."

36. **C.** *Fee simple estate* refers to the rights to ownership of a property that is free and clear of any leases. It is the most complete form of ownership as well as the most common.

37. **C.** The four sections of the Ethics Rule are: conduct, management, confidentiality, and record keeping.

38. **C.** An encroachment is the extension of some improvement or object across the boundary of an adjoining tract, and it may reduce the size or value of the intruded property.

39. **B.** The appropriate term identifying other properties used to indicate the value of the subject property is *comparables* (sometimes shortened to *comps*). The property being appraised is the subject. The term *outliers* is a term in statistical analysis referring to data that is not like the rest. For example, if regression analysis was being used, a property that was an outlier might be excluded from the analysis.

40. **B.** An appraisal is an unbiased opinion of the nature, quality, value, or utility of an interest in real estate and related personalty. The definitions of valuation and evaluation are not the same as the definition of an appraisal.

41. **D.** Neighborhood boundaries surround the area that influences the value of a property. These boundaries often coincide with changes in land use, natural terrain, type of occupant, availability, and type of transportation.

42. **A.** S.R.1-5 requires an appraiser to analyze all agreements of sale, options, and listings of the subject property.

43. **C.** The property being appraised is referred to as the subject property. Comparable properties are those that are similar to the subject property and are being used to estimate the value of the subject property. Assessed property refers to the valuation of property for tax purposes.

44. **B.** The collection and analysis of data is the means by which an appraiser brings about a thorough and efficient appraisal assignment. The other choices are all steps in the appraisal process.

45. **A.** The first step that should be undertaken in any appraisal assignment is a definition of the problem. Both the collection and analysis of data as well as an analysis of highest and best use are part of the process, but both are done after the definition of the problem.

46. **C.** A common inclusion in form appraisal reports is the statement "I estimate the market value, as defined, of subject property as of _____, 20___ to be $_____." Normally this date refers to the last time the property was inspected by the appraiser, which may or may not be the date the appraisal assignment was accepted or delivered.

47. **B.** An appraisal is an estimate of value. An appraiser does not determine asking price or establish loan value.

48. **C.** Economic base analysis, which involves addressing both basic and nonbasic industry sources, attempts to measure the present as well as the future economic activity and growth potential of an area.

49. **B.** When the sales comparison approach is employed, the comparables are adjusted to the subject property. If the comparable is superior to the subject property in regard to a certain feature, such as location, the

correct step would be to adjust the comparable downward.

50. **B.** Adjustments under the sales comparison
approach are always made to the comparables and never to the subject property.
In this example, an adjustment of subtracting $10,000 from the comparable
would be in order since the comparable has a two-car garage estimated to
have added $10,000 to the value of the
comparable.

51. **D.** To accurately and successfully use the
sales comparison approach, the appraiser
needs access to reliable market data.

52. **B.** There are numerous elements of comparison that may be appropriate for the
appraiser to use when employing the sales
comparison approach. One of the com-
parisons involves an adjustment for time,
which allows for any changes in value
between the date of sale of a comparable
and the date of the appraisal of the subject
property.

53. **C.** $100 \times 180 = 18,000$ square feet. Y_C
(sales price) $= 10,000 + 1 (18,000)$. Y_C
$= \$28,000$.

54. **D.** The adjusted sales prices for the three
comparables would be: comparable 1—
$15,002; comparable 2—$14,999; and
comparable 3—$14,997. An estimate of
the subject property would be $15,000.

55. **C.** A comparable property used as part of
the sales comparison approach must
be adjusted to reflect any differences
between the subject property and the
comparable. In the case of favorable
financing for a comparable, the sales price
would have to be adjusted for cash equivalency and the adjustment explained.

56. **B.** Unless it is extreme, deferred maintenance should be curable. If the extent of
the deferred maintenance is such that the
increment to the value of the property
is less than the cost to cure, it becomes
incurable.

57. **B.** Excess land is the portion of land not
needed for the existing improvements.
This land is not necessarily underimproved, and it would be rare for it to be
useless. It may not be adding "plottage"
value and is most likely being held by the
owner for future development. Its interim
highest and best use may very well be as
vacant land.

58. **A.** The specific term that explains the effect
on value of location where two streets
intersect is *corner influence.* In some
sense, corner influence might be considered an externality because it is a factor
external to the property that affects its
value, and perhaps an amenity if the
externality is positive. The effect can be
positive or negative depending on the
specific location and type of property; it is
dangerous to generalize.

59. **A.** *Site* refers to land that has been improved
for a specific purpose. Site improvements
may be onsite or offsite and include items
such as drainage systems, utility lines,
and access to roads. Raw land with no
improvements is referred to as a parcel,
lot, plot, or tract.

60. **A.** Functional obsolescence is caused by
defects in design or outdated design,
such as a ceiling that is too high. Maintenance items are considered physical
deterioration.

61. **C.** Reproduction cost is the current cost of
constructing an exact duplicate of the
property being appraised. Replacement
cost is the estimated cost at current prices
to construct an equivalent building using
current standards, materials, design, and
layout.

62. **B.** The quantity survey method computes
material costs and labor hours required.
Then these costs are used to estimate unit
and total costs. Entrepreneurial profit is
added to costs. This approach has limited use because of the time and expense
involved.

63. **B.** Use of the cost approach to value tends to be more accurate when the improvements are newer and when the land is being used under its highest and best use. The older improvements or the unknown replacement cost can result in a less accurate use of the cost approach. Vacant land is not appraised using the cost approach.

64. **C.** The cost of acquisition is not part of the cost approach to value. The remaining three choices are all part of the cost approach.

65. **B.** 2,200 × 800 = 1,760,000 sq. ft.; 1,760,000 ÷ 43,560 = 40.404 acres; 40.404 × $32,000 = $1,293,000 (rounded).

66. **A.** The cost approach to value requires an estimate of the land's value as if vacant. None of the other approaches requires this step.

67. **C.** Economic obsolescence or locational obsolescence is always considered incurable; whereas with both physical deterioration and functional obsolescence, the loss in value can be either curable or incurable.

68. **D.** Accrued depreciation is defined as a loss in value caused by physical deterioration, functional obsolescence, or economic obsolescence. The highest and best use of a site may not be residential even though it is currently being used as such. When using the cost approach to value, the exterior measurements are used rather than the interior measurements. A newly constructed house can indeed suffer from depreciation, such as functional or economic obsolescence.

69. **D.** Plottage is often illustrated when a square block in a metropolitan area is assembled into single ownership. In such a case, the value of the assembled parcels is often greater than the total value of the land when divided into, for example, 20 parcels, each owned by a different person.

70. **B.** Functional obsolescence allows for conditions within the structure that make the building outdated compared with a new building. Functional obsolescence also includes features not fully valued by the market.

71. **A.** Chronological age and actual age both refer to the historical age of a building; for example, a building constructed five years ago is five years old in actual age.

72. **B.** 2,200 × $125 = $275,000; $275,000 × 0.94 = $258,500; $258,500 × 1.05 = $271,425.

73. **B.** 15 ÷ 25 = 60 percent deterioration; $10,000 × 0.60 = $6,000.

74. **A.** Numerous techniques are used to estimate replacement or reproduction cost. The comparative unit method measures the total square footage or cubic footage and multiplies that total by the current cost per square or cubic foot.

75. **B.** V = I ÷ R denotes value, income, and rate of capitalization.

76. **C.** Amortization refers to the repayment of an obligation over a period of time. Real estate mortgages are normally either fully amortized or partially amortized.

77. **B.** $500 × 12 = $6,000 per year. $57,000 ÷ $6,000 = 9.5.

78. **B.** The relationship between the term of the loan and the payment due is inverse, which means the longer the term, the less the periodic payment.

79. **B.** The minimum period for considering and analyzing sales of the subject property is three years for all property types.

80. **D.** The gross rent multiplier equals sales price divided by the monthly gross rent. $6,000 ÷ 12 = $500 monthly rent. $100,000 ÷ $500 = 200 GRM. The property tax and mortgage payment

information given in this problem are not needed in determining the GRM.

81. **C.** $0.09 \div 12 = 0.0075 =$ monthly interest; $30,000 \times 0.0075 = \$225$.

82. **A.** Negative amortization occurs when the interest on a loan is greater than the payment. This situation sometimes occurs in loans with graduated payments. In this case, the loan payment would start at a lower payment level and then increase at some time in the future. When the loan payments are increased, the loan payment will be larger than the interest, and negative amortization will cease to occur; thus the principal will eventually be paid off.

83. **C.** Standard 1 does not cover the form of the appraisal report. Reports are the subject of Standard 2.

84. **B.** If residential property in a neighborhood is selling between $100,000 and $130,000, then the range is $30,000, which is the difference between the lowest and the highest values.

85. **A.** A leasehold is the legal interest that a tenant has in the property as a result of a lease. Once the tenant's legal interest is terminated, whatever legal interest that exists "reverts" to the landlord who therefore has a reversionary interest.

86. **D.** Certification is addressed in Standard 2.

87. **A.** The leasehold interest is not likely to have any value because the lessee is in an unfavorable situation. In fact, the lessee may be willing to pay to get out of the lease, which means that the leasehold position has a negative value. The above-market rents could result in a leased fee estate that is more valuable (not less valuable) because of the additional rent being collected.

88. **B.** Assessed value is used primarily in the calculation of property taxes. The assessed value is usually based on the market value but does not have to equal the market value.

89. **C.** The term used to refer to a lease used to sublease a property is a *sandwich lease*, and the legal interest that is created is sometimes referred to as a *sandwich position*.

90. **C.** A sale of property such as a home sold by a father to his daughter is normally not considered an arm's-length transaction, but is *distorted* in terms of what the sale tells you in regard to market activity. To use such a sale as a comparable in the sales comparison approach, the specifics of the sale would need to be known.

91. **C.** The sales comparison approach is based on information acquired from the market from comparable properties that have sold. Such information is, by definition, historical data and may have to be adjusted to accurately reflect current market conditions.

92. **C.** $\$100,000 \times (1.06)^2 = \$112,360$. During the two years, the time adjustment would be $12,360.

93. **D.** Disclosing any lack of knowledge or experience to a client is part of the Competency Rule.

94. **A.** The Scope of Work Rule covers all appraisal assignments, whether or not the report is oral or written.

95. **D.** Standard 2 does not require the appraiser to state all prior sales of the subject property.

96. **C.** Standard 2 requires the appraiser to communicate each analysis, opinion, and conclusion in a manner that is not misleading.

97. **C.** The mean denotes the average selling price. $\$150,000 + \$145,000 + \$150,000 + \$155,000 + \$152,500 = \$752,500 \div 5 = \$150,500$.

98. **B.** The median selling price is the price in the middle. In this example, $150,000 is the middle selling price.

99. **B.** Mean price per square foot is calculated by dividing each of the five sales prices by the size for that particular sale. The five price-per-square-foot figures are $75.00, $80.56, $75.00, $70.45, and $72.62. Thus, the mean or average would be $74.73.

100. **B.** The mode selling price refers to the sales price that occurs with the most frequency. In this example, $150,000 occurred twice. No other sales price occurred more than once.

101. **B.** 35 years/50 years = 0.70. Therefore, there is 0.30 depreciation. $475,000 × 0.30 = $142,500.

102. **B.** 2,500 sq. ft. × $190 = $475,000; $475,000 × 0.30 = $142,500; air-conditioning replacement cost = $10,000; $475,000 − $142,500 − $10,000 = $322,500.

103. **C.** $322,500 + $60,000 = $382,500.

104. **D.** Since the value gained by the air-conditioning ($15,000) is greater than the cost of adding the air-conditioning ($10,000), the lack of air-conditioning is functional obsolescence—curable.

105. **B.** Accrued depreciation is the difference between the reproduction cost new of the improvements and the present value (market value) of the improvements.

CHAPTER 13

Licensed/Certified Residential Exam B

1. Which principle of value suggests that the value of a property is equal to the present value of the property's projected income?
   A. Balance
   B. Anticipation
   C. Opportunity cost
   D. Substitution

2. Which action is *NOT* characteristic of market value?
   A. Sale as soon as possible
   B. Well-informed buyers
   C. Typical financing
   D. Typically motivated sellers

3. What term applies to the difference between the purchase price and the net proceeds from any mortgage(s) used to purchase the property?
   A. Asset
   B. Reversion
   C. Capital gain
   D. Equity

4. Which factor is *NOT* normally considered to affect the supply of real estate?
   A. Volume of new construction
   B. Standing stock
   C. Land use and city growth
   D. Competition

5. The relationship of a property to other properties in terms of time and distance preferences is referred to as
   A. linkage.
   B. externality.
   C. district.
   D. neighborhood.

6. What term *BEST* describes the effect of a power plant on the value of a nearby home?
   A. Balance
   B. Externalities
   C. Contribution
   D. Conformity

7. The demand for new homes in a market area is estimated to be 500 per year. Developer Abel's new subdivision, when completed, is expected to capture 10 percent of the market. Therefore Abel's subdivision has an expected absorption rate of
   A. 50 percent.
   B. 5 percent.
   C. 50 homes per year.
   D. 10 homes per year.

8. Which appraisal principle holds that market value is indicated by the value of another property with similar utility?
   A. Supply and demand
   B. Substitution
   C. Competition
   D. Balance

9. The market value of a property and the selling price of that same property could be equal under which condition?
   A. They are always equal.
   B. They are never equal.
   C. They are sometimes equal.
   D. They are equal only with rental property.

10. The specific use of a parcel of land that gives that land the greatest residual of income is referred to as the land's
    A. intrinsic use.
    B. highest and best use.
    C. income-producing use.
    D. efficient use.

11. Which economic principle is the underlying justification as to why the adjustment process is used in the sales comparison (market) approach?
    A. Anticipation
    B. Contribution
    C. Highest and best use
    D. Opportunity cost

12. The proper or most correct placement of an improvement to land, such as the construction of a house, is normally strongly influenced by the application of which economic principle?
    A. Conformity
    B. Encroachment
    C. Escheat
    D. Substitution

13. _____ refers to that possible and legal use of land that will preserve the land's utility and generate a net income that forms, when capitalized, the greatest present value of the land.
    A. Linkage
    B. Present value
    C. Market use
    D. Highest and best use

14. The term lenders often use to refer to the relative amount of money they will lend on a specific parcel of property is known as
    A. gross rent multiplier.
    B. debt-to-equity ratio.
    C. value-to-loan ratio.
    D. loan-to-value ratio.

15. Which written appraisal report is recognized in Standard 2 of the USPAP?
    A. Self-contained
    B. Restricted user
    C. Limited departure
    D. Summarized

16. Effective demand in the marketplace for housing varies most directly with which condition?
    A. Purchasing power
    B. Interest rates
    C. Building codes
    D. Building cycles

17. Appraisers may find themselves involved in the appraisal of a mobile home. A common term used to denote a mobile home is
    A. condominium.
    B. manufactured housing.
    C. PUD.
    D. cooperative.

18. In the USPAP, the Scope of Work Rule requires the appraiser to identify which assignment element?
    A. Type and definition of value
    B. Assignment conditions
    C. Client and other intended users
    D. All of the above

19. A fixture, such as the central air-conditioning system in a building, is legally treated as
    A. personalty.
    B. realty.
    C. intangible property.
    D. escheat.

20. In regard to an easement, which statement is correct?
    A. An easement is a personal property right rather than a real property right.
    B. An easement must always be in writing.
    C. An easement, once created, becomes a life estate.
    D. An easement may be terminated once the purpose for which it was created no longer exists.

21. A worn path crosses an owner's property.
    What legal doctrine would require a potential
    purchaser to take note of the fact that there
    may be an unrecorded prescriptive easement
    against that property?
    A. Actual notice
    B. Constructive notice
    C. Lis pendens
    D. Escheat

22. An irregularly shaped lot is located in an area
    where the zoning setback requirement of
    15 feet would result in a planned building not
    properly fitting on the lot. To seek relief from
    the harshness of this requirement, the owner
    may seek what type of adjustment from the
    local authority?
    A. Nonconforming use
    B. Exception
    C. Variance
    D. Special-use permit

23. An individual owner of a condominium unit
    is in default on payment of the property
    taxes to the local government. Which is the
    only choice legally available to the taxing
    authority?
    A. Levy the tax on the entire condominium
       project
    B. Foreclose against the individual
       unit
    C. Place a lien on the common areas
    D. Foreclose against the homeowners'
       association

24. A parcel of land has a market value of
    $80,000. The local taxing authority tax rate is
    $2 per $100 of assessed value, and the parcel
    of land is assessed at $40,000. In regard
    to this specific parcel, which statement is
    incorrect?
    A. The assessment ratio is one-half.
    B. The tax rate is 20 mills.
    C. The tax due is $800.
    D. The tax due is 2 percent of market
       value.

25. When a parcel of real estate is used as the
    collateral for a loan, the borrower is referred
    to as the _____, and the lender is referred
    to as the _____.
    A. mortgagor, mortgagee
    B. mortgagee, mortgagor
    C. mortgagee, financial institution
    D. principal, agent

26. In referring to various parties in a deed, the
    grantee is the
    A. seller.
    B. buyer.
    C. broker.
    D. escrow agent.

27. The legal right of government to acquire pri-
    vate property for a public use or purpose with
    just compensation is known as
    A. police power.
    B. eminent domain.
    C. condemnation.
    D. escheat.

28. A vacant lot 100 feet by 140 feet sold for
    $17,500. What was its selling price per
    square foot?
    A. $1.00
    B. $1.25
    C. $1.40
    D. $1.75

29. The walls located between two condominium
    units are normally considered
    A. individual unit elements.
    B. limited common elements.
    C. public elements.
    D. proprietary lease elements.

30. In regard to the legal concept of land, what
    is a landowner entitled to in addition to the
    surface rights?
    A. Nothing
    B. Air rights only
    C. Everything below the surface only
    D. Everything above and below the surface

31. In determining whether an item is real property or personal property, which test is normally considered?
    A. Manner of attachment, intention of the party who made the attachment, purpose for which the item is used
    B. Manner of attachment, age of the item, cost of the item
    C. Number of items in question, current market value, purpose for which the item is used
    D. Actual owner, cost of the item, current market value

32. The term *real estate* is generally used to refer to the physical land and improvements, whereas the term *real property* denotes
    A. air and subsurface rights.
    B. surface rights only.
    C. machinery and equipment.
    D. legal interests and rights inherent in ownership.

33. The private rights and privileges of real property ownership are limited by what four powers of government?
    A. Police power, eminent domain, taxation, escheat
    B. Police power, adverse possession, taxation, escheat
    C. Eminent domain, zoning, condemnation, taxation
    D. Zoning, police power, escheat, adverse possession

34. Which activity is *NOT* a public limitation on real estate?
    A. Building codes
    B. Zoning
    C. Adverse possession
    D. Fire codes

35. A written instrument, usually under seal, conveying some property interest from a grantor to a grantee is a common definition of
    A. mortgage.
    B. lease.
    C. deed.
    D. sales contract.

36. If the metes-and-bounds method of legally describing land is being used, which statement is correct?
    A. The starting point must be a natural benchmark.
    B. There must be a definite point of beginning.
    C. Monuments cannot be used as part of the description.
    D. No other method, such as lot-and-block, can be used as part of the description.

37. A current land use that existed prior to the establishment of a zoning district and is *NOT* consistent with the current restrictions imposed on land uses in that district is called a(n)
    A. variance.
    B. nonconforming use.
    C. illegal use.
    D. transitional use.

38. Which term refers to the legal interest belonging to a person who is leasing property from someone else?
    A. Leased fee estate
    B. Leasehold estate
    C. Fee simple estate
    D. Lessee's estate

39. In the valuation process, when does the reconciliation of value indications to a final value estimate take place?
    A. After completion of each approach
    B. After completion of all three approaches
    C. After the legal description is complete
    D. Periodically during the appraisal process

40. Which term refers to the stages that a neighborhood goes through over time?
    A. Revitalization
    B. Growth cycle
    C. Life cycle
    D. Change

41. Which statement is correct in regard to the range of value used in the final value estimate?
    A. There should be a single point estimate, not a range of values.
    B. A good range in values is plus or minus 5 percent.
    C. The range of value depends on the precision associated with the estimates and the confidence the appraiser has in the value.
    D. The price should be given in whole numbers.

42. The term *appraisal* refers to
    A. the process of estimating the market value of a property.
    B. the valuation of a market and how it affects property values.
    C. the process of estimating the most likely sales price of a property.
    D. the act or process of developing an opinion of value.

43. Comparing the physical components of the subject property with those of comparable properties is part of what step in the appraisal process?
    A. Defining the problem
    B. Collecting the data
    C. Analyzing data via the sales comparison approach
    D. Reconciling the value approaches

44. Why is it necessary for an appraiser to state the objective of the appraisal assignment clearly and in writing?
    A. It relieves the appraiser of any liability if he or she is sued.
    B. It defines the problem and identifies the specific type of value sought.
    C. All FHA and VA appraisals require it.
    D. It permits the appraiser to use only one of the traditional approaches to value.

45. The date of valuation for an appraisal is determined by
    A. the actual date the appraisal is signed.
    B. the date the appraisal assignment is accepted.
    C. the date the property is actually inspected.
    D. whatever date is specified in the appraisal report.

46. Which guideline is the primary one that should be followed by an appraiser in regard to the collection and analysis of data used in the appraisal process?
    A. They should be limited to public land records.
    B. They should be primary data only.
    C. They should be current.
    D. They should have a bearing or influence on the estimate of value.

47. What is the primary purpose of economic base analysis?
    A. To forecast future economic growth in an area and divide that growth between basic and nonbasic industries
    B. To forecast changes in local zoning ordinances
    C. To determine property tax rates and the likely amount of taxes due on property
    D. To forecast inflation rates

48. The valuation process has numerous steps that should be followed. Which step is *NOT* a normally acceptable one undertaken by an appraiser in the appraisal process?
    A. Definition of the problem
    B. Collection and analysis of data
    C. Averaging of the three approaches to value
    D. Report of the defined value

49. In using the sales comparison approach, the appraiser finds that in terms of location, sale #1 and sale #2 are superior to the subject. The correct procedure would be to adjust
    A. both sales down to the subject property.
    B. both sales up to the subject property.
    C. sale #1 down and sale #2 up.
    D. sale #1 up and sale #2 down.

50. Which statement *BEST* describes how the adjustment process is used in the sales comparison approach?
    A. The subject property is adjusted to the comparables to make it as similar as possible.
    B. The comparables are adjusted to the subject property to make them as similar as possible.
    C. The subject property is valued using its highest and best use.
    D. Accrued depreciation is subtracted from replacement cost to estimate the value of the subject property.

51. A single-family residence located on a busy street rents for $50 per month less than similar rental properties located on other streets in the same area. The average gross rent multiplier in this neighborhood is 110. What is the lump-sum dollar adjustment for the locational obsolescence of the residence?
    A. $50
    B. $600
    C. $5,000
    D. $5,500

52. Numerous elements of comparison are used by appraisers in the sales comparison approach. Which element is *NOT* one that should be employed in this approach?
    A. Conditions of sale
    B. Property rights being conveyed
    C. Cost
    D. Location

53. The adjustment in the sales comparison approach that involves comparing two properties with similar features and characteristics but different dates of sale is referred to as the
    A. loan closing adjustment.
    B. time adjustment (market conditions).
    C. appreciation in value adjustment.
    D. time value of money adjustment.

54. An appraiser is attempting to estimate the value of a house. The subject property has four bedrooms and a swimming pool. The appraiser has found three comparables that have recently sold:

Comparable	Sales Price	Bedrooms	Swimming Pool
1	$220,000	5	No
2	$200,000	4	No
3	$205,000	3	Yes

The appraiser estimates that each bedroom has a worth of $20,000 and a swimming pool a worth of $25,000.

Given the above information, what is the estimated value of the subject property using the average derived from the comparables?
    A. $200,000
    B. $220,000
    C. $225,000
    D. $240,000

55. A sales comparable sold one year ago for $62,000. Real estate values have increased 8 percent during the past year. The comparable is considered to be 15 percent more valuable than the subject property due to location and size. What is the estimated value of the subject property?
    A. $58,226
    B. $66,019
    C. $66,960
    D. $77,004

56. _____ cost is the estimated cost at current prices to construct an equivalent building using current standards, materials, design, and layout.
    A. Replacement
    B. Unit-in-place
    C. Reproduction
    D. Market

57. The building cost estimate method that finds the costs of the component parts of a building through standard cost estimates and then adjusts for the condition of the component, time, and location is known as the
    A. unit-in-place method.
    B. quantity survey method.
    C. break-down method.
    D. comparative unit method.

58. For functional obsolescence to be curable, the
    A. cost of replacing the feature must be less than the value of the feature.
    B. feature as improved must contribute to the income of the property.
    C. cost of replacing the feature must be the same as or less than the anticipated increase in value.
    D. contribution of the improved feature to the income of the property must be greater than the cost to install it.

59. Smith's house was built 12 years ago. Because he keeps it in excellent condition, it shows only as much wear as a typical five-year-old house. Smith's house therefore has an effective age of
    A. 5 years.
    B. 7 years.
    C. 12 years.
    D. 17 years.

60. The term *frontage* refers to the
    A. curb length along the perimeter of a property.
    B. width of a site.
    C. linear distance of a piece of land along a lake, river, street, or highway.
    D. distance between the front of a site and the back of the site.

61. Which set of terms best describes how functional obsolescence can be classified?
    A. Curable or incurable
    B. Curable or economic
    C. Incurable or physical
    D. Physical or economic

62. Which method is the most detailed in estimating the costs of reproducing a building as part of the cost approach to value?
    A. Unit-in-place
    B. Quantity survey
    C. Comparative unit
    D. Trade break-down

63. A residential neighborhood may suffer from economic obsolescence as a result of which condition?
    A. An increase in mortgage interest rates
    B. Expansion of an airport runway on an adjoining property
    C. Highest and best use of the surrounding land
    D. A decrease in the millage rate used to calculate property taxes

64. The cost approach to value takes into consideration all of these factors *EXCEPT*
    A. value of the land.
    B. replacement (reproduction) cost of the improvements.
    C. original sales price.
    D. physical defects.

65. A lot measuring 100 feet by 210 feet costs $31,500. At the same rate per square foot, what would a lot measuring 125 feet by 250 feet cost?
    A. $31,250
    B. $31,500
    C. $39,375
    D. $46,875

66. When using the cost approach to value, an appraiser should value the land as though
    A. it has been improved with a building.
    B. it is currently being used with an interim use.
    C. it is vacant and available for highest and best use.
    D. zoning ordinances are not being enforced and the local government will allow whatever use the appraiser deems necessary.

67. The process of combining two or more parcels of land into single ownership with the result that the value of the assembled site is worth more than the sum of the values of the individual sites is known as
    A. syndication.
    B. plottage.
    C. highest and best use.
    D. assemblage.

68. Corner influence is most important to the appraiser under which condition?
    A. Traffic flow on the road fronting the property is only one way.
    B. The property is zoned highway commercial.
    C. Access to the property is readily available.
    D. Investigation and analysis show corners to be more valuable.

69. The various traditional approaches to value involve the use of different techniques. In which approach(es) is the site valued separately from the valuation of the improvements?
    A. Cost approach
    B. Sales comparison approach
    C. Income approach
    D. Cost approach and sales comparison approach

70. A tract of land containing four acres recently sold for $6 per square foot. What is the estimated land value?
    A. $43,560
    B. $261,360
    C. $522,720
    D. $1,045,440

71. A house with a total living area of 2,500 square feet would cost $110 per square foot to reproduce new. It has an expected economic life of 50 years and is estimated to have an effective age of five years. The lot has a market value of $50,000. What is the estimated value of the property using the cost approach?
    A. $247,500
    B. $271,000
    C. $297,000
    D. $321,000

72. A residence has a physical deterioration that can be corrected for $5,000. However, if the correction is made, the value added will only be $3,000. How would an appraiser classify this item of depreciation when using the cost approach to value?
    A. Physical deterioration, incurable
    B. Physical deterioration, curable
    C. Physical deficiency, functionally incurable
    D. Physical deficiency, functionally curable

73. What is the correct percentage of accrued depreciation for a 15-year-old building if the building has an effective age of 20 years and a remaining economic life of 30 years?
    A. 20 percent
    B. 30 percent
    C. 40 percent
    D. 60 percent

74. In estimating accrued depreciation, the appraiser needs to know the historical or chronological age of the subject property. Such a period is commonly referred to as the building's
    A. actual age.
    B. effective age.
    C. economic age.
    D. remaining economic age.

75. When using the income approach to value, value is measured by estimating the present worth of the
    A. gross sales price.
    B. net operating income.
    C. outstanding mortgage balance.
    D. gross income multiplier.

76. The technique of capitalization is employed by the appraiser primarily in which approach?
    A. Sales comparison approach
    B. Cost approach
    C. Income approach
    D. Gross rent multiplier approach

77. You have assembled the following data on a comparable rental property, which you intend to use in estimating the gross rent multiplier for rental properties in a certain neighborhood:

Sales price:	$88,000
Annual rent:	$6,000
Property tax (monthly):	$75
Mortgage payment (monthly):	$700

   What is the monthly gross rent multiplier as indicated by this property?
   A. 14.7
   B. 100
   C. 110
   D. 176

78. In regard to the amortization of debt, which statement is incorrect?
   A. Amortization involves both payment of interest and repayment of principal.
   B. A loan may be fully amortized or partially amortized.
   C. Loan amortization always increases the equity that an investor has in the property.
   D. The amount of amortization is influenced by the length of time over which the loan is to be repaid.

79. The actual amount of rent specified in a lease is referred to as
   A. economic rent.
   B. market rent.
   C. contract rent.
   D. leaseback rent.

80. What payment period is normally used in calculating a gross rent multiplier for single-family residential rental property?
   A. Daily
   B. Weekly
   C. Monthly
   D. Annually

81. The income approach is probably most reliable when estimating the value for which type of property?
   A. Condominium
   B. Vacant land
   C. Office building
   D. Single-family residence

82. The Definitions section of the USPAP references an appraisal practice by three terms. *Appraisal practice,* as defined, includes
   A. market analysis.
   B. brokerage activities.
   C. appraisal consulting.
   D. investment analysis.

83. Even though important, which "product" of the Appraisal Standards Board has the *LEAST* direct impact on an appraiser?
   A. Advisory opinions
   B. Statements on standards
   C. Standards rules
   D. Standards

84. In regard to various statistical tests undertaken by appraisers, which statement is correct with respect to the median?
   A. The median and the mode are always the same.
   B. The median is the most commonly occurring value in a group.
   C. The median is the middle value in a group.
   D. The median is always greater than the mean.

85. A house with exterior dimensions of 60 feet by 49 feet has an area of
   A. 2,490 square feet.
   B. 2,940 square feet.
   C. 2,940 feet square.
   D. 2,940 cubic feet.

86. What term applies to the rent specified in a lease?
   A. Base rent
   B. Market rent
   C. Contract rent
   D. Gross rent

87. An assessment of real property refers to a(n)
   A. estimate of the interests in real property.
   B. determination of value.
   C. estimate of value.
   D. value for property tax purposes.

88. If the ad valorem tax is 1 percent, the property tax would be
    A. $1.
    B. $1 per $100 of assessed value.
    C. $1 per $100 of market value.
    D. 1 percent of the sales price.

89. The term *ground lease* applies to what type of lease?
    A. A lease that applies to the ground floor of a structure
    B. Any lease that includes land
    C. A lease allowing something to be removed from the land
    D. A lease that applies to the land only

90. The sales comparison approach is said to be the most reliable when which market exists?
    A. Active market
    B. Inactive market
    C. Buyer's market
    D. Seller's market

91. In the sales comparison approach, the correct steps for the appraiser to follow would be to _____ the dollar value of a feature present in the comparables but not in the subject property, while _____ the dollar value of a feature present in the subject property but not in the comparables.
    A. subtract, adding
    B. subtract, subtracting
    C. add, subtracting
    D. add, adding

92. A comparable property sold six months ago for $125,000. Market investigation indicates the following:

Location adjustment:	+5 percent
Time adjustment:	+6 percent
Age adjustment:	–7 percent

    Given the above information, what is the indicated value based on the comparable property?
    A. $123,225
    B. $129,386
    C. $130,000
    D. $132,500

93. Numerous elements should be identified when an appraiser is attempting to use the sales comparison approach to value. Which list best explains those elements of comparison?
    A. Demand, supply, utility, transferability
    B. Physical, functional, economic, locational
    C. Date of sale, location, physical condition, condition of sale
    D. Location, location, location, location

94. Under the Competency Rule of the USPAP, the appraiser must
    A. advise the client that he or she is a competent appraiser.
    B. have the knowledge and experience necessary to complete the assignment.
    C. disclose any extraordinary assumption or limiting condition that affects value.
    D. clearly and accurately set forth the appraisal in a manner that will not be misleading.

95. Which requirement is *NOT* a part of the USPAP Standard 1?
    A. The appraiser must not commit a substantial error of omission that significantly affects the appraisal.
    B. The appraisal must define the value being considered.
    C. The appraiser may not render appraisal services in a careless or negligent manner.
    D. The appraisal must contain sufficient information to enable intended users of the appraisal to understand the report properly.

96. Under the USPAP, the correct definition of a *report* is
    A. any written communication of an appraisal, review, or consulting service.
    B. any oral communication of an appraisal, review, or consulting service.
    C. any communication, written or oral, of an appraisal, appraisal review, or appraisal consulting service that is transmitted to the client upon completion of an assignment.
    D. the reporting of the value to the client.

97. Which statement is *NOT* required to be included in the certification statement per Standard 2 of the USPAP?
    A. The appraiser's compensation is not contingent upon the development or reporting of a predetermined value.
    B. The effective date of the appraisal and the date of the report are as stated.
    C. No one provided significant real property appraisal assistance to the person signing this certification.
    D. The appraiser has or has not made a personal inspection of the property that is the subject of this report.

APPLICATION-STYLE QUESTIONS

Questions 98 through 100 are based on the following information:

A property is owned by Abel and leased to Baker. Baker then leases the property to Collins.

98. Which term identifies the legal position of Abel?
    A. Leased fee
    B. Sandwich position
    C. Lessee
    D. Leasehold

99. What is the position of Baker?
    A. Leased fee
    B. Sandwich position
    C. Fee simple
    D. Lessor only

100. What is the position of Collins?
    A. Fee simple
    B. Subleasehold
    C. Sandwich position
    D. Lessor

Questions 101 through 105 are based on the following information:

Your current appraisal assignment involves a four-bedroom, three-bath home in an established neighborhood. Comparable properties with the exception of the house next door have been selling for between $290,000 and $340,000.

101. Comparable #1 is similar to the subject property except that it only has three bedrooms. If you believe a bedroom is worth $35,000, then the necessary adjustment should be to
    A. increase comp #1 by $35,000.
    B. decrease comp #1 by $35,000.
    C. increase subject property by $35,000.
    D. decrease subject property by $35,000.

102. Comparable #2 was built by the same builder as the subject property and is very similar to it except that it sold six months ago for $300,000 in a very active market where values are increasing 10 percent annually. A proper time adjustment for you to make would be to
    A. increase the adjustment for the subject property by $15,000.
    B. decrease the adjustment for the subject property by $15,000.
    C. increase the adjustment for comp #2 by $15,000.
    D. decrease the adjustment for comp #2 by $15,000.

103. The property next door sold one month ago
for $200,000. However, in researching the
sale you discover that a couple who had
lived in the house for ten years sold it to their
recently married son. Thus, it may be difficult
to adjust this sale in the adjustment process
due to
A. proximity of the subject property.
B. age of house.
C. age of buyer.
D. non-arm's-length transaction.

104. If similar properties in the neighborhood are
selling for between $290,000 and $340,000,
and if the subject property appraises within
this range of value, then on which economic
principle is this market action based?
A. Regression
B. Increasing and decreasing returns
C. Anticipation
D. Substitution

105. In appraising this property, the element of
comparison that would explain why the prop-
erty next door that sold from parents to son
might not be a comparable would be
A. date of sale.
B. location.
C. condition of sale.
D. unit of comparison.

ANSWERS TO RESIDENTIAL EXAM B

1. **B.** The principle of anticipation suggests that the value of a property is equal to the present value of the property's projected income. The principle of substitution applies indirectly in that the discount rate should reflect the opportunity cost associated with other investment opportunities.

2. **A.** Market value assumes a reasonable time on the market, not sale as soon as possible, which might reflect a discount for a distressed sale by a seller not typically motivated.

3. **C.** Equity refers to the amount of money invested in the property by the owner, whereas debt refers to the mortgage.

4. **D.** Competition affects the demand for real estate. For example, as other competing properties are constructed, the demand for the subject property will drop.

5. **A.** A time-distance relationship between one point and another is referred to as linkage.

6. **B.** The term *externalities* refers to the idea that influences outside a property's boundaries may have an effect on its value.

7. **C.** 10 percent of 500 = 50 homes per year.

8. **B.** The principle of substitution holds that whenever similar products are available, the product with the lowest price will attract the largest demand.

9. **C.** The two terms refer to entirely different things. However, under certain conditions the selling price of a property and the market value of that same property could be equal.

10. **B.** The use of a parcel of land that gives that land its greatest residual compensation is known as the highest and best use. While the particular use of a parcel of land may,

and often does, change, each and every parcel of land has a highest and best use.

11. **B.** The principle of contribution states that the value of a component part of a piece of property, such as an extra bathroom in a house, is equal to what that component adds to the total value, less any costs incurred.

12. **A.** The principle of conformity would explain why the correct placement of the house would influence value. Encroachment and escheat are not economic principles. The principle of substitution has to do with the cost of acquiring equally desirable substitutes.

13. **D.** The basic definition of highest and best use is that possible and legal use of land that will preserve the land's utility and generate the greatest income.

14. **D.** The relationship between the amount of money borrowed and the value of the property is known as the loan-to-value ratio. For example, a $100,000 property with a $75,000 loan would be referred to as having a 75 percent loan-to-value ratio.

15. **A.** The three types of appraisal reports are self-contained, summary, and restricted use.

16. **A.** Effective demand varies directly with purchasing power. As purchasing power increases, effective demand also increases. Likewise, a decrease in purchasing power would result in less demand.

17. **B.** *Manufactured housing* is a term used to denote what some people refer to as a mobile home. Condominiums and cooperatives are forms of ownership. A PUD (planned unit development) is a type of special land use permitted under many modern zoning ordinances.

18. **D.** The Scope of Work Rule requires the appraiser to identify certain assignment elements.

19. **B.** A fixture is treated as realty. Technically it is chattel real, which has become part of the real property and is thus realty.

20. **D.** An easement may be terminated. For example, an easement by necessity could be terminated if the need for creating the easement no longer exists. Such an easement would not have to be in writing, although it should be. Easements are real property rights and are not life estates because they run with the land.

21. **B.** Constructive notice is knowledge that the law assumes a person has about a particular fact, such as a worn path, regardless of whether the person actually knows about the fact. Actual notice would occur if the person actually knew the path existed. Lis pendens and escheat are legal terms not related to the subject matter of this question.

22. **C.** A variance is a type of safety valve provided through the zoning ordinance that allows a property owner who is unfairly burdened by a zoning restriction to seek relief; an irregularly shaped lot would be an example of such a burden. The remaining choices are all related to public limitations on real estate, but none of them answers the question.

23. **B.** Each individual owner is responsible for the taxes on his or her unit. Because each owner in a condominium project holds separate title, failure to pay property taxes may result in the taxing authority placing a lien on the individual unit.

24. **D.** The tax due is $800 ($40,000 × $2 ÷ $100). $800 is only 1 percent of the market value of $80,000.

25. **A.** The borrower is using the property as collateral; therefore the borrower is "giving" the lender a mortgage (security) against the property and is thus the mortgagor. The lender is the mortgagee.

26. **B.** The grantee is the buyer, while the grantor is the seller.

27. **B.** Eminent domain is the right of government to acquire private property. Condemnation is the process by which the property is taken. Police power and escheat are other government rights.

28. **B.** 100 × 140 = 14,000 square feet. $17,500 ÷ 14,000 = $1.25 per square foot.

29. **B.** Those portions of a condominium jointly owned by all unit owners but under the exclusive control or possession of only some of the owners are referred to as limited common elements. Walls between two units would be an example, as would balconies and enclosed courtyards.

30. **D.** Ownership of land encompasses three-dimensional space. This space consists of the land's surface, the space beneath, and the space above.

31. **A.** A fixture is broadly defined as personal property that has become real property. The tests used by courts include the manner of attachment, intention of the party who made the attachment, and the purpose for which the item is used. Age, cost, and/or market value are not considered in making this determination.

32. **D.** The term *real property* denotes the aggregate of rights, powers, and privileges inherent in the ownership of real estate.

33. **A.** The four limitations of the public sector placed on the rights and interests of real property are police power, eminent domain, taxation, and escheat.

34. **C.** Adverse possession is not a public limitation on real estate; rather, it is a method of acquiring title to real property by possession for a statutory period of time. Building codes, zoning, and fire codes

are all examples of the police power of government.

35. **C.** A deed conveys property interest from a grantor to a grantee. None of the other choices involves a transfer of legal interest from a grantor to a grantee.

36. **B.** One of the necessary requirements when land is being surveyed by the metes-and-bounds method is that a definite point of beginning be established. In addition to beginning at that point, the description will normally end with the wording, "and back to the point of beginning."

37. **B.** Quite often when a zoning district is created, some uses may exist that are not consistent with the current zoning ordinance. A nonconforming use may ordinarily remain; however, certain restrictions are usually imposed.

38. **B.** The leasehold estate is the legal interest of the tenant (lessee) and grants the tenant the right to possess the real property.

39. **B.** The purpose of reconciliation is to resolve the results of each approach to make a final value estimate. Thus it is done only after all three approaches are complete.

40. **C.** The neighborhood life cycle includes four periods of change: growth, stability, decline, and revitalization.

41. **C.** The type of final value estimate given depends on the precision of the data and confidence of the appraiser on the accuracy of the data. If the appraiser is not confident in the accuracy of the data, a value range should be used. The more inaccurate the data, the larger the range should be.

42. **D.** An appraisal is the act or process of developing an opinion of value. This does not have to be market value.

43. **C.** Part of the analysis undertaken in the sales comparison approach involves comparing the physical components of the subject property with those similar features in the comparables.

44. **B.** A necessary part of any completed appraisal assignment is a statement of the objective. This way, the appraiser can define the problem and identify the specific type of value (for example, market value) being sought in the appraisal assignment.

45. **D.** The actual date specified in the appraisal report determines the date of valuation.

46. **D.** Data collected and analyzed by an appraiser should have a bearing or influence on the estimated value; otherwise, there would be no reason to collect and analyze the data.

47. **A.** Economic base analysis is a technique used by market analysts and appraisers that attempts to measure the current economic activity and expected future economic growth in a specific geographic area.

48. **C.** While there are certain accepted steps that should be taken as part of the appraisal process, the averaging of the three approaches to value is not an acceptable step in that process. In many instances, the specific appraisal assignment will not involve the use of all three appraisal approaches, and never is the averaging of the three approaches an absolute part of the process.

49. **A.** Because both sale #1 and sale #2 are superior to the subject property, the correct procedure would be to adjust both of them down to the subject property. The fact that the two comparables are not equal to each other would possibly influence the amount of adjustment made for each.

50. **B.** In the sales comparison approach, the comparables are adjusted to the subject property to make them as similar as possible.

51. **D.** $50 × 110 = $5,500. In this instance, the economic obsolescence would be $5,500.

52. **C.** Cost is employed in the cost approach to value. In the sales comparison approach, cost is not an element of comparison as are conditions of sale, property rights being conveyed, and location.

53. **B.** The time adjustment allows for the difference in sales price as a result of sales occurring at different times. This adjustment is especially critical in markets where prices are moving quickly and where, within a reasonable period of time, prices change.

54. **C.** The adjusted sales prices for the three comparables would be: comparable 1—$225,000; comparable 2—$225,000; and comparable 3—$225,000. If the three comparables are average, the estimated value would be $225,000.

55. **A.** $62,000 × 1.08 = $66,960; $66,960 ÷ 1.15 = $58,226.

56. **A.** Replacement cost is the current cost of constructing a new building having utility equal to that of the property being approved. Reproduction cost is the cost at current prices to construct an exact duplicate or replica of the building being appraised using the same standards, materials, design, and layout.

57. **A.** The unit-in-place method or segregated cost method uses unit costs for building components and adds the labor cost. This is then multiplied by the area or volume measurement to find a total value. The total value of each of the components is summed to find the total value of the property.

58. **C.** Curable functional obsolescence is measured by the cost to cure the condition. If the property increases in value by more than what it costs to cure the condition, then the obsolescence is curable.

59. **A.** Effective age is measured by the condition and utility of the structure.

60. **C.** The frontage may be the same as the width of the site if it is regularly shaped. It is more precisely defined as the footage of a site along a lake, river, street, or other facility.

61. **A.** All functional obsolescence, as well as all physical deterioration, is classified either as curable or incurable.

62. **B.** The quantity survey method of estimating cost requires calculating the quantity and cost of each material item plus the total cost of installation.

63. **B.** Economic obsolescence is defined as a loss in value due to factors outside the subject property. An expansion of an airport runway on an adjoining property would be the only choice that could possibly result in economic obsolescence.

64. **C.** The original sales price of the property is not considered in estimating value based on the cost approach to value. All of the remaining choices are included in the cost approach.

65. **D.** 100 × 210 = 21,000 square feet; $31,500 ÷ 21,000 = $1.50 per square foot; 125 × 250 = 31,250 square feet; 31,250 × $1.50 = $46,875.

66. **C.** In the cost approach to value, the land is valued separately from any improvements and is thus valued based on an opinion of its highest and best use.

67. **D.** Assemblage results from the combining of two or more adjoining lots into one larger tract resulting in an increase in the total value of the assembled lots.

68. **D.** Corner influence refers to the additional value that a parcel of land has because of a corner location. For the corner lot to be valued as worth more, investigation and analysis would have to show that corner influence does exist.

69. **A.** The cost approach requires the appraisal of the site as if vacant and available at its highest and best use. Neither the sales comparison approach nor the income approach requires a separate appraisal of the site as part of the approach.

70. **D.** $43,560 \times \$6 = \$261,360$ per acre; $\$261,360 \times 4 = \$1,045,440$.

71. **C.** $2,500 \times \$110 = \$271,000$; $5 \div 50 = 1 \div 10$ or 0.10 deterioration; $\$271,000 \times 0.90 = \$247,500$ value of improvements; $\$247,500 + \$50,000 = \$297,500$ value of property.

72. **A.** An item of accrued depreciation is considered incurable if the cost to correct the defect is greater than the value added as a result of correcting the defect.

73. **C.** Accrued depreciation is defined as any loss in utility or value from the time of initial construction to the present. A building with an effective age of 20 years and a remaining economic life of 30 years suffers from 40 percent ($20 \div 50$) accrued depreciation.

74. **A.** The historical or chronological age of an improvement is commonly referred to as the improvement's actual age.

75. **B.** Under the income approach to value, value is defined as the present worth of income and, as such, the net operating income of the property is analyzed.

76. **C.** Capitalization of income is employed in the income approach.

77. **D.** $\$6,000 \div 12 = \$500$ monthly rent; $\$88,000 \div \$500 = 176$ monthly gross rent multiplier.

78. **C.** *Equity* is defined as the excess of a property's market value over and above the outstanding indebtedness. Thus a repayment of debt that is more than offset by a reduction in the property's value due to market forces will mean less equity for the investor.

79. **C.** The amount of rent due from the tenant according to the terms of the lease agreement is referred to as contract rent, as opposed to economic rent, which is the amount that would be received in an open, competitive market.

80. **C.** Normally a gross rent multiplier (GRM) is calculated based on a monthly collection of rent.

81. **C.** An office building is obviously most likely to be purchased on the basis of its rental income. Although some buildings are owner-occupied, office buildings are typically bought by investors and leased to tenants. Condominiums and single-family residences can be rented but are often (if not typically) bought to be occupied by the owner.

82. **C.** An appraisal practice is defined by three terms in the USPAP: *appraisal, appraisal review,* and *appraisal consulting.*

83. **A.** Advisory opinions do not establish new standards and are not enforceable; however, they have become exceedingly important.

84. **C.** The median is defined as the middle value of a group. The mean is the average value, and the mode is the most commonly occurring value in a group.

85. **B.** $60 \times 49 = 2,940$ square feet. Square feet is entirely different from either cubic feet or feet square.

86. **C.** Contract rent is the actual rent paid by the lessee. Contract rent does not always equal market rent.

87. **D.** An assessment of real property refers to a value for property tax purposes. The assessed value does not necessarily equal the market value. It is, however, based on market data.

88. **B.** Property tax is based on the assessed value, not the market value. However, the assessed value is usually based on the

market value. An ad valorem tax of 1 percent would mean $1 per $100 of assessed value.

89. **D.** A ground lease is a lease that applies to the land only. One method of finding land value is to capitalize the ground lease by a market-derived capitalization rate.

90. **A.** The sales comparison approach is considered a better indicator of market value when the market is active. The more activity, the more reliable is the data collected in the market.

91. **A.** In using the sales comparison approach, features present in the comparable and not in the subject property are subtracted, while the dollar value of a feature present in the subject property but not in the comparables is added. Remember, the comparables are always adjusted to the subject property; the subject property is never adjusted to the comparables.

92. **B.** $125,000 \times 1.06 = \$132,500$; $132,500 \times 1.05 \times 0.93 = \$129,386$.

93. **C.** In the sales comparison approach, the primary elements of comparison are normally divided into the categories of date of sale, location, physical condition, and the condition of sale.

94. **B.** The Competency Rule requires the appraiser to have the knowledge and experience necessary to complete the assignment.

95. **D.** The requirement that the appraisal must contain sufficient information to enable the intended users of the appraisal to understand the report properly is part of Standard Rule 2-1(b).

96. **C.** A report is defined as any communication, written or oral, of an appraisal, appraisal review, or appraisal consulting service that is transmitted to the client upon completion of an assignment.

97. **B.** The effective date of the appraisal and the date of the report are not required to be included in the certification. B is taken from S.R. 2-2(a). A, C, and D are from S.R. 2-3.

98. **A.** Abel has a leased fee estate. He is entitled to the rent received from Baker during the lease and then to the reversion at the end of the lease.

99. **B.** Baker is both a lessee and a lessor and thus has a sandwich position.

100. **B.** Collins is a sublessee and has a subleasehold position.

101. **A.** The comp is always adjusted, never the subject property. In this case, Comp #1 should be adjusted upward by $35,000.

102. **C.** To make the property time adjustment, comp #2 should be increased by $15,000 ($300,000 \times 0.10 \times 0.5 = \$15,000$).

103. **D.** Market value assumes arm's-length transactions. In this case, the selling of property to a family member is not an arm's-length transaction, and therefore it may be difficult to use this sale as a comparable.

104. **D.** The principle of substitution is based on the premise that a buyer will pay no more for a property than the cost of obtaining an equally desirable substitute. In this instance, the cost would be somewhere between $290,000 and $340,000.

105. **C.** Condition of sale is an element of comparison that refers to the motivations of the buyer and seller in a sales transaction. An example would include the relationship between the two parties—in this case, parents selling to their son.

Certified General
Exam A

1. Data obtained from published sources are referred to as
   A. primary data.
   B. secondary data.
   C. general data.
   D. specific data.

2. What term is used to describe tangible and intangible factors that enhance the desirability and thus add to the value of real estate?
   A. Amenities
   B. Goodies
   C. Enhancements
   D. Negative externalities

3. Market rental rates tend to be set at the rate that prevails for equally desirable space. This is a reflection of what appraisal principle?
   A. Anticipation
   B. Balance
   C. Substitution
   D. Competition

4. In the short run, which condition has the most effect on real estate prices?
   A. More changes in demand than changes in supply
   B. More changes in supply than changes in demand
   C. More inflation than demand
   D. More sellers than buyers

5. The process of identifying and analyzing sub-markets of a larger market is known as
   A. extraction.
   B. market allocation.
   C. market segmentation.
   D. substitution.

6. What term is used to describe the value to a typical investor?
   A. Market value
   B. Investment value
   C. Sale value
   D. Use value

7. The term *absorption rate* refers to
   A. an estimate of the expected annual sales or new occupancy of a particular type of land use.
   B. an estimate of the rate at which a type of real estate space will be sold or occupied.
   C. the rate at which the cash flow from a property will cover the initial investment in the property.
   D. the rate of return used to convert future payments into present cash values.

8. The proximity of a parcel of land to a supporting land use is referred to as
   A. location quotient.
   B. linkage.
   C. highest and best use.
   D. land efficiency.

9. If an appraiser is asked to render an opinion of value based on the specific requirements and needs of a purchaser or investor, the appraiser is more than likely estimating which value?
   A. Market value
   B. Investment value
   C. Value in exchange
   D. Sales value

10. When a property's highest and best use is in a stage of transition, which action is required of the appraiser?
   A. Consider interim use
   B. Ignore interim use
   C. Consider interim use only if it results in a higher value
   D. Consider interim use only if it results in a lower value

11. Which statement applies to a property with a nonconforming use?
   A. The existing nonconforming use is the highest and best use.
   B. A nonconforming use is likely to arise from changes in zoning.
   C. A nonconforming-use property may be underimproved but cannot be overimproved.
   D. In the sales comparison approach, an appraiser does not have to make a separate adjustment for the nonconforming use.

12. Which type of legal description method is *NOT* commonly found in urban or metropolitan areas?
   A. Metes-and-bounds
   B. Recorded plat
   C. Lot-and-block
   D. Monuments

13. The common areas in a condominium project normally are owned by whom?
   A. The developer
   B. The homeowners' association
   C. Each individual unit owner
   D. The board of directors of the homeowners' association

14. Owner *A* gives owner *B* an easement across *A*'s land to shorten the distance *B* has to travel to reach land he owns. The land *B* owns has benefited by this easement and is known as the
   A. dominant estate.
   B. servient estate.
   C. lien estate.
   D. estate in gross.

15. A strip of land used to separate two adjoining parcels of land that have incompatible uses, such as a residential subdivision and an industrial park, is referred to as a
   A. buffer zone.
   B. planned unit development.
   C. nonconforming use.
   D. variance.

16. The annual property tax on a parcel of land you are appraising is $756. The taxing authority assesses land at 60 percent of market value. If the tax rate is $1.80 per $100 (18 mills), what is the estimated market value of the land?
   A. $42,000
   B. $58,800
   C. $70,000
   D. $75,600

17. A parcel of land 440 feet by 792 feet contains how many acres?
   A. 4
   B. 8
   C. 12
   D. 36

18. In regard to an unpaid property tax that has become due and payable, which statement is *NOT* correct?
   A. The property tax is a specific lien against the property.
   B. The claim of the taxing authority is superior to any private claim.
   C. The property may be sold to satisfy the claim.
   D. Any other property owned by the individual owner may be sold to satisfy the claim against the property in question.

19. A description of the surface features of a parcel of land such as elevation or drainage is known as its
    A. location.
    B. plottage.
    C. topography.
    D. restrictive covenant.

20. Which test would be appropriate for determining when personal property becomes real property?
    A. Items attached are personal property if not classified as trade fixtures.
    B. Items attached are personal property if attached by the lessee.
    C. Items attached are personal property if the tenant is on a month-to-month lease.
    D. Items attached are personal property if they can be removed without damage.

21. A proprietary lease is often used in conjunction with which type of real estate ownership?
    A. Condominium
    B. Cooperative
    C. Time-sharing
    D. Life estate

22. In appraising a condominium, an appraiser should consider which approach(es) to value?
    A. Cost approach
    B. Sales comparison approach
    C. Income capitalization
    D. All three approaches

23. An owner of a parcel of land leases the land to a tenant for ten years. The next day the owner sells the land to a third party. Which statement is correct?
    A. The new owner has an option as to whether to accept the terms of the lease.
    B. The tenant may voluntarily terminate the lease.
    C. The tenant's leasehold is not affected.
    D. The tenant's legal interest is automatically terminated by operation of law.

24. Which statement in regard to zoning is *NOT* correct?
    A. Zoning is based on police power.
    B. Zoning is ordinarily compensatory in nature.
    C. Zoning power is ordinarily granted from the state to local government through enabling legislation.
    D. Zoning may be both directive and protective.

25. Which statement is correct for the purpose of estimating vacancy rates in an appraisal used to estimate the value of a fee simple estate?
    A. Projects that are the highest and best use of the site normally would have no vacancy.
    B. The vacancy rate used in an appraisal normally should be the vacancy rate currently experienced by the project.
    C. The vacancy rate used in an appraisal should reflect the typical vacancy rate for comparable properties.
    D. The vacancy rate should never be zero.

26. An appraiser calculates the present value of income based on the contract rent and adds the present value of the reversion at the end of the lease. What legal interest is being valued?
    A. Life estate
    B. Leased fee estate
    C. Fee simple estate
    D. Leasehold estate

27. When valuing a property as a fee simple estate, which rent should be used?
    A. Market rent
    B. Contract rent
    C. Percentage rent
    D. Overage rent

28. When a property's highest and best use can reasonably be expected to change in the near future, the prevailing highest and best use is referred to as a(n)
    A. interim use.
    B. temporary use.
    C. secondary use.
    D. current use.

29. The purpose of an appraisal assignment is usually to estimate which type of value?
    A. Investment value
    B. Market value
    C. Value in use
    D. Replacement value

30. Which approach(es) to value uses market data?
    A. Income approach
    B. Direct sales comparison approach
    C. Cost approach
    D. All three approaches

31. An appraisal report can either be
    A. oral or based on the complete analysis required for a written report.
    B. oral or in writing.
    C. based on market data or based on the highest and best use.
    D. narrative or in writing.

32. To be the highest and best use of an improved site, the current use must
    A. conform to the interim use.
    B. be the same as anticipated future uses.
    C. conform to current building codes.
    D. have no obsolescence.

33. An appraiser's final estimate of value of income property should be based on
    A. the average of the value from the three approaches.
    B. the approach with the highest value.
    C. a reconciliation of the three approaches to value.
    D. the approach with the most conservative value.

34. The level of vacancy of five-bedroom apartments in a particular city provides which type of information (data) to an appraiser?
    A. Supply information
    B. General data
    C. Demand information
    D. Secondary data

35. Which concept *BEST* describes the process of gentrification?
    A. A period of diminishing demand
    B. The process of identifying and analyzing submarkets within a larger market
    C. The perception that value is created by the expectation of benefits to be received in the future
    D. A period where neighborhood properties are renovated and improved

36. As an appraiser you attempt to render an opinion of value of a particular residential property using the listing price of similar properties included in a multiple listing service. Without any adjustments on your part, the derived value based solely on this information would more than likely be
    A. below market value.
    B. above market value.
    C. approximately equal to market value.
    D. 6 percent greater due to the commission rate.

37. In the sales comparison approach to value, physical units of comparison are often used to adjust for which condition?
    A. Location
    B. Scenic view
    C. Size
    D. Surrounding land uses

38. In appraising a house, the appraiser finds that comparable *A* is similar to the subject property and sold for $90,000. Comparable *B* is also similar except it has one additional bedroom and sold for $98,000. In regard to the extra bedroom, what adjustment is made?
    A. Add $8,000 to the subject property.
    B. Add $8,000 to the comparable.
    C. Subtract $8,000 from the subject property.
    D. Subtract $8,000 from the comparable.

39. The comparable sales (market) approach to value is generally considered to be the *MOST* reliable when
    A. the improvements are new and unoccupied.
    B. a ready access to current market data exists.
    C. the land is vacant and the rate of inflation is high.
    D. functional obsolescence does not exist.

40. A lot on a commercially zoned street contains 105,000 square feet and has a depth of 300 feet. Commercial land in the area is currently selling for $400 per front foot. What is the indicated value of the lot?
    A. $43,560
    B. $105,000
    C. $120,000
    D. $140,000

41. The process of assembling two or more sites under a single ownership so that a value increment is derived is referred to as
    A. zoning.
    B. highest and best use.
    C. plottage.
    D. linkage.

42. The estimated period of time over which improvements continue to contribute to property value is known as the
    A. total physical life.
    B. remaining economic life.
    C. remaining physical life.
    D. total useful life.

43. The age-life method of computing depreciation uses which period of time to estimate depreciation?
    A. Effective age and remaining economic life
    B. Actual age and remaining economic life
    C. Effective age and actual age
    D. Actual age and remaining physical life

44. What term is used to show the relationship between the number of off-street parking spaces and the number of building units in a particular development?
    A. Building ratio
    B. Floor area ratio
    C. Parking ratio
    D. External ratio

45. Which statement is correct in regard to a building's age?
    A. A building's effective age is always equal to or less than its actual age.
    B. A building's effective age equals the number of years since construction was completed.
    C. Physical age is determined by the condition and utility of the building.
    D. A building's effective age may be greater than its actual age.

46. After deducting the cost to cure physically curable items, the cost of incurable physical deterioration is measured by
    A. applying the ratio of effective age to estimated total physical life to the reproduction or replacement cost of each component.
    B. calculating the cost of restoring a component to new or reasonably new condition, i.e., the cost to cure.
    C. calculating the cost of installing the modern component minus the remaining value of the existing component.
    D. calculating the reproduction cost of the item minus any physical deterioration already charged plus the cost to install a normally adequate or standard item.

47. The difference between a particular building's actual layout and the building's ideal layout is referred to as
    A. physical disfiguration.
    B. functional obsolescence.
    C. locational obsolescence.
    D. economic obsolescence.

48. Which type of property should *NEVER* be appraised by using only the cost approach to value?
    A. Vacant land
    B. Vacant warehouses
    C. Government buildings
    D. Historic buildings

49. Which statement is *NOT* correct in regard to the chronological age of a building?
    A. Chronological age and actual age refer to the same period of time.
    B. Chronological age may be greater than or less than effective age.
    C. Chronological age is normally easier to establish than effective age.
    D. Chronological age and economic life refer to the same period of time.

50. The cost approach to value would have the *MOST* application and reliability under which situation?
    A. The improvements have suffered significant depreciation and are more than 20 years of age.
    B. Numerous comparables are in the immediate area, and the market is currently very active.
    C. The property being appraised is vacant.
    D. The improvements are new, and the site is being used under its highest and best use.

51. Numerous methods and techniques are used to estimate replacement or reproduction cost. The method that measures the total square footage or cubic footage of a building and then multiplies this total by a current cost per square foot or cubic foot factor is known as the
    A. quantity survey method.
    B. unit-in-place method.
    C. comparative unit method.
    D. price index method.

52. In using the cost approach to value, the cost method in which the appraiser groups the cost of a building into major components such as the foundation, walls, and heating is referred to as the
    A. square-foot method.
    B. unit-in-place method.
    C. quantity survey method.
    D. index method.

53. You have accepted an appraisal assignment to estimate the value of a square city block that has suffered from total fire damage. Your client is interested in selling the property. Which step should you take?
    A. Apply the comparable sales approach
    B. Estimate the highest and best use of the land
    C. Apply the cost approach and make adjustments to physical deterioration for the fire damage
    D. Find out how long it will take to rebuild the buildings and use the income approach to estimate the expected income stream

54. A lot measures 600 feet by 800 feet. What is its total land value if the land is worth $15,000 per acre?
    A. $15,000
    B. $43,560
    C. $48,000
    D. $165,300

55. An office building has a leasable area of 45,000 square feet. Its current reproduction cost is $130 per square foot. The building is on one acre of land. Comparable land costs $30 per square foot. Because the building is poorly designed, the building suffers a loss of $250,000 in functional obsolescence. What is the total value of the property using the cost approach?
    A. $5,600,000
    B. $5,850,000
    C. $6,906,800
    D. $4,566,800

56. An industrial building has a physical deterioration that can be corrected for $50,000. If the correction is made, the value added to the property will be $100,000. How would an appraiser classify this item of depreciation when using the cost approach to value?
    A. Physical deterioration, incurable
    B. Physical deterioration, curable
    C. Physical deficiency, functionally incurable
    D. Physical deficiency, functionally curable

57. As the degree of risk and uncertainty associated with the income potential of property increases, the income generated by that property may be capitalized at a higher rate. This action will bring about which result?
    A. A higher capitalization rate will mean a higher value.
    B. A higher capitalization rate will mean a lower value.
    C. A change in the capitalization rate will have no bearing on the estimate of value.
    D. A change in the capitalization rate will have an effect on value only if the property is being used under its highest and best use.

58. Which estimate would result in a capitalization rate of 20 percent?
    A. Potential gross income $100,000; value $500,000
    B. Effective gross income $100,000; value $500,000
    C. Net operating income $100,000; value $500,000
    D. Cash flow $100,000; value $500,000

59. An office building has 10,000 square feet of net leasable space. The owner has an annual mortgage payment of $75,000 and expects operating expenses to be $25,000. If the owner wants a before-tax cash flow of $50,000, what should the gross rent per square foot be on a monthly basis?
    A. $1.00
    B. $1.25
    C. $1.50
    D. $15.00

60. Why is the gross income multiplier normally *NOT* subject to adjustments by the appraiser?
    A. It is impossible to make adjustments when using income data.
    B. Relative desirability is presumed to be reflected in the gross income generated in the marketplace.
    C. Any differences between properties would be insignificant.
    D. The income approach never allows for adjustments of any kind.

61. In estimating the net operating income of a building, one of the necessary steps is the calculation of "other income." Which item is *NOT* considered other income?
    A. Parking fees
    B. Telephone switchboard services
    C. TV closed-circuit connection fees
    D. Escalation clauses in leases

62. Which statement is correct in regard to a mortgage constant?
    A. It is equal to the interest rate being paid.
    B. If the loan is being amortized, then it is always greater than the interest rate.
    C. If the loan is being amortized, then it is always less than the interest rate.
    D. The amount of the mortgage constant increases as the term of the loan increases.

63. Which estimate will result in a capitalization rate of 10 percent?
    A. Value $500,000; gross income $50,000
    B. Value $500,000; effective gross income $50,000
    C. Value $500,000; net operating income $50,000
    D. Value $500,000; cash flow $50,000

64. Suppose a property's NOI and value are not expected to change over an investment holding period. What would be the relationship between the overall rate and the property yield rate?
    A. The overall rate would be less than the property yield rate.
    B. The overall rate would be equal to the property yield rate.
    C. The overall rate would be greater than the property yield rate.
    D. More information is required to determine the relationship between the overall rate and the property yield rate.

65. What information is *NOT* needed to apply the building residual technique?
    A. Building value
    B. Land value
    C. Net operating income
    D. Land and building capitalization rates

66. Which term *BEST* describes a pattern of income or cash flow that is regular and predictable?
    A. Reversion
    B. Lease
    C. Annuity
    D. Payment

67. Which calculation is *NOT* a type of yield rate?
    A. Internal rate of return
    B. Discount rate
    C. Overall capitalization rate
    D. Interest rate

68. If interest rates were 8 percent but they rose by 50 basis points, what would the new rate be?
    A. 8.5 percent
    B. 12.0 percent
    C. 13.0 percent
    D. 58.0 percent

69. What term is used to denote the difference, if any, between the present value of expected benefits, or positive cash flows, and the present value of capital outlays, or negative cash flows?
    A. Profitability index
    B. Net present value
    C. Internal rate of return
    D. Net cash flow

70. A property has NOI of $10,000, interest payments of $8,000, and principal payments of $1,000. What is the debt coverage ratio?
    A. 0.80
    B. 0.90
    C. 1.11
    D. 1.25

71. Given the following information:

    Building capitalization rate: 0.11
    Land capitalization rate: 0.09
    Land value as a percent of
       total value: 35 percent

    What is the overall capitalization rate by using the band of investment approach?
    A. 0.097
    B. 0.100
    C. 0.103
    D. 0.110

72. Which term *BEST* explains the technique of adjusting a sales price downward to reflect the effect that favorable financing probably had on the sales price of a property?
    A. Comparison unit technique
    B. Break-down technique
    C. Cash equivalency technique
    D. Extraction technique

73. A small restaurant contains an oven and a freezer, each of which costs $7,000 and has an estimated useful life of ten years. Carpeting costs $4,900 and has an estimated useful life of seven years. What annual reserve for replacement would be appropriate for these items?
    A. $1,400
    B. $1,890
    C. $2,100
    D. $18,900

74. Given the following information, what is the building capitalization rate for the subject property?

Land value:	$60,000
Net operating income:	$25,000
Land capitalization rate:	8 percent
Overall capitalization rate:	9 percent

    A. 10.9 percent
    B. 9.3 percent
    C. 8.4 percent
    D. 8.8 percent

75. If a property has a net income ratio of 0.75 and a gross income multiplier of 9, what is the indicated overall capitalization rate?
    A. 2.78 percent
    B. 6.75 percent
    C. 8.33 percent
    D. 12.00 percent

76. If a property has an overall capitalization rate of 0.095 and a mortgage at a 75 percent loan-to-value ratio having an annual mortgage constant of 0.11, what is the equity dividend rate?
    A. 0.05
    B. 0.06
    C. 0.07
    D. 0.09

77. The appraiser collects the following information for a proposed new building assumed to be the highest and best use of the site:

Net operating income:	$150,000
Land capitalization rate:	0.09
Building capitalization rate:	0.11
Building value (based on cost):	$1,100,000

    What is the *BEST* estimate of the value of the property?
    A. $1,221,000
    B. $1,250,000
    C. $1,422,222
    D. $1,500,000

78. Two properties currently have the same NOI and the appraiser feels that each would probably be purchased on the basis of the same required rate of return over a five-year holding period. However, due to existing leases, the NOI for property *A* will not increase during the five years, whereas the NOI for property *B* is expected to increase over the five years. What would be *TRUE* for the overall capitalization rates for the two properties when they are purchased?
    A. The capitalization rate for property *A* should be lower than that for *B*.
    B. The capitalization rate for property *A* should be higher than that for *B*.
    C. The capitalization rate could be higher or lower for *A* versus *B*.
    D. The capitalization rates should be the same for *A* and *B*.

79. What is the present value of an annuity of $100 per year for the next five years using a 10 percent discount rate?
    A. $379.08
    B. $450.00
    C. $550.00
    D. $772.17

80. A discount rate of 10 percent applied to a $100 sum expected to be received in one year results in a present value of
    A. $90.
    B. $90.90.
    C. $100.
    D. $110.

81. The term *effective rate* refers to the
    A. loan constant on a mortgage.
    B. true rate of return considering all relevant financing expenses.
    C. interest rate after inflation is considered.
    D. rate at which future payments are discounted to present cash flows.

82. An investment requires a $10,000 negative cash flow for the first three years, then offers $8,500 of cash inflows for years 4–10. Using a "safe rate" of 5 percent, the negative cash flows have a present value of $27,232. If cash inflows are reinvested at 10 percent, the cash inflows will have a future value of $80,641. What is the FMRR?
    A. 6.97 percent
    B. 8.06 percent
    C. 8.74 percent
    D. 11.47 percent

83. The term *holding period* usually refers to the
    A. time span in which improvements continue to contribute to value.
    B. period of time over which net income remains greater than operating expenses.
    C. time span of ownership.
    D. period of time that has elapsed since construction of the improvements.

84. The following income statement is provided the appraiser by the building owner:

Rental income		$10,000
Less:		
Utilities	$1,500	
Property taxes	1,000	
Management fee	500	
Maintenance expenses	2,000	
Interest	2,000	
Depreciation allowance	1,000	
Income taxes	1,000	
Subtotal		– 9,000
Net income		$1,000

    What is the NOI?
    A. $1,000
    B. $2,000
    C. $4,000
    D. $5,000

85. An income-producing property requires a $10,000 investment. The property promises a $1,000 annual return for five years, then resale proceeds of $15,000. What is the IRR (nearest percent)?
    A. 10 percent
    B. 14 percent
    C. 15 percent
    D. 17 percent

86. A tenant has signed a lease in which the rent is based on the appraised value of the property. During the first year the property is appraised for $400,000 and the rent is $36,000. If during the second year the property increases in value to $440,000, what is the annual rent for the second year?
    A. $36,000
    B. $36,600
    C. $39,600
    D. $44,000

87. In an office building where there are a number of different tenants, which ratio defines the amount of net rentable area to the total gross area?
    A. Net income ratio
    B. Efficiency ratio
    C. Use ratio
    D. Net efficient ratio

88. A commercial building leases for $3,000 per month. If the building's dimensions are 60 feet by 80 feet, what is the annual rent per square foot?
    A. $0.63
    B. $1.00
    C. $7.50
    D. $12.00

89. What term would apply to a lease that requires the lessor to pay all operating expenses associated with the real estate?
    A. Index lease
    B. Gross lease
    C. Net lease
    D. Pass-through lease

90. Which explanation applies to the term *base rent?*
    A. The actual rent specified in a lease
    B. The minimum rent payable under a percentage lease
    C. The typical rent paid for comparable properties
    D. The minimum rent multiplied by an index to find the actual rent in an index lease

91. Discount Foods is leasing a store for $10,000 per month rent. If the landlord could rent the store on a new lease now, it would command $15,000 per month. What is the contract rent?
    A. $6,000
    B. $10,000
    C. $14,000
    D. $15,000

92. Standard 1 of the USPAP states that
    A. the appraiser must communicate each analysis, opinion, and conclusion in a manner that is not misleading.
    B. the appraiser must be aware of, understand, and correctly employ those recognized methods and techniques that are necessary to produce a credible appraisal.
    C. the appraiser must carefully consider the knowledge and experience that will be required to complete the assignment competently.
    D. the analyst must be aware of, understand, and correctly employ those recognized methods and techniques necessary to produce a credible analysis.

93. Clearly and accurately disclosing all assumptions, extraordinary assumptions, hypothetical conditions, and limiting conditions that directly affect the appraisal and indicating impact on value is a requirement of which USPAP standard or rule?
    A. The Scope of Work Rule
    B. Standard 1
    C. Standard 2
    D. Standard 3

94. All of these actions are requirements of USPAP Standard 1 *EXCEPT*
    A. considering the extent of the data-collection process.
    B. defining the value to be estimated.
    C. stating the name(s) of anyone providing significant professional assistance to the person signing the certification.
    D. identifying any hypothetical conditions in the assignment.

95. The USPAP Ethics Rule contains four sections. Which activity is part of the Ethics Rule?
    A. Scope of work
    B. Confidentiality
    C. Jurisdictional exception
    D. Competency

96. Standard 1 of the USPAP contains numerous requirements. All of these actions are requirements of Standard 1 *EXCEPT*
    A. defining the value being considered.
    B. identifying the real property interest.
    C. considering leases, easements, or other items of a similar nature.
    D. using and explaining all three traditional approaches to value.

97. With regard to the certification statement required by the USPAP in each written real property appraisal report, which statement is *TRUE?*
    A. If anyone provided significant real property appraisal assistance to the person signing the report, the appraiser signing the report may want to include the name of the person who offered the assistance.
    B. The appraiser signing the certification must certify that he or she personally accepted the subject property.
    C. The appraiser must certify that his or her compensation is contingent on the reporting of a predetermined value that favors the cause of the client.
    D. The appraiser should state whether he or she has any present or prospective interest in the property that is the subject of the report.

98. According to Standard 2 of the USPAP, an appraiser who signs any part of the appraisal report, including a letter of transmittal, must also
    A. be a certified general appraiser.
    B. sign the certification.
    C. personally inspect the property before signing the report.
    D. receive at least 50 percent of the appraisal fee.

99. "Having the knowledge and experience necessary to complete the assignment" is part of which USPAP rule?
    A. Departure Rule
    B. Ethics Rule
    C. Competency Rule
    D. Jurisdictional Exception Rule

100. Standard 2 of the USPAP requires the appraiser to "clearly and conspicuously state all extraordinary assumptions and hypothetical conditions and state that their use might have affected the assignment results." Which condition would be an example of such activity?
    A. Completion of off-site improvements
    B. Execution of a personal property bill of sale for one of the comps
    C. Revocation of an appraiser's certification by the state appraisal board
    D. Atypical financing of the properties in the neighborhood

101. In regard to analyzing current agreements of sale of the subject property current as of the effective date of the appraisal, which statement is *TRUE?*
    A. This requirement is always optional.
    B. The information, if available to the appraiser in the normal course of business, must be analyzed.
    C. The time frame cited in the requirement is maximum.
    D. The minimum period to be covered for all property types is one year.

APPLICATION-STYLE QUESTIONS

Questions 102 through 105 are based on the following data collected by an appraiser in regard to office space and the annual rent paid on a square-foot basis:

Office Building	Rent per Square Foot
1	$12
2	$17
3	$14
4	$15
5	$15
6	$16
7	$17
8	$17
9	$18
10	$19

102. What is the mean?
    A. $15
    B. $15.7
    C. $16
    D. $16.5

103. What is the median?
    A. $15
    B. $15.7
    C. $16
    D. $17

104. What is the mode?
    A. $15
    B. $15.7
    C. $16
    D. $17

105. What is the range?
    A. $0
    B. $6
    C. $12
    D. $18

Questions 106 through 110 are based on the following information in regard to the appraisal of an apartment complex:

You have been asked to appraise a 50-unit apartment complex. Thirty of the units rent for $700 per month and the remaining units rent for $600 per month. The vacancy rate is 5 percent and the operating expenses are 35 percent of EGI.

106. What is the annual NOI?
    A. $244,530
    B. $252,000
    C. $396,000
    D. $376,200

107. Using direct capitalization, what is the estimated value of the property if you assume a 12 percent market cap rate?
    A. $1,349,600
    B. $2,037,750
    C. $3,135,000
    D. $3,300,000

108. If the property sells for $2 million, what is the estimated ROI?
    A. 8.5%
    B. 10%
    C. 12.2%
    D. 15.5%

109. If the property sells for $2 million and is financed with an 80 percent, 20-year, 9 percent interest rate fully amortized loan, what is the BTCF?
    A. $82,579
    B. $161,951
    C. $244,530
    D. $396,000

110. Given the information calculated above, what is the break-even ratio?
    A. 5%
    B. 35%
    C. 66%
    D. 74%

ANSWERS TO GENERAL EXAM A

1. **B.** Secondary data are published by other sources, whereas primary data are gathered by the appraiser.

2. **A.** The term *amenities* refers to positive factors that enhance property value. An example would be an excellent view of a golf course from a residence. An amenity might also be referred to as a *positive externality.*

3. **C.** The principle of substitution is the best answer. It is one of the appraisal principles cited in most textbooks and expresses the concept that the price of an economic good, in this case space (e.g., rent), depends on the price of substitute goods.

4. **A.** The supply of real estate is measured by the amount of property for lease or sale. Because the amount of available real estate can change only as quickly as it can be built or renovated, supply changes more slowly than demand.

5. **C.** Markets can be subdivided into submarkets by price, location, and type of purchaser. The process of identifying and analyzing these submarkets is called *market segmentation.* Allocation and extraction refer to methods of land valuation.

6. **A.** Market value is the value to a typical investor, whereas investment value is the value to a specific investor.

7. **B.** An absorption rate is the measure of the rate at which a type of real estate space will be sold or occupied.

8. **B.** Linkage refers to the location, as measured in time and distance, of a particular parcel of land to supporting land uses.

9. **B.** Investment value is defined as the worth of investment property to a specific investor. This will change from investor to investor and from situation to situation.

10. **A.** The interim use of the property, regardless of its effect on value, should be considered by the appraiser.

11. **B.** A nonconforming use is a use that was formerly legally permissible but is not acceptable under current zoning.

12. **D.** The monuments method of legally describing land is often found in older descriptions in rural or nonurban areas where the land has not been platted for development. Such a method is not common in urban areas. In some jurisdictions the monuments method, if it is the only one being used, will not be accepted as having sufficiently described the land.

13. **C.** The common areas in a condominium are owned on a pro rata basis by each individual unit owner.

14. **A.** The estate that benefits from the creation of an easement is known as the dominant estate. Owner *A*'s land is the servient estate since it is burdened by the creation of the easement.

15. **A.** The purpose of the buffer zone is to provide for the "blending" of the two incompatible uses with each other. All three of the other choices are terms found in zoning discussion, but each has an entirely different meaning than the term *buffer zone.*

16. **C.** $756 \div 0.018 = \$42,000$; $\$42,000 \div 0.6 = \$70,000$.

17. **B.** $440 \times 792 = 348,480$ square feet; $348,480 \div 43,560 = 8$ acres.

18. **D.** A property tax is a specific lien and is thus levied against a specific property. Other property of the owner cannot be sold to satisfy the financial claim. A property tax claim that has not been paid may result in the property being sold to satisfy the lien.

19. **C.** Topography refers to the surface features of a parcel of land.

20. **D.** One of the tests applied by courts in regard to whether an item is personal property or real property is the manner in which the item is attached. If the items can be removed without damage to the real property, then they are considered personal property.

21. **B.** A proprietary lease is used in a cooperative apartment. Such a lease gives the tenant the right to occupy a certain apartment unit.

22. **D.** Even though a condominium is a unique form of ownership, the appraisal of a condominium does not limit the appraiser to only one approach; thus the appraiser should consider all three approaches. The appropriate technique(s) employed would need to be determined by the appraiser.

23. **C.** A lease creates rights and liabilities between the landlord and the tenant and operates both as a conveyance of property interest and as a contract between the landlord and the tenant. Thus the selling of property currently being leased does not affect the tenant's leasehold.

24. **B.** When police power such as zoning is used, the governing agency is not required to compensate a property owner for any loss in property values as a result of the regulation.

25. **C.** The appraiser should attempt to determine what vacancy rate is typical for comparable properties. This is what the vacancy rate is likely to be for the subject property under normal management and market rental rates. Although highly unlikely, it is conceivable that the typical vacancy rate is zero due to unusually high demand with preleasing of space. Thus we cannot say it would never be zero.

26. **B.** The leased fee estate has the rights to the contract rent and reversion at the end of the lease. The value of a fee simple estate would be based on market rent.

27. **A.** Market rent is used for a fee simple estate, which is the value unencumbered by any leases.

28. **A.** Interim use refers to the existing use when the property's highest and best use can reasonably be expected to change.

29. **B.** In most cases the purpose is to estimate market value, e.g., the most probable selling price. The price a particular buyer will pay may be less (if he or she can get a good deal) or more (if necessary and justified by a higher investment value or value in use).

30. **D.** The direct sales comparison approach was formerly referred to (and still is by some) as the market data approach. However, this is somewhat of a misnomer because data from the market is used for all three approaches to estimate value. For example, the income approach uses market data about rents, expenses, and discount rates. The cost approach uses market data about construction costs and market perceptions about how functional obsolescence affects value.

31. **B.** An appraisal report can either be oral or in writing. A narrative report is a type of written report. Other types of written reports include letter and form reports. An oral report is no less detailed than a written report and must be based on the same type of data as a written report.

32. **C.** The criteria used to determine whether a property is at its highest and best use are: (1) physically possible, (2) legally permissible, (3) financially feasible, and (4) maximally productive. Legally permissible includes conforming to current building codes. The highest and best use of a property may be expected to change in the future. In this case the property could have an interim use until the future

highest and best use is achievable. This could happen if, for instance, demand for the property is expected to change in the future. The interim use may or may not contribute value to the site.

33. **C.** When reconciling the final value estimate, inconsistencies between the different approaches should be examined and resolved. When determining a final value estimate, the appraiser should rely most heavily on the approach that is most applicable, significant, and defensible. A weighted average of the different approaches would be more appropriate than a simple average.

34. **A.** Vacancy levels are an indication of market supply for that type of space; such information could be either primary or secondary data, depending on whether the data were gathered by the appraiser or by another party and published.

35. **D.** Gentrification often occurs in areas of a city where middle-income to upper-income investors purchase older properties and restore them.

36. **B.** Normally the listing price of property placed in a multiple listing service is somewhat higher than the actual selling price. Use of such information without any investigation or adjustment would certainly be unfounded.

37. **C.** Of these four choices, size of the comparables is the only factor that could be adjusted using physical units of comparison.

38. **D.** In using the sales comparison (market) approach, the differences or units of comparison are always added to or subtracted from the comparables and not from the subject property. In this example, since the comparable has an extra bedroom, the comparable is adjusted downward to reflect the subject property.

39. **B.** The comparable sales approach to value is based primarily on the proper analysis of current market data. Without access to current market data, the appraiser should not try to employ this approach.

40. **D.** 105,000 ÷ 300 = 350 feet wide; 350 × $400 = $140,000.

41. **C.** The term *plottage* refers to the concept of increasing value by combining sites. This may or may not be the highest and best use, depending on how the sites are used.

42. **B.** Remaining economic life is the estimated number of remaining years of usefulness of a structure or component. The economic age may differ from the actual age.

43. **A.** In using the age-life method of computing depreciation, the estimated effective age (based on condition) is added to the remaining economic life. The effective age is then divided by that sum to obtain the total percent of depreciation to date.

44. **C.** Parking ratio shows the relationship between the number of available parking spaces and the number of building units or rentable square feet in a particular development. Minimum parking ratios are sometimes specified by local zoning codes.

45. **D.** Effective age is determined by the condition and utility of the building. Actual age is the number of years since construction was completed. Effective age can be greater than actual age if the building is not maintained well. The effective age could also be less than the actual age if it has above-average maintenance or renovations.

46. **A.** Incurable physical deterioration refers to items that cannot be corrected due to practical or economic reasons. Because the cost to cure curable physical items is first deducted from the reproduction or replacement cost, the cost of incurable physical deterioration cannot be applied to the total cost estimate. Incur-

able physical deterioration is broken into short-lived and long-lived components. Both are measured as indicated in answer A. However, the short-lived deterioration must be deducted before the long-lived deduction. The long-lived deduction is then applied to the cost after curable physical obsolescence and short-lived incurable physical deterioration are deducted.

47. **B.** Functional obsolescence can be the result of numerous occurrences, including the layout of the building. For example, a house with a poorly designed floor plan suffers from functional obsolescence.

48. **A.** The cost approach to value should not be employed to appraise vacant land. The other examples could all be appraised by the cost approach.

49. **D.** Chronological age and actual age are one and the same. While the actual age may be greater or less than the effective age, actual or chronological age is normally easier to establish. Economic life is the time period over which an improvement such as a building earns more income than the cost incurred in generating the income, and it is not the same as chronological age.

50. **D.** The reliability of the cost approach is strengthened when the site is being used under its highest and best use and the improvements are new with little or no depreciation. Vacant land is never valued using the cost approach. The older the improvements, for example 20 years, the less reliable the cost approach becomes. A market where there are numerous comparables might suggest use of the sales comparison approach.

51. **C.** The comparative unit method is a common way in which replacement cost is estimated. For example, a house with 2,000 square feet located in an area where similar construction costs $90 per square foot would have an estimated replacement cost of 2,000 × $90, or $180,000. The

other choices in this problem are all ways by which replacement or reproduction costs can be estimated.

52. **B.** The unit-in-place method of estimating cost is a common means of deriving an estimate of replacement or reproduction costs. This method involves grouping the major functional parts of the structure and estimating the appropriate cost of each.

53. **B.** If you are appraising property that has been totally destroyed by fire, the correct approach would be to estimate the highest and best use of the land.

54. **D.** 600 × 800 = 480,000 square feet; 480,000 ÷ 43,560 = 11.02 acres; $15,000 × 11.02 = $165,300.

55. **C.** 45,000 × $130 = $5,800,000 reproduction cost; $5,850,000 − $250,000 = $5,600,000; value of the improvements; 43,560 × $30 = $1,306,800, the value of the land; $5,600,000 + $1,306,800 = $6,906,800, value of the property.

56. **B.** An item of accrued depreciation is considered to be curable if the cost to correct the defect is equal to or less than the value added as a result of correcting the defect.

57. **B.** An increase in the capitalization rate (associated with higher risk and uncertainty) will result in a lower value. This is based on the basic capitalization formula $V = I \div R$.

58. **C.** In the basic capitalization formula $R = I \div V$, I refers to net operating income. $100,000 \div $500,000 = 0.20.

59. **B.** $75,000 + $25,000 + $50,000 = $150,000; $150,000 ÷ 10,000 = $15 per square foot per year; $15 ÷ 12 = $1.25 per month.

60. **B.** The gross income multiplier is a rule of thumb used in estimating the sales price. As its name implies, a gross income multiplier is based on gross income. As such,

an assumption made when employing such a multiplier is that any differences that may exist in the marketplace will be reflected by differences in the gross income multipliers derived for specific properties.

61. **D.** If any of the leases for income-producing property contain escalation clauses, then the increases in rent will be calculated as part of the gross income of the project. Other income includes those sources of income that are not part of the rent generated. In this example, the remaining three choices are all examples of income generated other than gross income.

62. **B.** A mortgage constant is the relationship between an annual or monthly loan requirement and the initial mortgage loan principal expressed as a decimal or a percentage. Because the loan is being amortized, and thus contains both principal and interest, the mortgage constant will always be greater than the interest rate.

63. **C.** The basic formula V = I ÷ R denotes net operating income. Net operating income of $50,000 divided by a value of $500,000 would result in a capitalization rate of 10 percent.

64. **B.** The overall rate equals the yield rate plus the relative change in property value if the value increases, or minus the relative change in property value if the property value decreases. Because no change in property value occurred in this example, the overall rate would equal the yield rate.

65. **A.** The building value does not need to be known before applying the technique. The purpose of the building value technique is to estimate the building value. The net operating income and land value must be known. Also, land and building capitalization rates are needed for the standard application of the building residual technique.

66. **C.** An annuity is a regular and predictable income pattern. It is normally level, although some would also use the term *annuity* for an income pattern that increases or decreases by a regular pattern. For example, an annuity might increase at a compound rate of 3 percent per year. There are usually formulas to calculate the present value of annuities because the income pattern is regular and predictable in a manner that can be described mathematically. Although a lease or a mortgage payment might be examples of annuity, there is no guarantee that either would have a regular and predictable pattern. A reversion is always a single receipt, whereas an annuity is a series of income flows.

67. **C.** An overall capitalization rate is not a yield rate. It is a ratio of one year's net operating income to the value of the property. Yield rates are annualized rates of return that consider income over a holding period. An internal rate of return is a yield rate, as is a discount rate. The discount rate used for finding the present value of future income is the yield rate that reflects the rate of return needed to justify waiting to receive the income. An interest rate is a yield rate to the lender. (Note: There are a few books that refer to an overall rate as a *current yield*. However, this is not common practice.)

68. **A.** A basis point is 1 ÷ 100 of 1 percent. Thus 8 percent + 0.50 ÷ 100 of 1 percent = 8.5 percent.

69. **B.** The net present value is a present value that is net of all cash flows (positive and negative) discounted to the present value. The term *net cash flow* by itself does not imply that the cash flow has been discounted. Profitability index is the ratio of the present value of expected benefits to the present value of capital outlays.

70. **C.** Debt coverage ratio equals net operating income divided by the mortgage payment. The mortgage payment includes interest and principal. $10,000 ÷ $9,000 = 1.11.

71. **C.** $R_O = L \times R_L + B \times R_B$

    $R_O = 0.35(0.09) + 0.65(0.11) = 0.103$ or 10.3 percent.

72. **C.** If a property is purchased with below-market rate financing, the purchaser will probably have paid more for the property to receive the favorable financing. The cash equivalency technique is used to adjust a property with different financing so that it can be compared to the subject property. The exact adjustments used depend on the type of financing involved. However, the basic procedure is to adjust the sales price by the present value of the favorable financing.

73. **C.** Carpeting reserve = $\$4,900 \div 7$ $= \$700$

    Oven reserve = $\$7,000 \div 10$ $= \$700$

    Freezer reserve = $\$7,000 \div 10$ $= \underline{\$700}$

    Total annual reserve $= \$2,100$

74. **B.** $\$25,000 \div 0.09 = \$277,778$ = Total value of property

    $R_O = L \times R_L + (1 - L) \times R_B$

    $L = \$60,000 \div \$277,778 = 0.216$

    $0.09 = 0.216 \times 0.08 + 0.784 \times R_B$

    $0.073 = 0.784 \times R_B$

    $0.093 = R_B$

75. **C.** NIR = Net income ratio

    GIM = Gross income multiplier

    NOI = Net operating income

    $R_O = $ NIR $\div$ GIM, since NIR = NOI $\div$ gross income and GIM = Value $\div$ gross income and $R_O = $ NOI $\div$ Value

    $R_O = 0.75 \div 9 = 0.0833$

76. **A.** $R_O = M \times R_M + (1 - M) \div R_E$

    $0.095 = 0.75 \times 0.11 + 0.25 \times R_E$

    $0.0125 = 0.25 \times R_E$

    $0.05 = R_E$

77. **C.** $\$1,100,000 \times 0.11 = \$121,000 =$ Income to the building

    $\$150,000 - \$121,000 = \$29,000 =$ Residual income to the land

    $\$29,000 \div 0.09 = \$322,222$

    $\$1,100,000 + \$322,222 = \$1,422,222$

78. **B.** If the investor is going to receive the same rate of return for properties *A* and *B* over the holding period, then less must be paid for property *A* because its NOI is not increasing. This will result in a higher overall capitalization rate for property *A*.

79. **A.** PV = PMT $\times$ (PVIFA, 10 percent, 5 years); PV = $\$100 \times 3.790787 = \$379.08$.

80. **B.** The *present value of one* factor for one year is 0.909.

81. **B.** If there are no financing costs, the effective rate equals the interest rate of the loan. Financing costs will cause the effective rate to be higher than the loan's interest rate.

82. **D.** 11.47 percent is the rate at which $27,232 would grow to $80,641 in ten years with compound interest.

83. **C.** The term *holding period* refers to the timespan of ownership.

84. **D.** $\$10,000 - \$1,500 - \$1,000 - \$500 - \$2,000 = \$5,000$. Income taxes, interest, and depreciation allowance are not included in the net operating income. Interest, depreciation, and income taxes are not included in the NOI calculations.

85. **D.** $\$10,000 = \$1,000 \times$ (PVIFA, ? percent, 4 years) + $\$16,000 \times$ (PVIF, ? percent, 5 years) ? percent = 17 percent from tables.

86. **C.** $\$36,000 \div \$400,000 = 0.09$; $\$440,000 \times 0.09 = \$39,600$.

87. **B.** The efficiency ratio expresses the relationship between leasable space and total space. For example, a 10,000-square-foot building with 25 percent of the space used for halls and elevators has an efficiency ratio of 75 percent.

88. **C.** $60 \times 80 = 4,800$ square feet; $\$3,000 \times 12 = \$36,000$ annual rent; $\$36,000 \div 4,800 = \$7.50$ per square foot.

89. **B.** If the lessor has to pay the expenses, it is a gross lease. If the lessee (tenant) pays the expenses it is a net lease. The term *pass-through* is sometimes used to refer to passing through expenses to a tenant.

90. **B.** The base rent is the minimum rent payable under a percentage lease. Base rent and percentage rent typically are used in retail leases where the tenant pays a base rent plus a percent of sales.

91. **A.** The $10,000 is the contract rent and the $15,000 is the market (economic) rent.

92. **B.** Standard 1 requires the appraiser to be aware of, understand, and correctly employ those methods that are necessary to produce a credible appraisal. A is Standard 2, C is the Competency Rule, D is Standard 4.

93. **C.** S.R. 2-1(c) addresses the issue of disclosing all assumptions, extraordinary assumptions, hypothetical conditions, and limiting conditions used in the assignment.

94. **C.** The requirement of stating the name(s) of anyone who provided significant professional assistance to the person signing the certification is not a part of Standard 1; rather, it is a part of Standards Rule 2-3.

95. **B.** The four sections of the Ethics Rule are: conduct, management, confidentiality, and record keeping.

96. **D.** Standard 1 does not require that all three traditional approaches to value be used; rather, the appraiser should consider whether each approach is appropriate for the specific appraisal assignment.

97. **D.** Standard 2-3 requires that the name of each individual providing significant real property appraisal assistance to the person signing the certification must be stated. The appraiser may or may not have inspected the property. Appraiser compensation must not be contingent on predetermined opinions of value.

98. **B.** Per Standards Rule 2-3, an appraiser who signs any part of the appraisal report, including a letter of transmittal, must also sign the certification.

99. **C.** The Competency Rule requires the appraiser to have the knowledge and experience necessary to complete the assignment competently.

100. **A.** The revocation of an appraiser's certification by an appraisal board is not an example of an extraordinary assumption or limiting condition as intended in Standard 2. Atypical financing of the subject property should be included.

101. **B.** The minimum period to be analyzed for all types of property is three years. This is a requirement under Standards Rule 1-5.

102. **B.** $\$12 + \$17 + \$14 + \$15 + \$15 + \$16 + \$17 + \$17 + \$18 + \$16 = \$157$; $\$157 \div 10 = \$15.70$.

103. **C.** The median is the number that is exactly in the middle. In this instance, $16 is the average of the two middle observations.

104. **D.** The mode is the number that occurs the most number of times. In this sample, $17 was the rent per square foot in three instances.

105. **B.** Range $= \$18 - \$12 = \$6$.

106. **A.**

30 units × $700 × 12 =	$252,000
20 units × 600 × 12 =	$144,000
Effective income =	$396,000
– Vacancy rate (5%)	–19,800
Effective gross income	$376,200
– Op. exp.	–$131,670
Net operating income	$244,530

107. **B.** V = I/R; $244,530/0.12 = $2,037,750.

108. **C.** $244,530/$2,000,000 = 12.22%.

109. **A.** Monthly mortgage payment of
$13,495.89 = ADS of $161,951;
$244,530 – $161,951 = $82,579.

110. **D.** Break-even ratio = Op. exp. + ADS/Gross
income; $131,670 + $161,951/$396,000
= 0.74 or 74%.

Certified General Exam B

1. Which appraisal principle states that economic factors outside the property may have a positive or negative effect on the property's value?
   A. Anticipation
   B. Substitution
   C. Contribution
   D. Externalities

2. What term is used to explain the appraisal principle that states that value is based on the concept that the more a property or its components are in harmony with the surrounding properties or components, the greater the contributory value?
   A. Substitution
   B. Conformity
   C. Anticipation
   D. Contribution

3. What value concept applies when the value of a property includes the benefit of a proven business operating on the property?
   A. Going-concern value
   B. Investment value
   C. Market value
   D. Use value

4. When does investment value equal market value?
   A. When the property is the highest and best use of the site
   B. Only by coincidence
   C. When market demand equals market supply
   D. When the assessed value equals the investment value

5. Market value is best described as the
   A. price asked by the seller.
   B. most probable selling price in an open market.
   C. price offered by the buyer.
   D. actual price paid.

6. Building measurements gathered by an appraiser are an example of which type of data?
   A. General data
   B. Secondary data
   C. Primary data
   D. Improvement cost data

7. What does linkage refer to?
   A. The amount of the monthly mortgage payment going toward reducing the principal
   B. Time-distance cost necessary to access a supporting facility
   C. Relationship between gross income and net income for income-producing property
   D. Percent of an area's employment engaged in basic industries

8. The market value of property and the most probable sales price of that property could be equal
   A. always.
   B. never.
   C. sometimes.
   D. only with owner-occupied residential property.

9. The cost approach to value is based primarily on which economic principle?
   A. Highest and best use
   B. Supply and demand
   C. Substitution
   D. Conformity

10. The highest and best use of a parcel of land is that use that will result in the
    A. highest building value.
    B. highest occupancy rate of the building.
    C. highest present value of the property.
    D. lowest total investment.

11. A homeowners' association in a condominium project is normally directly responsible for certain payments. Which expense would be the direct responsibility of the homeowners' association?
    A. Maintenance expenses in individual units
    B. Property taxes for the limited common areas
    C. Premiums for a package liability insurance policy
    D. Brokerage fees incurred in the marketing of individual units

12. Which statement is *NOT* correct in regard to a life estate created in real estate?
    A. It may be leased.
    B. It may be sold to a third party.
    C. It may be mortgaged.
    D. It is inheritable.

13. Which USPAP standard is directed toward the substantive aspect of developing a competent appraisal of real property?
    A. Standard 1
    B. Standard 2
    C. Standard 4
    D. Standard 5

14. A lien and an easement are both legal interest in real estate. Which statement is correct in regard to both a lien and an easement?
    A. They both must be in writing to be legal.
    B. They are both encumbrances.
    C. They must be recorded in the public land records to be legal.
    D. They can be imposed against the property only after all parties involved have agreed to same.

15. The definitions section of the USPAP would classify an item such as furnishings or machinery and equipment as
    A. real property.
    B. personal property.
    C. personal estate.
    D. real estate.

16. The floor area ratio adopted by a local government as part of its zoning ordinance is 4:1. What is the maximum height a building could be constructed if the structure covers one-third of the land?
    A. 1 story
    B. 4 stories
    C. 12 stories
    D. The height of the structure cannot be regulated by zoning.

17. A land use that existed before a certain zoning district was established and is currently not consistent with the restrictions imposed on land uses in that district is referred to as a
   A. variance.
   B. nonconforming use.
   C. transitional use.
   D. planned unit development.

18. A *mill* is a unit of measure used in many taxing jurisdictions for the purpose of levying property taxes. A mill is equal to
   A. 0.10 of a dollar.
   B. 0.01 of a dollar.
   C. 0.001 of a dollar.
   D. 0.0001 of a dollar.

19. Which item normally would *NOT* be considered a fixture?
   A. Bathtub
   B. Storm doors
   C. Refrigerator
   D. Wall-to-wall carpeting

20. A vacant lot measures 200 feet by 381 feet. What is its estimated worth if the land is valued at $20,000 per acre?
   A. $20,000
   B. $28,800
   C. $33,500
   D. $35,000

21. The process of a local government in exercising its power of eminent domain is known as
   A. police power.
   B. condemnation.
   C. escheat.
   D. urban renewal.

22. First Realty Corporation owns an office building that was subject to a property tax of $57,000 last year. At that time, the property had an assessed value of $1,500,000. This year the taxing authority has increased the assessed value to $2,000,000 and has also increased the millage rate by 6 mills. What will the property tax be this year?
   A. $57,000
   B. $66,000
   C. $76,000
   D. $88,000

23. In regard to leases, which statement is correct?
   A. A lease is both a conveyance of an interest in land and a contract.
   B. In a percentage lease, the percentage is always based on gross sales.
   C. A graduated lease is entirely different from a step-up lease.
   D. Assignment and subleasing refer to the same thing.

24. In which legal interest does the benefit "run with the land"?
   A. License
   B. Easement in gross
   C. Easement in net
   D. Easement appurtenant

25. Which right of government is based on police power?
   A. Eminent domain
   B. Taxation
   C. Escheat
   D. Zoning

26. What rent should the appraiser use in making a gross income estimate on a free-and-clear, no-lease valuation?
   A. Contract rent
   B. Economic (market) rent
   C. Contract rent as the upset level
   D. Net rental called for in the lease

27. The benefit of having a contract rent lower than the market rent goes to which estate?
   A. Leased fee estate
   B. Leasehold estate
   C. Fee simple absolute estate
   D. Fee simple determinable estate

28. The value of a site that is currently improved with a building should be based on
   A. its value under the highest and best use as if vacant.
   B. its residual value after determining the value of the building.
   C. the property residual technique.
   D. prorating the total value of the land and building.

29. Multifamily, commercial, and industrial areas are generally referred to as
    A. districts.
    B. neighborhoods.
    C. nonresidential.
    D. parks.

30. Land utilization studies, supply and demand studies, economic feasibility studies, and highest and best use analysis are all examples of which action?
    A. Review
    B. Mass appraisal
    C. Appraisal
    D. Investment analysis

31. Reconciliation is defined as the process of
    A. calculating the average of the three approaches to value to find the final value of a property.
    B. analyzing different conclusions to arrive at a final value.
    C. arbitrating a price between a buyer and seller.
    D. reviewing the appraisal to ensure that data and techniques are valid and consistent.

32. Which statement expresses the difference between valuation and evaluation?
    A. Evaluation is the process of finding an estimated value of a property at a given time; valuation refers to an analysis of the market without necessarily giving an estimate of value.
    B. Valuation refers to the estimate of a market value; evaluation refers to an estimate of value other than the market value.
    C. Valuation is the process of finding an estimated value of a property at a given time; evaluation refers to an analysis of the market without necessarily giving an estimate of value.
    D. Valuation refers to an estimate of the value of real property; evaluation refers to an estimate of the value of real estate.

33. Units of comparison can be used in which approach(es) to value?
    A. All three approaches
    B. The sales comparison (market) approach only
    C. The cost approach only
    D. The cost and sales comparison approaches only

34. When attempting to use the sales comparison approach, the appraiser *MUST* complete which action?
    A. Have at least three comparable sales
    B. Find comparable sales within three months of the valuation date
    C. Confirm all pertinent factors for each comparable used
    D. Use comparables only within the same neighborhood

35. In the analysis of sales data as part of the sales comparison approach, *conditions of sales* refers to the
    A. validity of the sales contract.
    B. amount of interest paid on an assumed mortgage.
    C. motives, intention, and knowledge of the parties.
    D. amount of personal property included.

36. The adjustment process used in the sales comparison approach could *BEST* be described by which action?
    A. The subject property is adjusted to make it as similar as possible to the comparables.
    B. The comparables are adjusted to make them equal to the subject property.
    C. Properties currently available for sale are adjusted to the subject property.
    D. The subject property is adjusted to make it as similar as possible to highest and best use.

37. Which set of terms *BEST* describes the four elements of sale that need to be identified and compared in the sales comparison approach?
    A. Date of sale, location, physical condition, condition of sale
    B. Location, legal, physical, social
    C. Physical, social, legal, economic
    D. Physical, functional, economic, locational

38. How would an appraiser *MOST* likely be able to use the assessed values found in the public land records for properties in a particular area?
    A. As a starting point to derive an opinion of value
    B. As a true indication of local property values
    C. As input in calculating property taxes needed in the income approach to value
    D. As an indication of gross rent multipliers for the area

39. The use of multiple regression analysis denotes a statistical technique used to
    A. measure the relationship between two variables.
    B. measure the relationship among three or more variables.
    C. determine the mean of a sample.
    D. measure the likelihood of highest and best use being obtained.

40. When land is improved to the extent that it is ready to be used for the purpose for which it was intended, it is known as a
    A. plot.
    B. site.
    C. parcel.
    D. lot.

41. Excess land is land that is
    A. not as valuable because it is not necessary to accommodate a site's highest and best use.
    B. not needed to support the existing improvement.
    C. always used for expansion of the existing improvement.
    D. not included in the estimated value of the improvements.

42. Which statement *MOST* correctly explains the impact of corner lots?
    A. They have a higher value than other lots.
    B. They have a lower value than other lots.
    C. They may have a higher or lower value than other lots depending on the local market.
    D. They have a higher utility than other lots.

43. The term *plottage* refers to
    A. value created by land that is not necessary for the primary improvements.
    B. the incremental value that results when two sites are combined.
    C. the results of a survey that is plotted on a map.
    D. the steps taken to determine which approach to value should be used.

44. Curable physical deterioration is measured by
    A. applying the ratio of effective age to estimated total physical life to the reproduction or replacement cost of each component.
    B. calculating the cost of restoring a component to new or reasonably new condition, i.e., the cost to cure.
    C. calculating the cost of installing the modern component minus the remaining value of the existing component.
    D. calculating the reproduction cost of the item minus any physical deterioration already charged, plus the cost to install a normally adequate or standard item.

45. Curable superadequate features are measured by
    A. applying the ratio of effective age to estimated total physical life to the reproduction or replacement cost of each component.
    B. calculating the cost of restoring a component to new or reasonably new condition, i.e., the cost to cure.
    C. calculating the cost of installing the modern component minus the remaining value of the existing component.
    D. calculating the reproduction cost of the item minus any physical deterioration already charged, plus the cost to install a normally adequate or standard item.

46. The period of time over which an improvement to land, such as a building, earns more income than the cost incurred in generating that income is known as the property's
    A. physical life.
    B. economic life.
    C. loan period.
    D. highest and best use life.

47. An item of accrued depreciation is said to be curable under which situation?
    A. The cost to cure is no greater than the expected increase in value.
    B. The cost to cure is no greater than the replacement cost of the item.
    C. The item can be physically replaced without damaging the property.
    D. The cost to cure does not change the assessed value of the property.

48. A lot measuring 130 feet by 200 feet recently sold for $71,500. What was the selling price per square foot?
    A. $2.75
    B. $5.50
    C. $275
    D. $550

49. The cost approach to value utilizes cost new of the existing improvements as of what date?
    A. Original construction
    B. Date of last purchase
    C. Date of value
    D. Date of depreciation for federal income tax purposes

50. One of the necessary steps in the cost approach to value is to place a value on the site. The site value assumes which condition?
    A. The site is vacant.
    B. The site is not available for any use.
    C. The site has suffered from complete depreciation.
    D. The site has numerous possible uses.

51. You are appraising a warehouse using the cost approach to value method. You have estimated that the effective age of the building is 15 years and the remaining economic life is 45 years. Using the age-life method, total depreciation expressed as a percentage is (rounded) to
    A. 25 percent.
    B. 33.3 percent.
    C. 66.7 percent.
    D. 75 percent.

52. A house has a living area of 1,900 square feet. An attached garage has a total area of 420 square feet. The building has an expected life of 50 years and an effective age of five years. The lot is worth $50,000. If it costs $110 to reproduce the living area and $50 to reproduce the garage on a square-foot basis, what is the indicated value of the property?
    A. $207,000
    B. $230,000
    C. $257,000
    D. $280,000

53. What is the correct way for an appraiser to measure *economic obsolescence*?
    A. The capitalized value of the loss in rent due to the condition
    B. The absolute cost incurred to cure the condition
    C. The absolute cost incurred to cure the condition times the gross rent multiplier
    D. The capitalized value of the total property income

54. A warehouse has a market value of $3,000,000. It generates an annual gross income of $500,000. Annual operating expenses are also $500,000. What is the gross income multiplier?
    A. 4
    B. 5
    C. 6
    D. 6.5

55. Inflation, interest rates, and thus the cost of mortgage money affect property values. How is this relationship indicated in the appraisal process?
    A. Capitalization rates may be adjusted up or down.
    B. When mortgage rates are high, the cost approach is used exclusively.
    C. When interest rates are low, the sales comparison approach is used exclusively.
    D. When interest rates are expected to change, the income approach is never used.

56. When using the income approach, what is the initial step the appraiser must take in reconstructing an operating statement?
    A. Estimate gross income
    B. Estimate operating expenses
    C. Estimate net operating income
    D. Select an appropriate capitalization rate

57. The net operating income of $60,000 of a property capitalized at a rate of 14 percent indicates a value _____ the value indicated by capitalizing a net operating income of $30,000 at a rate of 7 percent.
    A. less than
    B. equal to
    C. greater than
    D. exactly twice

58. The performance of a real property consulting service by an appraiser is the subject matter of which USPAP standard?
    A. Standard 1
    B. Standard 4
    C. Standard 7
    D. Standard 9

59. A property sold for $145,000 with $30,000 down and the balance in the form of a purchase-money mortgage (seller financing) at 8 percent for 15 years with monthly payments. Shortly after the sale of the property, the seller sold the mortgage to an investor for $105,000. The price paid by the investor for the mortgage was based on the current market rate for mortgages. What does this indicate is the cash equivalent selling price for the property?
    A. $105,000
    B. $115,000
    C. $132,391
    D. $135,000

60. A property has a gross income multiplier of 9 and a net income ratio of 0.75. What does this indicate for the overall capitalization rate?
    A. 6.75 percent
    B. 8.33 percent
    C. 9.00 percent
    D. 12.00 percent

61. What is the annual debt service on a $75,000 loan with monthly payments over 20 years at a nominal annual rate of 13 percent?
    A. $879
    B. $1,353
    C. $10,544
    D. $10,676

62. A property is projected to have level NOI of $25,000 per year for the next five years. The property value is projected to increase a total of 15 percent over the five years. The appraiser determines that an appropriate discount rate is 12 percent. What is the value of the property?
    A. $90,119
    B. $166,667
    C. $208,333
    D. $259,367

63. A property is leased as follows:

    Years 1–5, $10,000 per year
    Years 6–10, $15,000 per year

    Using a 10 percent discount rate, what is the present value of the lease payments assuming they are paid at the *end* of each year?
    A. $64,175
    B. $73,215
    C. $92,176
    D. $94,770

64. Refer to the preceding question. What is the present value assuming the payments are made at the *beginning* of each year?
    A. $73,215
    B. $80,536
    C. $94,247
    D. $104,247

65. The subject property's net income is $15,000 per year. Comparable investments sold as follows:

Comparable	Net Income	Sales Price
1	$14,400	$120,000
2	$14,000	$147,400
3	$13,500	$122,700
4	$14,500	$152,600

All of the above sales are recent. Comparables 2 and 4 were most similar to the subject. Using direct capitalization with an overall rate, what is the *BEST* estimate of the value of the subject property?
A. $125,000
B. $137,000
C. $143,000
D. $158,000

66. When doing a discounted cash flow analysis to estimate value, how is the effect of sale at the end of a holding period treated?
A. The difference between the sales price and the original purchase price is discounted to its present value.
B. Discounted cash flow analysis does not consider sale of the property.
C. The cash flow available from sale is discounted to its present value.
D. The average annual increase in price is added to the NOI each year before discounting.

67. The equity dividend rate is measured against which amount?
A. Market value
B. Purchase price
C. Mortgage amount
D. Initial equity investment

68. Given the following information, what is the indicated land value (using the land residual technique)?

Building value: $600,000
Net operating income: $88,000
Building capitalization rate: 11 percent
Land capitalization rate: 9 percent

A. $22,000
B. $309,091
C. $377,778
D. $244,444

69. If the overall rate is 0.10, the annual mortgage constant is 0.11, and the mortgage ratio is 70 percent, what is the indicated debt coverage ratio?
A. 0.77
B. 1.57
C. 1.30
D. 0.64

70. What is the overall capitalization rate of a property with a land-to-value ratio of 0.1, land capitalization rate of 0.09, and building capitalization rate of 0.12?
A. 9.3 percent
B. 10.5 percent
C. 11.7 percent
D. 12.0 percent

71. What is the relationship between the annual mortgage constant and the annual interest rate for a mortgage that is fully amortized over the loan term?
A. The mortgage constant must be lower than the interest rate.
B. The mortgage constant must be higher than the interest rate.
C. The mortgage constant can be higher or lower than the interest rate depending on the length of the loan term.
D. The mortgage constant will be equal to the interest rate.

72. Which calculation is *NOT* needed to use the band of investment technique?
A. Reversion
B. Loan-to-value ratio
C. Equity dividend rate
D. Mortgage constant

73. A landlord leases property for five years. The rent of $9,000, payable at the beginning of each period, constitutes an annuity in advance. What is the present value using a 10 percent discount rate?
    A. $34,117
    B. $37,529
    C. $40,500
    D. $49,500

74. An appraisal report must contain certain minimum requirements per Standards Rule 2-2. Which item is required (as a minimum) in every appraisal report?
    A. Intended use of the appraisal
    B. Name of previous owners
    C. Definition of market value
    D. Effective date of the expected title transfer

75. Per the requirements of the USPAP, which statement is *TRUE* in regard to contingency compensation?
    A. The acceptance of compensation contingent on the reporting of a predetermined value in an appraisal is unethical.
    B. Contingency fees are addressed in the Record Keeping section of the Ethics Rule.
    C. Restrictions on contingency compensation do not apply to appraisal review assignments where the review appraiser did not conduct the original appraisal.
    D. Contingency compensation in an appraisal consulting practice is unethical.

76. According to the Confidentiality section of the Ethics Rule of the USPAP, certain persons may have confidential factual data from an appraisal assignment disclosed to them. Which persons are clearly recognized under the Confidentiality section?
    A. All persons who read the appraisal report
    B. Appraisers who have previously valued the property
    C. Parties authorized under due process of law
    D. All members of the appraiser's local organization

77. In the USPAP, the Scope of Work Rule requires the appraiser to identify all of these assignment elements *EXCEPT*
    A. the client and any other intended users.
    B. the type and definition of value.
    C. the effective date of the appraiser's opinions and conclusions.
    D. all three approaches to value.

78. The term *book value* refers to which of the following amounts?
    A. The purchase price less accrued appreciation
    B. The carrying amount of an asset, as shown on the books of a company; generally the amount paid for an asset, less depreciation
    C. The sales price less the mortgage balance
    D. The before-tax cash flow less the tax on capital gain

79. What is meant by the term *discount rate?*
    A. The difference between the face amount of an obligation and the amount advanced or received
    B. The interest rate associated with the loan on a property
    C. A compound interest rate used to convert expected future income into a present value
    D. The annual mortgage payment divided by the loan principal

80. What term is used for the method of measuring investment performance that is a variation on the internal rate of return method where the user specifies more than one reinvestment rate: a safe rate obtainable for liquid deposits and a run-of-the-mill rate, which can be earned from typical investments over a long term?
    A. Internal rate of return (IRR)
    B. Financial management rate of return (FMRR)
    C. Discounted cash flow analysis (DCF)
    D. Yield capitalization

81. An interest rate that incorporates the effects
of discount points is referred to as a(n)
   A. discount rate.
   B. effective rate.
   C. internal rate of return.
   D. financial management rate of return.

82. Jones sells land for $20,000 that he bought
four years earlier for $10,000. There were no
carrying charges or transaction costs. What
was Jones's IRR (nearest percent)?
   A. 17 percent
   B. 19 percent
   C. 25 percent
   D. 100 percent

83. A property produces rental income of
$100,000 during the year. The expenses
incurred are as follows:

   Operating expenses:
Maintenance	$20,000
Insurance	5,000
Property taxes	10,000
Management	10,000
Utilities	15,000
	$60,000

   Debt service:
Interest	$18,000
Principal	2,000
	$20,000

   | Income taxes: | ($5,000) |

   What is the NOI?
   A. $20,000
   B. $22,000
   C. $40,000
   D. $50,000

84. When a portion of a landowner's property is
being taken for public use such as the expansion of an airport runway, _____ damages
may be awarded in addition to the payment
for the land actually being taken.
   A. condemnation
   B. consequential
   C. severance
   D. escheat

85. A single-story office building 100 feet by
80 feet rents for $18 per square foot per year.
If a tenant agrees to sign a four-year lease,
no rent is due for the first six months. Under
these conditions, what is the average rent paid
per month over the full term of the lease?
   A. $3,000
   B. $10,500
   C. $12,000
   D. $42,000

86. A rental concession is defined as a(n)
   A. increase in the amount of rent.
   B. service or discount offered by the landlord to induce a would-be tenant to sign
a lease.
   C. percent of gross sales being paid to
the lessor.
   D. participation agreement by the
lender in a land lease.

87. The ratio of net rentable area to gross area in
a multitenant building is normally referred
to as
   A. floor area ratio.
   B. net operating ratio.
   C. efficiency ratio.
   D. variance ratio.

88. What term is used to describe the additional
rent paid by retail tenants on a percentage
lease that is above the specified minimum
rent?
   A. Base rent
   B. Overage rent
   C. Excess rent
   D. Market rent

89. What term is used to explain what occurs
when prospective tenants are given a discount
by a landlord to induce them to sign a lease?
   A. Bribe
   B. Concession
   C. Kickback
   D. Freebie

90. When estimating the value of a fee simple estate, which definition of rent would be used?
    A. Fee rent
    B. Contract rent
    C. Market rent
    D. Simple rent

91. According to the USPAP, at a minimum, how long must an appraiser retain his or her work-file after preparation of the appraisal report?
    A. No set minimum time
    B. One year
    C. Two years
    D. Five years

92. The USPAP standard or rule that requires the appraiser to clearly and accurately set forth the appraisal in a manner that will not be misleading is addressed in
    A. Standard 1.
    B. Standard 2.
    C. Standard 3.
    D. the Scope of Work Rule.

93. An appraiser who signs a real property appraisal certification prepared by another, even under the label of "review appraiser," *MUST*
    A. receive one-half of the compensation.
    B. contribute at least one-half of the time spent collecting and analyzing data.
    C. physically inspect the subject property.
    D. accept full responsibility for all elements of the certification.

94. An appraiser should group the assumptions and limiting conditions in an identified section of the appraisal report. Which statement is an example of an assumption or limiting condition?
    A. This report is prepared in compliance with the USPAP.
    B. I have made a personal inspection of the subject property.
    C. I assume there are no hidden defects in the property that would render it more or less valuable.
    D. No one offered significant real property appraisal assistance to the person preparing the report.

95. The definition of market value in the USPAP is based on a number of conditions. All of these conditions are assumed in the definition *EXCEPT*
    A. all parties are acting in their best interest.
    B. a maximum time is allowed for exposure in the open market.
    C. both parties are well informed.
    D. the buyer and the seller are typically motivated.

96. In regard to the Preamble of the USPAP, which statement is *TRUE?*
    A. The USPAP reflects the current standards of the appraisal profession.
    B. The USPAP was developed by the Appraisal Subcommittee for the purpose of regulating appraisers.
    C. The standards include advisory opinions.
    D. The standards deal with the procedures to be followed in performing an appraisal or appraisal review but not an appraisal consulting service.

97. According to the definitions in the USPAP, "that which is contrary to what exists but is supposed for the purpose of analysis" is referred to as a(n)
    A. extraordinary assumption.
    B. extraordinary condition.
    C. hypothetical assumption.
    D. hypothetical condition.

98. Standard 2 of the USPAP addresses the application and use of the traditional approaches to value. In terms of how the approaches to value are used, which statement *BEST* describes what Standards Rule 2-2(a) requires for a self-contained appraisal report?
    A. If the appraisal report concerns residential property, the sales comparison approach must have been used.
    B. The appraisal must justify the use of any approach used in the report.
    C. The appraiser must explain and support the reason for excluding any of the usual valuation approaches.
    D. One of the usual approaches cannot be eliminated simply because the data collected do not support the use of that approach.

APPLICATION-STYLE QUESTIONS

Questions 99 and 100 are based on the following information:

	Apartment	Office	Retail/ Commercial
Cost to Construct Improvements	$5,900,000	$8,600,000	$4,300,000
Net Operating Income	$850,000	$1,204,000	$650,000

Building capitalization rate, 12 percent; land capitalization rate, 10 percent

99. The highest and best use of the site is a(n)
   A. apartment.
   B. office.
   C. retail/commercial use.
   D. apartment or office.

100. The land value would be
   A. $860,000.
   B. $1,340,000.
   C. $1,420,000.
   D. $1,720,000.

Questions 101 and 102 are based on the following information:

A property is projected to have the following cash flows:

Year 1: $5,000
Year 2: $7,000
Year 3: $9,000
Year 4: $9,000
Year 5: $110,000

The cash flow in year 5 includes the reversion.

101. What is the present value of the cash flows using a 10 percent discount rate?
   A. $85,896
   B. $91,541
   C. $92,224
   D. $102,273

102. Assume the property is purchased by an investor for $100,000. What is the investor's net present value?
   A. – $7,776
   B. $8,459
   C. – $8,459
   D. $10,000

Questions 103 through 105 are based on the following seven residential sales prices.

Parcel	Sales Price
1	$80,000
2	$81,300
3	$81,600
4	$82,500
5	$84,000
6	$84,000
7	$86,800

103. What is the mean selling price of the sample?
   A. $81,300
   B. $82,886
   C. $83,666
   D. $84,000

104. What is the median selling price of the sample?
   A. $80,000
   B. $82,500
   C. $82,886
   D. $84,000

105. What is the mode selling price of the sample?
   A. $80,000
   B. $82,500
   C. $82,886
   D. $84,000

Questions 106 through 110 are based on the following information:

You have been asked to appraise a 20,000-square-foot office building that is currently under a long-term triple net lease. The space rents for $18 per square foot. Property taxes and property insurance are $18,000 annually.

106. What is the monthly rent due from the tenants?
     A. $18,000
     B. $27,000
     C. $30,000
     D. $36,667

107. Due to the inferior location of this office building, you find that other buildings in the city are renting for $22 per square foot. What is the monthly rent of the subject property?
     A. $18,000
     B. $27,000
     C. $30,000
     D. $36,667

108. What would be the net montly rent to the landlord if the lease were a gross lease instead of a triple net lease?
     A. $28,500
     B. $30,000
     C. $31,500
     D. $36,000

109. Capitalizing the existing income at a 14 percent cap rate results in an indicated value of
     A. $2,143,000.
     B. $2,333,000.
     C. $2,443,000.
     D. $2,571,000.

110. If the owner finances the property with a fully amortized $2 million loan for 15 years with a 9 percent interest rate, what is the ROE?
     A. 9%
     B. 12%
     C. 16%
     D. 20%

ANSWERS TO GENERAL EXAM B

1. **D.** Externalities are economies or diseconomies outside or external to the property that may affect the property's value.

2. **B.** The principle of conformity states that value is created when a property conforms to the environment due to economic pressures, zoning, similar preferences of neighbors, etc.

3. **A.** The value of a proven business adds going-concern value. Investment value is value to a specific investment but does not necessarily include the benefits of a property operation. Use value is value to the user of the property but, as with investment value, does not necessarily imply that there is a business operating on the property.

4. **B.** Investment value is the value of a property to a particular investor. Because market value is the value of a property to a typical investor, investment value will equal market value only when the investor's preferences equal the market's preferences (i.e., by coincidence).

5. **B.** Market value is the most probable selling price of a property in a competitive and open market, where the buyer and seller are each acting prudently, knowledgeably, and assuming the price is not affected by undue stimulus.

6. **C.** Primary data are gathered by the appraiser, whereas secondary data are gathered by another party and available to the appraiser through published sources.

7. **B.** *Linkage* is defined as the proximity of a parcel of land to a supporting land use and refers to the time and distance necessary to reach the supporting facility.

8. **C.** The terms *market value* and *most probable sales price* do not refer to the same thing. However, it is possible that under certain conditions the market value of property could be equal to its most probable or likely sales price.

9. **C.** The principle of substitution is the basis on which the cost approach to value is formed. This principle states that the value of a parcel is set by the cost of acquiring an equally desirable substitute.

10. **C.** *Highest and best use* is defined as that legal use of a parcel of land which, when capitalized, will generate the greatest net present value of income.

11. **C.** Premiums for a package insurance policy would be the responsibility of the homeowners' association. Any expenses such as maintenance or brokerage fees incurred by individual units are the responsibility of the owner(s) of that unit. Owners of the limited common areas would be assessed on a pro rata share of their ownership in the limited common areas.

12. **D.** A life estate is not inheritable. However, it may be leased, sold to a third party, or mortgaged. Nevertheless, it would still remain as a life estate.

13. **A.** Standard 1 is directed toward the substantive aspect of developing a competent appraisal of real property.

14. **B.** Liens and easements are both encumbrances. While they *may* be in writing and may be recorded, they do not *have* to be. A lien could be placed against property without the knowledge or consent of all parties involved.

15. **B.** Personal property is defined in the USPAP as identifiable, trangible objects that are considered by the general public as being "personal" and includes such items as furnishings or machinery and equipment.

16. **C.** A floor area ratio (FAR) of 4:1 means that four square feet of space can be

constructed for each one square foot of land. Thus if the building is constructed on one-third of the land, the maximum height allowed would be 12 stories (4 × 3).

17. **B.** Quite often when a zoning district is created, some uses may exist that are not consistent with the zoning ordinance. A nonconforming use may ordinarily remain; however, certain restrictions may be imposed.

18. **C.** A mill is equal to 0.001 of a dollar or one-tenth of a penny.

19. **C.** A refrigerator is not normally attached in such a manner as to be considered attached to the property; thus it is personal property.

20. **D.** 200 × 381 = 76,200 square feet; 76,200 ÷ 43,560 = 1.75 acres; 1.75 × $20,000 = $35,000.

21. **B.** Condemnation is the process of taking private property for public use through the power of eminent domain. Police power and escheat are rights of the public sector against the private ownership of property. Urban renewal is an example of a government program to upgrade or develop land use.

22. **D.** $57,000 ÷ $1,500,000 = 0.038 millage rate; 0.038 + 6 mills = 0.044 new millage rate; $2,000,000 × 0.044 = $88,000.

23. **A.** A lease is both a conveyance of an interest in land as well as a contract.

24. **D.** An easement appurtenant is one that belongs to and passes with a particular tract of land. An easement appurtenant "runs with the land," which means that when the land is sold or otherwise conveyed, the easement is also one of the legal rights conveyed.

25. **D.** Police power is the inherent right of the state to regulate land use for the purpose of promoting health, safety, welfare, and morality. This right is the basis for zoning, building codes, and subdivision regulations.

26. **B.** Because a lease interest is not being valued, the market rent should be used to estimate income. By using market rent (the typical rent found in comparable properties) instead of the actual rent of the property, the appraiser will be estimating the value to a typical investor, or market value.

27. **B.** The below-market rent benefits the tenant whose legal rights are referred to as a leasehold estate.

28. **A.** Land is always valued under its highest and best use as if vacant, even when it is currently improved. The theory is that any loss in value due to an improper improvement is borne by the improvements.

29. **A.** Multifamily, commercial, and industrial areas are generally referred to as districts.

30. **C.** An appraisal is an estimate of value and can take numerous forms.

31. **B.** The reconciliation process begins with a review of the appraisal; then this analysis is used to arrive at a final value estimate. The final value estimate is not necessarily an average of the different approaches.

32. **C.** The type of value does not determine whether the process is valuation or evaluation. Evaluation does not necessarily give an estimate of value, whereas valuation does.

33. **A.** Although probably most used in the sales comparison approach, units of comparison can be used in all three approaches; for example, cost/square foot for the cost approach and net income/price for the income approach.

34. **C.** When using the sales comparison approach, the appraiser must confirm all pertinent factors for each comparable

used. There is no set minimum or absolute location for the comparables that will be used.

35. **C.** In the sales comparison approach, the term *conditions of sales* refers to the motives, intention, and knowledge of the parties. For example, a "hurried" sale due to a job relocation could result in the property actually selling for less than what it would normally bring. This condition would need to be included in the analysis undertaken by the appraiser if the sales comparison approach is used.

36. **B.** When using the sales comparison approach, the appraiser always adjusts the comparables to the subject property. The subject property is never adjusted to the comparables.

37. **A.** In the sales comparison approach, the principal factors for which adjustments generally will be made can be divided into four categories: date of sale, location, physical condition, and condition of sale.

38. **C.** An appraiser should be careful in regard to using assessed value information for anything other than as input in calculating property taxes. The assessed value of property as found in the public land records should not be used as an indicator of market value or probable sales price.

39. **B.** Multiple regression is a statistical technique used to measure the relationship among three or more variables. Such a technique is often used by appraisers when numerous independent variables such as square footage, number of rooms, age of structure, etc., can be quantified and a dependent variable such as likely sales price is being estimated.

40. **B.** A site refers to improved land. Plot, parcel, and lot refer to unimproved land.

41. **B.** Excess land is land not needed to support the existing improvement. Excess land should be identified in highest and best use analysis and valued separately if appropriate. In some situations, the site may be too large for the existing improvement but not considered to contain excess land. This situation occurs when the extra land cannot be used separately.

42. **C.** Corner lots may have a higher or lower value than other lots depending on the use of the lot. For instance, in a residential area a corner lot at the intersection of two busy streets may have a lower value if buyers do not want the extra noise near their homes. A restaurant owner, however, may prefer a corner lot to allow easier access for customers.

43. **B.** Plottage refers to the incremental value that results when extra utility is gained by combining two or more sites. If extra utility is not gained by combining sites, there is no plottage value.

44. **B.** Curable physical deterioration refers to items of deferred maintenance. Therefore the depreciation equals the cost to restore the item to a new or reasonably new condition.

45. **D.** A superadequacy or overimprovement is an item whose cost exceeds its value. Superadequate features are a type of functional obsolescence and may be curable or incurable. The superadequacy is curable if the cost of correcting it is currently economically feasible.

46. **B.** This is simply the definition of economic life, which may be entirely different from the property's physical life.

47. **A.** Accrued depreciation can be either curable or incurable. An item is curable if the cost to correct the defect is no greater than the expected increase in value as a result of the correction.

48. **A.** $130 \times 200 = 26,000$ sq. ft.; $71,500 $\div$ 26,000 = 2.75 per square foot.

49. **C.** In the cost approach to value, one of the necessary steps is to estimate the cost of the existing improvements. This estimate is made as of the date of the value.

50. **A.** When using the cost approach to value, the value of the site is appraised as if vacant and available for construction at its highest and best use. By adding the site value to the building value estimate, the total property value can be estimated.

51. **A.** $15 \div (15 + 45) = 15 \div 60 = 0.25$ or 25 percent.

52. **C.** $(1,900 \times \$110) + (420 \times \$50) = \$230,000$; $\$230,000 \times 0.9 = \$207,000$ value of improvements; $\$207,000 + \$50,000 = \$257,000$.

53. **A.** *Economic obsolescence* is defined as any loss in value due to factors outside the subject property. When economic obsolescence exists, the total impact of the loss can be quantified by capitalizing the loss in rent due to the condition.

54. **C.** $\$3,000,000 \div \$500,000 = 6$.

55. **A.** The various approaches to value are not avoided or used exclusively just because interest rates have gone up or down. A change in rates does, however, affect the capitalization rate that will be used in the income approach.

56. **A.** The first step necessary in the income approach to value is to calculate estimated gross income, which is defined as the amount of income generated if all the space is rented all of the time.

57. **B.** The basic valuation formula used for income-producing property is $V = I \div R$. $\$60,000 \div 0.14 = \$428,571$; $\$30,000 \div 0.07 = \$428,571$. Decreasing both the net operating income and the capitalization rate by one-half resulted in the same value estimate.

58. **B.** Standard 4 of the USPAP addresses the performance of a real property consulting service.

59. **D.** The value of the mortgage, $\$105,000$, plus the value of the equity, $\$30,000$, equals the value of the property or $\$135,000$.

60. **B.** The overall rate is equal to the net income ratio divided by the gross income multiplier. Thus $0.75/9 = 0.0833$ or 8.33 percent.

61. **C.** $\$75,000 =$ Monthly payment $\times$ (MPVIFA, 13 percent, 20 years); $\$75,000 =$ Monthly payment $\times$ 85.355132 (from table); $\$75,000 \div 85.355132 = \$878.68$.

    Annual payment = Monthly payment $\times$ 12; Annual payment $= \$878.68 \times 12 = \$10,544$.

62. **D.** $V =$ Value of property (or present value of cash flows); $V = \$25,000 \times$ (PVIFA, 12 percent, 5 years) $+ 1.15 \times V \times$ (PVF, 12 percent, 5 years)

    $V = (\$25,000 \times 3.604776) + (1.15 \times V \times 0.567427)$

    $V = \$90,119.40 + 0.6525 \times V$

    $V - 0.6525 \times V = \$90,119.40$

    $0.3475 \times V = \$90,119.40$

    $V = \$90,119.40 \div 0.3475 = \$259,367$

63. **B.** $(\$10,000 \times$ [PVIFA, 10 percent, 5 years]$)$ $+ (\$15,000 \times$ (PVIFA, 10 percent, 5 years) $\times$ (PVF, 10 percent, 5 years) $=$ Present value $(\$10,000 \times 3.790787)$ $+ (\$15,000 \times 3.790787 \times 0.620921)$ $= \$73,215$.

64. **B.** $\$10,000 + (\$10,000 \times$ [PVIFA, 10 percent, 4 years]$) + (\$15,000 \times$ ([PVIFA, 10 percent, 5 years]$) \times$ (PVF, 10 percent, 4 years) $=$ Present value.

    $\$10,000 + (\$10,000 \times 3.169865)$ $+ (\$15,000 \times 3.790787 \times 0.683013)$ $= \$80,536$.

65. **D.** $R_O = NOI/V$

Comparable	Net Income	Sales Price	R_O
1	$14,400	$120,000	0.12
2	$14,000	$147,400	0.095
3	$13,500	$122,700	0.11
4	$14,500	$152,600	0.095

Because comparables 2 and 4 are the most similar, the capitalization rates from these properties will be considered more heavily in determining the value of the subject property. $15,000 ÷ 0.095 = $157,895, rounded to $158,000.

66. **C.** Discounted cash flow analysis discounts cash flows from the time they are actually received. Thus whatever cash flow is received by the investor from sale is discounted to its present value. Some appraisers deduct selling expenses (cash expenses) from the sales price before discounting. Furthermore, if financing is being considered in the discounted cash flow analysis, then the mortgage balance must be deducted from the sale proceeds.

67. **D.** The equity dividend rate equals the cash flow available to the equity investor. Therefore it is compared to the initial cash outflow from the equity investor. The equity dividend rate is equal to the net operating income minus mortgage payments, and is also called the cash-on-cash rate.

68. **D.** $600,000 × 0.11 = $66,000 = income to the building. $88,000 − $66,000 = $22,000 = income to the land. $22,000 ÷ 0.09 = $244,444.

69. **C.** $R_O = M \times R_M \times DCR$

$0.10 = 0.7 \times 0.11 \times DCR$

$0.10 = 0.077 \times DCR$

$1.30 = DCR$

70. **C.** $R_O = L \times R_L + (1 - L) \times R_B$

$R_O = 0.1 \times 0.09 + 0.9 \times 0.12 = 0.117$

71. **B.** The mortgage constant must be higher than the interest rate to allow for amortization of the loan. If the mortgage constant were equal to the interest rate then the loan would be interest only, and if the mortgage constant were less than the interest rate then the loan would have negative amortization.

72. **A.** The band of investment technique does not explicitly consider the reversion (sale) of the property. It is simply a weighted average of the equity dividend rate and mortgage constant. The loan-to-value ratio is used for the weighting.

73. **B.** PV = $9,000 + $9,000 × (PVIFA, 10 percent, 4 years); PV = $9,000 + $9,000 × 3.169865 = $37,529.

74. **A.** The USPAP requires that value be defined. The effective date of the appraisal must be included. The names of previous owners are not required to be included in the appraisal report.

75. **A.** Contingency compensation in an appraisal consulting practice is unethical. Review appraisers are not permitted to accept contingency compensation. Contingency fees are addressed in the Management section of the Ethics Rule.

76. **C.** The Confidentiality section includes parties authorized by due process of law.

77. **D.** The approaches to value are required to be used only when they are necessary for credible assignment results.

78. **B.** Book value denotes the carrying amount of an asset as shown on the books of a company. The book value is not necessarily the same as the sales price or original cost.

79. **C.** If the net present value of the cash flows equals zero, the discount rate equals the internal rate of return. If the net present value of the cash flows is positive, the discount rate is less than the internal rate of return and vice versa.

80. **B.** The financial management rate of return (FMRR) is a variation of the internal rate of return (IRR) that uses a safe rate to discount negative cash flows and a run-of-the-mill rate to reinvest positive cash flows. The FMRR is usually lower than the IRR because the run-of-the-mill investment rate is lower than the IRR.

81. **B.** The effective rate can be calculated by finding the internal rate of return of the actual cash flows in a loan schedule. Payments are based on the full amount loaned. However, the amount of money received includes the financing costs. The effective rate will be higher than the interest rate on loans with financing costs. If no financing costs are involved, the effective rate will equal the interest rate.

82. **B.** 19 percent is the annual rate at which compound interest must be paid for $10,000 to become $20,000 in four years.

83. **C.** NOI (net operating income) = $100,000 – $60,000 = $40,000.

84. **C.** Severance damage is the loss in value to the remaining tract or parcel of land resulting from a partial taking of land through the power of eminent domain.

85. **B.** 100 × 80 × $18 × 3.5 ÷ 48 = $10,500 per month.

86. **B.** A rental concession is a service or discount offered by the landlord or representative of the landlord, such as the property manager, to a tenant to induce the tenant to sign a lease. Reasons for offering concessions might include the desire to rent up a certain amount of space prior to completion of the project or as an effort to retain existing tenants upon the expiration of their leases.

87. **C.** The efficiency ratio shows the relationship between leasable space and total space. A building with 50,000 square feet of total space but only 35,000 square feet of space that can be rented has an efficiency ratio of 70 percent.

88. **B.** The technical term for the amount of rent above the minimum rent is *overage rent*, which results from a percentage lease. It may or may not be the market rent.

89. **B.** A concession is a service or a discount offered by the landlord to a tenant to induce the tenant into signing a lease. Examples of concessions include reduced or "free" rent for a specified time period or improvements made by the owner on behalf of the tenant.

90. **C.** The value of a fee simple estate is based on market rent (sometimes referred to as economic rent). Contract rent is used for the value of a leased fee estate.

91. **D.** Workfiles must, as a minimum, be retained for five years after preparation of the appraisal report.

92. **B.** S.R. 2-2(a) addresses the requirement of containing sufficient information.

93. **D.** According to S.R. 2-3, an appraiser who signs a real property appraisal certification prepared by another, even under the label of "review appraiser," must accept full responsibility for all elements of the certification.

94. **C.** Assumptions and limiting conditions would include such a statement as "I assume there are no hidden defects in the property that would render it more or less valuable." The other statements would be included in the appraiser's certification.

95. **B.** The conditions assumed under the definition of market value include exposure in the open market for a reasonable amount of time.

96. **A.** The USPAP was developed by the appraisal profession rather than by a regulatory agency. The standards are for appraisers and the users of appraisal services.

97. **D.** A hypothetical condition is defined as "that which is contrary to what exists but is supposed for the purpose of analysis."

98. **C.** The appraiser should use his or her judgment and therefore should know if and when a particular approach to value is not appropriate for a specific appraisal assignment. Standards Rule 2-2(a)(viii) requires the appraiser to explain the exclusion of any of the usual valuation approaches.

99. **B.**

	Apartment	Office	Retail/ Commercial
Cost to Construct Improvements	$5,900,000	$8,600,000	$4,300,000
Net Operating Income	$850,000	$1,204,000	$650,000
Return to Building (12 percent)	−$708,000	−$1,032,000	−$516,000
Return to Land	$142,000	−$172,000	$134,000

The office building has the highest return to the land.

100. **D.** $172,000 ÷ 0.10 = $1,720,000.

101. **B.** PV = $5,000 × (PVIF, 10 percent, 1 year) + $7,000 × (PVIF, 10 percent, 2 years) + $9,000 × (PVIF, 10 percent, 3 years) + $9,000 × (PVIF, 10 percent, 4 years) + $110,000 × (PVIF, 10 percent, 5 years).

PV = ($5,000 × 0.909091) + ($7,000 × 0.826446) + ($9,000 × 0.751315) + ($9,000 × 0.683013) + ($110,000 × 0.620921).

PV = $91,541

102. **C.** $91,541 − $100,000 = − $8,459.

103. **B.** $80,000 + $81,300 + $81,600 + $82,500 + $84,000 + $84,000 + $86,800 = $580,200 ÷ 7 = $82,886.

104. **B.** $82,500 is the median or "middle" sales price in the sample.

105. **D.** The mode is the value that occurs the most number of times. In this sample, $84,000 occurred twice. No other sales price occurred more than once.

106. **C.** 20,000 sq. ft. × $18 = $360,000/12 = $30,000.

107. **C.** 20,000 sq. ft. × $18 = $360,000/12 = $30,000. The contract rent, regardless of the market rent, is still $18 per sq. ft.

108. **A.** $360,000 − $18,000 = $342,000/12 = $28,500.

109. **D.** $360,000/0.14 = $2,571,000.

110. **D.** ADS = $20,285.33 × 12 = $243,424; $360,000 − $243,424 = $116,576 BTCF; $116,576/$571,000 = 0.20 or 20%.

State Real Estate Appraisal Boards

Alabama

Lisa Brooks
Executive Director
Alabama Real Estate Appraiser Board
PO Box 304355
Montgomery, AL 36130
(334) 242-8747 (O)
(334) 242-8749 (F)
http://reab.state.al.us

Alaska

Wanda Fleming
Licensing Examiner
Alaska Board of Certified Real Estate Appraisers
PO Box 110806
Juneau, AK 99811-0806
(907) 465-2542 (O)
(907) 465-2974 (F)
www.commerce.state.ak.us/occ

Arizona

Deborah Pearson
Executive Director
Arizona Board of Appraisal
1400 West Washington, Suite 360
Phoenix, AZ 85007
(602) 542-1543 (O)
(602) 542-1598 (F)
www.appraisal.state.az.us

Arkansas

Jim Martin
Executive Director
Arkansas Appraiser Licensing and Certification
    Board
101 E. Capitol Street, Suite 430
Little Rock, AR 72202
(501) 296-1843 (O)
(501) 296-1844 (F)
www.state.ar.us/alcb

California

Anthony Majewski
Director
Office of Real Estate Appraisers
1102 Q Street, Suite 4100
Sacramento, CA 95833
(916) 440-7878 (O)
(916) 440-7406 (F)
www.orea.ca.gov

Colorado

Stewart A. Leach
Program Administrator
Colorado Board of Real Estate Appraisers
1900 Grant Street, Suite 600
Denver, CO 80203
(303) 894-2424 (O)
(303) 894-2683 (F)
www.dora.state.co.us/real_estate

Connecticut
Lauren Rubino
Real Estate Examiner
Real Estate Appraisal Commission
165 Capitol Avenue, Room 110
Hartford, CT 06106-1630
(860) 713-6150 (O)
(860) 713-7230 (F)
www.state.ct.us/licensing/realestate

Delaware
Dana Spruill
Administrative Specialist
Delaware Council on Real Estate Appraisers
Professional Regulation Division
861 Silver Lake Blvd., Suite 203
Dover, DE 19904
(302) 744-4500 (O)
(302) 739-2711 (F)
www.dpr.delaware.gov

District of Columbia
Dorothy Thomas
Administrator
DCRA/OPLA
941 N. Capitol St. N.E., Suite 7200
Washington, DC 20002
(202) 442-4472 (O)
(202) 442-4528 (F)
www.dcra.dc.gov/dcra

Florida
Michael E. Murphy
Division Director
Florida Real Estate Appraisal Board
400 West Robinson Street
North Tower, Suite N 801
Orlando, FL 32801-1757
(407) 481-5662 (O)
(407) 317-7245 (F)
www.state.fl.us/dbpr/re/freab_welcome.shtml

Georgia
Charles Clark
Real Estate Commissioner
Georgia Real Estate Appraisers Board
International Tower, Suite 1000
229 Peachtree Street NE
Atlanta, GA 30303-1605
(404) 656-3916 (O)
(404) 656-6650 (F)
www.state.ga.us/Ga.Real_Estate

Hawaii
Candace Ito
Executive Officer
Hawaii Real Estate Appraiser Committee
PO Box 3469
Honolulu, HI 96801
(808) 586-2704 (O)
(808) 586-2689 (F)
www.hawaii.gov/dcca/pv

Idaho
Sandy Hitesman
Bureau Chief
Idaho Real Estate Appraisers Board
Bureau of Occupational Licenses
1109 Main St., Suite 220
Boise, ID 83702-5642
(208) 334-3233 (O)
(208) 334-3945 (F)
www2.state.id.us/ibol/rea.htm

Illinois
Michael Brown
Director
Illinois Office of Banks and Real Estate
310 S. Michigan Ave., Suite 2130
Chicago, IL 60604
(217) 793-7254 (O)
(217) 793-8720 (F)
www.obre.state.il.us/realest/appraisal.htm

Indiana
Nick Rhoad
Executive Director
Indiana Professional Licensing Agency
302 W. Washington, Room EO 12
Indianapolis, IN 46204-2700
(317) 234-3009 (O)
(317) 232-2312 (F)
www.in.gov/pla/bandc/appraiser

Iowa
Susan Griffel
Executive Officer
Professional Licensing and Regulation Division
Department of Commerce
1918 Southeast Hulsizer Avenue
Ankeny, IA 50021-3941
(515) 281-7417 (O)
(515) 281-7411 (F)
*www.state.ia.us/government/com/prof/realappr/
    realappr.htm*

Kansas

Sally Pritchett
Executive Director
Kansas Real Estate Appraisal Board
1100 S.W. Wanamaker Rd., Suite 104
Topeka, KS 66604
(785) 271-3371 (O)
(785) 271-3370 (F)
www.accesskansas.org/kreab

Kentucky

Larry Disney
Executive Director
2480 Fortune Dr., Suite 120
Lexington, KY 40509
(859) 543-8943 (O)
(859) 543-0028 (F)
www.kyappraisersboard.com

Louisiana

J.C. Willie
Executive Director
Louisiana Real Estate Appraisers Board
    of Certification
9071 Interline Ave.
Baton Rouge, LA 70898-4785
(225) 765-0191 (O)
(225) 765-0637 (F)
www.reab.state.la.us

Maine

Carol Leighton
Administrator
Maine Board of Real Estate Appraisers
State House Station #35
Augusta, ME 04333-0035
(207) 624-8520 (O)
(207) 624-8637 (F)
www.state.me.us/pfr/lolr/categories/cat37.htm

Maryland

Charles Kazlo
Executive Director
Maryland Real Estate Appraisers Commission
500 N. Calvert St., Room 302
Baltimore, MD 21202
(410) 333-6328 (O)
(410) 333-6314 (F)
www.dllr.state.md.us/license/occprof/reappr.html

Massachusetts

Judith H. Meltzer
Program Coordinator
Board of Registration of Real Estate Appraisers
239 Causway St., Suite 500
Boston, MA 02114
(617) 727-3055 (O)
(617) 727-2197 (F)
www.state.ma.us/reg/boards/ra

Michigan

Joseph Campbell
Licensing Administrator
Michigan Board of Real Estate Appraisers
PO Box 30018
Lansing, MI 48909
(517) 241-9201 (O)
(517) 241-9280 (F)
www.michigan.gov/cis

Minnesota

Susan Bergh
Licensing Director
Department of Commerce
85 N. 7th Place #500
St. Paul, MN 55101
(651) 296-6319 (O)
(651) 284-4107 (F)
www.commerce.state.mn.us

Mississippi

Robert Praytor
Administrator
Mississippi Real Estate Appraiser and
    Certification Board
2506 Lakeland Dr., Suite 300
Jackson, MS 39232
(601) 932-9191 (O)
(601) 932-3880 (F)
www.mrec.state.ms.us/

Missouri

Kristi Klamet
Executive Director
Missouri Real Estate Appraisers Commission
PO Box 1335
Jefferson City, MO 65102-1335
(573) 751-0038 (O)
(573) 526-3489 (F)
www.pr.mo.gov/appraisers.asp

Montana

Grace Berger
Board Administrator
Montana Board of Real Estate Appraisers
PO Box 200513
Helena, MT 59620-0513
(406) 841-2386 (O)
(406) 841-2305 (F)
www.commerce.mt.gov/licensing

Nebraska

Jim Ekstein
Director
Nebraska Real Estate Appraiser Board
State Office Bldg., 3rd Floor
Lincoln, NE 68509-4963
(402) 471-9015 (O)
(402) 471-9017 (F)
www.linuxlo.nrc.state.ne.us/appraiser

Nevada

Brenda Kindred-Kipling
Appraisal Officer
Department of Business and Industry
Nevada Real Estate Division
788 Fairview Dr., Suite 200
Carson City, NV 89702
(775) 687-4280 (O)
(775) 687-4868 (F)
www.red.state.nv.us

New Hampshire

Maureen Jully
Executive Secretary
Real Estate Appraiser Board
State House Annex, Room 426
25 Capitol Street
Concord, NH 03301-6312
(603) 271-6186 (O)
(603) 271-6513 (F)

New Jersey

James Hsu
Executive Director
State Board of Real Estate Appraisers
Department of Law and Public Safety
124 Halsey Street, 3rd Floor
Newark, NJ 07101
(973) 504-6480 (O)
(973) 504-6458 (F)
www.state.nj.us/LPs/ca/real

New Mexico

Renee Romero
Executive Director
New Mexico Real Estate Appraisers Board
PO Box 25101
Santa Fe, NM 87504
(505) 476-7082 (O)
(505) 476-7094 (F)
www.state.mn.us/rld/asd

New York

Al Jurczynski
Deputy Secretary to the Board
New York Board of Real Estate Appraisers
84 Holland Ave.
Albany, NY 12208-3490
(518) 474-4429 (O)
(518) 473-6648 (F)
www.dos.state.ny.us/lcns/appraise.html

North Carolina

Philip Humphries
Director
North Carolina Appraisal Board
PO Box 20500
Raleigh, NC 27619-0500
(919) 420-7920 (O)
(919) 420-7925 (F)
www.ncappraisalboard.org

North Dakota

Jodie R. Campbell
Executive Director
North Dakota Appraisal Board
PO Box 1336
Bismarck, ND 58502-1336
(701) 222-1051 (O)
(701) 222-8083 (F)
ndapprb@btigate.com

Ohio

Kelly Davids
Superintendent
Ohio Real Estate Appraiser Board
77 S. High Street, 20th Floor
Columbus, OH 43215
(614) 466-6297 (O)
(216) 787-4449 (F)
www.com.state.oh.us/odoc/real/appmain.htm

Oklahoma
George Stirman
Director
Oklahoma Real Estate Appraiser Board
PO Box 53408
Oklahoma City, OK 73152-3408
(405) 521-6636 (O)
(405) 522-6909 (F)
www.oid.state.ok.us/agentbrokers/realesta.html

Oregon
Robert A. Keith
Administrator
Appraiser Certification & Licensure Board
1860 Hawthorne Ave. N.E., #200
Salem, OR 97303
(503) 485-2555 (O)
(503) 485-2559 (F)
www.oregonaclb.org

Pennsylvania
Michelle Smey
Board Administrator
State Board of Certified Real Estate Appraisers
124 Pine Street, 1st Floor
Harrisburg, PA 17101
(717) 783-4866 (O)
(717) 705-5540 (F)
www.dos.state.pa.us/real

Rhode Island
Valerie Voccio
Administrator
Rhode Island Real Estate Appraisers Board
233 Richmond Street, Room 230
Providence, RI 02903-4230
(401) 277-2262 (O)
(401) 277-6654 (F)

South Carolina
John R. Pitts
Administrator
Real Estate Appraisers Board
PO Box 11847
Columbia, SC 29211-1847
(803) 896-4400 (O)
(803) 896-4404 (F)
www.llr.state.sc.us/pol/realestateappraisers

South Dakota
Sherry Bren
Executive Director
Appraiser Certification Program
Department of Commerce/Regulation
445 East Capitol Avenue
Pierre, SD 57501-3185
(605) 773-4608 (O)
(605) 773-5369 (F)
www.state.sd.us/appraisers

Tennessee
Kay Searcy
Administrative Director
Tennessee Real Estate Appraiser Commission
500 James Roberson Parkway, Ste. 620
Nashville, TN 37243-1166
(615) 741-1831 (O)
(615) 253-1692 (F)
www.state.tn.us/commerce/boards

Texas
Wayne Thorburn
Commissioner
Appraiser Licensing and Certification Board
PO Box 12188
Austin, TX 78711-2188
(512) 465-3950 (O)
(512) 465-3953 (F)
www.talcb.capnet.state.tx.us

Utah
Derek Miller
Director
Utah Department of Commerce
Division of Real Estate
160 East 300 South
Salt Lake City, UT 84114-6711
(801) 530-6762 (O)
(801) 530-6749 (F)
www.commerce.state.ut.gov/dre/applicensing.html

Vermont
Theodore McKnight
Board Administrator
Vermont Real Estate Appraisers Board
81 River St., Heritage 1 Bldg.
Montpelier, VT 05609-1106
(802) 828-3228 (O)
(802) 828-2368 (F)
www.vtprofessionals.org/opr1/appraisers

Virginia

Christine Martine
Executive Director
Real Estate Appraiser Board
Department of Professional and Occupational
    Registration
3600 West Broad Street, 5th Floor
Richmond, VA 23230-4817
(804) 367-2039 (O)
(804) 367-6946 (F)
www.state.va.us/dpor/indexne.html

Washington

Ralph C. Birkedahl
Program Manager
Real Estate Appraiser Section
Business and Professions Division
PO Box 9015
Olympia, WA 98507-9015
(360) 664-6504 (O)
(360) 570-4981 (F)
www.dol.wa.gov/app/appfront.htm

West Virginia

Sharon Knotts
Executive Director
Appraiser Licensing and Certification Board
2110 Kanawha Blvd, Suite 101
Charleston, WV 25311
(304) 558-3919 (O)
(304) 558-3983 (F)
www.state.wv.us/appraise

Wisconsin

Tim Wellnitz
Bureau Director
Wisconsin Real Estate Appraisers Board
1400 E. Washington
Madison, WI 53708-8935
(608) 261-4486 (O)
(608) 267-0644 (F)
www.drl.state.wi.us

Wyoming

Donna Rice
Executive Director
Certified Real Estate Appraiser Board
2020 Carey Avenue, Suite 100
Cheyenne, WY 82002-0180
(307) 777-7141 (O)
(307) 777-3796 (F)
http://realestate.state.wy.us

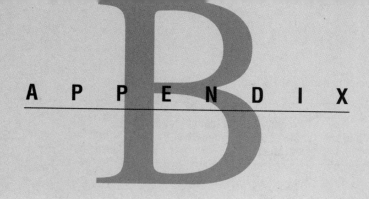

Compound Interest Tables *

---

* The tables on the following pages include the six functions of a dollar. Two sets of tables are provided. The first set of tables is based on annual compounding and the second set is based on monthly compounding. Solutions to some of the problems in the sample exams, especially those that deal with the income approach, are based on the use of these tables.

Annual Compound Interest Tables

6.00% Annual Interest Rate

	1	2	3	4	5	6	
	Future Value of $1	Future Value Annuity of $1 Per Year	Sinking Fund Factor	Present Value of $1 (Reversion)	Present Value Annuity of $1 Per Year	Payment to Amortize $1	
Years							Years
1	1.060000	1.000000	1.000000	0.943396	0.943396	1.060000	1
2	1.123600	2.060000	0.485437	0.889996	1.833393	0.545437	2
3	1.191016	3.183600	0.314110	0.839619	2.673012	0.374110	3
4	1.262477	4.374616	0.228592	0.792094	3.465106	0.288592	4
5	1.338226	5.637093	0.177396	0.747258	4.212364	0.237396	5
6	1.418519	6.975319	0.143363	0.704960	4.917324	0.203363	6
7	1.503630	8.393838	0.119135	0.665057	5.582381	0.179135	7
8	1.593848	9.897468	0.101036	0.627412	6.209794	0.161036	8
9	1.689479	11.491316	0.087022	0.591898	6.801692	0.147022	9
10	1.790848	13.180795	0.075868	0.558395	7.360087	0.135868	10
11	1.898299	14.971643	0.066793	0.526787	7.886875	0.126793	11
12	2.012196	16.869941	0.059277	0.496969	8.383844	0.119277	12
13	2.132928	18.882138	0.052960	0.468839	8.852683	0.112960	13
14	2.260904	21.015066	0.047585	0.442301	9.294984	0.107585	14
15	2.396558	23.275970	0.042963	0.417265	9.712249	0.102963	15
16	2.540352	25.672528	0.038952	0.393646	10.105895	0.098952	16
17	2.692773	28.212880	0.035445	0.371364	10.477260	0.095445	17
18	2.854339	30.905653	0.032357	0.350344	10.827603	0.092357	18
19	3.025600	33.759992	0.029621	0.330513	11.158117	0.089621	19
20	3.207135	36.785591	0.027185	0.311805	11.469921	0.087185	20
21	3.399564	39.992727	0.025005	0.294155	11.764077	0.085005	21
22	3.603537	43.392290	0.023046	0.277505	12.041582	0.083046	22
23	3.819750	46.995828	0.021278	0.261797	12.303379	0.081278	23
24	4.048935	50.815577	0.019679	0.246978	12.550358	0.079679	24
25	4.291871	54.864512	0.018227	0.232998	12.783356	0.078227	25
26	4.549383	59.156383	0.016904	0.219810	13.003166	0.076904	26
27	4.822346	63.705766	0.015697	0.207368	13.210534	0.075697	27
28	5.111687	68.528112	0.014593	0.195630	13.406164	0.074593	28
29	5.418388	73.639798	0.013580	0.184557	13.590721	0.073580	29
30	5.743491	79.058186	0.012649	0.174110	13.764831	0.072649	30
31	6.088101	84.801677	0.011792	0.164255	13.929086	0.071792	31
32	6.453387	90.889778	0.011002	0.154957	14.084043	0.071002	32
33	6.840590	97.343165	0.010273	0.146186	14.230230	0.070273	33
34	7.251025	104.183755	0.009598	0.137911	14.368141	0.069598	34
35	7.686087	111.434780	0.008974	0.130105	14.498246	0.068974	35
36	8.147252	119.120867	0.008395	0.122741	14.620987	0.068395	36
37	8.636087	127.268119	0.007857	0.115793	14.736780	0.067857	37
38	9.154252	135.904206	0.007358	0.109239	14.846019	0.067358	38
39	9.703507	145.058458	0.006894	0.103055	14.949075	0.066894	39
40	10.285718	154.761966	0.006462	0.097222	15.046297	0.066462	40
41	10.902861	165.047684	0.006059	0.091719	15.138016	0.066059	41
42	11.557033	175.950545	0.005683	0.086527	15.224543	0.065683	42
43	12.250455	187.507577	0.005333	0.081630	15.306173	0.065333	43
44	12.985482	199.758032	0.005006	0.077009	15.383182	0.065006	44
45	13.764611	212.743514	0.004701	0.072650	15.455832	0.064701	45
46	14.590487	226.508125	0.004415	0.068538	15.524370	0.064415	46
47	15.465917	241.098612	0.004148	0.064658	15.589028	0.064148	47
48	16.393872	256.564529	0.003898	0.060998	15.650027	0.063898	48
49	17.377504	272.958401	0.003664	0.057546	15.707572	0.063664	49
50	18.420154	290.335905	0.003444	0.054288	15.761861	0.063444	50

Annual Compound Interest Tables

8.00% Annual Interest Rate

	1	2	3	4	5	6	
	Future Value of $1	**Future Value Annuity of $1 Per Year**	**Sinking Fund Factor**	**Present Value of $1 (Reversion)**	**Present Value Annuity of $1 Per Year**	**Payment to Amortize $1**	
Years							Years
1	1.080000	1.000000	1.000000	0.925926	0.925926	1.080000	1
2	1.166400	2.080000	0.480769	0.857339	1.783265	0.560769	2
3	1.259712	3.246400	0.308034	0.793832	2.577097	0.388034	3
4	1.360489	4.506112	0.221921	0.735030	3.312127	0.301921	4
5	1.469328	5.866601	0.170456	0.680583	3.992710	0.250456	5
6	1.586874	7.335929	0.136315	0.630170	4.622880	0.216315	6
7	1.713824	8.922803	0.112072	0.583490	5.206370	0.192072	7
8	1.850930	10.636628	0.094015	0.540269	5.746639	0.174015	8
9	1.999005	12.487558	0.080080	0.500249	6.246888	0.160080	9
10	2.158925	14.486562	0.069029	0.463193	6.710081	0.149029	10
11	2.331639	16.645487	0.060076	0.428883	7.138964	0.140076	11
12	2.518170	18.977126	0.052695	0.397114	7.536078	0.132695	12
13	2.719624	21.495297	0.046522	0.367698	7.903776	0.126522	13
14	2.937194	24.214920	0.041297	0.340461	8.244237	0.121297	14
15	3.172169	27.152114	0.036830	0.315242	8.559479	0.116830	15
16	3.425943	30.324283	0.032977	0.291890	8.851369	0.112977	16
17	3.700018	33.750226	0.029629	0.270269	9.121638	0.109629	17
18	3.996020	37.450244	0.026702	0.250249	9.371887	0.106702	18
19	4.315701	41.446263	0.024128	0.231712	9.603599	0.104128	19
20	4.660957	45.761964	0.021852	0.214548	9.818147	0.101852	20
21	5.033834	50.422921	0.019832	0.198656	10.016803	0.099832	21
22	5.436540	55.456755	0.018032	0.183940	10.200744	0.098032	22
23	5.871464	60.893296	0.016422	0.170315	10.371059	0.096422	23
24	6.341181	66.764759	0.014978	0.157699	10.528758	0.094978	24
25	6.848475	73.105940	0.013679	0.146018	10.674776	0.093679	25
26	7.396353	79.954415	0.012507	0.135202	10.809978	0.092507	26
27	7.988061	87.350768	0.011448	0.125187	10.935165	0.091448	27
28	8.627106	95.338830	0.010489	0.115914	11.051079	0.090489	28
29	9.317275	103.965936	0.009619	0.107327	11.158406	0.089619	29
30	10.062657	113.283211	0.008827	0.099377	11.257783	0.088827	30
31	10.867669	123.345868	0.008107	0.092016	11.349799	0.088107	31
32	11.737083	134.213537	0.007451	0.085200	11.434999	0.087451	32
33	12.676050	145.950620	0.006852	0.078889	11.513888	0.086852	33
34	13.690134	158.626670	0.006304	0.073045	11.586934	0.086304	34
35	14.785344	172.316804	0.005803	0.067634	11.654568	0.085803	35
36	15.968172	187.102148	0.005345	0.062625	11.717193	0.085345	36
37	17.245626	203.070320	0.004924	0.057986	11.775179	0.084924	37
38	18.625276	220.315945	0.004539	0.053690	11.828869	0.084539	38
39	20.115298	238.941221	0.004185	0.049713	11.878582	0.084185	39
40	21.724522	259.056519	0.003860	0.046031	11.924613	0.083860	40
41	23.462483	280.781040	0.003562	0.042621	11.967235	0.083562	41
42	25.339482	304.243523	0.003287	0.039464	12.006699	0.083287	42
43	27.366640	329.583005	0.003034	0.036541	12.043240	0.083034	43
44	29.555972	356.949646	0.002802	0.033834	12.077074	0.082802	44
45	31.920449	386.505617	0.002587	0.031328	12.108402	0.082587	45
46	34.474085	418.426067	0.002390	0.029007	12.137409	0.082390	46
47	37.232012	452.900152	0.002208	0.026859	12.164267	0.082208	47
48	40.210573	490.132164	0.002040	0.024869	12.189136	0.082040	48
49	43.427419	530.342737	0.001886	0.023027	12.212163	0.081886	49
50	46.901613	573.770156	0.001743	0.021321	12.233485	0.081743	50

Annual Compound Interest Tables

9.00% Annual Interest Rate

	1	2	3	4	5	6	
	Future Value of $1	Future Value Annuity of $1 Per Year	Sinking Fund Factor	Present Value of $1 (Reversion)	Present Value Annuity of $1 Per Year	Payment to Amortize $1	
Years							Years
1	1.090000	1.000000	1.000000	0.917431	0.917431	1.090000	1
2	1.188100	2.090000	0.478469	0.841680	1.759111	0.568469	2
3	1.295029	3.278100	0.305055	0.772183	2.531295	0.395055	3
4	1.411582	4.573129	0.218669	0.708425	3.239720	0.308669	4
5	1.538624	5.984711	0.167092	0.649931	3.889651	0.257092	5
6	1.677100	7.523335	0.132920	0.596267	4.485919	0.222920	6
7	1.828039	9.200435	0.108691	0.547034	5.032953	0.198691	7
8	1.992563	11.028474	0.090674	0.501866	5.534819	0.180674	8
9	2.171893	13.021036	0.076799	0.460427	5.995247	0.166799	9
10	2.367364	15.192930	0.065820	0.422410	6.417658	0.155820	10
11	2.580426	17.560293	0.056947	0.387532	6.805191	0.146947	11
12	2.812665	20.140720	0.049651	0.355534	7.160725	0.139651	12
13	3.065805	22.953385	0.043567	0.326178	7.486904	0.133567	13
14	3.341727	26.019189	0.038433	0.299246	7.786150	0.128433	14
15	3.642482	29.360916	0.034059	0.274538	8.060688	0.124059	15
16	3.970306	33.003399	0.030300	0.251869	8.312558	0.120300	16
17	4.327633	36.973705	0.027046	0.231073	8.543631	0.117046	17
18	4.717120	41.301338	0.024212	0.211993	8.755625	0.114212	18
19	5.141661	46.018458	0.021730	0.194489	8.950115	0.111730	19
20	5.604411	51.160120	0.019546	0.178431	9.128546	0.109546	20
21	6.108808	56.764530	0.017617	0.163698	9.292244	0.107617	21
22	6.658600	62.873338	0.015905	0.150181	9.442425	0.105905	22
23	7.257874	69.531939	0.014382	0.137781	9.580207	0.104382	23
24	7.911083	76.789813	0.013023	0.126405	9.706612	0.103023	24
25	8.623081	84.700896	0.011806	0.115968	9.822580	0.101806	25
26	9.399158	93.323977	0.010715	0.106392	9.928972	0.100715	26
27	10.245082	102.723135	0.009735	0.097608	10.026580	0.099735	27
28	11.167140	112.968217	0.008852	0.089548	10.116128	0.098852	28
29	12.172182	124.135356	0.008056	0.082154	10.198283	0.098056	29
30	13.267678	136.307539	0.007336	0.075371	10.273654	0.097336	30
31	14.461770	149.575217	0.006686	0.069148	10.342802	0.096686	31
32	15.763329	164.036987	0.006096	0.063438	10.406240	0.096096	32
33	17.182028	179.800315	0.005562	0.058200	10.464441	0.095562	33
34	18.728411	196.982344	0.005077	0.053395	10.517835	0.095077	34
35	20.413968	215.710755	0.004636	0.048986	10.566821	0.094636	35
36	22.251225	236.124723	0.004235	0.044941	10.611763	0.094235	36
37	24.253835	258.375948	0.003870	0.041230	10.652993	0.093870	37
38	26.436680	282.629783	0.003538	0.037826	10.690820	0.093538	38
39	28.815982	309.066463	0.003236	0.034703	10.725523	0.093236	39
40	31.409420	337.882445	0.002960	0.031837	10.757360	0.092960	40
41	34.236268	369.291865	0.002708	0.029209	10.786569	0.092708	41
42	37.317532	403.528133	0.002478	0.026797	10.813366	0.092478	42
43	40.676110	440.845665	0.002268	0.024584	10.837951	0.092268	43
44	44.336960	481.521775	0.002077	0.022554	10.860505	0.092077	44
45	48.327286	525.858735	0.001902	0.020692	10.881197	0.091902	45
46	52.676742	574.186021	0.001742	0.018984	10.900181	0.091742	46
47	57.417649	626.862762	0.001595	0.017416	10.917597	0.091595	47
48	62.585237	684.280411	0.001461	0.015978	10.933575	0.091461	48
49	68.217908	746.865648	0.001339	0.014659	10.948234	0.091339	49
50	74.357520	815.083556	0.001227	0.013448	10.961683	0.091227	50

Annual Compound Interest Tables

10.00% Annual Interest Rate

	1	2	3	4	5	6	
Years	Future Value of $1	Future Value Annuity of $1 Per Year	Sinking Fund Factor	Present Value of $1 (Reversion)	Present Value Annuity of $1 Per Year	Payment to Amortize $1	Years
1	1.100000	1.000000	1.000000	0.909091	0.909091	1.100000	1
2	1.210000	2.100000	0.476190	0.826446	1.735537	0.576190	2
3	1.331000	3.310000	0.302115	0.751315	2.486852	0.402115	3
4	1.464100	4.641000	0.215471	0.683013	3.169865	0.315471	4
5	1.610510	6.105100	0.163797	0.620921	3.790787	0.263797	5
6	1.771561	7.715610	0.129607	0.564474	4.355261	0.229607	6
7	1.948717	9.487171	0.105406	0.513158	4.868419	0.205406	7
8	2.143589	11.435888	0.087444	0.466507	5.334926	0.187444	8
9	2.357948	13.579477	0.073641	0.424098	5.759024	0.173641	9
10	2.593742	15.937425	0.062745	0.385543	6.144567	0.162745	10
11	2.853117	18.531167	0.053963	0.350494	6.495061	0.153963	11
12	3.138428	21.384284	0.046763	0.318631	6.813692	0.146763	12
13	3.452271	24.522712	0.040779	0.289664	7.103356	0.140779	13
14	3.797498	27.974983	0.035746	0.263331	7.366687	0.135746	14
15	4.177248	31.772482	0.031474	0.239392	7.606080	0.131474	15
16	4.594973	35.949730	0.027817	0.217629	7.823709	0.127817	16
17	5.054470	40.544703	0.024664	0.197845	8.021553	0.124664	17
18	5.559917	45.599173	0.021930	0.179859	8.201412	0.121930	18
19	6.115909	51.159090	0.019547	0.163508	8.364920	0.119547	19
20	6.727500	57.275000	0.017460	0.148644	8.513564	0.117460	20
21	7.400250	64.002499	0.015624	0.135131	8.648694	0.115624	21
22	8.140275	71.402749	0.014005	0.122846	8.771540	0.114005	22
23	8.954302	79.543024	0.012572	0.111678	8.883218	0.112572	23
24	9.849733	88.497327	0.011300	0.101526	8.984744	0.111300	24
25	10.834706	98.347059	0.010168	0.092296	9.077040	0.110168	25
26	11.918177	109.181765	0.009159	0.083905	9.160945	0.109159	26
27	13.109994	121.099942	0.008258	0.076278	9.237223	0.108258	27
28	14.420994	134.209936	0.007451	0.069343	9.306567	0.107451	28
29	15.863093	148.630930	0.006728	0.063039	9.369606	0.106728	29
30	17.449402	164.494023	0.006079	0.057309	9.426914	0.106079	30
31	19.194343	181.943425	0.005496	0.052099	9.479013	0.105496	31
32	21.113777	201.137767	0.004972	0.047362	9.526376	0.104972	32
33	23.225154	222.251544	0.004499	0.043057	9.569432	0.104499	33
34	25.547670	245.476699	0.004074	0.039143	9.608575	0.104074	34
35	28.102437	271.024368	0.003690	0.035584	9.644159	0.103690	35
36	30.912681	299.126805	0.003343	0.032349	9.676508	0.103343	36
37	34.003949	330.039486	0.003030	0.029408	9.705917	0.103030	37
38	37.404343	364.043434	0.002747	0.026735	9.732651	0.102747	38
39	41.144778	401.447778	0.002491	0.024304	9.756956	0.102491	39
40	45.259256	442.592556	0.002259	0.022095	9.779051	0.102259	40
41	49.785181	487.851811	0.002050	0.020086	9.799137	0.102050	41
42	54.763699	537.636992	0.001860	0.018260	9.817397	0.101860	42
43	60.240069	592.400692	0.001688	0.016600	9.833998	0.101688	43
44	66.264076	652.640761	0.001532	0.015091	9.849089	0.101532	44
45	72.890484	718.904837	0.001391	0.013719	9.862808	0.101391	45
46	80.179532	791.795321	0.001263	0.012472	9.875280	0.101263	46
47	88.197485	871.974853	0.001147	0.011338	9.886618	0.101147	47
48	97.017234	960.172338	0.001041	0.010307	9.896926	0.101041	48
49	106.718957	1057.189572	0.000946	0.009370	9.906296	0.100946	49
50	117.390853	1163.908529	0.000859	0.008519	9.914814	0.100859	50

Annual Compound Interest Tables

11.00% Annual Interest Rate

	1	2	3	4	5	6	
	Future Value of $1	Future Value Annuity of $1 Per Year	Sinking Fund Factor	Present Value of $1 (Reversion)	Present Value Annuity of $1 Per Year	Payment to Amortize $1	
Years							Years
1	1.110000	1.000000	1.000000	0.900901	0.900901	1.110000	1
2	1.232100	2.110000	0.473934	0.811622	1.712523	0.583934	2
3	1.367631	3.342100	0.299213	0.731191	2.443715	0.409213	3
4	1.518070	4.709731	0.212326	0.658731	3.102446	0.322326	4
5	1.685058	6.227801	0.160570	0.593451	3.695897	0.270570	5
6	1.870415	7.912860	0.126377	0.534641	4.230538	0.236377	6
7	2.076160	9.783274	0.102215	0.481658	4.712196	0.212215	7
8	2.304538	11.859434	0.084321	0.433927	5.146123	0.194321	8
9	2.558037	14.163972	0.070602	0.390925	5.537048	0.180602	9
10	2.839421	16.722009	0.059801	0.352184	5.889232	0.169801	10
11	3.151757	19.561430	0.051121	0.317283	6.206515	0.161121	11
12	3.498451	22.713187	0.044027	0.285841	6.492356	0.154027	12
13	3.883280	26.211638	0.038151	0.257514	6.749870	0.148151	13
14	4.310441	30.094918	0.033228	0.231995	6.981865	0.143228	14
15	4.784589	34.405359	0.029065	0.209004	7.190870	0.139065	15
16	5.310894	39.189948	0.025517	0.188292	7.379162	0.135517	16
17	5.895093	44.500843	0.022471	0.169633	7.548794	0.132471	17
18	6.543553	50.395936	0.019843	0.152822	7.701617	0.129843	18
19	7.263344	56.939488	0.017563	0.137678	7.839294	0.127563	19
20	8.062312	64.202832	0.015576	0.124034	7.963328	0.125576	20
21	8.949166	72.265144	0.013838	0.111742	8.075070	0.123838	21
22	9.933574	81.214309	0.012313	0.100669	8.175739	0.122313	22
23	11.026267	91.147884	0.010971	0.090693	8.266432	0.120971	23
24	12.239157	102.174151	0.009787	0.081705	8.348137	0.119787	24
25	13.585464	114.413307	0.008740	0.073608	8.421745	0.118740	25
26	15.079865	127.998771	0.007813	0.066314	8.488058	0.117813	26
27	16.738650	143.078636	0.006989	0.059742	8.547800	0.116989	27
28	18.579901	159.817286	0.006257	0.053822	8.601622	0.116257	28
29	20.623691	178.397187	0.005605	0.048488	8.650110	0.115605	29
30	22.892297	199.020878	0.005025	0.043683	8.693793	0.115025	30
31	25.410449	221.913174	0.004506	0.039354	8.733146	0.114506	31
32	28.205599	247.323624	0.004043	0.035454	8.768600	0.114043	32
33	31.308214	275.529222	0.003629	0.031941	8.800541	0.113629	33
34	34.752118	306.837437	0.003259	0.028775	8.829316	0.113259	34
35	38.574851	341.589555	0.002927	0.025924	8.855240	0.112927	35
36	42.818085	380.164406	0.002630	0.023355	8.878594	0.112630	36
37	47.528074	422.982490	0.002364	0.021040	8.899635	0.112364	37
38	52.756162	470.510564	0.002125	0.018955	8.918590	0.112125	38
39	58.559340	523.266727	0.001911	0.017077	8.935666	0.111911	39
40	65.000867	581.826066	0.001719	0.015384	8.951051	0.111719	40
41	72.150963	646.826934	0.001546	0.013860	8.964911	0.111546	41
42	80.087569	718.977896	0.001391	0.012486	8.977397	0.111391	42
43	88.897201	799.065465	0.001251	0.011249	8.988646	0.111251	43
44	98.675893	887.962666	0.001126	0.010134	8.998780	0.111126	44
45	109.530242	986.638559	0.001014	0.009130	9.007910	0.111014	45
46	121.578568	1096.168801	0.000912	0.008225	9.016135	0.110912	46
47	134.952211	1217.747369	0.000821	0.007410	9.023545	0.110821	47
48	149.796954	1352.699580	0.000739	0.006676	9.030221	0.110739	48
49	166.274619	1502.496534	0.000666	0.006014	9.036235	0.110666	49
50	184.564827	1668.771152	0.000599	0.005418	9.041653	0.110599	50

Annual Compound Interest Tables

12.00% Annual Interest Rate

	1	2	3	4	5	6	
	Future Value of $1	Future Value Annuity of $1 Per Year	Sinking Fund Factor	Present Value of $1 (Reversion)	Present Value Annuity of $1 Per Year	Payment to Amortize $1	
Years							Years
1	1.120000	1.000000	1.000000	0.892857	0.892857	1.120000	1
2	1.254400	2.120000	0.471698	0.797194	1.690051	0.591698	2
3	1.404928	3.374400	0.296349	0.711780	2.401831	0.416349	3
4	1.573519	4.779328	0.209234	0.635518	3.037349	0.329234	4
5	1.762342	6.352847	0.157410	0.567426	3.604776	0.277410	5
6	1.973823	8.115189	0.123226	0.506631	4.111407	0.243226	6
7	2.210681	10.089012	0.099118	0.452349	4.563757	0.219118	7
8	2.475963	12.299693	0.081303	0.403883	4.967640	0.201303	8
9	2.773079	14.775656	0.067679	0.360610	5.328250	0.187679	9
10	3.105848	17.548735	0.056984	0.321973	5.650223	0.176984	10
11	3.478550	20.654583	0.048415	0.287476	5.937699	0.168415	11
12	3.895976	24.133133	0.041437	0.256675	6.194374	0.161437	12
13	4.363493	28.029109	0.035677	0.229174	6.423548	0.155677	13
14	4.887112	32.392602	0.030871	0.204619	6.628168	0.150871	14
15	5.473566	37.279715	0.026824	0.182696	6.810864	0.146824	15
16	6.130394	42.753280	0.023390	0.163121	6.973986	0.143390	16
17	6.866041	48.883674	0.020457	0.145644	7.119631	0.140457	17
18	7.689966	55.749715	0.017937	0.130039	7.249670	0.137937	18
19	8.612762	63.439681	0.015763	0.116106	7.365777	0.135763	19
20	9.646293	72.052442	0.013879	0.103666	7.469444	0.133879	20
21	10.803848	81.698736	0.012240	0.092559	7.562003	0.132240	21
22	12.100310	92.502584	0.010811	0.082642	7.644646	0.130811	22
23	13.552347	104.602894	0.009560	0.073788	7.718434	0.129560	23
24	15.178629	118.155241	0.008463	0.065882	7.784316	0.128463	24
25	17.000064	133.333870	0.007500	0.058823	7.843139	0.127500	25
26	19.040072	150.333934	0.006652	0.052521	7.895660	0.126652	26
27	21.324881	169.374007	0.005904	0.046893	7.942554	0.125904	27
28	23.883866	190.698887	0.005244	0.041869	7.984423	0.125244	28
29	26.749930	214.582754	0.004660	0.037383	8.021806	0.124660	29
30	29.959922	241.332684	0.004144	0.033378	8.055184	0.124144	30
31	33.555113	271.292606	0.003686	0.029802	8.084986	0.123686	31
32	37.581726	304.847719	0.003280	0.026609	8.111594	0.123280	32
33	42.091533	342.429446	0.002920	0.023758	8.135352	0.122920	33
34	47.142517	384.520979	0.002601	0.021212	8.156564	0.122601	34
35	52.799620	431.663497	0.002317	0.018939	8.175504	0.122317	35
36	59.135574	484.463116	0.002064	0.016910	8.192414	0.122064	36
37	66.231843	543.598690	0.001840	0.015098	8.207513	0.121840	37
38	74.179664	609.830533	0.001640	0.013481	8.220993	0.121640	38
39	83.081224	684.010197	0.001462	0.012036	8.233030	0.121462	39
40	93.050970	767.091420	0.001304	0.010747	8.243777	0.121304	40
41	104.217087	860.142391	0.001163	0.009595	8.253372	0.121163	41
42	116.723137	964.359478	0.001037	0.008567	8.261939	0.121037	42
43	130.729914	1081.082615	0.000925	0.007649	8.269589	0.120925	43
44	146.417503	1211.812529	0.000825	0.006830	8.276418	0.120825	44
45	163.987604	1358.230032	0.000736	0.006098	8.282516	0.120736	45
46	183.666116	1522.217636	0.000657	0.005445	8.287961	0.120657	46
47	205.706050	1705.883752	0.000586	0.004861	8.292822	0.120586	47
48	230.390776	1911.589803	0.000523	0.004340	8.297163	0.120523	48
49	258.037670	2141.980579	0.000467	0.003875	8.301038	0.120467	49
50	289.002190	2400.018249	0.000417	0.003460	8.304498	0.120417	50

Annual Compound Interest Tables

13.00% Annual Interest Rate

	1	2	3	4	5	6	
	Future Value of $1	Future Value Annuity of $1 Per Year	Sinking Fund Factor	Present Value of $1 (Reversion)	Present Value Annuity of $1 Per Year	Payment to Amortize $1	
Years							Years
1	1.130000	1.000000	1.000000	0.884956	0.884956	1.130000	1
2	1.276900	2.130000	0.469484	0.783147	1.668102	0.599484	2
3	1.442897	3.406900	0.293522	0.693051	2.361153	0.423522	3
4	1.630474	4.849797	0.206194	0.613319	2.974471	0.336194	4
5	1.842435	6.480271	0.154315	0.542761	3.517231	0.284315	5
6	2.081952	8.322706	0.120153	0.480319	3.997550	0.250153	6
7	2.352605	10.404658	0.096111	0.425061	4.422610	0.226111	7
8	2.658444	12.757263	0.078387	0.376161	4.798770	0.208387	8
9	3.004042	15.415707	0.064869	0.332886	5.131655	0.194869	9
10	3.394567	18.419749	0.054290	0.294589	5.426243	0.184290	10
11	3.835861	21.814317	0.045841	0.260698	5.686941	0.175841	11
12	4.334523	25.650178	0.038986	0.230707	5.917647	0.168986	12
13	4.898011	29.984701	0.033350	0.204165	6.121812	0.163350	13
14	5.534753	34.882712	0.028668	0.180677	6.302488	0.158668	14
15	6.254270	40.417464	0.024742	0.159891	6.462379	0.154742	15
16	7.067326	46.671735	0.021426	0.141497	6.603875	0.151426	16
17	7.986078	53.739060	0.018608	0.125219	6.729093	0.148608	17
18	9.024268	61.725138	0.016201	0.110813	6.839905	0.146201	18
19	10.197423	70.749406	0.014134	0.098065	6.937969	0.144134	19
20	11.523088	80.946829	0.012354	0.086783	7.024752	0.142354	20
21	13.021089	92.469917	0.010814	0.076799	7.101550	0.140814	21
22	14.713831	105.491006	0.009479	0.067964	7.169513	0.139479	22
23	16.626629	120.204837	0.008319	0.060145	7.229658	0.138319	23
24	18.788091	136.831465	0.007308	0.053226	7.282883	0.137308	24
25	21.230542	155.619556	0.006426	0.047102	7.329985	0.136426	25
26	23.990513	176.850098	0.005655	0.041683	7.371668	0.135655	26
27	27.109279	200.840611	0.004979	0.036888	7.408556	0.134979	27
28	30.633486	227.949890	0.004387	0.032644	7.441200	0.134387	28
29	34.615839	258.583376	0.003867	0.028889	7.470088	0.133867	29
30	39.115898	293.199215	0.003411	0.025565	7.495653	0.133411	30
31	44.200965	332.315113	0.003009	0.022624	7.518277	0.133009	31
32	49.947090	376.516078	0.002656	0.020021	7.538299	0.132656	32
33	56.440212	426.463168	0.002345	0.017718	7.556016	0.132345	33
34	63.777439	482.903380	0.002071	0.015680	7.571696	0.132071	34
35	72.068506	546.680819	0.001829	0.013876	7.585572	0.131829	35
36	81.437412	618.749325	0.001616	0.012279	7.597851	0.131616	36
37	92.024276	700.186738	0.001428	0.010867	7.608718	0.131428	37
38	103.987432	792.211014	0.001262	0.009617	7.618334	0.131262	38
39	117.505798	896.198445	0.001116	0.008510	7.626844	0.131116	39
40	132.781552	1013.704243	0.000986	0.007531	7.634376	0.130986	40
41	150.043153	1146.485795	0.000872	0.006665	7.641040	0.130872	41
42	169.548763	1296.528948	0.000771	0.005898	7.646938	0.130771	42
43	191.590103	1466.077712	0.000682	0.005219	7.652158	0.130682	43
44	216.496816	1657.667814	0.000603	0.004619	7.656777	0.130603	44
45	244.641402	1874.164630	0.000534	0.004088	7.660865	0.130534	45
46	276.444784	2118.806032	0.000472	0.003617	7.664482	0.130472	46
47	312.382606	2395.250816	0.000418	0.003201	7.667683	0.130418	47
48	352.992345	2707.633422	0.000369	0.002833	7.670516	0.130369	48
49	398.881350	3060.625767	0.000327	0.002507	7.673023	0.130327	49
50	450.735925	3459.507117	0.000289	0.002219	7.675242	0.130289	50

Annual Compound Interest Tables

14.00% Annual Interest Rate

	1	2	3	4	5	6	
	Future Value of $1	Future Value Annuity of $1 Per Year	Sinking Fund Factor	Present Value of $1 (Reversion)	Present Value Annuity of $1 Per Year	Payment to Amortize $1	
Years							Years
1	1.140000	1.000000	1.000000	0.877193	0.877193	1.140000	1
2	1.299600	2.140000	0.467290	0.769468	1.646661	0.607290	2
3	1.481544	3.439600	0.290731	0.674972	2.321632	0.430731	3
4	1.688960	4.921144	0.203205	0.592080	2.913712	0.343205	4
5	1.925415	6.610104	0.151284	0.519369	3.433081	0.291284	5
6	2.194973	8.535519	0.117158	0.455587	3.888668	0.257158	6
7	2.502269	10.730491	0.093192	0.399637	4.288305	0.233192	7
8	2.852586	13.232760	0.075570	0.350559	4.638864	0.215570	8
9	3.251949	16.085347	0.062168	0.307508	4.946372	0.202168	9
10	3.707221	19.337295	0.051714	0.269744	5.216116	0.191714	10
11	4.226232	23.044516	0.043394	0.236617	5.452733	0.183394	11
12	4.817905	27.270749	0.036669	0.207559	5.660292	0.176669	12
13	5.492412	32.088654	0.031164	0.182069	5.842362	0.171164	13
14	6.261349	37.581065	0.026609	0.159710	6.002072	0.166609	14
15	7.137938	43.842414	0.022809	0.140097	6.142168	0.162809	15
16	8.137249	50.980352	0.019615	0.122892	6.265060	0.159615	16
17	9.276464	59.117601	0.016915	0.107800	6.372859	0.156915	17
18	10.575169	68.394066	0.014621	0.094561	6.467420	0.154621	18
19	12.055693	78.969235	0.012663	0.082948	6.550369	0.152663	19
20	13.743490	91.024928	0.010986	0.072762	6.623131	0.150986	20
21	15.667578	104.768418	0.009545	0.063826	6.686957	0.149545	21
22	17.861039	120.435996	0.008303	0.055988	6.742944	0.148303	22
23	20.361585	138.297035	0.007231	0.049112	6.792057	0.147231	23
24	23.212207	158.658620	0.006303	0.043081	6.835137	0.146303	24
25	26.461916	181.870827	0.005498	0.037790	6.872927	0.145498	25
26	30.166584	208.332743	0.004800	0.033149	6.906077	0.144800	26
27	34.389906	238.499327	0.004193	0.029078	6.935155	0.144193	27
28	39.204493	272.889233	0.003665	0.025507	6.960662	0.143665	28
29	44.693122	312.093725	0.003204	0.022375	6.983037	0.143204	29
30	50.950159	356.786847	0.002803	0.019627	7.002664	0.142803	30
31	58.083181	407.737006	0.002453	0.017217	7.019881	0.142453	31
32	66.214826	465.820186	0.002147	0.015102	7.034983	0.142147	32
33	75.484902	532.035012	0.001880	0.013248	7.048231	0.141880	33
34	86.052788	607.519914	0.001646	0.011621	7.059852	0.141646	34
35	98.100178	693.572702	0.001442	0.010194	7.070045	0.141442	35
36	111.834203	791.672881	0.001263	0.008942	7.078987	0.141263	36
37	127.490992	903.507084	0.001107	0.007844	7.086831	0.141107	37
38	145.339731	1030.998076	0.000970	0.006880	7.093711	0.140970	38
39	165.687293	1176.337806	0.000850	0.006035	7.099747	0.140850	39
40	188.883514	1342.025099	0.000745	0.005294	7.105041	0.140745	40
41	215.327206	1530.908613	0.000653	0.004644	7.109685	0.140653	41
42	245.473015	1746.235819	0.000573	0.004074	7.113759	0.140573	42
43	279.839237	1991.708833	0.000502	0.003573	7.117332	0.140502	43
44	319.016730	2271.548070	0.000440	0.003135	7.120467	0.140440	44
45	363.679072	2590.564800	0.000386	0.002750	7.123217	0.140386	45
46	414.594142	2954.243872	0.000339	0.002412	7.125629	0.140339	46
47	472.637322	3368.838014	0.000297	0.002116	7.127744	0.140297	47
48	538.806547	3841.475336	0.000260	0.001856	7.129600	0.140260	48
49	614.239464	4380.281883	0.000228	0.001628	7.131228	0.140228	49
50	700.232988	4994.521346	0.000200	0.001428	7.132656	0.140200	50

Annual Compound Interest Tables

15.00% Annual Interest Rate

	1	2	3	4	5	6	
	Future Value of $1	Future Value Annuity of $1 Per Year	Sinking Fund Factor	Present Value of $1 (Reversion)	Present Value Annuity of $1 Per Year	Payment to Amortize $1	
Years							Years
1	1.150000	1.000000	1.000000	0.869565	0.869565	1.150000	1
2	1.322500	2.150000	0.465116	0.756144	1.625709	0.615116	2
3	1.520875	3.472500	0.287977	0.657516	2.283225	0.437977	3
4	1.749006	4.993375	0.200265	0.571753	2.854978	0.350265	4
5	2.011357	6.742381	0.148316	0.497177	3.352155	0.298316	5
6	2.313061	8.753738	0.114237	0.432328	3.784483	0.264237	6
7	2.660020	11.066799	0.090360	0.375936	4.160420	0.240360	7
8	3.059023	13.726819	0.072850	0.326901	4.487322	0.222850	8
9	3.517876	16.785842	0.059574	0.284262	4.771584	0.209574	9
10	4.045558	20.303718	0.049252	0.247184	5.018769	0.199252	10
11	4.652391	24.349276	0.041069	0.214943	5.233712	0.191069	11
12	5.350250	29.001667	0.034481	0.186907	5.420619	0.184481	12
13	6.152788	34.351917	0.029110	0.162527	5.583147	0.179110	13
14	7.075706	40.504705	0.024688	0.141328	5.724476	0.174688	14
15	8.137062	47.580411	0.021017	0.122894	5.847370	0.171017	15
16	9.357621	55.717473	0.017948	0.106865	5.954235	0.167948	16
17	10.761264	65.075093	0.015367	0.092926	6.047161	0.165367	17
18	12.375454	75.836357	0.013186	0.080805	6.127966	0.163186	18
19	14.231772	88.211811	0.011336	0.070265	6.198231	0.161336	19
20	16.366537	102.443583	0.009761	0.061100	6.259331	0.159761	20
21	18.821518	118.810120	0.008417	0.053130	6.312462	0.158417	21
22	21.644746	137.631638	0.007266	0.046200	6.358663	0.157266	22
23	24.891458	159.276384	0.006278	0.040174	6.398837	0.156278	23
24	28.625176	184.167841	0.005430	0.034934	6.433771	0.155430	24
25	32.918953	212.793017	0.004699	0.030377	6.464149	0.154699	25
26	37.856796	245.711970	0.004070	0.026415	6.490564	0.154070	26
27	43.535315	283.568766	0.003526	0.022970	6.513534	0.153526	27
28	50.065612	327.104080	0.003057	0.019974	6.533508	0.153057	28
29	57.575454	377.169693	0.002651	0.017368	6.550877	0.152651	29
30	66.211772	434.745146	0.002300	0.015103	6.565980	0.152300	30
31	76.143538	500.956918	0.001996	0.013133	6.579113	0.151996	31
32	87.565068	577.100456	0.001733	0.011420	6.590533	0.151733	32
33	100.699829	664.665525	0.001505	0.009930	6.600463	0.151505	33
34	115.804803	765.365353	0.001307	0.008635	6.609099	0.151307	34
35	133.175523	881.170156	0.001135	0.007509	6.616607	0.151135	35
36	153.151852	1014.345680	0.000986	0.006529	6.623137	0.150986	36
37	176.124630	1167.497532	0.000857	0.005678	6.628815	0.150857	37
38	202.543324	1343.622161	0.000744	0.004937	6.633752	0.150744	38
39	232.924823	1546.165485	0.000647	0.004293	6.638045	0.150647	39
40	267.863546	1779.090308	0.000562	0.003733	6.641778	0.150562	40
41	308.043078	2046.953854	0.000489	0.003246	6.645025	0.150489	41
42	354.249540	2354.996933	0.000425	0.002823	6.647848	0.150425	42
43	407.386971	2709.246473	0.000369	0.002455	6.650302	0.150369	43
44	468.495017	3116.633443	0.000321	0.002134	6.652437	0.150321	44
45	538.769269	3585.128460	0.000279	0.001856	6.654293	0.150279	45
46	619.584659	4123.897729	0.000242	0.001614	6.655907	0.150242	46
47	712.522358	4743.482388	0.000211	0.001403	6.657310	0.150211	47
48	819.400712	5456.004746	0.000183	0.001220	6.658531	0.150183	48
49	942.310819	6275.405458	0.000159	0.001061	6.659592	0.150159	49
50	1083.657442	7217.716277	0.000139	0.000923	6.660515	0.150139	50

Annual Compound Interest Tables

16.00% Annual Interest Rate

	1	2	3	4	5	6	
	Future Value of $1	Future Value Annuity of $1 Per Year	Sinking Fund Factor	Present Value of $1 (Reversion)	Present Value Annuity of $1 Per Year	Payment to Amortize $1	
Years							Years
1	1.160000	1.000000	1.000000	0.862069	0.862069	1.160000	1
2	1.345600	2.160000	0.462963	0.743163	1.605232	0.622963	2
3	1.560896	3.505600	0.285258	0.640658	2.245890	0.445258	3
4	1.810639	5.066496	0.197375	0.552291	2.798181	0.357375	4
5	2.100342	6.877135	0.145409	0.476113	3.274294	0.305409	5
6	2.436396	8.977477	0.111390	0.410442	3.684736	0.271390	6
7	2.826220	11.413873	0.087613	0.353830	4.038565	0.247613	7
8	3.278415	14.240093	0.070224	0.305026	4.343591	0.230224	8
9	3.802961	17.518508	0.057082	0.262953	4.606544	0.217082	9
10	4.411435	21.321469	0.046901	0.226684	4.833227	0.206901	10
11	5.117265	25.732904	0.038861	0.195417	5.028644	0.198861	11
12	5.936027	30.850169	0.032415	0.168463	5.197107	0.192415	12
13	6.885791	36.786196	0.027184	0.145227	5.342334	0.187184	13
14	7.987518	43.671987	0.022898	0.125195	5.467529	0.182898	14
15	9.265521	51.659505	0.019358	0.107927	5.575456	0.179358	15
16	10.748004	60.925026	0.016414	0.093041	5.668497	0.176414	16
17	12.467685	71.673030	0.013952	0.080207	5.748704	0.173952	17
18	14.462514	84.140715	0.011885	0.069144	5.817848	0.171885	18
19	16.776517	98.603230	0.010142	0.059607	5.877455	0.170142	19
20	19.460759	115.379747	0.008667	0.051386	5.928841	0.168667	20
21	22.574481	134.840506	0.007416	0.044298	5.973139	0.167416	21
22	26.186398	157.414987	0.006353	0.038188	6.011326	0.166353	22
23	30.376222	183.601385	0.005447	0.032921	6.044247	0.165447	23
24	35.236417	213.977607	0.004673	0.028380	6.072627	0.164673	24
25	40.874244	249.214024	0.004013	0.024465	6.097092	0.164013	25
26	47.414123	290.088267	0.003447	0.021091	6.118183	0.163447	26
27	55.000382	337.502390	0.002963	0.018182	6.136364	0.162963	27
28	63.800444	392.502773	0.002548	0.015674	6.152038	0.162548	28
29	74.008515	456.303216	0.002192	0.013512	6.165550	0.162192	29
30	85.849877	530.311731	0.001886	0.011648	6.177199	0.161886	30
31	99.585857	616.161608	0.001623	0.010042	6.187240	0.161623	31
32	115.519594	715.747465	0.001397	0.008657	6.195897	0.161397	32
33	134.002729	831.267059	0.001203	0.007463	6.203359	0.161203	33
34	155.443166	965.269789	0.001036	0.006433	6.209792	0.161036	34
35	180.314073	1120.712955	0.000892	0.005546	6.215338	0.160892	35
36	209.164324	1301.027028	0.000769	0.004781	6.220119	0.160769	36
37	242.630616	1510.191352	0.000662	0.004122	6.224241	0.160662	37
38	281.451515	1752.821968	0.000571	0.003553	6.227794	0.160571	38
39	326.483757	2034.273483	0.000492	0.003063	6.230857	0.160492	39
40	378.721159	2360.757241	0.000424	0.002640	6.233497	0.160424	40
41	439.316544	2739.478399	0.000365	0.002276	6.235773	0.160365	41
42	509.607191	3178.794943	0.000315	0.001962	6.237736	0.160315	42
43	591.144341	3688.402134	0.000271	0.001692	6.239427	0.160271	43
44	685.727436	4279.546475	0.000234	0.001458	6.240886	0.160234	44
45	795.443826	4965.273911	0.000201	0.001257	6.242143	0.160201	45
46	922.714838	5760.717737	0.000174	0.001084	6.243227	0.160174	46
47	1070.349212	6683.432575	0.000150	0.000934	6.244161	0.160150	47
48	1241.605086	7753.781787	0.000129	0.000805	6.244966	0.160129	48
49	1440.261900	8995.386873	0.000111	0.000694	6.245661	0.160111	49
50	1670.703804	10435.648773	0.000096	0.000599	6.246259	0.160096	50

Annual Compound Interest Tables

17.00% Annual Interest Rate

	1	2	3	4	5	6	
	Future Value of $1	Future Value Annuity of $1 Per Year	Sinking Fund Factor	Present Value of $1 (Reversion)	Present Value Annuity of $1 Per Year	Payment to Amortize $1	
Years							Years
1	1.170000	1.000000	1.000000	0.854701	0.854701	1.170000	1
2	1.368900	2.170000	0.460830	0.730514	1.585214	0.630830	2
3	1.601613	3.538900	0.282574	0.624371	2.209585	0.452574	3
4	1.873887	5.140513	0.194533	0.533650	2.743235	0.364533	4
5	2.192448	7.014400	0.142564	0.456112	3.199346	0.312564	5
6	2.565164	9.206848	0.108615	0.389839	3.589185	0.278615	6
7	3.001242	11.772012	0.084947	0.333196	3.922380	0.254947	7
8	3.511453	14.773255	0.067690	0.284783	4.207163	0.237690	8
9	4.108400	18.284708	0.054691	0.243404	4.450566	0.224691	9
10	4.806828	22.393108	0.044657	0.208038	4.658604	0.214657	10
11	5.623989	27.199937	0.036765	0.177810	4.836413	0.206765	11
12	6.580067	32.823926	0.030466	0.151974	4.988387	0.200466	12
13	7.698679	39.403993	0.025378	0.129893	5.118280	0.195378	13
14	9.007454	47.102672	0.021230	0.111019	5.229299	0.191230	14
15	10.538721	56.110126	0.017822	0.094888	5.324187	0.187822	15
16	12.330304	66.648848	0.015004	0.081101	5.405288	0.185004	16
17	14.426456	78.979152	0.012662	0.069317	5.474605	0.182662	17
18	16.878953	93.405608	0.010706	0.059246	5.533851	0.180706	18
19	19.748375	110.284561	0.009067	0.050637	5.584488	0.179067	19
20	23.105599	130.032936	0.007690	0.043280	5.627767	0.177690	20
21	27.033551	153.138535	0.006530	0.036991	5.664758	0.176530	21
22	31.629255	180.172086	0.005550	0.031616	5.696375	0.175550	22
23	37.006228	211.801341	0.004721	0.027023	5.723397	0.174721	23
24	43.297287	248.807569	0.004019	0.023096	5.746493	0.174019	24
25	50.657826	292.104856	0.003423	0.019740	5.766234	0.173423	25
26	59.269656	342.762681	0.002917	0.016872	5.783106	0.172917	26
27	69.345497	402.032337	0.002487	0.014421	5.797526	0.172487	27
28	81.134232	471.377835	0.002121	0.012325	5.809851	0.172121	28
29	94.927051	552.512066	0.001810	0.010534	5.820386	0.171810	29
30	111.064650	647.439118	0.001545	0.009004	5.829390	0.171545	30
31	129.945641	758.503768	0.001318	0.007696	5.837085	0.171318	31
32	152.036399	888.449408	0.001126	0.006577	5.843663	0.171126	32
33	177.882587	1040.485808	0.000961	0.005622	5.849284	0.170961	33
34	208.122627	1218.368395	0.000821	0.004805	5.854089	0.170821	34
35	243.503474	1426.491022	0.000701	0.004107	5.858196	0.170701	35
36	284.899064	1669.994496	0.000599	0.003510	5.861706	0.170599	36
37	333.331905	1954.893560	0.000512	0.003000	5.864706	0.170512	37
38	389.998329	2288.225465	0.000437	0.002564	5.867270	0.170437	38
39	456.298045	2678.223794	0.000373	0.002192	5.869461	0.170373	39
40	533.868713	3134.521839	0.000319	0.001873	5.871335	0.170319	40
41	624.626394	3668.390552	0.000273	0.001601	5.872936	0.170273	41
42	730.812881	4293.016946	0.000233	0.001368	5.874304	0.170233	42
43	855.051071	5023.829827	0.000199	0.001170	5.875473	0.170199	43
44	1000.409753	5878.880897	0.000170	0.001000	5.876473	0.170170	44
45	1170.479411	6879.290650	0.000145	0.000854	5.877327	0.170145	45
46	1369.460910	8049.770061	0.000124	0.000730	5.878058	0.170124	46
47	1602.269265	9419.230971	0.000106	0.000624	5.878682	0.170106	47
48	1874.655040	11021.500236	0.000091	0.000533	5.879215	0.170091	48
49	2193.346397	12896.155276	0.000078	0.000456	5.879671	0.170078	49
50	2566.215284	15089.501673	0.000066	0.000390	5.880061	0.170066	50

Annual Compound Interest Tables

18.00% Annual Interest Rate

	1	2	3	4	5	6	
	Future Value of $1	**Future Value Annuity of $1 Per Year**	**Sinking Fund Factor**	**Present Value of $1 (Reversion)**	**Present Value Annuity of $1 Per Year**	**Payment to Amortize $1**	
Years							**Years**
1	1.180000	1.000000	1.000000	0.847458	0.847458	1.180000	1
2	1.392400	2.180000	0.458716	0.718185	1.565642	0.638716	2
3	1.643032	3.572400	0.279924	0.608632	2.174273	0.459924	3
4	1.938778	5.215432	0.191739	0.515790	2.690062	0.371739	4
5	2.287758	7.154210	0.139778	0.437110	3.127171	0.319778	5
6	2.699554	9.441968	0.105910	0.370433	3.497603	0.285910	6
7	3.185474	12.141522	0.082362	0.313926	3.811528	0.262362	7
8	3.758859	15.326996	0.065244	0.266039	4.077566	0.245244	8
9	4.435454	19.085855	0.052395	0.225457	4.303022	0.232395	9
10	5.233836	23.521309	0.042515	0.191065	4.494086	0.222515	10
11	6.175926	28.755144	0.034776	0.161920	4.656005	0.214776	11
12	7.287593	34.931070	0.028628	0.137220	4.793225	0.208628	12
13	8.599359	42.218663	0.023686	0.116288	4.909513	0.203686	13
14	10.147244	50.818022	0.019678	0.098550	5.008062	0.199678	14
15	11.973748	60.965266	0.016403	0.083517	5.091578	0.196403	15
16	14.129023	72.939014	0.013710	0.070777	5.162354	0.193710	16
17	16.672247	87.068036	0.011485	0.059980	5.222334	0.191485	17
18	19.673251	103.740283	0.009639	0.050831	5.273164	0.189639	18
19	23.214436	123.413534	0.008103	0.043077	5.316241	0.188103	19
20	27.393035	146.627970	0.006820	0.036506	5.352747	0.186820	20
21	32.323781	174.021005	0.005746	0.030937	5.383683	0.185746	21
22	38.142061	206.344785	0.004846	0.026218	5.409901	0.184846	22
23	45.007632	244.486847	0.004090	0.022219	5.432120	0.184090	23
24	53.109006	289.494479	0.003454	0.018829	5.450949	0.183454	24
25	62.668627	342.603486	0.002919	0.015957	5.466906	0.182919	25
26	73.948980	405.272113	0.002467	0.013523	5.480429	0.182467	26
27	87.259797	479.221093	0.002087	0.011460	5.491889	0.182087	27
28	102.966560	566.480890	0.001765	0.009712	5.501601	0.181765	28
29	121.500541	669.447450	0.001494	0.008231	5.509831	0.181494	29
30	143.370638	790.947991	0.001264	0.006975	5.516806	0.181264	30
31	169.177353	934.318630	0.001070	0.005911	5.522717	0.181070	31
32	199.629277	1103.495983	0.000906	0.005009	5.527726	0.180906	32
33	235.562547	1303.125260	0.000767	0.004245	5.531971	0.180767	33
34	277.963805	1538.687807	0.000650	0.003598	5.535569	0.180650	34
35	327.997290	1816.651612	0.000550	0.003049	5.538618	0.180550	35
36	387.036802	2144.648902	0.000466	0.002584	5.541201	0.180466	36
37	456.703427	2531.685705	0.000395	0.002190	5.543391	0.180395	37
38	538.910044	2988.389132	0.000335	0.001856	5.545247	0.180335	38
39	635.913852	3527.299175	0.000284	0.001573	5.546819	0.180284	39
40	750.378345	4163.213027	0.000240	0.001333	5.548152	0.180240	40
41	885.446447	4913.591372	0.000204	0.001129	5.549281	0.180204	41
42	1044.826807	5799.037819	0.000172	0.000957	5.550238	0.180172	42
43	1232.895633	6843.864626	0.000146	0.000811	5.551049	0.180146	43
44	1454.816847	8076.760259	0.000124	0.000687	5.551737	0.180124	44
45	1716.683879	9531.577105	0.000105	0.000583	5.552319	0.180105	45
46	2025.686977	11248.260984	0.000089	0.000494	5.552813	0.180089	46
47	2390.310633	13273.947961	0.000075	0.000418	5.553231	0.180075	47
48	2820.566547	15664.258594	0.000064	0.000355	5.553586	0.180064	48
49	3328.268525	18484.825141	0.000054	0.000300	5.553886	0.180054	49
50	3927.356860	21813.093666	0.000046	0.000255	5.554141	0.180046	50

Annual Compound Interest Tables

19.00% Annual Interest Rate

	1	2	3	4	5	6	
	Future Value of $1	Future Value Annuity of $1 Per Year	Sinking Fund Factor	Present Value of $1 (Reversion)	Present Value Annuity of $1 Per Year	Payment to Amortize $1	
Years							Years
1	1.190000	1.000000	1.000000	0.840336	0.840336	1.190000	1
2	1.416100	2.190000	0.456621	0.706165	1.546501	0.646621	2
3	1.685159	3.606100	0.277308	0.593416	2.139917	0.467308	3
4	2.005339	5.291259	0.188991	0.498668	2.638586	0.378991	4
5	2.386354	7.296598	0.137050	0.419049	3.057635	0.327050	5
6	2.839761	9.682952	0.103274	0.352142	3.409777	0.293274	6
7	3.379315	12.522713	0.079855	0.295918	3.705695	0.269855	7
8	4.021385	15.902028	0.062885	0.248670	3.954366	0.252885	8
9	4.785449	19.923414	0.050192	0.208967	4.163333	0.240192	9
10	5.694684	24.708862	0.040471	0.175602	4.338935	0.230471	10
11	6.776674	30.403546	0.032891	0.147565	4.486500	0.222891	11
12	8.064242	37.180220	0.026896	0.124004	4.610504	0.216896	12
13	9.596448	45.244461	0.022102	0.104205	4.714709	0.212102	13
14	11.419773	54.840909	0.018235	0.087567	4.802277	0.208235	14
15	13.589530	66.260682	0.015092	0.073586	4.875863	0.205092	15
16	16.171540	79.850211	0.012523	0.061837	4.937700	0.202523	16
17	19.244133	96.021751	0.010414	0.051964	4.989664	0.200414	17
18	22.900518	115.265884	0.008676	0.043667	5.033331	0.198676	18
19	27.251616	138.166402	0.007238	0.036695	5.070026	0.197238	19
20	32.429423	165.418018	0.006045	0.030836	5.100862	0.196045	20
21	38.591014	197.847442	0.005054	0.025913	5.126775	0.195054	21
22	45.923307	236.438456	0.004229	0.021775	5.148550	0.194229	22
23	54.648735	282.361762	0.003542	0.018299	5.166849	0.193542	23
24	65.031994	337.010497	0.002967	0.015377	5.182226	0.192967	24
25	77.388073	402.042492	0.002487	0.012922	5.195148	0.192487	25
26	92.091807	479.430565	0.002086	0.010859	5.206007	0.192086	26
27	109.589251	571.522372	0.001750	0.009125	5.215132	0.191750	27
28	130.411208	681.111623	0.001468	0.007668	5.222800	0.191468	28
29	155.189338	811.522831	0.001232	0.006444	5.229243	0.191232	29
30	184.675312	966.712169	0.001034	0.005415	5.234658	0.191034	30
31	219.763621	1151.387481	0.000869	0.004550	5.239209	0.190869	31
32	261.518710	1371.151103	0.000729	0.003824	5.243033	0.190729	32
33	311.207264	1632.669812	0.000613	0.003213	5.246246	0.190613	33
34	370.336645	1943.877077	0.000514	0.002700	5.248946	0.190514	34
35	440.700607	2314.213721	0.000432	0.002269	5.251215	0.190432	35
36	524.433722	2754.914328	0.000363	0.001907	5.253122	0.190363	36
37	624.076130	3279.348051	0.000305	0.001602	5.254724	0.190305	37
38	742.650594	3903.424180	0.000256	0.001347	5.256071	0.190256	38
39	883.754207	4646.074775	0.000215	0.001132	5.257202	0.190215	39
40	1051.667507	5529.828982	0.000181	0.000951	5.258153	0.190181	40
41	1251.484333	6581.496488	0.000152	0.000799	5.258952	0.190152	41
42	1489.266356	7832.980821	0.000128	0.000671	5.259624	0.190128	42
43	1772.226964	9322.247177	0.000107	0.000564	5.260188	0.190107	43
44	2108.950087	11094.474141	0.000090	0.000474	5.260662	0.190090	44
45	2509.650603	13203.424228	0.000076	0.000398	5.261061	0.190076	45
46	2986.484218	15713.074831	0.000064	0.000335	5.261396	0.190064	46
47	3553.916219	18699.559049	0.000053	0.000281	5.261677	0.190053	47
48	4229.160301	22253.475268	0.000045	0.000236	5.261913	0.190045	48
49	5032.700758	26482.635569	0.000038	0.000199	5.262112	0.190038	49
50	5988.913902	31515.336327	0.000032	0.000167	5.262279	0.190032	50

Monthly Compound Interest Tables

	1	2	3	4	5	6	
6.00% Annual Interest Rate					**0.5000% Monthly Effective Interest Rate**		
	Future Value of $1	**Future Value Annuity of $1 Per Year**	**Sinking Fund Factor**	**Present Value of $1 (Reversion)**	**Present Value Annuity of $1 Per Year**	**Payment to Amortize $1**	
Months							**Months**
1	1.005000	1.000000	1.000000	0.995025	0.995025	1.005000	1
2	1.010025	2.005000	0.498753	0.990075	1.985099	0.503753	2
3	1.015075	3.015025	0.331672	0.985149	2.970248	0.336672	3
4	1.020151	4.030100	0.248133	0.980248	3.950496	0.253133	4
5	1.025251	5.050251	0.198010	0.975371	4.925866	0.203010	5
6	1.030378	6.075502	0.164595	0.970518	5.896384	0.169595	6
7	1.035529	7.105879	0.140729	0.965690	6.862074	0.145729	7
8	1.040707	8.141409	0.122829	0.960885	7.822959	0.127829	8
9	1.045911	9.182116	0.108907	0.956105	8.779064	0.113907	9
10	1.051140	10.228026	0.097771	0.951348	9.730412	0.102771	10
11	1.056396	11.279167	0.088659	0.946615	10.677027	0.093659	11
12	1.061678	12.335562	0.081066	0.941905	11.618932	0.086066	12
Years							**Months**
1	1.061678	12.335562	0.081066	0.941905	11.618932	0.086066	12
2	1.127160	25.431955	0.039321	0.887186	22.562866	0.044321	24
3	1.196681	39.336105	0.025422	0.835645	32.871016	0.030422	36
4	1.270489	54.097832	0.018485	0.787098	42.580318	0.023485	48
5	1.348850	69.770031	0.014333	0.741372	51.725561	0.019333	60
6	1.432044	86.408856	0.011573	0.698302	60.339514	0.016573	72
7	1.520370	104.073927	0.009609	0.657735	68.453042	0.014609	84
8	1.614143	122.828542	0.008141	0.619524	76.095218	0.013141	96
9	1.713700	142.739900	0.007006	0.583533	83.293424	0.012006	108
10	1.819397	163.879347	0.006102	0.549633	90.073453	0.011102	120
11	1.931613	186.322629	0.005367	0.517702	96.459599	0.010367	132
12	2.050751	210.150163	0.004759	0.487626	102.474743	0.009759	144
13	2.177237	235.447328	0.004247	0.459298	108.140440	0.009247	156
14	2.311524	262.304766	0.003812	0.432615	113.476990	0.008812	168
15	2.454094	290.818712	0.003439	0.407482	118.503515	0.008439	180
16	2.605457	321.091337	0.003114	0.383810	123.238025	0.008114	192
17	2.766156	353.231110	0.002831	0.361513	127.697486	0.007831	204
18	2.936766	387.353194	0.002582	0.340511	131.897876	0.007582	216
19	3.117899	423.579854	0.002361	0.320729	135.854246	0.007361	228
20	3.310204	462.040895	0.002164	0.302096	139.580772	0.007164	240
21	3.514371	502.874129	0.001989	0.284546	143.090806	0.006989	252
22	3.731129	546.225867	0.001831	0.268015	146.396927	0.006831	264
23	3.961257	592.251446	0.001688	0.252445	149.510979	0.006688	276
24	4.205579	641.115782	0.001560	0.237779	152.444121	0.006560	288
25	4.464970	692.993962	0.001443	0.223966	155.206864	0.006443	300
26	4.740359	748.071876	0.001337	0.210954	157.809106	0.006337	312
27	5.032734	806.546875	0.001240	0.198699	160.260172	0.006240	324
28	5.343142	868.628484	0.001151	0.187156	162.568844	0.006151	336
29	5.672696	934.539150	0.001070	0.176283	164.743394	0.006070	348
30	6.022575	1004.515042	0.000996	0.166042	166.791614	0.005996	360
31	6.394034	1078.806895	0.000927	0.156396	168.720844	0.005927	372
32	6.788405	1157.680906	0.000864	0.147310	170.537996	0.005864	384
33	7.207098	1241.419693	0.000806	0.138752	172.249581	0.005806	396
34	7.651617	1330.323306	0.000752	0.130691	173.861732	0.005752	408
35	8.123552	1424.710299	0.000702	0.123099	175.380226	0.005702	420
36	8.624594	1524.918875	0.000656	0.115947	176.810504	0.005656	432
37	9.156540	1631.308097	0.000613	0.109212	178.157690	0.005613	444
38	9.721296	1744.259173	0.000573	0.102867	179.426611	0.005573	456
39	10.320884	1864.176825	0.000536	0.096891	180.621815	0.005536	468
40	10.957454	1991.490734	0.000502	0.091262	181.747584	0.005502	480

Monthly Compound Interest Tables

8.00% Annual Interest Rate				0.6666% Monthly Effective Interest Rate		
1	2	3	4	5	6	
Future Value of $1	Future Value Annuity of $1 Per Year	Sinking Fund Factor	Present Value of $1 (Reversion)	Present Value Annuity of $1 Per Year	Payment to Amortize $1	
Months						**Months**
1	1.006667	1.000000	1.000000	0.993377	0.993377	1.006667	1
2	1.013378	2.006667	0.498339	0.986799	1.980176	0.505006	2
3	1.020134	3.020044	0.331121	0.980264	2.960440	0.337788	3
4	1.026935	4.040178	0.247514	0.973772	3.934212	0.254181	4
5	1.033781	5.067113	0.197351	0.967323	4.901535	0.204018	5
6	1.040673	6.100893	0.163910	0.960917	5.862452	0.170577	6
7	1.047610	7.141566	0.140025	0.954553	6.817005	0.146692	7
8	1.054595	8.189176	0.122112	0.948232	7.765237	0.128779	8
9	1.061625	9.243771	0.108181	0.941952	8.707189	0.114848	9
10	1.068703	10.305396	0.097037	0.935714	9.642903	0.103703	10
11	1.075827	11.374099	0.087919	0.929517	10.572420	0.094586	11
12	1.083000	12.449926	0.080322	0.923361	11.495782	0.086988	12
Years						**Months**
1	1.083000	12.449926	0.080322	0.923361	11.495782	0.086988	12
2	1.172888	25.933190	0.038561	0.852596	22.110544	0.045227	24
3	1.270237	40.535558	0.024670	0.787255	31.911806	0.031336	36
4	1.375666	56.349915	0.017746	0.726921	40.961913	0.024413	48
5	1.489846	73.476856	0.013610	0.671210	49.318433	0.020276	60
6	1.613502	92.025325	0.010867	0.619770	57.034522	0.017533	72
7	1.747422	112.113308	0.008920	0.572272	64.159261	0.015586	84
8	1.892457	133.868583	0.007470	0.528414	70.737971	0.014137	96
9	2.049530	157.429535	0.006352	0.487917	76.812497	0.013019	108
10	2.219640	182.946035	0.005466	0.450523	82.421481	0.012133	120
11	2.403869	210.580392	0.004749	0.415996	87.600600	0.011415	132
12	2.603389	240.508387	0.004158	0.384115	92.382800	0.010825	144
13	2.819469	272.920390	0.003664	0.354677	96.798498	0.010331	156
14	3.053484	308.022574	0.003247	0.327495	100.875784	0.009913	168
15	3.306922	346.038222	0.002890	0.302396	104.640592	0.009557	180
16	3.581394	387.209149	0.002583	0.279221	108.116871	0.009249	192
17	3.878648	431.797244	0.002316	0.257822	111.326733	0.008983	204
18	4.200574	480.086128	0.002083	0.238063	114.290596	0.008750	216
19	4.549220	532.382966	0.001878	0.219818	117.027313	0.008545	228
20	4.926803	589.020416	0.001698	0.202971	119.554292	0.008364	240
21	5.335725	650.358746	0.001538	0.187416	121.887607	0.008204	252
22	5.778588	716.788127	0.001395	0.173053	124.042099	0.008062	264
23	6.258207	788.731114	0.001268	0.159790	126.031475	0.007935	276
24	6.777636	866.645333	0.001154	0.147544	127.868388	0.007821	288
25	7.340176	951.026395	0.001052	0.136237	129.564523	0.007718	300
26	7.949407	1042.411042	0.000959	0.125796	131.130668	0.007626	312
27	8.609204	1141.380571	0.000876	0.116155	132.576786	0.007543	324
28	9.323764	1248.564521	0.000801	0.107253	133.912076	0.007468	336
29	10.097631	1364.644687	0.000733	0.099033	135.145031	0.007399	348
30	10.935730	1490.359449	0.000671	0.091443	136.283494	0.007338	360
31	11.843390	1626.508474	0.000615	0.084435	137.334707	0.007281	372
32	12.826386	1773.957801	0.000564	0.077964	138.305357	0.007230	384
33	13.890969	1933.645350	0.000517	0.071989	139.201617	0.007184	396
34	15.043913	2106.586886	0.000475	0.066472	140.029190	0.007141	408
35	16.292550	2293.882485	0.000436	0.061378	140.793338	0.007103	420
36	17.644824	2496.723526	0.000401	0.056674	141.498923	0.007067	432
37	19.109335	2716.400273	0.000368	0.052330	142.150433	0.007035	444
38	20.695401	2954.310082	0.000338	0.048320	142.752013	0.007005	456
39	22.413109	3211.966288	0.000311	0.044617	143.307488	0.006978	468
40	24.273386	3491.007831	0.000286	0.041197	143.820392	0.006953	480

Monthly Compound Interest Tables

	1	2	3	4	5	6	
	Future Value of $1	**Future Value Annuity of $1 Per Year**	**Sinking Fund Factor**	**Present Value of $1 (Reversion)**	**Present Value Annuity of $1 Per Year**	**Payment to Amortize $1**	
Months							**Months**
1	1.007500	1.000000	1.000000	0.992556	0.992556	1.007500	1
2	1.015056	2.007500	0.498132	0.985167	1.977723	0.505632	2
3	1.022669	3.022556	0.330846	0.977833	2.955556	0.338346	3
4	1.030339	4.045225	0.247205	0.970554	3.926110	0.254705	4
5	1.038067	5.075565	0.197022	0.963329	4.889440	0.204522	5
6	1.045852	6.113631	0.163569	0.956158	5.845598	0.171069	6
7	1.053696	7.159484	0.139675	0.949040	6.794638	0.147175	7
8	1.061599	8.213180	0.121756	0.941975	7.736613	0.129256	8
9	1.069561	9.274779	0.107819	0.934963	8.671576	0.115319	9
10	1.077583	10.344339	0.096671	0.928003	9.599580	0.104171	10
11	1.085664	11.421922	0.087551	0.921095	10.520675	0.095051	11
12	1.093807	12.507586	0.079951	0.914238	11.434913	0.087451	12
Years							**Months**
1	1.093807	12.507586	0.079951	0.914238	11.434913	0.087451	12
2	1.196414	26.188471	0.038185	0.835831	21.889146	0.045685	24
3	1.308645	41.152716	0.024300	0.764149	31.446805	0.031800	36
4	1.431405	57.520711	0.017385	0.698614	40.184782	0.024885	48
5	1.565681	75.424137	0.013258	0.638700	48.173374	0.020758	60
6	1.712553	95.007028	0.010526	0.583924	55.476849	0.018026	72
7	1.873202	116.426928	0.008589	0.533845	62.153965	0.016089	84
8	2.048921	139.856164	0.007150	0.488062	68.258439	0.014650	96
9	2.241124	165.483223	0.006043	0.446205	73.839382	0.013543	108
10	2.451357	193.514277	0.005168	0.407937	78.941693	0.012668	120
11	2.681311	224.174837	0.004461	0.372952	83.606420	0.011961	132
12	2.932837	257.711570	0.003880	0.340967	87.871092	0.011380	144
13	3.207957	294.394279	0.003397	0.311725	91.770018	0.010897	156
14	3.508886	334.518079	0.002989	0.284991	95.334564	0.010489	168
15	3.838043	378.405769	0.002643	0.260549	98.593409	0.010143	180
16	4.198078	426.410427	0.002345	0.238204	101.572769	0.009845	192
17	4.591887	478.918252	0.002088	0.217775	104.296613	0.009588	204
18	5.022638	536.351674	0.001864	0.199099	106.786856	0.009364	216
19	5.493796	599.172747	0.001669	0.182024	109.063531	0.009169	228
20	6.009152	667.886870	0.001497	0.166413	111.144954	0.008997	240
21	6.572851	743.046852	0.001346	0.152141	113.047870	0.008846	252
22	7.189430	825.257358	0.001212	0.139093	114.787589	0.008712	264
23	7.863848	915.179777	0.001093	0.127164	116.378106	0.008593	276
24	8.601532	1013.537539	0.000987	0.116258	117.832218	0.008487	288
25	9.408415	1121.121937	0.000892	0.106288	119.161622	0.008392	300
26	10.290989	1238.798495	0.000807	0.097172	120.377014	0.008307	312
27	11.256354	1367.513925	0.000731	0.088839	121.488172	0.008231	324
28	12.312278	1508.303750	0.000663	0.081220	122.504035	0.008163	336
29	13.467255	1662.300631	0.000602	0.074254	123.432776	0.008102	348
30	14.730576	1830.743483	0.000546	0.067886	124.281866	0.008046	360
31	16.112406	2014.987436	0.000496	0.062064	125.058136	0.007996	372
32	17.623861	2216.514743	0.000451	0.056741	125.767832	0.007951	384
33	19.277100	2436.946701	0.000410	0.051875	126.416664	0.007910	396
34	21.085425	2678.056697	0.000373	0.047426	127.009850	0.007873	408
35	23.063384	2941.784474	0.000340	0.043359	127.552164	0.007840	420
36	25.226888	3230.251735	0.000310	0.039640	128.047967	0.007810	432
37	27.593344	3545.779215	0.000282	0.036241	128.501250	0.007782	444
38	30.181790	3890.905350	0.000257	0.033133	128.915659	0.007757	456
39	33.013050	4268.406696	0.000234	0.030291	129.294526	0.007734	468
40	36.109902	4681.320273	0.000214	0.027693	129.640902	0.007714	480

Monthly Compound Interest Tables

10.00% Annual Interest Rate				0.8333% Monthly Effective Interest Rate		
1	**2**	**3**	**4**	**5**	**6**	
Future Value of $1	Future Value Annuity of $1 Per Year	Sinking Fund Factor	Present Value of $1 (Reversion)	Present Value Annuity of $1 Per Year	Payment to Amortize $1	
Months						**Months**
1	1.008333	1.000000	1.000000	0.991736	0.991736	1.008333	1
2	1.016736	2.008333	0.497925	0.983539	1.975275	0.506259	2
3	1.025209	3.025069	0.330571	0.975411	2.950686	0.338904	3
4	1.033752	4.050278	0.246897	0.967350	3.918036	0.255230	4
5	1.042367	5.084031	0.196694	0.959355	4.877391	0.205028	5
6	1.051053	6.126398	0.163228	0.951427	5.828817	0.171561	6
7	1.059812	7.177451	0.139325	0.943564	6.772381	0.147659	7
8	1.068644	8.237263	0.121400	0.935765	7.708146	0.129733	8
9	1.077549	9.305907	0.107459	0.928032	8.636178	0.115792	9
10	1.086529	10.383456	0.096307	0.920362	9.556540	0.104640	10
11	1.095583	11.469985	0.087184	0.912756	10.469296	0.095517	11
12	1.104713	12.565568	0.079583	0.905212	11.374508	0.087916	12
Years						**Months**
1	1.104713	12.565568	0.079583	0.905212	11.374508	0.087916	12
2	1.220391	26.446915	0.037812	0.819410	21.670855	0.046145	24
3	1.348182	41.781821	0.023934	0.741740	30.991236	0.032267	36
4	1.489354	58.722492	0.017029	0.671432	39.428160	0.025363	48
5	1.645309	77.437072	0.012914	0.607789	47.065369	0.021247	60
6	1.817594	98.111314	0.010193	0.550178	53.978665	0.018526	72
7	2.007920	120.950418	0.008268	0.498028	60.236667	0.016601	84
8	2.218176	146.181076	0.006841	0.450821	65.901488	0.015174	96
9	2.450448	174.053713	0.005745	0.408089	71.029355	0.014079	108
10	2.707041	204.844979	0.004882	0.369407	75.671163	0.013215	120
11	2.990504	238.860493	0.004187	0.334392	79.872986	0.012520	132
12	3.303649	276.437876	0.003617	0.302696	83.676528	0.011951	144
13	3.649584	317.950102	0.003145	0.274004	87.119542	0.011478	156
14	4.031743	363.809201	0.002749	0.248032	90.236201	0.011082	168
15	4.453920	414.470346	0.002413	0.224521	93.057439	0.010746	180
16	4.920303	470.436376	0.002126	0.203240	95.611259	0.010459	192
17	5.435523	532.262780	0.001879	0.183975	97.923008	0.010212	204
18	6.004693	600.563216	0.001665	0.166536	100.015633	0.009998	216
19	6.633463	676.015601	0.001479	0.150751	101.909902	0.009813	228
20	7.328074	759.368836	0.001317	0.136462	103.624619	0.009650	240
21	8.095419	851.450244	0.001174	0.123527	105.176801	0.009508	252
22	8.943115	953.173779	0.001049	0.111818	106.581856	0.009382	264
23	9.879576	1065.549097	0.000938	0.101219	107.853730	0.009272	276
24	10.914097	1189.691580	0.000841	0.091625	109.005045	0.009174	288
25	12.056945	1326.833403	0.000754	0.082940	110.047230	0.009087	300
26	13.319465	1478.335767	0.000676	0.075078	110.990629	0.009010	312
27	14.714187	1645.702407	0.000608	0.067962	111.844605	0.008941	324
28	16.254954	1830.594523	0.000546	0.061520	112.617635	0.008880	336
29	17.957060	2034.847259	0.000491	0.055688	113.317392	0.008825	348
30	19.837399	2260.487925	0.000442	0.050410	113.950820	0.008776	360
31	21.914634	2509.756117	0.000398	0.045632	114.524207	0.008732	372
32	24.209383	2785.125947	0.000359	0.041306	115.043244	0.008692	384
33	26.744422	3089.330596	0.000324	0.037391	115.513083	0.008657	396
34	29.544912	3425.389447	0.000292	0.033847	115.938387	0.008625	408
35	32.638650	3796.638052	0.000263	0.030639	116.323377	0.008597	420
36	36.056344	4206.761236	0.000238	0.027734	116.671876	0.008571	432
37	39.831914	4659.829677	0.000215	0.025106	116.987340	0.008548	444
38	44.002836	5160.340305	0.000194	0.022726	117.272903	0.008527	456
39	48.610508	5713.260935	0.000175	0.020572	117.531398	0.008508	468
40	53.700663	6324.079581	0.000158	0.018622	117.765391	0.008491	480

Monthly Compound Interest Tables

| 11.00% Annual Interest Rate | | | | 0.9167% Monthly Effective Interest Rate | | |

	1	2	3	4	5	6	
	Future Value of $1	**Future Value Annuity of $1 Per Year**	**Sinking Fund Factor**	**Present Value of $1 (Reversion)**	**Present Value Annuity of $1 Per Year**	**Payment to Amortize $1**	
Months							**Months**
1	1.009167	1.000000	1.000000	0.990917	0.990917	1.009167	1
2	1.018417	2.009167	0.497719	0.981916	1.972832	0.506885	2
3	1.027753	3.027584	0.330296	0.972997	2.945829	0.339463	3
4	1.037174	4.055337	0.246589	0.964158	3.909987	0.255755	4
5	1.046681	5.092511	0.196367	0.955401	4.865388	0.205533	5
6	1.056276	6.139192	0.162888	0.946722	5.812110	0.172055	6
7	1.065958	7.195468	0.138976	0.938123	6.750233	0.148143	7
8	1.075730	8.261427	0.121044	0.929602	7.679835	0.130211	8
9	1.085591	9.337156	0.107099	0.921158	8.600992	0.116266	9
10	1.095542	10.422747	0.095944	0.912790	9.513783	0.105111	10
11	1.105584	11.518289	0.086818	0.904499	10.418282	0.095985	11
12	1.115719	12.623873	0.079215	0.896283	11.314565	0.088382	12
Years							**Months**
1	1.115719	12.623873	0.079215	0.896283	11.314565	0.088382	12
2	1.244829	26.708566	0.037441	0.803324	21.455619	0.046608	24
3	1.388879	42.423123	0.023572	0.720005	30.544874	0.032739	36
4	1.549598	59.956151	0.016679	0.645329	38.691421	0.025846	48
5	1.728916	79.518080	0.012576	0.578397	45.993034	0.021742	60
6	1.928984	101.343692	0.009867	0.518408	52.537346	0.019034	72
7	2.152204	125.694940	0.007956	0.464640	58.402903	0.017122	84
8	2.401254	152.864085	0.006542	0.416449	63.660103	0.015708	96
9	2.679124	183.177212	0.005459	0.373256	68.372043	0.014626	108
10	2.989150	216.998139	0.004608	0.334543	72.595275	0.013775	120
11	3.335051	254.732784	0.003926	0.299846	76.380487	0.013092	132
12	3.720979	296.834038	0.003369	0.268747	79.773109	0.012536	144
13	4.151566	343.807200	0.002909	0.240873	82.813859	0.012075	156
14	4.631980	396.216042	0.002524	0.215890	85.539231	0.011691	168
15	5.167988	454.689575	0.002199	0.193499	87.981937	0.011366	180
16	5.766021	519.929596	0.001923	0.173430	90.171293	0.011090	192
17	6.433259	592.719117	0.001687	0.155442	92.133576	0.010854	204
18	7.177708	673.931757	0.001484	0.139320	93.892337	0.010651	216
19	8.008304	764.542228	0.001308	0.124870	95.468685	0.010475	228
20	8.935015	865.638038	0.001155	0.111919	96.881539	0.010322	240
21	9.968965	978.432537	0.001022	0.100311	98.147856	0.010189	252
22	11.122562	1104.279485	0.000906	0.089907	99.282835	0.010072	264
23	12.409652	1244.689295	0.000803	0.080582	100.300098	0.009970	276
24	13.845682	1401.347165	0.000714	0.072225	101.211853	0.009880	288
25	15.447889	1576.133301	0.000634	0.064734	102.029044	0.009801	300
26	17.235500	1771.145485	0.000565	0.058020	102.761478	0.009731	312
27	19.229972	1988.724252	0.000503	0.052002	103.417947	0.009670	324
28	21.455242	2231.480981	0.000448	0.046609	104.006328	0.009615	336
29	23.938018	2502.329236	0.000400	0.041775	104.533685	0.009566	348
30	26.708098	2804.519736	0.000357	0.037442	105.006346	0.009523	360
31	29.798728	3141.679369	0.000318	0.033558	105.429984	0.009485	372
32	33.247002	3517.854723	0.000284	0.030078	105.809684	0.009451	384
33	37.094306	3937.560650	0.000254	0.026958	106.150002	0.009421	396
34	41.386816	4405.834459	0.000227	0.024162	106.455024	0.009394	408
35	46.176050	4928.296368	0.000203	0.021656	106.728409	0.009370	420
36	51.519489	5511.216962	0.000181	0.019410	106.973440	0.009348	432
37	57.481264	6161.592447	0.000162	0.017397	107.193058	0.009329	444
38	64.132929	6887.228628	0.000145	0.015593	107.389897	0.009312	456
39	71.554317	7696.834582	0.000130	0.013975	107.566320	0.009297	468
40	79.834499	8600.127195	0.000116	0.012526	107.724446	0.009283	480

Monthly Compound Interest Tables

	1	2	3	4	5	6	
	Future Value of $1	Future Value Annuity of $1 Per Year	Sinking Fund Factor	Present Value of $1 (Reversion)	Present Value Annuity of $1 Per Year	Payment to Amortize $1	
Months							**Months**
1	1.010000	1.000000	1.000000	0.990099	0.990099	1.010000	1
2	1.020100	2.010000	0.497512	0.980296	1.970395	0.507512	2
3	1.030301	3.030100	0.330022	0.970590	2.940985	0.340022	3
4	1.040604	4.060401	0.246281	0.960980	3.901966	0.256281	4
5	1.051010	5.101005	0.196040	0.951466	4.853431	0.206040	5
6	1.061520	6.152015	0.162548	0.942045	5.795476	0.172548	6
7	1.072135	7.213535	0.138628	0.932718	6.728195	0.148628	7
8	1.082857	8.285671	0.120690	0.923483	7.651678	0.130690	8
9	1.093685	9.368527	0.106740	0.914340	8.566018	0.116740	9
10	1.104622	10.462213	0.095582	0.905287	9.471305	0.105582	10
11	1.115668	11.566835	0.086454	0.896324	10.367628	0.096454	11
12	1.126825	12.682503	0.078849	0.887449	11.255077	0.088849	12
Years							**Months**
1	1.126825	12.682503	0.078849	0.887449	11.255077	0.088849	12
2	1.269735	26.973465	0.037073	0.787566	21.243387	0.047073	24
3	1.430769	43.076878	0.023214	0.698925	30.107505	0.033214	36
4	1.612226	61.222608	0.016334	0.620260	37.973960	0.026334	48
5	1.816697	81.669670	0.012244	0.550450	44.955038	0.022244	60
6	2.047099	104.709931	0.009550	0.488496	51.150391	0.019550	72
7	2.306723	130.672274	0.007653	0.433515	56.648453	0.017653	84
8	2.599273	159.927293	0.006253	0.384723	61.527703	0.016253	96
9	2.928926	192.892579	0.005184	0.341422	65.857790	0.015184	108
10	3.300387	230.038689	0.004347	0.302995	69.700522	0.014347	120
11	3.718959	271.895856	0.003678	0.268892	73.110752	0.013678	132
12	4.190616	319.061559	0.003134	0.238628	76.137157	0.013134	144
13	4.722091	372.209054	0.002687	0.211771	78.822939	0.012687	156
14	5.320970	432.096982	0.002314	0.187936	81.206434	0.012314	168
15	5.995802	499.580198	0.002002	0.166783	83.321664	0.012002	180
16	6.756220	575.621974	0.001737	0.148012	85.198824	0.011737	192
17	7.613078	661.307751	0.001512	0.131353	86.864708	0.011512	204
18	8.578606	757.860630	0.001320	0.116569	88.343095	0.011320	216
19	9.666588	866.658830	0.001154	0.103449	89.655089	0.011154	228
20	10.892554	989.255365	0.001011	0.091806	90.819416	0.011011	240
21	12.274002	1127.400210	0.000887	0.081473	91.852698	0.010887	252
22	13.830653	1283.065279	0.000779	0.072303	92.769683	0.010779	264
23	15.584726	1458.472574	0.000686	0.064165	93.583461	0.010686	276
24	17.561259	1656.125905	0.000604	0.056944	94.305647	0.010604	288
25	19.788466	1878.846626	0.000532	0.050534	94.946551	0.010532	300
26	22.298139	2129.813909	0.000470	0.044847	95.515321	0.010470	312
27	25.126101	2412.610125	0.000414	0.039799	96.020075	0.010414	324
28	28.312720	2731.271980	0.000366	0.035320	96.468019	0.010366	336
29	31.903481	3090.348134	0.000324	0.031345	96.865546	0.010324	348
30	35.949641	3494.964133	0.000286	0.027817	97.218331	0.010286	360
31	40.508956	3950.895567	0.000253	0.024686	97.531410	0.010253	372
32	45.646505	4464.650520	0.000224	0.021907	97.809252	0.010224	384
33	51.435625	5043.562459	0.000198	0.019442	98.055822	0.010198	396
34	57.958949	5695.894923	0.000176	0.017254	98.274641	0.010176	408
35	65.309595	6430.959471	0.000156	0.015312	98.468831	0.010156	420
36	73.592486	7259.248603	0.000138	0.013588	98.641166	0.010138	432
37	82.925855	8192.585529	0.000122	0.012059	98.794103	0.010122	444
38	93.442929	9244.292939	0.000108	0.010702	98.929828	0.010108	456
39	105.293832	10429.383172	0.000096	0.009497	99.050277	0.010096	468
40	118.647725	11764.772510	0.000085	0.008428	99.157169	0.010085	480

Monthly Compound Interest Tables

	1	2	3	4	5	6	
	Future Value of $1	**Future Value Annuity of $1 Per Year**	**Sinking Fund Factor**	**Present Value of $1 (Reversion)**	**Present Value Annuity of $1 Per Year**	**Payment to Amortize $1**	
Months							**Months**
1	1.010833	1.000000	1.000000	0.989283	0.989283	1.010833	1
2	1.021784	2.010833	0.497306	0.978680	1.967963	0.508140	2
3	1.032853	3.032617	0.329748	0.968192	2.936155	0.340582	3
4	1.044043	4.065471	0.245974	0.957815	3.893970	0.256807	4
5	1.055353	5.109513	0.195713	0.947550	4.841520	0.206547	5
6	1.066786	6.164866	0.162210	0.937395	5.778915	0.173043	6
7	1.078343	7.231652	0.138281	0.927349	6.706264	0.149114	7
8	1.090025	8.309995	0.120337	0.917410	7.623674	0.131170	8
9	1.101834	9.400020	0.106383	0.907578	8.531253	0.117216	9
10	1.113770	10.501854	0.095221	0.897851	9.429104	0.106055	10
11	1.125836	11.615624	0.086091	0.888229	10.317333	0.096924	11
12	1.138032	12.741460	0.078484	0.878710	11.196042	0.089317	12
Years							**Months**
1	1.138032	12.741460	0.078484	0.878710	11.196042	0.089317	12
2	1.295118	27.241655	0.036708	0.772130	21.034112	0.047542	24
3	1.473886	43.743348	0.022861	0.678478	29.678917	0.033694	36
4	1.677330	62.522811	0.015994	0.596185	37.275190	0.026828	48
5	1.908857	83.894449	0.011920	0.523874	43.950107	0.022753	60
6	2.172341	108.216068	0.009241	0.460333	49.815421	0.020074	72
7	2.472194	135.894861	0.007359	0.404499	54.969328	0.018192	84
8	2.813437	167.394225	0.005974	0.355437	59.498115	0.016807	96
9	3.201783	203.241525	0.004920	0.312326	63.477604	0.015754	108
10	3.643733	244.036917	0.004098	0.274444	66.974419	0.014931	120
11	4.146687	290.463399	0.003443	0.241156	70.047103	0.014276	132
12	4.719064	343.298242	0.002913	0.211906	72.747100	0.013746	144
13	5.370448	403.426010	0.002479	0.186204	75.119613	0.013312	156
14	6.111745	471.853363	0.002119	0.163619	77.204363	0.012953	168
15	6.955364	549.725914	0.001819	0.143774	79.036253	0.012652	180
16	7.915430	638.347406	0.001567	0.126336	80.645952	0.012400	192
17	9.008017	739.201542	0.001353	0.111012	82.060410	0.012186	204
18	10.251416	853.976825	0.001171	0.097548	83.303307	0.012004	216
19	11.666444	984.594826	0.001016	0.085716	84.395453	0.011849	228
20	13.276792	1133.242353	0.000882	0.075319	85.355132	0.011716	240
21	15.109421	1302.408067	0.000768	0.066184	86.198412	0.011601	252
22	17.195012	1494.924144	0.000669	0.058156	86.939409	0.011502	264
23	19.568482	1714.013694	0.000583	0.051103	87.590531	0.011417	276
24	22.269568	1963.344717	0.000509	0.044904	88.162677	0.011343	288
25	25.343491	2247.091520	0.000445	0.039458	88.665428	0.011278	300
26	28.841717	2570.004599	0.000389	0.034672	89.107200	0.011222	312
27	32.822810	2937.490172	0.000340	0.030467	89.495389	0.011174	324
28	37.353424	3355.700690	0.000298	0.026771	89.836495	0.011131	336
29	42.509410	3831.637843	0.000261	0.023524	90.136227	0.011094	348
30	48.377089	4373.269783	0.000229	0.020671	90.399605	0.011062	360
31	55.054699	4989.664524	0.000200	0.018164	90.631038	0.011034	372
32	62.654036	5691.141761	0.000176	0.015961	90.834400	0.011009	384
33	71.302328	6489.445641	0.000154	0.014025	91.013097	0.010987	396
34	81.144365	7397.941387	0.000135	0.012324	91.170119	0.010969	408
35	92.344923	8431.839055	0.000119	0.010829	91.308095	0.010952	420
36	105.091522	9608.448184	0.000104	0.009516	91.429337	0.010937	432
37	119.597566	10947.467591	0.000091	0.008361	91.535873	0.010925	444
38	136.105914	12471.315170	0.000080	0.007347	91.629487	0.010914	456
39	154.892951	14205.503212	0.000070	0.006456	91.711747	0.010904	468
40	176.273210	16179.065533	0.000062	0.005673	91.784030	0.010895	480

Monthly Compound Interest Tables

14.00% Annual Interest Rate **1.1667% Monthly Effective Interest Rate**

	1	2	3	4	5	6	
	Future Value of $1	Future Value Annuity of $1 Per Year	Sinking Fund Factor	Present Value of $1 (Reversion)	Present Value Annuity of $1 Per Year	Payment to Amortize $1	
Months							**Months**
1	1.011667	1.000000	1.000000	0.988468	0.988468	1.011667	1
2	1.023469	2.011667	0.497100	0.977069	1.965537	0.508767	2
3	1.035410	3.035136	0.329475	0.965801	2.931338	0.341141	3
4	1.047490	4.070546	0.245667	0.954663	3.886001	0.257334	4
5	1.059710	5.118036	0.195387	0.943654	4.829655	0.207054	5
6	1.072074	6.177746	0.161871	0.932772	5.762427	0.173538	6
7	1.084581	7.249820	0.137934	0.922015	6.684442	0.149601	7
8	1.097235	8.334401	0.119985	0.911382	7.595824	0.131651	8
9	1.110036	9.431636	0.106026	0.900872	8.496696	0.117693	9
10	1.122986	10.541672	0.094862	0.890483	9.387179	0.106528	10
11	1.136088	11.664658	0.085729	0.880214	10.267392	0.097396	11
12	1.149342	12.800746	0.078120	0.870063	11.137455	0.089787	12
Years							**Months**
1	1.149342	12.800746	0.078120	0.870063	11.137455	0.089787	12
2	1.320987	27.513180	0.036346	0.757010	20.827743	0.048013	24
3	1.518266	44.422800	0.022511	0.658646	29.258904	0.034178	36
4	1.745007	63.857736	0.015660	0.573064	36.594546	0.027326	48
5	2.005610	86.195125	0.011602	0.498601	42.977016	0.023268	60
6	2.305132	111.868425	0.008939	0.433815	48.530168	0.020606	72
7	2.649385	141.375828	0.007073	0.377446	53.361760	0.018740	84
8	3.045050	175.289927	0.005705	0.328402	57.565549	0.017372	96
9	3.499804	214.268826	0.004667	0.285730	61.223111	0.016334	108
10	4.022472	259.068912	0.003860	0.248603	64.405420	0.015527	120
11	4.623197	310.559534	0.003220	0.216301	67.174230	0.014887	132
12	5.313634	369.739871	0.002705	0.188195	69.583269	0.014371	144
13	6.107184	437.758319	0.002284	0.163742	71.679284	0.013951	156
14	7.019243	515.934780	0.001938	0.142466	73.502950	0.013605	168
15	8.067511	605.786272	0.001651	0.123954	75.089654	0.013317	180
16	9.272330	709.056369	0.001410	0.107848	76.470187	0.013077	192
17	10.657079	827.749031	0.001208	0.093834	77.671337	0.012875	204
18	12.248630	964.167496	0.001037	0.081642	78.716413	0.012704	216
19	14.077865	1120.958972	0.000892	0.071034	79.625696	0.012559	228
20	16.180283	1301.166005	0.000769	0.061804	80.416829	0.012435	240
21	18.596680	1508.285522	0.000663	0.053773	81.105164	0.012330	252
22	21.373947	1746.336688	0.000573	0.046786	81.704060	0.012239	264
23	24.565976	2019.938898	0.000495	0.040707	82.225136	0.012162	276
24	28.234710	2334.401417	0.000428	0.035417	82.678506	0.012095	288
25	32.451340	2695.826407	0.000371	0.030815	83.072966	0.012038	300
26	37.297691	3111.227338	0.000321	0.026811	83.416171	0.011988	312
27	42.867805	3588.665088	0.000279	0.023328	83.714781	0.011945	324
28	49.269772	4137.404359	0.000242	0.020296	83.974591	0.011908	336
29	56.627822	4768.093467	0.000210	0.017659	84.200641	0.011876	348
30	65.084738	5492.970967	0.000182	0.015365	84.397320	0.011849	360
31	74.804628	6326.103143	0.000158	0.013368	84.568442	0.011825	372
32	85.976107	7283.656968	0.000137	0.011631	84.717330	0.011804	384
33	98.815957	8384.213825	0.000119	0.010120	84.846871	0.011786	396
34	113.573337	9649.130077	0.000104	0.008805	84.959580	0.011770	408
35	130.534615	11102.951488	0.000090	0.007661	85.057645	0.011757	420
36	150.028925	12773.889538	0.000078	0.006665	85.142967	0.011745	432
37	172.434556	14694.368868	0.000068	0.005799	85.217202	0.011735	444
38	198.186290	16901.656478	0.000059	0.005046	85.281792	0.011726	456
39	227.783842	19438.584899	0.000051	0.004390	85.337989	0.011718	468
40	261.801553	22354.383358	0.000045	0.003820	85.386883	0.011711	480

Monthly Compound Interest Tables

15.00% Annual Interest Rate				1.2500% Monthly Effective Interest Rate		
1	2	3	4	5	6	
Future Value of $1	Future Value Annuity of $1 Per Year	Sinking Fund Factor	Present Value of $1 (Reversion)	Present Value Annuity of $1 Per Year	Payment to Amortize $1	
Months						**Months**
1 1.012500	1.000000	1.000000	0.987654	0.987654	1.012500	1
2 1.025156	2.012500	0.496894	0.975461	1.963115	0.509394	2
3 1.037971	3.037656	0.329201	0.963418	2.926534	0.341701	3
4 1.050945	4.075627	0.245361	0.951524	3.878058	0.257861	4
5 1.064082	5.126572	0.195062	0.939777	4.817835	0.207562	5
6 1.077383	6.190654	0.161534	0.928175	5.746010	0.174034	6
7 1.090850	7.268038	0.137589	0.916716	6.662726	0.150089	7
8 1.104486	8.358888	0.119633	0.905398	7.568124	0.132133	8
9 1.118292	9.463374	0.105671	0.894221	8.462345	0.118171	9
10 1.132271	10.581666	0.094503	0.883181	9.345526	0.107003	10
11 1.146424	11.713937	0.085368	0.872277	10.217803	0.097868	11
12 1.160755	12.860361	0.077758	0.861509	11.079312	0.090258	12
Years						**Months**
1 1.160755	12.860361	0.077758	0.861509	11.079312	0.090258	12
2 1.347351	27.788084	0.035987	0.742197	20.624235	0.048487	24
3 1.563944	45.115506	0.022165	0.639409	28.847267	0.034665	36
4 1.815355	65.228388	0.015331	0.550856	35.931481	0.027831	48
5 2.107181	88.574508	0.011290	0.474568	42.034592	0.023790	60
6 2.445920	115.673621	0.008645	0.408844	47.292474	0.021145	72
7 2.839113	147.129040	0.006797	0.352223	51.822185	0.019297	84
8 3.295513	183.641059	0.005445	0.303443	55.724570	0.017945	96
9 3.825282	226.022551	0.004424	0.261419	59.086509	0.016924	108
10 4.440213	275.217058	0.003634	0.225214	61.982847	0.016134	120
11 5.153998	332.319805	0.003009	0.194024	64.478068	0.015509	132
12 5.982526	398.602077	0.002509	0.167153	66.627722	0.015009	144
13 6.944244	475.539523	0.002103	0.144004	68.479668	0.014603	156
14 8.060563	564.845011	0.001770	0.124061	70.075135	0.014270	168
15 9.356335	668.506759	0.001496	0.106879	71.449643	0.013996	180
16 10.860408	788.832603	0.001268	0.092078	72.633794	0.013768	192
17 12.606267	928.501369	0.001077	0.079326	73.653950	0.013577	204
18 14.632782	1090.622520	0.000917	0.068340	74.532823	0.013417	216
19 16.985067	1278.805378	0.000782	0.058875	75.289980	0.013282	228
20 19.715494	1497.239481	0.000668	0.050722	75.942278	0.013168	240
21 22.884848	1750.787854	0.000571	0.043697	76.504237	0.013071	252
22 26.563691	2045.095272	0.000489	0.037645	76.988370	0.012989	264
23 30.833924	2386.713938	0.000419	0.032432	77.405455	0.012919	276
24 35.790617	2783.249347	0.000359	0.027940	77.764777	0.012859	288
25 41.544120	3243.529615	0.000308	0.024071	78.074336	0.012808	300
26 48.222525	3777.802015	0.000265	0.020737	78.341024	0.012765	312
27 55.974514	4397.961118	0.000227	0.017865	78.570778	0.012727	324
28 64.972670	5117.813598	0.000195	0.015391	78.768713	0.012695	336
29 75.417320	5953.385616	0.000168	0.013260	78.939236	0.012668	348
30 87.540995	6923.279611	0.000144	0.011423	79.086142	0.012644	360
31 101.613606	8049.088447	0.000124	0.009841	79.212704	0.012624	372
32 117.948452	9355.876140	0.000107	0.008478	79.321738	0.012607	384
33 136.909198	10872.735858	0.000092	0.007304	79.415671	0.012592	396
34 158.917970	12633.437629	0.000079	0.006293	79.496596	0.012579	408
35 184.464752	14677.180163	0.000068	0.005421	79.566313	0.012568	420
36 214.118294	17049.463544	0.000059	0.004670	79.626375	0.012559	432
37 248.538777	19803.102194	0.000051	0.004024	79.678119	0.012551	444
38 288.492509	22999.400699	0.000043	0.003466	79.722696	0.012543	456
39 334.868983	26709.518627	0.000037	0.002986	79.761101	0.012537	468
40 388.700685	31016.054774	0.000032	0.002573	79.794186	0.012532	480

Monthly Compound Interest Tables

16.00% Annual Interest Rate				1.3333% Monthly Effective Interest Rate		
1	2	3	4	5	6	
Future Value of $1	Future Value Annuity of $1 Per Year	Sinking Fund Factor	Present Value of $1 (Reversion)	Present Value Annuity of $1 Per Year	Payment to Amortize $1	
Months						**Months**
1	1.013333	1.000000	1.000000	0.986842	0.986842	1.013333	1
2	1.026844	2.013333	0.496689	0.973857	1.960699	0.510022	2
3	1.040537	3.040178	0.328928	0.961043	2.921743	0.342261	3
4	1.054410	4.080713	0.245055	0.948398	3.870141	0.258389	4
5	1.068467	5.135123	0.194737	0.935919	4.806060	0.208071	5
6	1.082715	6.203591	0.161197	0.923604	5.729665	0.174530	6
7	1.097151	7.286306	0.137244	0.911452	6.641116	0.150577	7
8	1.111779	8.383457	0.119283	0.899459	7.540575	0.132616	8
9	1.126603	9.495236	0.105316	0.887624	8.428199	0.118649	9
10	1.141624	10.621839	0.094146	0.875945	9.304144	0.107479	10
11	1.156846	11.763463	0.085009	0.864419	10.168563	0.098342	11
12	1.172271	12.920310	0.077398	0.853045	11.021608	0.090731	12
Years						**Months**
1	1.172271	12.920310	0.077398	0.853045	11.021608	0.090731	12
2	1.374219	28.066412	0.035630	0.727686	20.423539	0.048963	24
3	1.610957	45.821745	0.021824	0.620749	28.443811	0.035157	36
4	1.888477	66.635803	0.015007	0.529527	35.285465	0.028340	48
5	2.213807	91.035516	0.010985	0.451711	41.121706	0.024318	60
6	2.595181	119.638587	0.008359	0.385330	46.100283	0.021692	72
7	3.042255	153.169132	0.006529	0.328704	50.347235	0.019862	84
8	3.566347	192.476010	0.005195	0.280399	53.970077	0.018529	96
9	4.180724	238.554316	0.004192	0.239193	57.060524	0.017525	108
10	4.900941	292.570569	0.003418	0.204043	59.696816	0.016751	120
11	5.745230	355.892244	0.002810	0.174058	61.945692	0.016143	132
12	6.734965	430.122395	0.002325	0.148479	63.864085	0.015658	144
13	7.895203	517.140233	0.001934	0.126659	65.500561	0.015267	156
14	9.255316	619.148703	0.001615	0.108046	66.896549	0.014948	168
15	10.849737	738.730255	0.001354	0.092168	68.087390	0.014687	180
16	12.718830	878.912215	0.001138	0.078624	69.103231	0.014471	192
17	14.909912	1043.243434	0.000959	0.067070	69.969789	0.014292	204
18	17.478455	1235.884123	0.000809	0.057213	70.709003	0.014142	216
19	20.489482	1461.711177	0.000684	0.048806	71.339585	0.014017	228
20	24.019222	1726.441638	0.000579	0.041633	71.877501	0.013913	240
21	28.157032	2036.777427	0.000491	0.035515	72.336367	0.013824	252
22	33.007667	2400.575011	0.000417	0.030296	72.727801	0.013750	264
23	38.693924	2827.044294	0.000354	0.025844	73.061711	0.013687	276
24	45.359757	3326.981781	0.000301	0.022046	73.346552	0.013634	288
25	53.173919	3913.043898	0.000256	0.018806	73.589534	0.013589	300
26	62.334232	4600.067404	0.000217	0.016043	73.796809	0.013551	312
27	73.072600	5405.444997	0.000185	0.013685	73.973624	0.013518	324
28	85.660875	6349.565632	0.000158	0.011674	74.124454	0.013491	336
29	100.417742	7456.330682	0.000134	0.009958	74.253120	0.013467	348
30	117.716787	8753.759030	0.000114	0.008495	74.362878	0.013448	360
31	137.995952	10274.696396	0.000097	0.007247	74.456506	0.013431	372
32	161.768625	12057.646856	0.000083	0.006182	74.536375	0.013416	384
33	189.636635	14147.747615	0.000071	0.005273	74.604507	0.013404	396
34	222.305489	16597.911700	0.000060	0.004498	74.662626	0.013394	408
35	260.602233	19470.167508	0.000051	0.003837	74.712205	0.013385	420
36	305.496388	22837.229116	0.000044	0.003273	74.754498	0.013377	432
37	358.124495	26784.337116	0.000037	0.002792	74.790576	0.013371	444
38	419.818887	31411.416562	0.000032	0.002382	74.821352	0.013365	456
39	492.141422	36835.606677	0.000027	0.002032	74.847605	0.013360	468
40	576.923018	43194.226353	0.000023	0.001733	74.870000	0.013356	480

Monthly Compound Interest Tables

	1	2	3	4	5	6	
	Future Value of $1	Future Value Annuity of $1 Per Year	Sinking Fund Factor	Present Value of $1 (Reversion)	Present Value Annuity of $1 Per Year	Payment to Amortize $1	
Months							**Months**
1	1.014167	1.000000	1.000000	0.986031	0.986031	1.014167	1
2	1.028534	2.014167	0.496483	0.972258	1.958289	0.510650	2
3	1.043105	3.042701	0.328655	0.958676	2.916965	0.342822	3
4	1.057882	4.085806	0.244750	0.945285	3.862250	0.258916	4
5	1.072869	5.143688	0.194413	0.932080	4.794330	0.208580	5
6	1.088068	6.216557	0.160861	0.919060	5.713391	0.175027	6
7	1.103482	7.304625	0.136900	0.906222	6.619613	0.151066	7
8	1.119115	8.408107	0.118933	0.893563	7.513176	0.133100	8
9	1.134969	9.527222	0.104962	0.881081	8.394257	0.119129	9
10	1.151048	10.662191	0.093789	0.868774	9.263031	0.107956	10
11	1.167354	11.813238	0.084651	0.856638	10.119669	0.098817	11
12	1.183892	12.980593	0.077038	0.844672	10.964341	0.091205	12
Years							**Months**
1	1.183892	12.980593	0.077038	0.844672	10.964341	0.091205	12
2	1.401600	28.348209	0.035276	0.713471	20.225611	0.049442	24
3	1.659342	46.541802	0.021486	0.602648	28.048345	0.035653	36
4	1.964482	68.081048	0.014688	0.509040	34.655988	0.028855	48
5	2.325733	93.581182	0.010686	0.429972	40.237278	0.024853	60
6	2.753417	123.770579	0.008079	0.363185	44.951636	0.022246	72
7	3.259747	159.511558	0.006269	0.306772	48.933722	0.020436	84
8	3.859188	201.825006	0.004955	0.259122	52.297278	0.019121	96
9	4.568860	251.919548	0.003970	0.218873	55.138379	0.018136	108
10	5.409036	311.226062	0.003213	0.184876	57.538177	0.017380	120
11	6.403713	381.438553	0.002622	0.156159	59.565218	0.016788	132
12	7.581303	464.562540	0.002153	0.131903	61.277403	0.016319	144
13	8.975442	562.972341	0.001776	0.111415	62.723638	0.015943	156
14	10.625951	679.478890	0.001472	0.094109	63.945231	0.015638	168
15	12.579975	817.410030	0.001223	0.079491	64.977077	0.015390	180
16	14.893329	980.705566	0.001020	0.067144	65.848648	0.015186	192
17	17.632089	1174.029800	0.000852	0.056715	66.584839	0.015018	204
18	20.874484	1402.904761	0.000713	0.047905	67.206679	0.014879	216
19	24.713129	1673.867935	0.000597	0.040464	67.731930	0.014764	228
20	29.257669	1994.658995	0.000501	0.034179	68.175595	0.014668	240
21	34.637912	2374.440878	0.000421	0.028870	68.550346	0.014588	252
22	41.007538	2824.061507	0.000354	0.024386	68.866888	0.014521	264
23	48.548485	3356.363651	0.000298	0.020598	69.134261	0.014465	276
24	57.476150	3986.551756	0.000251	0.017399	69.360104	0.014418	288
25	68.045538	4732.626240	0.000211	0.014696	69.550868	0.014378	300
26	80.558550	5615.897651	0.000178	0.012413	69.712000	0.014345	312
27	95.372601	6661.595368	0.000150	0.010485	69.848104	0.014317	324
28	112.910833	7899.588246	0.000127	0.008857	69.963067	0.014293	336
29	133.674202	9365.237774	0.000107	0.007481	70.060174	0.014273	348
30	158.255782	11100.408126	0.000090	0.006319	70.142196	0.014257	360
31	187.357711	13154.661953	0.000076	0.005337	70.211479	0.014243	372
32	221.811244	15586.676066	0.000064	0.004508	70.270000	0.014231	384
33	262.600497	18465.917458	0.000054	0.003808	70.319431	0.014221	396
34	310.890557	21874.627526	0.000046	0.003217	70.361184	0.014212	408
35	368.060758	25910.171179	0.000039	0.002717	70.396451	0.014205	420
36	435.744087	30687.817929	0.000033	0.002295	70.426241	0.014199	432
37	515.873821	36344.034396	0.000028	0.001938	70.451403	0.014194	444
38	610.738749	43040.382285	0.000023	0.001637	70.472657	0.014190	456
39	723.048553	50968.133160	0.000020	0.001383	70.490609	0.014186	468
40	856.011201	60353.731845	0.000017	0.001168	70.505773	0.014183	480

Monthly Compound Interest Tables

	1	2	3	4	5	6	
	Future Value of $1	Future Value Annuity of $1 Per Year	Sinking Fund Factor	Present Value of $1 (Reversion)	Present Value Annuity of $1 Per Year	Payment to Amortize $1	
Months							**Months**
1	1.015000	1.000000	1.000000	0.985222	0.985222	1.015000	1
2	1.030225	2.015000	0.496278	0.970662	1.955883	0.511278	2
3	1.045678	3.045225	0.328383	0.956317	2.912200	0.343383	3
4	1.061364	4.090903	0.244445	0.942184	3.854385	0.259445	4
5	1.077284	5.152267	0.194089	0.928260	4.782645	0.209089	5
6	1.093443	6.229551	0.160525	0.914542	5.697187	0.175525	6
7	1.109845	7.322994	0.136556	0.901027	6.598214	0.151556	7
8	1.126493	8.432839	0.118584	0.887711	7.485925	0.133584	8
9	1.143390	9.559332	0.104610	0.874592	8.360517	0.119610	9
10	1.160541	10.702722	0.093434	0.861667	9.222185	0.108434	10
11	1.177949	11.863263	0.084294	0.848933	10.071118	0.099294	11
12	1.195618	13.041211	0.076680	0.836387	10.907505	0.091680	12
Years							**Months**
1	1.195618	13.041211	0.076680	0.836387	10.907505	0.091680	12
2	1.429503	28.633521	0.034924	0.699544	20.030405	0.049924	24
3	1.709140	47.275969	0.021152	0.585090	27.660684	0.036152	36
4	2.043478	69.565219	0.014375	0.489362	34.042554	0.029375	48
5	2.443220	96.214652	0.010393	0.409296	39.380269	0.025393	60
6	2.921158	128.077197	0.007808	0.342330	43.844667	0.022808	72
7	3.492590	166.172636	0.006018	0.286321	47.578633	0.021018	84
8	4.175804	211.720235	0.004723	0.239475	50.701675	0.019723	96
9	4.992667	266.177771	0.003757	0.200294	53.313749	0.018757	108
10	5.969323	331.288191	0.003019	0.167523	55.498454	0.018019	120
11	7.137031	409.135393	0.002444	0.140114	57.325714	0.017444	132
12	8.533164	502.210922	0.001991	0.117190	58.854011	0.016991	144
13	10.202406	613.493716	0.001630	0.098016	60.132260	0.016630	156
14	12.198182	746.545446	0.001340	0.081979	61.201371	0.016340	168
15	14.584368	905.624513	0.001104	0.068567	62.095562	0.016104	180
16	17.437335	1095.822335	0.000913	0.057348	62.843452	0.015913	192
17	20.848395	1323.226308	0.000756	0.047965	63.468978	0.015756	204
18	24.926719	1595.114630	0.000627	0.040118	63.992160	0.015627	216
19	29.802839	1920.189249	0.000521	0.033554	64.429743	0.015521	228
20	35.632816	2308.854370	0.000433	0.028064	64.795732	0.015433	240
21	42.603242	2773.549452	0.000361	0.023472	65.101841	0.015361	252
22	50.937210	3329.147335	0.000300	0.019632	65.357866	0.015300	264
23	60.901454	3993.430261	0.000250	0.016420	65.572002	0.015250	276
24	72.814885	4787.658998	0.000209	0.013733	65.751103	0.015209	288
25	87.058800	5737.253308	0.000174	0.011486	65.900901	0.015174	300
26	104.089083	6872.605521	0.000146	0.009607	66.026190	0.015146	312
27	124.450799	8230.053258	0.000122	0.008035	66.130980	0.015122	324
28	148.795637	9853.042439	0.000102	0.006721	66.218625	0.015102	336
29	177.902767	11793.517795	0.000085	0.005621	66.291930	0.015085	348
30	212.703781	14113.585393	0.000071	0.004701	66.353242	0.015071	360
31	254.312506	16887.500372	0.000059	0.003932	66.404522	0.015059	372
32	304.060653	20204.043526	0.000050	0.003289	66.447412	0.015050	384
33	363.540442	24169.362788	0.000041	0.002751	66.483285	0.015041	396
34	434.655558	28910.370554	0.000035	0.002301	66.513289	0.015035	408
35	519.682084	34578.805589	0.000029	0.001924	66.538383	0.015029	420
36	621.341343	41356.089521	0.000024	0.001609	66.559372	0.015024	432
37	742.887000	49459.133344	0.000020	0.001346	66.576927	0.015020	444
38	888.209197	59147.279782	0.000017	0.001126	66.591609	0.015017	456
39	1061.959056	70730.603711	0.000014	0.000942	66.603890	0.015014	468
40	1269.697544	84579.836287	0.000012	0.000788	66.614161	0.015012	480

Monthly Compound Interest Tables

1.5833% Monthly Effective Interest Rate

	1	2	3	4	5	6	
	Future Value of $1	Future Value Annuity of $1 Per Year	Sinking Fund Factor	Present Value of $1 (Reversion)	Present Value Annuity of $1 Per Year	Payment to Amortize $1	
Months							**Months**
1	1.015833	1.000000	1.000000	0.984413	0.984413	1.015833	1
2	1.031917	2.015833	0.496073	0.969070	1.953483	0.511906	2
3	1.048256	3.047751	0.328111	0.953965	2.907449	0.343944	3
4	1.064853	4.096007	0.244140	0.939096	3.846545	0.259974	4
5	1.081714	5.160860	0.193766	0.924459	4.771004	0.209599	5
6	1.098841	6.242574	0.160190	0.910050	5.681054	0.176024	6
7	1.116239	7.341415	0.136214	0.895865	6.576920	0.152047	7
8	1.133913	8.457654	0.118236	0.881902	7.458822	0.134069	8
9	1.151866	9.591566	0.104258	0.868156	8.326978	0.120092	9
10	1.170104	10.743433	0.093080	0.854625	9.181602	0.108913	10
11	1.188631	11.913537	0.083938	0.841304	10.022906	0.099771	11
12	1.207451	13.102168	0.076323	0.828191	10.851097	0.092157	12
Years							**Months**
1	1.207451	13.102168	0.076323	0.828191	10.851097	0.092157	12
2	1.457938	28.922395	0.034575	0.685900	19.837878	0.050409	24
3	1.760389	48.024542	0.020823	0.568056	27.280649	0.036656	36
4	2.125583	71.089450	0.014067	0.470459	33.444684	0.029900	48
5	2.566537	98.939196	0.010107	0.389630	38.549682	0.025941	60
6	3.098968	132.566399	0.007543	0.322688	42.777596	0.023377	72
7	3.741852	173.169599	0.005775	0.267247	46.279115	0.021608	84
8	4.518103	222.195973	0.004501	0.221332	49.179042	0.020334	96
9	5.455388	281.392918	0.003554	0.183305	51.580735	0.019387	108
10	6.587114	352.870328	0.002834	0.151812	53.569796	0.018667	120
11	7.953617	439.175798	0.002277	0.125729	55.217118	0.018110	132
12	9.603603	543.385424	0.001840	0.104128	56.581415	0.017674	144
13	11.595879	669.213441	0.001494	0.086238	57.711314	0.017328	156
14	14.001456	821.144606	0.001218	0.071421	58.647086	0.017051	168
15	16.906072	1004.594042	0.000995	0.059150	59.422084	0.016829	180
16	20.413254	1226.100247	0.000816	0.048988	60.063930	0.016649	192
17	24.648004	1493.558135	0.000670	0.040571	60.595501	0.016503	204
18	29.761257	1816.500430	0.000551	0.033601	61.035743	0.016384	216
19	35.935259	2206.437425	0.000453	0.027828	61.400348	0.016287	228
20	43.390065	2677.267240	0.000374	0.023047	61.702310	0.016207	240
21	52.391377	3245.771169	0.000308	0.019087	61.952393	0.016141	252
22	63.260020	3932.211806	0.000254	0.015808	62.159509	0.016088	264
23	76.383375	4761.055238	0.000210	0.013092	62.331041	0.016043	276
24	92.229182	5761.843068	0.000174	0.010843	62.473102	0.016007	288
25	111.362218	6970.245332	0.000143	0.008980	62.590755	0.015977	300
26	134.464421	8429.331851	0.000119	0.007437	62.688195	0.015952	312
27	162.359199	10191.107326	0.000098	0.006159	62.768894	0.015931	324
28	196.040777	12318.364881	0.000081	0.005101	62.835728	0.015915	336
29	236.709632	14886.924139	0.000067	0.004225	62.891079	0.015901	348
30	285.815282	17988.333579	0.000056	0.003499	62.936920	0.015889	360
31	345.107947	21733.133503	0.000046	0.002898	62.974886	0.015879	372
32	416.700935	26254.795909	0.000038	0.002400	63.006328	0.015871	384
33	503.145960	31714.481694	0.000032	0.001988	63.032369	0.015865	396
34	607.524092	38306.784745	0.000026	0.001646	63.053935	0.015859	408
35	733.555571	46266.667644	0.000022	0.001363	63.071796	0.015855	420
36	885.732406	55877.836195	0.000018	0.001129	63.086589	0.015851	432
37	1069.478478	67482.851256	0.000015	0.000935	63.098840	0.015848	444
38	1291.342856	81495.338274	0.000012	0.000774	63.108986	0.015846	456
39	1559.233220	98414.729710	0.000010	0.000641	63.117389	0.015844	468
40	1882.697708	118844.065787	0.000008	0.000531	63.124348	0.015842	480

absorption rate An estimate of the rate at which a particular classification of properties for sale or lease can be successfully marketed in a given area; it is often requested in a feasibility study or an appraisal in connection with a request for financing.

abstraction A method of valuing land in which an appraiser establishes a typical ratio of site value to total property value from comparable improved properties. This ratio is then applied to the total value of the property being appraised to estimate the value of the land. Also called the allocation or extraction method.

accessibility The ease with which a person can enter or exit a particular tract of land.

accession The transfer of ownership of fixtures or land as a result of the attachment of those fixtures or land to another's property.

accrued depreciation The difference between an improvement's reproduction or replacement cost and its market value as of the date of the appraisal. It represents the total depreciation accumulated since the improvement was constructed.

accumulated depreciation (*See* accrued depreciation.)

accumulation of $1 per period ($S_n$) Column 2 of the compound interest tables in Appendix B. Also called future value interest factor—annuity, future worth of one per period, and FVIFA.

acre An area of land that measures 43,560 square feet; there are 640 acres of land in a section.

acreage property A large and, for the most part, unimproved tract of land; such land is often used for agricultural purposes.

actual age The number of years that have elapsed since construction was completed. Also called chronological or historical age.

adjacent land Land physically located close to or near another parcel of land.

adjusted sales price The estimated sales price of a comparable property after additions and/ or subtractions have been made to the actual sales price to allow for differences between the comparables and the subject property.

adjustments The dollar value or percentage amounts added to or subtracted from the sales price of a comparable property to arrive at an indicated value for the property being appraised (subject property). Real estate elements of comparison typically are adjusted in the following order: property rights, financing terms, conditions of sale, market conditions, location, and physical characteristics.

ad valorem A tax based on value. Real property tax is an ad valorem tax based on the assessed valuation of the property.

adverse possession The acquiring of title to real property owned by another by means of open, actual, continuous, and hostile possession for a statutory period of time.

after-tax cash flow (ATCF) The cash flow remaining after debt service and ordinary income tax on operations are subtracted from net operating income.

age-life depreciation An appraisal method of computing accrued depreciation. Under this method, depreciation is estimated by multiplying the reproduction or replacement cost by the ratio of the improvement's effective age to total economic life.

air rights The legal right to use and occupy the space above a particular parcel of real estate; air rights can be transferred legally through selling them, leasing them and, in some instances, creating an easement.

Akerson format A mortgage-equity procedure used to estimate an overall capitalization rate. The procedure substitutes an arithmetic format for the algebraic equation in the Ellwood formula.

allocation (*See* abstraction.)

amenities Features that enhance the value or desirability of real estate. Amenities may be tangible (such as a swimming pool) or intangible (such as a good view).

amortization The repayment or retiring of debt through scheduled, systematic repayment of principal over a set period of time.

amortization schedule A schedule that shows the amounts of principal and interest incurred and paid at each time period of a scheduled, systematic repayment of principal.

amount of $1 at compound interest ($S^n$) Column 1 of the compound interest tables (*see* Appendix B). The amount to which an investment of $1 grows with compound interest after a specified number of years at a specified interest rate. Also called *future value of one* and *future value interest factor.*

a_n (*See* present value of annuity.)

$1/a_n$ (*See* installment to amortize $1.)

anchor tenant   The major store within a shopping center that attracts or generates traffic for the facility. Anchors are strategically placed to maximize sales for all tenants. The type of anchor depends on the type of shopping center (e.g., a supermarket is a typical anchor for a neighborhood shopping center, whereas a major chain or department store is a typical anchor for a regional shopping mall).

annual debt service (ADS)   The total mortgage payments required in one year in regard to a particular loan.

annual loan constant   The ratio of annual debt service or yearly loan payment to the original principal on the loan.

annuity   A series of cash flows in which an equal payment occurs at regular or fixed intervals. Also sometimes used to refer to a series of equal payments that change according to a predictable pattern [e.g., increasing by a fixed dollar amount each year (straight-line annuity) or increasing by a constant percentage each year (constant-ratio annuity)]. Formulas can be used to find the present value or future value of these latter annuities.

annuity in advance   A series of cash flows in which an equal payment occurs at the beginning of each period.

anticipation   The appraisal principle that states that value is created by the expectation of benefits to be received in the future.

appraisal   The act or process of developing an opinion of value.

appraisal principles   Concepts that provide the rationale of market behavior, which affects value. Appraisal principles include anticipation, change, supply and demand, substitution, and balance.

appraisal process   The step-by-step analysis undertaken by an appraiser for the purpose of accurately developing an opinion of value.

appraisal report   A report, written or oral, that contains the results of an appraisal. A standard written report usually contains the following pieces of information: the definition of value to be applied, the estimate and effective date of the valuation, certifications and limiting conditions, description of the property and rights being appraised, supporting data, justification to support the value estimate, consideration of each of the three approaches, and the reconciliation. Oral reports should also include the above information when appropriate.

appraiser   A person who possesses the education, training, and experience necessary to accurately render an opinion as to the value of real estate.

appreciation   An increase in the value of an asset over some period of time; opposite of depreciation.

approaches to value   Various methods typically used by an appraiser in preparing an appraisal report. Of the three traditional approaches to value, the cost approach bases value on the reproduction or replacement cost of the improvements, less depreciation, plus the value of the land. The income approach bases value on the capitalization of future cash flows from a property at an acceptable market rate. The sales comparison approach bases value on a comparative analysis of recent sales prices of similar properties, after making adjustments for seller concessions, time, and other differences in the properties.

appurtenances   Items that have been affixed to a property and thus have become an inherent part of the property. Such items usually pass with the property when title is transferred although they are not part of the property (e.g., easements, water rights, condominium parking stalls).

arbitrator   One who mediates a dispute.

arm's-length transaction   A transaction occurring in a competitive market with reasonable exposure under conditions requisite to a fair sale, with a willing buyer and a willing seller each acting prudently, knowledgeably, and for self-interest. An arm's-length transaction assumes that neither buyer nor seller is under undue duress.

asking price   The price at which the owner offers to sell.

assemblage   The combining of two or more adjoining lots into one larger tract resulting in an increase in the total value of the combined lots.

assessed value   The value or worth of a property on which ad valorem taxes are based.

assessment   A valuation of real property for tax purposes in which the assessed value of the property is determined.

assessment ratio   The ratio of assessed value to full market value as set by the taxing authority; used by the tax assessor in determining the amount of property tax due on a parcel of real estate.

ATCF   (*See* after-tax cash flow.)

average deviation   A number arrived at by finding the average of a set of numbers, adding the absolute difference of this average with each value, and then dividing this sum by the total number of values in the set. Average deviation gives an indication of the variation in the set of numbers.

B   Ratio of building value to total value.

balance   The appraisal principle that states that property value is a function of contrasting, opposing, or interacting elements and their state of equilibrium.

band of investment   An appraisal technique used in the income approach where the overall rate is derived from the weighted-average rates attributable to the components of a capital investment. The technique can be based on mortgage-equity components or land-building components. Note, however, that the term is often used to refer *only* to the mortgage-equity approach. In this case, the overall rate is found by a weighted average of the mortgage loan constant and the equity dividend rate.

base rent   The minimum rent stipulated in a lease. It is typically associated with leases that also specify some sort of overage rent.

basic employment   Employment in basic industry. (*See* basic industry.)

basic industry   An industry that attracts income from outside the community; opposite of a nonbasic industry, which is a support industry for a basic industry.

basis point   One one-hundredth (1/100) of 1 percent. Used to indicate a change in interest rates. For example, if interest rates rise from 10 percent to 11 percent, then the increase would be 100 basis points.

before-tax cash flow (BTCF)   The cash flow remaining after deduction of debt service (principal and interest) and any other cash outflows from net operating income. BTCF considers all cash flows that could affect the investor except federal income taxes. For example, leasing commissions and the cost of tenant improvements would be subtracted in calculating BTCF. Also referred to as pretax cash flow.

before-tax income   (*See* before-tax cash flow.)

blanket mortgage   A loan secured by more than one property or lot. It is commonly used in construction financing for subdivision or condominium development.

book value   The amount at which property is carried on the books of a company. It usually equals the original cost less accounting depreciation plus any additions to capital.

borrower   One who has temporarily used funds from another through the use of debt financing.

break-down method   A method of estimating accrued depreciation in which each cause of depreciation is analyzed and measured separately. The different types of depreciation are then added to find the total depreciation.

break-even point   The point where the property's effective gross income is equal to the sum of its typical operating expenses plus debt service (principal and interest). This indicates the point-of-zero, before-tax cash flow.

BTCF (*See* before-tax cash flow.)

buffer zone   A strip of land separating one type of zoning from another. A buffer zone will sometimes be left vacant as a buffer from land uses that are incompatible.

builder's break-down method   (*See* quantity survey method.)

building capitalization rate (R_B)   The ratio of the building income to building value. In the income approach to value, the rate is used in both the band of investment and residual techniques to convert income into estimated value.

building cap rate   (*See* building capitalization rate.)

building codes   Rules and ordinances created by a municipal government to regulate the design, construction, quality, use, occupancy, location, and maintenance of buildings to provide minimum standards to safeguard public welfare.

Building codes are a part of a state's police power and are enforced by inspections and the issuance of building permits and certificates of occupancy.

building ratio The ratio of building value to total property value; used in band of investment techniques in the income approach to value.

building residual technique A method used to find property value in the income approach when the value of land and net operating income are known. The income attributable to land is subtracted from the net operating income to find the income attributable to improvements. This figure is then capitalized and added to the land value to estimate the property value.

building restrictions Limitations and regulations placed on a property that control the type and size of structures that can be constructed; examples would include zoning ordinances and deed restrictions.

bundle of rights A concept that describes real property by the legal rights associated with owning the property. It specifies rights such as the rights to sell, lease, occupy, and trade the property. The buyer in a sales transaction typically purchases the legal rights previously held by the seller, except those that are reserved or limited in the sale.

business risk The risk associated with unknown future variability in rents, vacancies, or operating expenses.

buydown A lump-sum payment to the lender that reduces the monthly payment of the borrower; it is sometimes used by developers to lower the effective interest rate on the buyer's loan. The cost of the buydown is usually reflected in the purchase price.

buyer's market A situation in which supply in the marketplace is greater than demand.

capital gain The gain arising from the resale of a capital asset. The capital gain equals the net proceeds from the sale minus the adjusted basis (original cost minus depreciation) of the asset. However, limits do exist on the amount of capital loss allowed to offset ordinary income.

capitalization A technique used in the income approach to convert income into an estimate of value. (*See* direct capitalization *and* yield capitalization.)

capitalization rate A rate used in the income approach to convert income into value; it equals the ratio of the net operating income to the property value or sales price. The rate reflects market conditions, property characteristics, etc. Also called a cap rate.

capitalize In *appraisal*, the process of expressing an opinion of value based on the income produced by the property. The value can be estimated by yield capitalization or by direct capitalization. In tax accounting, *capitalize* refers to including the cost of an item in the depreciable basis of the property as opposed to including the item as a current expense.

capital loss The loss arising when the net proceeds from the sale of a capital asset do not equal the adjusted basis (original cost minus depreciation) of the asset. Limits do exist on the amount of capital loss allowed to offset ordinary income.

cap rate Short for capitalization rate.

cash equivalency The process that adjusts the sales price of a comparable with atypical financing to reflect a sales price with typical market financing. This is necessary because any premium that results from atypical financing is not part of the value of the real property; the financing premium is intangible personal property.

cash flow The periodic income or loss arising from operations of the property; it is the income remaining after expenses and debt service are subtracted. The after-tax cash flow also subtracts income taxes.

cash on cash return (R_E) (*See* equity dividend rate.)

CBD (*See* central business district.)

central business district (CBD) A city's downtown area, which contains the business and governmental activities of the area.

central tendency The tendency of values in a set of numbers to cluster around a certain point in a frequency distribution; measures of central tendency are the mean, median, and mode.

certificate of reasonable value (CRV) A certificate issued by the Department of Veterans Affairs that states an estimate of the value of the property being appraised; a CRV must be issued on any property in which VA financing is used.

change   The appraisal principle that states that the cause and effect of economic and social forces are constantly causing property values to be in transition.

chattels real   All interests in real estate that do not constitute a freehold or fee estate in land such as leasehold estates.

chronological age   The true age of an item; also called actual age.

classical theory   A theory of value popular in the 1700s that based the value of an item on the cost of production. Scarcity and utility were also believed to affect value.

collection loss   A loss of income incurred when payment is not collected from tenants.

commercial property   Properties used for business purposes.

common elements   The part of the land and buildings in a condominium form of ownership that is jointly owned and used with other unit owners.

comparables   Properties used to express estimate of value for the subject property. Normally, such properties have been recently sold or leased and are similar to the property being evaluated. Comparables need not be identical to the subject but should be similar or relatively easy to adjust for differences in comparison. Also called comps.

comparable sale   (*See* comparables.)

comparative unit method   A method used to estimate building costs in which components of the building are totaled on a unit basis, such as dollars per square foot or cubic foot of area, and are based on known costs of similar structures adjusted for time and physical differences.

competition   An appraisal principle that states that competition is a function of supply and demand.

compound growth   The process of increasing in value by a certain percentage each period.

compound interest   Interest based on the original principal plus all accrued interest incurred before that time period. Each interest payment is added to the principal; the following period's interest is then multiplied by that sum to find the current interest incurred.

comps   (*See* comparables.)

concessions   A service or discount given to prospective tenants to induce them to lease specific properties.

condemnation   The exercise of the power of eminent domain by the government (i.e., the right of the government to take private property for public use).

conditions of sale   An element of comparison in the sales comparison approach that refers to the motivations of the buyer and seller in a sales transaction. Examples include the relationship between buyer and seller, financial needs of buyer and seller (a "quick" sale), and lack of exposure on the market.

condominium   A form of ownership in which persons hold fee simple title to individual units within the building and an undivided interest in common areas.

condominium conversion   The process of converting rental property, such as an apartment building, into a condominium form of ownership.

conformity   An appraisal principle that states that value is created when components of a property are in harmony with its surroundings.

consequential damages   The financial compensation made to a person who has suffered loss or injury as a result of a breach of contract that could not reasonably have been prevented.

consistent use   An appraisal concept that states that land and improvements to that land must be valued on the same basis; improvements to the land must contribute to the land value to have any value themselves.

constant   (*See* mortgage loan constant.)

constant amortization mortgage   A mortgage that requires equal periodic principal payments. Because the interest decreases as the loan is amortized, total payments decrease over the loan term.

construction cost   The expenses incurred to build a structure including direct costs of labor and materials plus the contractor's indirect costs (such as taxes and interest).

constructive notice   The legal presumption that a person is responsible for knowing certain facts that may be discovered by diligence or inquiry into the public records.

Consumer Price Index (CPI)   A statistical measure of the change in price levels of a predetermined mix of consumer goods and services; often used as a means of adjusting rental payments in a lease.

contractor's overhead   Direct costs other than costs of material and labor (e.g., job supervision costs, contractor's insurance, and workers' compensation).

contract rent   The actual rent specified in a lease.

contribution   The appraisal principle that states that the worth of a particular component is measured by the amount it contributes to the value of the whole property, regardless of the actual cost of the component; the value of the component may be measured as the amount by which its absence would detract from the entire property value.

conversion   The transformation of an income-producing property into another use.

convertible mortgage   A mortgage in which the lender may convert mortgage interests into equity interests at some time during the life of the loan in lieu of or by decreasing cash amortization payments.

cooperative ownership   A form of ownership in which each resident of a cooperative apartment building or housing corporation has purchased shares in a corporation that holds title to the building. The individual pays a proportionate share of operating expenses and debt service on the building owned by the corporation based on the amount of stock held in the corporation. In return for stock in the corporation, the individual receives a lease granting occupancy of a specific unit in the building.

corner influence   The effect on value when a property line abuts the intersection of two streets; the value may be greater or less than inside lots depending on the utility associated with being located on a corner.

corporation   In legal terms, an organization that acts as a single legal entity in performing certain activities; corporate status is held separately from the individuals involved.

cost   (*See* direct costs *and* indirect costs.)

cost approach   One of three traditional approaches to value in appraisal theory. In the cost approach, value is based on the estimated land value plus the current cost to reproduce or replace the existing structure, deducting for all accrued depreciation in the property.

cost-of-living index   A summary of general consumer prices through time.

cost service index   A regional table of factors used to convert historical costs into current costs.

coverage ratio   (*See* debt coverage ratio.)

CPI   (*See* Consumer Price Index.)

CPI adjustment   An adjustment used in leases in which the rent payment is periodically adjusted by a percentage of the increase in the Consumer Price Index (CPI); the CPI adjustment is used to help protect the lessor from unexpected increases in inflation.

CRV   (*See* certificate of reasonable value.)

curable   Reasonable and economically feasible to cure refers to an item of physical deterioration and functional obsolescence in which the cost to cure the item is less than or the same as the anticipated increase in value after the item is cured.

curable functional obsolescence   A defect caused by a flaw in the structure, material, or design in which the cost to cure the item is less than or the same as the anticipated increase in value after the item is cured.

curable physical deterioration   An item in need of repair; deferred maintenance. To be curable, the cost of curing the item must be reasonable and economically feasible.

current use   The use for which a property is presently designated; it may or may not be the highest and best use.

date of value   The date at which the value of a property is estimated in an appraisal report; it is not necessarily the same as the date of the report.

DCR   (*See* debt coverage ratio.)

debt coverage ratio (DCR)   The ratio of annual net operating income to annual debt service; often used as a criterion in underwriting income property loans.

debt equity ratio   The relationship between the total amount of the loan and the invested capital (equity) of the owner(s).

debt service   The dollar amount of the annual loan payment.

dedication   A voluntary transfer of privately owned property for some public use.

deed   A written, legal instrument by which an estate or ownership interest in real property is conveyed by a grantor to a grantee when it is executed and delivered. Many different types of deeds exist; the main difference being the covenant made by the grantor (e.g., warranty deeds, grant deeds, executor's deed, quitclaim deed).

deed of trust   A legal instrument, similar to a mortgage, that conveys title to property to a third-party trustee; the deed of trust secures an obligation owed by the borrower to the lender.

deed restriction   A clause in the deed of a property that limits the property's use.

default ratio   A ratio that divides the effective gross income by the sum of the operating expenses plus the mortgage payment; a ratio of less than 1 means that the property is not generating enough income to service the mortgage payment.

defect   An improperly performing feature in a structure that results in functional obsolescence.

deferred annuity   A stream of cash flows that begins at some time in the future.

deferred maintenance   Items in need of repair because the maintenance has been postponed, resulting in physical depreciation or loss in value of a building; this type of depreciation is usually curable.

deficiency   An inadequate feature in a structure that results in functional obsolescence.

demand   The quantity of real property desired at a certain price or rent at a specific time in a given market.

demographic data   Data regarding the population and its changes; specifically regarding the population size, density, and distribution (among others).

demolition costs   The expenses incurred to tear down and remove the improvements on a parcel of land; demolition costs may be considered in highest and best use analysis.

density of land development   The number of building units or occupants per unit of land area (acre, square mile); allowable density is commonly specified in zoning ordinances.

depreciable   Property subject to wear and tear and used in a trade or business or held for the production of income; land and personal residences are not depreciable.

depreciation   A loss in property value from any cause; the difference between reproduction cost or replacement cost and market value. In appraisal, depreciation is divided into three classes: physical deterioration, functional obsolescence, and external obsolescence. The term *depreciation* is also used to refer to tax depreciation, which is a deduction from NOI (*see* net operating income) when calculating taxable income. Tax depreciation is a function of the current tax law and not necessarily related to actual depreciation in the value of the asset.

depth tables   Uniform percentage tables that indicate the proportion of site value attributable to each additional amount of depth in the lot; typically used in urban areas where lot depths are often similar.

design and layout   The architectural arrangement of a property; if not up to current standards, design and layout may cause functional obsolescence.

deterioration   A loss in value due to wear and tear on the property.

developer   One who organizes and supervises the construction of improvements in an attempt to put land to its most profitable use.

developer's profit   The sum of money a developer expects to receive in addition to costs for the time and effort, coordination, and risk-bearing necessary to develop real estate. That portion associated with creation of the real estate by a developer is referred to as developer's profit. (*See* entrepreneurial profit.)

direct capitalization   In the income approach, the method used to convert a *single* year's income into an estimate of property value. This can be accomplished by dividing the net operating income by a market-derived overall capitalization rate or by multiplying the income by a market-derived income multiplier.

direct costs   Costs for labor and materials, including contractor's overhead and profit. Also called hard costs.

direct reduction mortgage   A mortgage in which both principal and interest are paid in periodic, usually equal, installments adequate for amortization over the loan's term.

discount   1. The fee paid at the origination of a debt for the use of capital during that period and commonly deducted from the principal when the funds are advanced. 2. Conversion of future payments to a present value with the use of a discount rate. (*See* discounted cash flow analysis.)

discounted cash flow analysis   In general, the use of discounting in appraisal or investment analysis to calculate a present value, net present value, IRR, or other measures that consider the time value of money. A procedure in which anticipated future cash flows are discounted to a net present value by the appropriate yield rate based on the assumption that benefits received in the future are worth less than benefits received now due to the time value of money.

discounting   (*See* discounted cash flow analysis.)

discount points   A fee paid to a lender at the origination of a loan where one discount point equals 1 percent of the principal of the loan.

discount rate   Used in the income approach; a compound interest rate used to convert expected future cash flows into a present value. It should represent the rate of return necessary to attract investment capital.

dispersion   The degree of scatter of values in a set of numbers; usually measured from a central value.

district   A type of neighborhood that represents homogeneous land use (e.g., multifamily, commercial, agricultural).

dollar adjustment   A means by which an adjustment is made to the sales price of a comparable property to reflect dollar differences between the comparable and the subject property.

dominant estate   The estate that derives benefit from the servient estate in an easement. For example, an easement road passes over an owner's land (servient estate) to another parcel of land (dominant estate).

dwelling   A structure designed for occupancy as living quarters.

dwelling units   A room or rooms containing a single kitchen and constituting an independent unit for living space of a single family; dwelling units do not include hotel or motel rooms.

easement   A legal interest in real property that conveys use or enjoyment but not ownership of the property.

easement in gross   A limited right of one person to use another's property when the right is not created for the benefit of land owned by the owner of the easement; such right is not attached to any particular estate or land, nor is it transferred through the conveyance of title. Examples would include pipelines and telephone lines.

economic age-life method   A method of estimating accrued depreciation in which the ratio of effective age to total economic life is multiplied by the reproduction or replacement cost to calculate the accrued depreciation.

economic base analysis   An analysis of the economic activity of a community that enables it to attract income from outside its boundaries. The relationship between basic and nonbasic employment is used to predict population, income, or other variables that affect real estate values or land utilization.

economic depreciation   Loss of value from all causes outside the boundaries of the property itself.

economic feasibility study   (*See* feasibility analysis.)

economic force   In appraisal theory, one type of force that affects property value; it includes factors such as supply and demand, employment, wage levels, industrial expansion, and availability of mortgage credit.

economic life   The time span during which improvements to real property contribute to value (i.e., the time in which income is expected to exceed operating expenses).

economic obsolescence   (*See* external obsolescence.)

economic rent   In appraisal practice this is considered synonymous with market rent.

effective age   The age of a property based on its condition and utility or wear and tear; it may be more or less than the actual age.

effective annual rate   The annual interest rate that is equivalent to a nominal annual rate that is compounded more frequently than annually. For example, if the nominal rate is 12 percent compounded monthly, the effective annual rate is $[1 + (0.12/12)]^{12} - 1 = 12.68$ percent.

effective gross income (EGI)   The income from all operations of real property less an adjustment for vacancy and collection losses.

effective gross income multiplier (EGIM)   The ratio of sales price or value to effective gross income.

effective yield   (*See* effective annual rate.)

efficiency ratio   The ratio between a building's net leasable area and gross area.

EGI   (*See* effective gross income.)

EGIM   (*See* effective gross income multiplier.)

egress   The means by which a person leaves or exits a property; the opposite of ingress.

elements of comparison   A categorization of property characteristics that cause real estate prices to vary. Examples include property rights, financing terms, conditions of sale, date of sale (or market conditions), location, and physical characteristics.

Ellwood formula   An algebraic formula used to calculate an overall capitalization rate. It is referred to as a mortgage-equity technique because it is based on assumptions about the mortgage financing (interest rate and loan term) as well as assumptions about the equity investor (Y_E and holding period). Changes in the property value over the investment holding period can also be considered. The value found with an Ellwood formula is equivalent to that found with a discounted cash flow analysis if the same assumptions are made.

emblements   A growing crop that is produced annually and is considered personal property.

eminent domain   The government right to take private property for public use upon the payment of just compensation to the property owner.

encroachment   A part of real estate that physically intrudes on, overlaps, or trespasses on the property of another.

encumbered   The legal term applied to a property that has attached to it a claim, lien, charge, or liability.

encumbrance   An interest or claim against the land of another that burdens or takes away from the value of the property. Mortgages, taxes, and easements are considered encumbrances.

entrepreneurial profit   The sum of money an entrepreneur expects to receive in addition to costs for the time and effort, coordination, and risk-bearing necessary to create a project. That portion associated with creation of the real estate by a developer is referred to as developer's profit. Properties that also include an operating business may include additional entrepreneurial profit that is reflected in the going-concern value of the property. (*See* going-concern value.)

environmental forces   In appraisal theory, one of four categories of forces that affect property value; environmental forces include climate, location, topography, natural barriers, and transportation systems.

environmental regulations   The Environmental Protection Agency (EPA), created by the federal government, sets standards to control air, water, and noise pollution and other environmental conditions.

equity   The owner's interest in property above all claims and liens against it. The term is often used to refer to the amount an investor initially invests in a project (e.g., the difference between the acquisition cost and the net proceeds from debt financing).

equity buildup   Refers to the increase in the owner's equity over time due to any repayment of principal on the loan and/or any increase in the value of the property. The owner receives the benefit of this equity buildup when the property is sold.

equity capitalization rate   (*See* equity dividend rate.)

equity dividend   The result of subtracting debt service (principal and interest) from NOI (*see* net operating income). This will equal before-tax cash flow if there are no other cash outflows. (*See* before-tax cash flow.)

equity dividend rate (R_E)   The ratio of before-tax cash flow to the equity investment. Also called equity capitalization rate and cash on cash return.

equity kicker   An equity interest in a property given to the mortgage lender.

equity residual   A technique used to estimate property value in the income approach when the value of the mortgage and net operating income are known. The annual debt service is subtracted from the net operating income to find the income attributable to equity. This figure is then capitalized and added to the value of the mortgage to find the property value.

equity yield rate (Y_E)   A rate of return on equity capital; the equity investor's internal rate of return based on before-tax cash flows and the equity investment.

escalation clause   A clause appearing in a contract in which the price or rent is based on some event or index. It is used to help offset increases in operating expenses.

escheat   The government right to transfer property ownership to the state when the owner dies without a will or any ascertainable heirs.

evaluation   An analysis of a parcel of real estate in which a value estimate is not necessarily required. The study may be based on the nature, quality, or utility of an interest in the parcel or the entire parcel.

excess land   On an unimproved site, land that is not needed to accommodate a site's highest and best use. On an improved site, the surplus land that is not needed to serve or support the existing improvement.

excess rent   The amount of contract rent over market rent; probably created by a favorable lease with a locational advantage, unusually good management, or lease origination in a strong market.

exculpatory clause   A clause that limits the recourse of one party against another in the event of default by limiting recovery to the property only.

expense ratio   The ratio of annual operating expenses to potential gross income or effective gross income.

expense stop   In a lease, a dollar amount (usually expressed on a per-square-foot basis) above which the tenant agrees to pay operating expenses; helps protect the lessor from unexpected increases in expenses from inflation or other factors. The amount paid by the tenant is said to "pass through" to the tenant. (*See* pass-through.)

exponential change   An increase by a certain percentage each period as opposed to a straight-line change, which increases by a constant dollar amount each period. Synonymous with compound change or constant ratio change.

externality   The appraisal principle that states that forces outside a property's boundaries may have a positive or negative effect on its value.

external obsolescence   A defect caused by negative influences outside the property itself; it is not considered curable. Also called economic obsolescence.

extrapolation   The process of forecasting future trends based on current and past data patterns and relationships. Assumes that the same economic factors that affected past trends are likely to continue over the forecasting period.

face amount   The value of a security as set forth in the document itself; the par value as shown on the document as opposed to the real value or market value, which may differ if interest rates have changed.

fair market rent   (*See* market rent.)

favorable leverage   (*See* positive leverage.)

feasibility analysis   An analysis of the ability of a project to satisfy the economic objectives of the investor.

feasibility study   (*See* feasibility analysis.)

Federal Fair Housing Law   Enacted as part of the Civil Rights Act in 1968, this law makes discrimination on the basis of race, color, sex, religion, or national origin illegal in regard to the sale or rental of housing properties. It does not affect commercial or industrial properties. The act was amended in 1988 to include families with children and handicap status as additional protected classes.

Federal Home Loan Bank Board (FHLBBA)   Administered by 12 regional banks, the FHLBB sets credit policies, administers reserve and liquidity requirements, and controls lending practices of member banks.

Federal Home Loan Mortgage Corporation (FHLMC)   An agency directed by the Federal Home Loan Bank Board for the purpose of increasing the availability of mortgage funds and providing greater flexibility for mortgage investors. It purchases single-family and condominium mortgages from approved financial institutions and resells its mortgage inventories. Commonly known as Freddie Mac.

federal income taxes   The tax rate at which ordinary income is taxed; cash flows from operating and selling a property are normally taxable at the income tax rate.

Federal National Mortgage Association (FNMA)   An independent agency that purchases mortgages from the primary markets and issues long-term debentures and short-term discount notes. Commonly known as Fannie Mae.

Federal Reserve System (FRS)   The central banking system of the United States that regulates money supply and member banks; it consists of 12 federal reserve banks and their branches, as well as banks that are members of the system.

fee appraiser   A person who charges a fee for rendering an opinion of value rather than basing compensation on the derived value.

fee simple estate   Ownership of a property that is unencumbered by any other interest or estate.

fee simple value   The value of the fee simple estate.

final estimate of value   A range of value or a single dollar amount given in an appraisal report that is derived by reconciling various approaches to value.

financial leverage   The use of debt to purchase real estate; the effect on an investor's return may be positive or negative.

financially feasible   A project that satisfies the economic objectives of the investor.

financing costs   The expense incurred to acquire capital to finance a project; in mortgages, often charged up front in the form of points or fees.

financial management rate of return (FMRR)   A variant of the internal rate of return in which negative cash flows are discounted to a present value at a safe rate (liquid rate) and positive cash flows are compounded forward to the end of the holding period at a reinvestment rate (run-of-the-mill rate). The FMRR is the rate that equates the present value to the future value of the positive cash flows.

financial risk   Uncertainty caused by financing an investment.

financial statements   A formal composite statement that reflects the financial status and net worth of an individual or entity as of a specified date; usually classifies assets, liabilities, income, and expenses.

first mortgage   A mortgage that has priority as a lien over all other mortgages. In cases of foreclosure, the first mortgage will be fully repaid plus legal expenses before other mortgages are satisfied.

fixed expenses   Operating expenses, such as property taxes, that do not vary with the occupancy level.

fixed-rate mortgage   A loan in which the interest rate is constant over the term of the loan.

fixture   Personal property that becomes real property because of the manner in which it is affixed, the character of the item, and/or the intention of the tenant who attached the item.

flat rental   A rent specified in a lease that remains constant throughout the lease term.

floor area ratio   The ratio of building area to land area.

FMRR   (*See* financial management rate of return.)

foreclosure   A legal process in which a default in payment or other terms of the mortgage note causes the property used as security for the mortgage to be sold to satisfy the debt; the title in the mortgage is passed to either the holder of the mortgage or to a third party.

form report   A specific format for presenting an appraisal report; typically required by financial institutions, insurance companies, and government agencies.

free and clear   Real property that is free of any liens, mortgages, or other encumbrances.

frontage   The linear distance of land that abuts a lake, river, street, or highway.

front foot   A measurement of land that abuts the street line or other landmark, such as a river or lake; typically used for lots of near uniform depth in urban areas.

fully amortized   (*See* fully amortized loan.)

fully amortized loan   A loan with equal, periodic payments that allow for both principal and interest to be recovered over the term of the loan.

functional depreciation   (*See* functional obsolescence.)

functional obsolescence   (*See* curable functional obsolescence *and* incurable functional obsolescence.)

future benefits   In appraisal, anticipated positive cash flows or appreciation in property value; a premise of the income approach.

future value annuity of one per period   (*See* accumulation of $1 per period [$S_n$]).

future value interest factor (FVIF)   (*See* amount of $1 at compound interest.)

future value interest factor annuity (FVIFA)   (*See* accumulation of $1 per period.)

future value of one   (*See* amount of $1 at compound interest.)

FVIF   Column 1 in the compound interest tables in Appendix B. (*See* future value interest factor.)

FVIFA   (*See* future value interest factor—annuity.)

general data   Information not specific to a certain property (e.g., interest rates, employment rates, and census information).

gentrification   A process in which neighborhood properties are purchased and renovated or rehabilitated.

geodetic survey system   A legal description of land maintained by the U.S. government as part of the rectangular survey system. Topographic maps, referred to as quadrangles, are created based on latitude and longitude, which consider the curvature of the earth's surface.

GIM   (*See* gross income multiplier.)

going-concern value   Value created by a business operation; includes an intangible value that is not considered as a part of the real estate.

going in capitalization rate   Used to refer to the capitalization rate that is calculated based on the NOI (*see* net operating income) at the time the property is purchased. When the term *capitalization rate* is used alone, it is assumed to be a going in capitalization rate. The term is used to contrast the going in capitalization rate with a *terminal capitalization rate*, which refers to a capitalization rate based on the NOI when the property is to be sold at the end of a holding period.

government forces   In appraisal theory, one of four forces thought to affect real estate value; includes government controls and regulations, public services, zoning, and building codes (among others).

Government National Mortgage Association (GNMA)   Agency that purchases mortgages through its secondary mortgage market operations and issues mortgage-backed federally insured securities called collateralized mortgage obligations (CMOs). Commonly known as Ginnie Mae.

government rectangular survey   A legal description of land that divides land into townships by range lines (north-south lines) and lines (east-west lines). These lines are based on true east-west lines (baselines) and true north-south lines (principal meridians). Townships are six miles square, each containing 36 sections that are one mile square or 640 acres.

graduated-payment mortgage (GPM)   A loan in which payments start low and increase over the term of the loan. It is designed to help borrowers match payments with projected increases in income.

graduated rental   Rent that graduates (usually increases) periodically during a lease term based on changes specified in the lease.

grantee   One to whom property is transferred by deed, trust instrument, or other document.

grantor   One who transfers property to another by deed, trust instrument, or other document.

graphic analysis   A method used in sensitivity analysis in which one variable is changed and the effect of this change on a second variable is plotted on a graph. By visually analyzing the graph the appraiser may be able to better determine if assumptions used in the appraisal are realistic.

GRM   (*See* gross rent multiplier.)

gross income   Total income from the operation of a property before operating expenses are deducted; effective gross income also subtracts an allowance for vacancy and collection loss, whereas potential gross income does not. "Other income" from sources such as vending machines is also included in gross income.

gross income multiplier (GIM)   The ratio of sales price or value to annual potential or effective gross income. Also called gross rent multiplier.

gross leasable area (GLA)   The total floor area designed for the occupancy of tenants; it does not include common areas.

gross lease   A lease that specifies that all or most property charges must be paid by the lessor (or landlord).

gross living area   Residential space measured by finished and habitable above-grade areas.

gross rent   (*See* gross income.)

gross rent multiplier (GRM)   (*See* gross income multiplier.)

ground lease   A lease that grants the right to use and occupy the land only.

ground rent   Rent paid for the right to use and occupy land.

highest and best use   The use that maximizes return to the land. Highest and best use must meet four criteria: it must be physically possible, financially feasible, legally permissible, and maximally productive.

historic district   A zoning classification referring to a geographic area that has been recognized as having historical significance.

holding period   The time span over which a property is owned.

homeowners' association   The organization in a condominium form of ownership responsible for maintaining the common areas of the condominium.

homestead exemption   A release from assessment of a portion of the value of the property declared as a homestead.

Hoskold capitalization rate   A factor derived by adding a speculative rate to a sinking-fund factor for a safe rate; this is based on the premise that a portion of the NOI (net operating income) is reinvested at a "safe rate" in order to periodically replace the asset. It has historically been used to capitalize the income produced by a wasting asset. This should not be confused with the concept of a modified IRR or FMRR, which applies a reinvestment rate to all the cash flow received by the investor. (*See* Hoskold premise.)

Hoskold premise   An appraisal theory designed to value the income stream of a wasting asset. Two separate interest rates are used: a speculative rate, representing a fair rate of return on capital, and a safe rate for a sinking fund, designed to return all the invested capital in a lump sum at the termination of the investment. (*See* Hoskold capitalization rate.)

hotel   A facility that offers temporary lodging and a few other services such as food, recreation, and sometimes retail shops; it is not considered residential property.

improved site   A parcel of land that has been modified or developed for use in constructing improvements.

improvement   A structure or building permanently attached to the land.

improvement ratio   A ratio that compares the value of the improvements to the total value of the property.

income approach   One of the three approaches to value in appraisal theory; property value is estimated based on the property's anticipated future benefits. Also called the income capitalization approach.

income capitalization   A method used in the income approach to convert income to a value estimate by either dividing a single income figure by the appropriate capitalization rate or by discounting the reversion and annual cash flows for the holding period at the appropriate yield rate.

increasing and decreasing returns, principle of   An economic principle that states that the addition of more factors of production will increase the output up to a certain point, which is the point of the asset's maximum value.

incurable depreciation   (*See* incurable functional obsolescence *and* incurable physical deterioration.)

incurable functional obsolescence   A defect that is caused by a deficiency or superadequacy in the structure, materials, or design and layout of a structure; the defect is deemed incurable if the cost to cure the defect is greater than the anticipated increase in value after the defect is cured.

incurable physical deterioration   A defect caused by physical wear and tear on the building that is considered unreasonable or uneconomic to correct.

index lease   A lease that specifies rent adjustments based on the change in a specific index (e.g., the CPI).

indirect costs   Construction expenses for items other than labor and materials (e.g., financing, taxes, administrative costs, etc.). Also called soft costs.

industrial property   Land and buildings used for manufacturing, processing, assembly, and storage of products or natural resources.

inflation index   A time series trend that tracks the erosion of the purchasing power of currency.

infrastructure   The core of development in a building or complex that serves as the source of utilities and support services.

ingress   Access or entrance into land; opposite of egress.

inside lot   A lot located between the corner lots on a specific block.

installment to amortize $1 (1/S$_n$)   (*See* payment to amortize $1.)

insurable value   The value of a property for insurance purposes.

interest   1. The cost of using money; a return on capital. 2. A type or extent of ownership.

interest expense   The periodic cost incurred through a debt.

interest only   (*See* interest-only loan.)

interest-only loan   A loan in which only interest is paid during the term of the loan and principal is recovered in a balloon payment at the loan maturity.

interest rate   A rate of return on capital; the cost of using money. Also known as a term loan.

interest rate risk   The uncertainty caused by a variation in interest rates.

interim use   A highest and best use expected to change in the future, although the future use is not currently financially or physically possible.

internal rate of return (IRR)   The annualized rate of return on capital that equates the value of cash returns over time with the cash invested; the discount rate that makes the net present value of an investment equal to zero.

interpolation   The estimation of a value within a range of data in a set of numbers.

investment analysis   An analysis of a proposed real estate investment for the purpose of determining the feasibility of the project for a particular investor. The focus is often on the relationship between acquisition price and anticipated future benefits.

investment value   The value of a property to a particular investor.

Inwood annuity factor   A factor that indicates the present value of a level-payment income stream when multiplied by the periodic payment; an annuity factor that represents the present worth of $1 per period for a given number of periods and can be found in Column 5 of the tables in Appendix A. (*See* Inwood premise.)

Inwood premise   An appraisal theory used to value an income stream of equal payments in which the present value of the income stream is based on a single discount figure; the basis for the present value of an ordinary annuity factor in compound interest tables. See Column 5 of the tables in Appendix A. (*See* Inwood annuity factor.)

IRR   (*See* internal rate of return.)

J factor   A factor that can be used to convert an increasing or decreasing stream of income into a level-payment equivalent. The J factor was historically developed to be used with the Ellwood formula. The income pattern implicit in the use of a J factor is similar, but not identical, to compound growth. Rather, the rate of change of the income pattern increases each year. For example, the rate of change might be 1 percent the first year, 2 percent the second year, and so forth.

joint tenancy   Joint ownership by two or more persons with right of survivorship in which each person has an identical interest and right of possession.

junior mortgage   A loan with less priority than the first mortgage as a lien in case of foreclosure. It may be a first, second, or third, etc., loan.

just compensation   Fair and reasonable compensation to both the private owner of property and the public when property is taken for public use through condemnation.

K factor   A factor that can be used to convert a stream of income that changes at a constant ratio (compound rate) into a level-payment equivalent. A way of stabilizing income. Sometimes used in conjunction with the Ellwood formula.

L   (*See* land ratio.)

land   The earth's surface and natural resources in their original state.

land building ratio   The ratio between the total land space and the gross building area.

land capitalization rate (R_L)   The ratio of the land income to land value; it is used in the income approach in residual techniques to convert income into estimated value.

landlocked   A parcel of land that belongs to one person and is completely surrounded by land belonging to another.

landlord   One who leases a property to another. Also called lessor.

land ratio (L)   The ratio of land value to total property value.

land residual technique   A technique used to find property value in the income approach when the value of the building and net operating income are known. The income attributable to the building is subtracted from the net operating income to find the income attributable to the land. This figure is then capitalized and added to the building value to find the total property value.

land use   The utilization of a site to produce revenue or other benefits.

land utilization studies   An analysis of the potential uses of a parcel of land and a determination of the highest and best use for that parcel.

lease   A contract that transfers the rights of possession of a property from the owner to another for a specific period of time in return for a specified rent.

leased fee   (*See* leased fee estate.)

leased fee estate   An ownership interest held by a landlord in which the right to use and occupy a property has been conveyed by lease to another.

leasehold   (*See* leasehold estate.)

leasehold estate   An ownership interest held by a tenant in which the right to use and occupy a property has been conveyed to the tenant by lease.

leasehold value   The value of a lease present when the market rental value is greater than the contract rent.

legal description   A description of a parcel of land complete enough to allow a competent surveyor to locate the exact boundaries of the land.

legally nonconforming use   A use that was once legal but no longer conforms to the zoning in which it is located; this usually occurs due to zoning changes.

legally permissible   That which is allowable by law. To be the highest and best use of a site, the use must be legally permissible.

lender   (*See* mortgagee.)

lessee   One who uses and occupies a property under a lease agreement; a tenant.

lessor   One who holds property title and rents the property to another under a lease agreement; a landlord.

letter report   A shortened appraisal report that states the conclusions of the appraiser's investigation and analysis. It typically contains an identification of the property, purpose of the appraisal, a description of the analysis, the date of valuation, and limiting conditions. Much of the data and reasoning are omitted.

leverage   The process of increasing purchasing power by using borrowed funds (debt) to acquire real estate. The debt may increase or decrease the rate of return on the investment.

license   A formal agreement from a constituted authority that allows an activity to be conducted.

lien   A charge created by agreement or law against a property as the security for a debt.

life estate   An estate limited to the lifetime of a designated party and conveys the rights to use, occupy, and control the property.

limited common elements   Items in a multiunit project that are available for use by one or more but not all units (e.g., parking stalls or storage units).

limiting conditions   Specifications in an appraisal report that restrict the assumptions in the report to certain situations (e.g., date and use of the appraisal, definition of value, definition of surveys used or not used).

linear regression   The analysis of one or more independent variables and their effect on a single dependent variable.

linkage   The time-distance relationship between a property or neighborhood and other destinations or originations.

liquidity   The ease of selling an asset for cash.

listing price   The asking price at which a property is listed for sale; it does not necessarily equal the market value.

loan balance   The amount of principal left to be paid on a loan at a specified period of time; it equals the present value of future payments.

loan constant   (*See* mortgage loan constant.)

loan term   The number of periods over which a loan will be held.

loan-to-value ratio (LTV)   The ratio of the loan principal to the total value of the property.

location   The time-distance relationship (linkage) between a property or neighborhood and all other origins and destinations.

locational obsolescence   (*See* economic obsolescence.)

lot   Land within a set of defined boundaries. Also called a parcel, plot, or tract.

lot-and-block survey system   A legal description of land in which land is subdivided and referred to by lot-and-block numbers that appear on survey maps.

LTV   (*See* loan-to-value ratio.)

maintenance   Procedures and expenditures necessary to keep a property in operating condition.

maintenance fee   The payments made by the individual owners in a condominium to the homeowners' association for expenses incurred in the maintenance and upkeep of the common areas.

mall   The area in a retail section or shopping center designated for pedestrian use only.

management fee   A fee paid for the administration and supervision of a property.

manufactured housing   Residential buildings that are partially assembled or completely assembled before being placed on a permanent site.

market analysis   An analysis of trends in market conditions (such as location, competition, and demand unit) that affect a property's value.

marketability study   An analysis of the ability of a property to be absorbed, sold, or leased under current or anticipated market conditions.

market approach   One of the three approaches to value in appraisal theory; value is estimated by comparing sales of similar properties sold recently to the subject property and adjusting the comparable sales for differences in characteristics to indicate a final value estimate for the subject property. Also known as the sales comparison approach.

market conditions   Characteristics of the market such as vacancy rates, interest rates, employment levels, etc.

market rent   The rent income a property would most probably command if offered in an open, competitive market.

market segmentation   An analysis of submarkets within a larger market.

market study   (*See* market analysis.)

market value   The cash value of a property to a well-informed, typical buyer in an open market. The most probable price a property should bring in a competitive and open market under all conditions requisite to a fair sale, with the buyer and seller each acting prudently and knowledgeably, and assuming the price is not affected by undue stimulus.

mass appraisal   An estimate of value for a large number of properties as of a given date; similar properties are valued in a uniform manner by property types with standard methodology.

maximally productive   One of four criteria in highest and best use analysis, it states that a use is the highest and best use if it produces the highest value or price.

mean   The average of a set of numbers.

median   The middle figure in a numerically ordered set of data such that an equal number of values lie above and below the middle figure.

mercantilism   A theory of value popular in the 18th and 19th centuries that stated that wealth is associated with a nation's power. It focused on maintaining a favorable balance of trade through strong economic controls to accumulate gold.

metes-and-bounds method   A legal description of land in which land boundaries are referred to by a point of beginning (POB), a line in a specified direction from this point (metes), and a point of change in direction in the boundary (bounds), until the line has returned to the point of beginning.

metropolitan statistical area (MSA)   A central city containing at least 50,000 people with a total metropolitan population of at least 100,000.

mill   One-tenth of one cent; often used in tax assessment.

minimum lot size   A provision in a zoning ordinance that stipulates the minimum dimensions of a lot necessary for construction of a building.

minimum rent   (*See* base rent.)

mode   The most frequent value in a set of numbers.

modified economic age-life method   A method of estimating accrued depreciation in which the ratio of effective age to total economic life is multiplied by the reproduction or replacement cost minus curable physical and functional obsolescence to calculate the accrued depreciation.

monthly present value interest factor—annuity (MPVIFA)   Column 5 of the monthly compound interest table; a number that discounts a monthly annuity to its present value for a given discount rate and number of payments.

monument   A natural or artificial visible object that is fixed in place and used by surveyors to establish real estate boundaries.

mortgage   A legal document in which real estate is named as the security or collateral for the repayment of the loan.

mortgage balance   (*See* loan balance.)

mortgagee   One who advances funds for a mortgage loan; the lender.

mortgage equity analysis   An analysis of income-producing property that studies the effect of mortgage terms and equity requirements on the property value.

mortgage interest   The cost of borrowing money through a mortgage; the rate can be fixed or variable.

mortgage loan constant (R_M)   The ratio of annual debt service to principal of the loan.

mortgage payment (PMT)   The outlay made to decrease the principal and/or interest on a mortgage.

mortgagor   One who gives a mortgage as security for a loan; the borrower.

most probable selling price   The most likely price at which a property should sell if exposed in a competitive market for a reasonable period of time, under the market conditions at the date of the appraisal. (*See* market value.)

MPVIFA   (*See* monthly present value interest factor—annuity.)

MSA   (*See* metropolitan statistical area.)

multifamily   A structure that is architecturally intended for habitation by more than one family.

multiple regression analysis   A statistical analysis that measures the influence of two or more independent variables on one dependent variable. Often used in mass appraisal of single-family residences.

narrative report   The most common and complete type of appraisal report; it includes an introduction, assumptions of the appraisal, presentation and analysis of data, and addenda.

negative amortization   The results of a loan payment that is less than the interest charged per period; in effect, the loan balance increases each period by the amount of interest unpaid. This generally occurs in mortgages with initially low payments that increase at some point in time.

negative cash flow   An expenditure or payment given to another party; occurs when operating expenses are greater than operating income.

negative externalities   Forces from outside the property's boundaries that cause the property value to decrease.

negative leverage   The result of borrowing at a cost of capital that exceeds the return on capital causing the return on equity to decrease.

neighborhood   An area characterized by complementary land uses.

neighborhood boundaries   Borders that surround the area that influences the value of a subject property; may coincide with changes in prevailing land use, occupant characteristics, or physical characteristics.

neighborhood life cycle   The changes that occur in a neighborhood over time; the cycle is defined by four stages: growth, stability, decline, and revitalization.

neoclassical theory   A theory of value popular in the late 19th and early 20th centuries that stressed supply and demand as factors for determining value.

net income   (*See* net operating income.)

net income multiplier (NIM)   The ratio of the property value or sales price to its net operating income for a given year. It is the reciprocal of the overall capitalization rate.

net income ratio (NIR)   The ratio of net operating income to effective gross income.

net lease   A lease in which the tenant pays expenses such as property taxes, insurance, and maintenance. Sometimes referred to as a net net net lease.

net leasable area   Floor space that can be rented to tenants; the space available for rent; generally excludes common areas.

net net net lease   A lease in which the tenant pays taxes, insurance, and maintenance. (*See* net lease.)

net operating income (NOI)   The income remaining after deducting all operating expenses and vacancy and collection loss from total potential income.

net present value (NPV)   The discounted value of all future cash flows minus the initial cash outlay. A discount rate must be specified to calculate an NPV.

net proceeds   Cash received after all liens and expenses have been paid.

net rentable area   (*See* net leasable area.)

net reversion   (*See* net proceeds.)

NIR   (*See* net income ratio.)

NOI   (*See* net operating income.)

nominal interest rate (I)   A stated annual rate of interest.

nonbasic industry   A service or support industry in an area; the opposite of a basic industry, which generates income from outside the area.

nonconforming use   (*See* legally nonconforming use.)

note   A legal document that acknowledges a promise to pay a specified debt.

NPV   (*See* net present value.)

obsolescence   A loss in value resulting from defects in design or forces outside the boundaries of a property; may be either functional or external.

occupancy   The level of units leased.

OER   (*See* operating expense ratio.)

office building   A building used primarily by companies to conduct business.

offsite improvements   Physical improvements that affect the use and the value of a parcel of land but are not directly located on the land;

examples for residential real estate would include streets, curbs, and open space.

one-hundred percent location   The particular area in a city considered to be the prime location.

onsite improvements   Physical improvements that are constructed within the boundaries of a parcel of land (e.g., buildings, structures, and other support facilities installed within the boundaries of the property).

open-end mortgage   A loan that allows the mortgagor to borrow additional sums based on specified conditions, such as minimum asset to debt ratios.

open space   Land that has not been improved with buildings; such land is often left by a developer in a subdivision for recreational use and enjoyment by all the property owners.

operating costs   (*See* operating expenses.)

operating expense ratio (OER)   The ratio of total operating expenses to effective gross income.

operating expenses   Expenditures necessary to maintain the real property and continue the production of income.

opportunity cost   The cost of options forgone or opportunities not chosen.

option   A legal contract that allows one to buy, sell, or lease real property within a specified time limit under specified terms.

oral report   A complete unwritten appraisal report; it must be based on the same facts and conclusions as a written report.

ordinary annuity   A level annuity for which all payments are received at the end of the period.

ordinary income   Income that is subject to income taxes at the owner's income tax rate.

original cost   The actual cost of a property to its present owner.

overage   (*See* overage rent.)

overage rent   A rent paid in addition to a fixed base rent; it is usually based on a variable figure such as a percent of sales or an index.

overall capitalization rate (R_o)   The ratio of net operating income from a single year or average of several years to sales price or property value.

overall rate   (*See* overall capitalization rate.)

overall yield rate (Y$_o$) The yield rate based on the NOI and resale proceeds (reversion). The discount rate that equates the present value of the NOI and resale proceeds with the purchase price. Sometimes referred to as a free-and-clear yield because it does not consider financing.

overimprovement (*See* superadequacy.)

paired data analysis A procedure used in the sales comparison approach to estimate values of specific property characteristics to find a value of the subject property; property sales are paired by similar property characteristics. Ideally the properties are exactly the same except for one characteristic; the difference in sales price can then be attributed to the difference in this characteristic. However, several adjustments usually must be made to paired sales to isolate the effect of one characteristic.

paired data sets (*See* paired data analysis.)

paired sales technique (*See* paired data analysis.)

parcel (*See* lot.)

parking ratio The number of available parking spaces divided by a unit of rentable area, usually per 1,000 square feet of rentable area.

partial release A mortgage clause in a blanket mortgage in which the lender agrees to release certain parcels from the mortgage lien upon payment by the mortgagor; frequently found in tract development construction loans.

participation mortgage A loan in which the lender shares part of the income or resale proceeds from a property in return for a reduction in periodic loan repayments.

partnership A business arrangement in which two or more persons co-own a business.

partnership interest An ownership interest in a partnership.

pass-through The tax advantage of a partnership or real estate investment trust that permits cash flows and deductions, especially depreciation, to "pass through" the legal structure of the partnership directly to the individual investors. The transfer of specified operating expenses to the tenant to be paid based on the terms of the lease. For example, the lease may specify that property taxes are passed through to the tenant to be paid.

payback period The time required for cumulative income from an investment to equal the amount initially invested. Usually calculated to the next whole year.

payment to amortize $1 The periodic payment necessary to repay a $1 loan with interest paid on the outstanding balance. Column 6 in the compound interest tables in Appendix B.

percentage adjustment A means by which an adjustment is made to the sales price of a comparable to reflect percentage differences between the comparable and the subject property.

percentage lease A lease that specifies a rent based on some percent of sales from the property, usually in addition to a base rent; frequently used in retail properties.

percentage rent Rent based on a percent of sales from the property. (*See* percentage lease.)

personal property Items not permanently affixed to real estate and not considered real property. Personal property can be tangible (such as furniture and fixtures) or intangible (such as a premium paid for below-market financing or going-concern value).

PGI (*See* potential gross income.)

PGIM (*See* potential gross income multiplier.)

physical age (*See* actual age.)

physical age-life method A method of estimating incurable physical deterioration in which the deterioration is calculated by multiplying the ratio of effective age divided by the total physical life of the item by the reproduction or replacement cost of the item minus any curable physical deterioration already charged. (*See* incurable physical deterioration.)

physical characteristics The tangible aspects of real estate.

physical depreciation (*See* curable physical deterioration and incurable physical deterioration.)

physical deterioration (*See* curable physical deterioration *and* incurable physical deterioration.)

physically possible One of four criteria in highest and best use analysis; for a use to be the highest and best use, the size, shape, and terrain of the property must be able to accommodate the use.

physiocrat Believer in a theory of value popular in the mid-18th century that stressed the use of land and agricultural productivity as the source of wealth.

PI (*See* profitability index.)

planned unit development (PUD) A zoning classification for a subdivision that sets a density limit and allows the dwelling units to be clustered to provide for common open space.

plat A map showing and identifying the location of land that has been subdivided into individual lots.

plottage An increment of value that results when extra utility is created by combining two or more sites under a single ownership.

plottage value (*See* plottage.)

PMT (*See* mortgage payment.)

police power The government right to regulate property to protect public safety, health, morals, and general welfare.

positive leverage The result of borrowing at a cost of capital less than the return on capital, causing the return on equity to increase.

potential gross income (PGI) The total operating income produced by a real property, assuming no vacancies or collection losses.

potential gross income multiplier (PGIM) The ratio of sales price or value to the potential gross income.

presales A sale by a developer that occurs before construction.

present value (PV) The current worth of a payment or payments based on the time value of money; future payments are discounted to an equivalent current value by a discount rate based on the premise that cash flows received sooner are more valuable than cash flows received later.

present value interest factor (PVIF) (*See* present value of one factor.)

present value interest factor annuity (PVIFA) (*See* present value of annuity.)

present value of annuity (a_n) The current worth of a level stream of future cash flows discounted to the present time period at a specified discount rate; Column 5 of the compound interest tables in Appendix B. Also called present value interest factor annuity.

present value of one factor ($1/S^n$) The current worth of a payment to be received in the future; the future payment is discounted to the current value through the present value of one factor, which can be found in compound interest tables (see Column 4 in Appendix B). Also called reversion factor, present value interest factor.

present value reversion of $1 (*See* present value of one factor.)

pretax cash flow (*See* before-tax cash flow.)

price The amount of money paid or asked for in exchange for an item.

primary data Information gathered by the appraiser that is not available in a published source.

principal (loan) The amount of capital borrowed or remaining to be paid on an investment. Also refers to that portion of a loan payment that reduces the balance of the loan.

principle (appraisal) The interactive factors that affect property value; includes concepts such as supply and demand, substitution, conformity, balance, and externalities.

profitability index (PI) The ratio of the present value of a cash flow to the initial cash outlay. A discount rate must be specified.

profit The right to remove something from the land of another.

profits The amount by which the proceeds of a transaction exceed the expenses.

pro forma statement Financial statements that show future expected cash flows.

projected income The amount of net cash flow forecasted for a future period; may be used in the income approach.

property Anything in which there is ownership; may refer to real property or personal property.

property insurance Protection by an owner/user against the risk of a certain loss or disastrous event.

property management The process of overseeing the financial, physical, and administrative aspects of property operations.

property managers One who oversees the operational activities of a property; including the leasing, marketing, maintenance, and the administration.

property residual technique   A historical term for estimating the property value by discounting the expected future NOI and the expected proceeds from sale of the property. This term is a misnomer because there is no true "residual" component as in other residual techniques. This technique is just a form of discounted cash flow analysis.

property rights   The privileges associated with the ownership of real estate; includes rights such as the right to sell, lease, occupy, or use. Such rights may be divided independently of the real estate itself.

property tax   An ad valorem tax issued by the government based on the assessed value of property.

property tax assessment   (*See* assessment.)

property value   The worth of a property; a property may have several different values depending on the interest or use involved. (*See* market value, investment value, insurable value, assessed value, leased fee value, *and* going-concern value.)

proprietary lease   In a multiunit building, the lease a corporation provides to the stockholders that allows them to use a specific unit under the conditions specified.

PUD   (*See* planned unit development.)

PV   (*See* present value.)

PVIF   (*See* present value interest factor.)

PVIFA   (*See* present value interest factor annuity.)

quantity survey method   The most comprehensive method of estimating building costs in which the quantity and quality of all materials and labor are estimated on a unit cost basis to arrive at a total cost estimate; it duplicates the contractor's method of developing a bid.

quantity survey system   (*See* quantity survey method.)

range   An interval in numbers ordered sequentially from the lowest to the highest number.

range lines   In the rectangular survey system, the north-south lines, spaced six miles apart, used to define a township.

range of value   In an appraisal report, the confidence interval in which the final estimate of a property's value may lie.

raw land   Land that has not been improved.

R$_B$ (*See* building capitalization rate.)

R$_E$ (*See* cash on cash return.)

real estate   The physical land and structures affixed to it. Usually differentiated from real property, which refers to the ownership rights in real estate.

real estate taxes   A levy issued to the property owner by the government based on the assessed value of the property.

real property   The bundle of rights inherent in the ownership of real estate. Distinct from personal property.

reappraisal lease   A lease that contains a provision providing for the amount of the rent to be based on the appraised value of the property.

reconciliation   In the appraisal process, the analysis of value indications from different appraisal approaches to arrive at a final value estimate.

reconstructed operating statement   A document that states estimated future income and expenses of a property in the proper format for appraisal purposes.

recreational property   An improvement constructed for entertainment purposes.

rectangular survey system   (*See* government rectangular survey.)

regional shopping center   An enclosed shopping area comprised of numerous stores including national and regional chains; such centers are located in areas with populations in excess of 250,000.

regression analysis   (*See* linear regression analysis *and* multiple regression analysis.)

remainder   A future possessory interest in real estate that becomes effective upon the termination of another estate in that property.

remaining economic life   The estimated time period during which operating income will be greater than operating expenses; the period over which improvements will continue to contribute to property value.

renewal options   A lease clause that allows the lessee to extend the lease under specified terms for a certain period of time.

rental concession   (*See* concessions.)

rentup   The process of finding tenants for a new building.

repairs   Minor alterations required to keep a building in operating condition.

replacement cost   The cost to construct a building with equivalent utility at current prices, materials, standards, design, and layout.

reproduction cost   The cost to construct an exact duplicate of a building at current prices using the same materials, standards, design, layout, and quality, and embodying all the subject's deficiencies, superadequacies, and obsolescence.

resale   Sale of a property at the termination of the holding period.

reserve for replacement   An accounting allowance to provide for the maintenance and replacement of short-lived items.

residential area   A locality characterized by residential use.

residential property   Units used for dwelling purposes, not of a transient nature.

residual   Value or income attributable to a component, such as financial, physical, or legal estate components, after deducting an amount necessary to meet a required return on the other component.

residual income   Income attributable to a component after the known income from other components is deducted from the total income.

residual techniques   Processes used in the income approach in which the unknown income from one component is derived by subtracting the known income from another component from the net operating income. The derived (residual) income is then capitalized to find the value of the corresponding component. Can be used for landbuilding or mortgage-equity components.

retail   Use of a property characterized by the sale of merchandise (e.g., shopping areas).

return of capital   The recovery of invested funds over time, either through net operating income or resale.

return on capital   Income that provides a rate of return to the investor on capital that has been invested. Analogous to an interest rate or IRR.

reverse annuity mortgage (RAM)   A loan for homeowners who owe little or nothing on their homes; typically allows owners to borrow against the value of their home in periodic payments to the borrower so that a supplemental income is provided.

reversion   A lessor's right to possess leased property at the termination of a lease. Also refers generally to sale of a property at the end of a holding period.

reversionary value   1. The worth of a lessor's right to possess leased property at the termination of the lease. 2. The value of a property at the end of a holding period.

review appraiser   An appraiser who inspects the reports of other appraisers to determine the validity of the conclusions and data given in the report.

rezoning   A change or amendment to a zoning map.

risk   Uncertainty arising from the probability that events will not occur as expected.

R_L (*See* land capitalization rate.)

R_M (*See* mortgage loan constant.)

R_O (*See* overall capitalization rate.)

sales adjustment grid   A grid used in the sales comparison approach in which the elements of comparison are listed by line for the subject property and comparable properties; it allows an easy comparison of different properties for adjustment to find the value of the subject property.

sales comparison approach   One of the three approaches to value in appraisal theory; value is estimated by comparing similar properties that have sold recently to the subject property.

sales price   The amount of money paid or asked for in a specific transaction; the sales price may include nonrealty items such as personal property or a financing premium.

sandwich estate   An estate that arises from a sandwich lease.

sandwich lease   A sublease that occurs when a lessee leases a property to another and becomes a lessor.

secondary data   Data that are obtained from published sources and have not been collected by the appraiser.

secondary mortgage market   A market that exists for the sale and purchase of existing mortgages; it provides more liquidity for the mortgage market.

second mortgage   A loan that is subordinate to the first mortgage; a type of junior mortgage.

section   In the rectangular survey method of legally describing land, it equals 640 acres, one square mile, or 1/36 of a township.

senior mortgage   A loan given precedence over another loan. In case of foreclosure, the senior mortgage will be fulfilled first.

sequence of adjustments   In the sales comparison approach, adjustments to comparable characteristics should be made in the following order to find the appropriate value of the subject property: property rights, financing terms, conditions of sale, market conditions, location, and physical characteristics.

severance damage   In an eminent domain proceeding in which part of a real property interest is taken for public use; it is a loss in market value of the remainder that arises as a result of the taking. It is compensable to the owner.

shared appreciation mortgage (SAM)   Participation loan in which the lender receives part of the increase in property value at the time of resale.

shopping center   A building that contains several retail stores, typically with one or more large department, discount, or grocery stores and a common parking area.

single-family unit   A structure intended and used for occupancy by one family.

single purpose property   A property whose highest and best use is unique to that site; land value in this case is based on the highest and best use of the property, regardless of the most likely use.

sinking fund (1/S_n)   An account in which equal installments of funds are periodically deposited to accumulate enough money to replace an asset or reach a specified target sum; usually assumes compound interest.

sinking fund factor   The periodic payment, at a specified compound interest and number of payments, that will grow to $1. The symbol $1/S_n$ is used to represent the sinking fund factor. This factor is in Column 3 of the compound interest tables in Appendix B.

site   A plot of land improved for a specific purpose.

six functions of a dollar   Refers to compound interest and present value factors that can be identified in compound interest tables; the functions are amount of $1, amount (accumulation) of $1 per period, sinking fund factor, present value of $1, present value of $1 per period, and partial payment (installment to amortize $1) factor. *See* the tables in Appendix B.

S^n   (*See* amount of $1 at compound interest.)

S_n   (*See* accumulation of $1 per period.)

$1/S^n$ (*See* present value of one factor.)

$1/S_n$ (*See* sinking fund factor.)

SMSA   (*See* standard metropolitan area.)

social characteristics   (*See* social forces.)

social forces   In appraisal theory, one of four forces thought to influence property value; refers to population characteristics such as population age and distribution.

soft costs   (*See* indirect costs.)

special assessment   A tax imposed only against those parcels of realty that will benefit from a proposed public improvement.

special purpose properties   A property appropriate for only one use or a very limited number of uses; its highest and best use will probably be continued at the current use, or the improvements will be demolished.

specific date   Data collected dealing with the subject property and the comparable properties.

speculative use   Property held primarily for future sale; value is based on the future highest and best use.

standard deviation   The square root of the arithmetic mean of the squares of the deviations from the arithmetic mean of the frequency distribution; it measures the extent of variability in a frequency distribution. It is often used as a measure of risk.

standard metropolitan statistical area (SMSA)   (*See* metropolitan statistical area.)

standing stock   The amount of real estate that has already been built; it is one indication of the supply of real estate.

straight-line capitalization   A method of developing an overall capitalization rate; the capitalization rate is calculated by adding an allowance for return of capital to the discount rate (return on capital). The allowance for return of capital assumes the capital is recaptured *evenly* over the holding period or economic life of the property. For example, if the economic life of the property is 50 years, the allowance for return of capital will be 1/50, or 2 percent. With a 10 percent discount rate the overall capitalization rate is 12 percent. This method, which is not commonly used today, implicitly assumes that the property's income is declining each year.

strip center   A commercial use of real estate, such as a neighborhood shopping center in which the buildings are adjoining and narrow in depth relative to their length.

structure   Any constructed improvement including buildings, kiosks, garages, fencing, and enclosures.

subdivision   A large plot of land divided into smaller lots for sale or lease.

subdivision regulations   A local ordinance that establishes minimum standards to be met before a subdivision will be approved for development; regulations include width of streets, size of lots, and drainage requirements.

subject building   The building being appraised.

subject property   The property being appraised.

sublease   An agreement in which the tenant (lessee) leases the property or part of the property to a third party, thus becoming a lessor.

subleasehold   The property interest associated with a sublease.

submarkets   A further division of a market based on the preferences of buyers and sellers.

subordinate   That which takes less precedence than another.

subordinated mortgage   A loan that takes less precedence (junior) to another loan.

subordination clause   A mortgage clause that gives priority to a subsequent mortgage.

substitution   The appraisal principle that states a buyer will pay no more for a property than the cost of obtaining an equally desirable substitute.

superadequacy   A type of functional obsolescence caused by a structural component that is too large or of a higher quality than what is needed for the highest and best use of the property; an item the cost of which exceeds its value; an overimprovement.

superadequate features   (*See* superadequacy.)

supply   The quantity of a product available on the market at a particular time as a function of different prices.

supply and demand   In appraisal, a principle that states that the value of a property depends on the quantity and price of the property type available in the market, and on the number of market participants and the price they are willing to pay.

supply and demand study   An analysis of the availability and desire for a specific type of property.

surplus productivity   The net income that remains after the costs of labor, capital, and coordination have been deducted from total income.

taxable income   On income-producing properties, net operating income minus depreciation and interest; should not be confused with after-tax income or before-tax cash flow.

tax assessment   (*See* assessment.)

tax depreciation   The loss in value of a building due to wear and tear, which is allowed to be subtracted from income and sale proceeds under tax law.

tax shelter   The ability of a property to shield income from taxes, usually through accounting losses arising from interest deductions and depreciation.

tenancy by the entireties   An equal indivisible estate held by a husband and wife in which neither has a disposable interest in the property during the lifetime of the other, except by joint action; the property passes to the survivor upon death of one spouse.

tenancy in common   An indivisible estate held by two or more persons who may have equal or unequal interests; the property passes to the heirs and not the survivor(s) on the death of one.

tenant   One who exclusively occupies or holds a property through a lease; a lessee.

tenant improvements   In construction projects, the installation of finished tenant space by lessee or lessor; also may refer to fixed improvements installed and paid for by a lessee.

terminal capitalization rate   The capitalization rate used to estimate the resale price for a property at the end of a holding period; it equals the estimated net operating income at the time of sale (or one year after the year of sale) divided by the sales price. The NOI for the year *following* the year of sale is often used when estimating value with a terminal capitalization rate because this is the *first* year of NOI for the buyer.

time-sharing   A sale of limited undivided ownership interests in a property in which each purchaser receives a deed conveying title to the unit for a specific period of time.

topography   The features and contour of the land.

township   In the rectangular survey system of legally describing land, an area six miles square containing 36 sections and 23,040 acres.

trade area   A defined geographic area from which a business attracts the majority of its customers.

trade fixtures   A type of personal property that is owned and attached to a rented space by the *tenant* and is used in conducting business; it is differentiated from a regular fixture, which is part of the real estate, by the manner in which it is affixed, the character of the item, and the intention of the tenant who attached the item. Whereas regular fixtures are real property, trade fixtures remain personal property.

transaction price   (*See* sales price.)

trend analysis   A study of changes in the environment of a property used particularly in the income approach to help forecast future changes in property income, sales price, and occupancy rates.

trustee   One who holds property in trust for another and controls legal title to property under a trust agreement.

trustor   One for whom property is held under a trust agreement.

UCIAR   (*See* Uniform Commercial-Industrial Appraisal Report.)

underimproved land   Land that, due to the fact it is not being used under its highest and best use, does not generate the maximum amount of income that could be generated.

unfavorable leverage   (*See* negative leverage.)

Uniform Commercial-Industrial Appraisal Report (UCIAR)   An appraisal form developed to provide a consistent report of the value of commercial and industrial properties.

Uniform Residential Appraisal Report (URAR)   An appraisal form requested by many federal agencies to value residential properties in a consistent manner.

Uniform Standards of Professional Appraisal Practice (USPAP)   A set of standards originally developed by a committee of nine appraisal associations to provide guidelines for the development of appraisal reports; updates to the standards are currently the responsibility of the Appraisal Standards Board of The Appraisal Foundation. All appraisal members of the foundation have adopted the standards.

unit-in-place method   A method of estimating building costs in which total building cost is estimated by summing prices for various building components as installed based on specific units of use such as square footage or cubic footage. Also called the segregated cost method.

units of comparison   A physical or economic measure that can be divided into the property's price to provide a more standardized comparison of the properties. The measure should be one that accounts for differences in the price typically paid for the properties, such as price per square foot (office building), price per seat (theater), or price per gallon of gas pumped (gas station). Income can also be a unit of comparison, such as when price is divided by effective gross income to obtain an effective gross income multiplier.

URAR   (*See* Uniform Residential Appraisal Report.)

useful life   The period of time over which a property is expected to remain economically feasible to the investor.

use value   (*See* value in use.)

utilities   Operating services required by a developed area, usually provided by public companies (e.g., electricity, telephone, water, and gas).

V   (*See* value.)

vacancies   Space available for rent that is not occupied.

vacancy allowance   In the income approach, a deduction from potential gross income for current or expected future space not rented due to tenant turnover or to lack of demand.

vacancy and collection loss   (*See* vacancy allowance *and* collection loss.)

valuation   The process of estimating a defined value of an identified interest in a specific parcel of real estate as of a given date.

value (V)   The monetary worth of rights arising from property ownership.

value in exchange   The value of a property in a typical market; market value.

value in use   The value of a property based on a specific use. This may differ from market value when the use is specialized and there is a limited market for the property based on that use.

variable expense   An operating expense that varies with the occupancy or use level of a property.

variance   In *statistics,* the arithmetic mean of the squares of the deviations from the arithmetic mean of the frequency distribution; it measures the extent of variability in a frequency distribution. In zoning, official permission to depart from the requirements of a zoning ordinance.

volume of new construction   The amount of property that has recently been built; it is one indication of the supply of real estate.

wear and tear   Physical deterioration of property due to weathering, aging, and use.

wraparound mortgage   A loan in which the lender takes over payments of a previous mortgage and in turn provides a mortgage in the amount of the previous mortgage plus an additional amount. It is subordinate to the previous loan.

Y_E (*See* equity yield rate.)

yield   The rate of return on an investment. Could be an overall yield for the property (Y_O), a yield for the equity investor (Y_E), or a yield for the lender (Y_M).

yield capitalization   A method used in the income approach to determine property value by discounting future cash flows at an appropriate discount rate (yield rate) that reflects the rate of return required by investors. The approach may or may not explicitly consider financing. (*See* discounted cash flow analysis.)

yield to maturity   (*See* internal rate of return.)

Y_O (*See* overall yield.)

zoning   An application of police power; a legal mechanism for local governments to regulate land use and density of development for privately owned real property.

zoning restrictions   Restrictions may be placed on issues such as height, density, use, or development of properties. (*See* zoning.)